More praise for *The Harlot by the Side of the Road*

"Jonathan Kirsch's new book is guaranteed to turn the heads of book-store browsers from coast to coast. In a time when so many decry biblical illiteracy, *The Harlot by the Side of the Road* is a welcome addition to the growing genre of Bible scholarship that has slowly been moving from the rarefied confines of universities and cloistered seminaries into the hands of everyday believers and skeptics alike."

—*Los Angeles Times*

"Fascinating reading . . . Demonstrating meticulous research and an enticing style."

—*Booklist*

"Kirsch succeeds in bringing these ancient stories to vivid life, and in revealing the human passions and frailties often left out of the telling of familiar Bible tales."

—*Publishers Weekly*

THE HARLOT BY THE SIDE OF THE ROAD

Forbidden Tales of the Bible

JONATHAN KIRSCH

BALLANTINE BOOKS
NEW YORK

A Ballantine Book
Published by The Ballantine Publishing Group

Grateful acknowledgement is made to the following for permission to reprint previously published material:

Esquire magazine and the Hearst Corporation: Excerpt from "If You Could Ask One Question about Life, What would the answer be?" by Isaac Bashevis Singer, first published in *Esquire* magazine, December 1974. Reprinted courtesy of *Esquire* magazine and the Hearst Corporation.

Cambridge University Press: Excerpts from THE NEW ENGLISH BIBLE WITH APOCRYPHA. Copyright © Oxford University Press and Cambridge University Press 1961, 1970. Reprinted by permission of Cambridge University Press.

http://www.randomhouse.com

Library of Congress Catalog Card Number: 97-97070

ISBN: 0-345-41882-4

Manufactured in the United States of America

Cover design by Kristine V. Mills-Noble
Cover illustration by Honi Werner

First Hardcover Edition: May 1997
First Trade Paperback Edition: March 1998

10 9 8 7 6 5 4 3 2 1

To Ann, Adam, and Jennifer
With love, as always.

Remember us in life,
and health, and strength,
O Lord who delighteth in life,
And inscribe us in the Book of Life . . .

"When the kings had died, a pauper, barefooted and hungry, came and sat on the throne. 'God,' he whispered, 'the eyes of man cannot bear to look directly at the sun, for they are blinded. How then, Omnipotent, can they look directly at you? Have pity, Lord; temper your strength, turn down your splendor so that I, who am poor and afflicted, may see you!' Then—listen, old man!—God became a piece of bread, a cup of cool water, a warm tunic, a hut, and in front of the hut, a woman giving suck to an infant. 'Thank you, Lord,' he whispered. 'You humbled yourself for my sake. You became bread, water, a warm tunic and my wife and son in order that I may see you. And I did see you. I bow down and worship your beloved many-faced face!' "

—*NIKOS KAZANTZAKIS*
THE LAST TEMPTATION OF CHRIST

CONTENTS

Contents

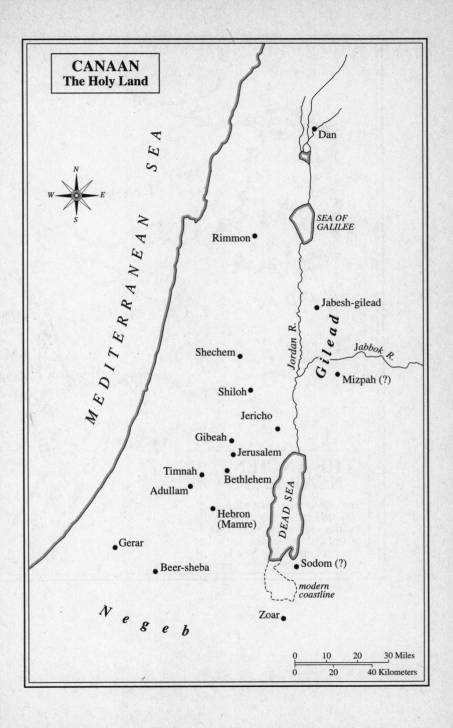

CANAAN
The Holy Land

MEDITERRANEAN SEA

N
W E
S

Dan

SEA OF
GALILEE

Rimmon

Jabesh-gilead

Shechem

Gilead

Jabbok R.

Jordan R.

Mizpah (?)

Shiloh

Jericho

Gibeah

Jerusalem

Timnah

Bethlehem

DEAD SEA

Adullam

Hebron
(Mamre)

Gerar

Sodom (?)

Beer-sheba

modern
coastline

N e g e b

Zoar

0   10   20   30 Miles

0   20   40 Kilometers

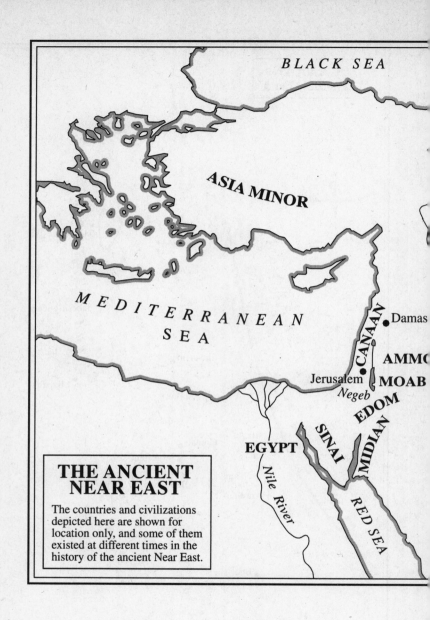

BLACK SEA

ASIA MINOR

MEDITERRANEAN
SEA

CANAAN

Damas

AMMO

Jerusalem   MOAB

Negeb

EDOM

EGYPT   SINAI   MIDIAN

Nile River

RED SEA

THE ANCIENT
NEAR EAST

The countries and civilizations
depicted here are shown for
location only, and some of them
existed at different times in the
history of the ancient Near East.

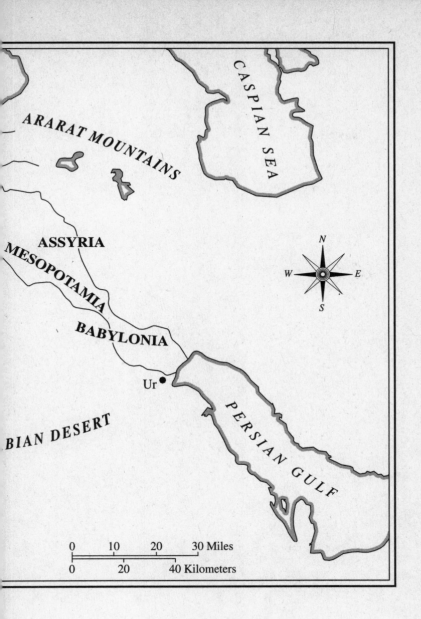

CHAPTER ONE

FORBIDDEN TALES OF THE BIBLE

THE NAKED NOAH ✤ THE FORBIDDEN BIBLE
THE FORGOTTEN BIBLE ✤ THE LIBERATING BIBLE
"A NEED TO TELL AND HEAR STORIES"

The stories you are about to read are some of the most violent and sexually explicit in all of Western literature. They are tales of human passion in all of its infinite variety: adultery, seduction, incest, rape, mutilation, assassination, torture, sacrifice, and murder. And yet every one of these stories is drawn directly from the pages of the Holy Bible.

"You mean that's in the *Bible?*" is the common reaction of the reader who knows the Bible, if at all, only from the occasional sermon or some dimly remembered Sunday school lesson.

Even readers who think they know the Bible may be unfamiliar with these stories precisely because embarrassed rabbis, priests, and ministers have sought to hide the plain language of the original Hebrew text behind fuzzy euphemisms, unlikely interpretations, or intentional mistranslations. Although the Bible is Holy Writ to three religions, a few of its most shocking stories have been banned outright by clergy who were not entirely comfortable with telling their congregants what *really* happens in the Bible.

As a result of these efforts at bowdlerizing, we are sometimes given the impression that the Bible is mostly a dry and preachy work—a list of stern "shalts" and "shalt nots" that condemn all but the narrowest range of human behavior, a forbidding black book with little to say to worldly men and women whose lives are far messier than what we imagine the Bible to allow. But the fact is that the Bible offers some surprising insights that we might profitably recall when confronting the toughest issues of our own times, from the debate over abortion to the search for peace in the Middle East, from sexual politics to world politics.

To be sure, the Hebrew Bible includes generous portions of strict moral instruction, starting with the Ten Commandments and bulking up to include some 613 other dos and don'ts. For that matter, there is little that one *cannot* find in the Bible, which is actually a fantastic grab bag of law, legend, history, politics, propaganda, poetry, prayer, ethics, genealogy, hygienic practices, military tactics, dietary advice, and carpentry instructions, among many other things. But, as we will see, the Bible is also a treasury of storytelling that recounts the lives of men and women who were thoroughly human, which is to say that they were as confused, conflicted, twisted, tortured, and vulnerable to the weaknesses of the flesh and failure of the spirit as any character in Homer, Shakespeare, Dostoyevsky, or any of the soap operas, bodice rippers, and tabloids that amount to the literature of our own times.

Nowadays, we have come to associate the Bible with bluenoses and "Bible-thumpers." We expect Bible readers to be narrow-minded and highly disapproving of the slightest degree of human misconduct, especially in sexual and spiritual matters. But, as we shall soon see, the Bible describes and even seems to encourage a range of human conduct that goes far beyond what is permitted in the Ten Commandments.

THE NAKED NOAH

I first discovered what is hidden away in the odd cracks and corners of the Holy Scriptures when, many years ago, I resolved to acquaint my young son with the Bible as a work of literature by reading aloud to him at bedtime from Genesis. I chose the New English Bible, with its plain-spoken translation of the hoary text, so that my five-year-old would understand what was actually going on in the stories without the impedimenta of the antique words and phrases that give the King James Version such grandeur but sometimes make it hard to follow.

We began *In the beginning*, of course, and we continued through the highly suggestive tale of Eve and the serpent, then the bloody murder of Abel by his brother, Cain. I already knew that Genesis was not exactly G-rated, but I reassured myself that we would soon reach the tale of Noah and the Ark, an unobjectionable Sunday school story that would distract my son from the more disturbing passages that we had just read. Nothing had prepared me for what we found there, right after the familiar moment when the animals come aboard the ark, two by two.

At the end of the story of Noah, after the flood has subsided and God has signaled his good intentions toward humanity by painting a rainbow across the sky, we came upon a scene that does not find its way into the storybooks or Sunday school lessons: Noah is lying alone in his tent, buck naked and drunk as a sailor on the wine from his own vineyards. One of his sons, Ham, blunders into the tent and finds himself staring at his nude and drunken father.

> When Ham, father of Canaan, saw his father naked, he told his two brothers outside. So Shem and Japheth took a cloak, put it on their shoulders and walked backwards, and so covered their father's naked body; their faces were turned the other way, so that they did not see their father naked (Gen. 9:20–24 NEB).*

After *that* scene, so comical and yet so disquieting to any parent mindful of Freud, I read the Bible more slowly, rephrasing certain passages as I went along and omitting others altogether. My son, already media wise at five, soon began to protest. If I paused too long over a troublesome passage, trying to figure out how to tone down or cut the earthier parts, he would sit up in bed and demand indignantly: "What are you leaving out?"

In a sense, his question prompted the book you are now reading. As I read the Bible aloud to my son, I found myself doing exactly what overweening and fearful clerics and translators have done for

*All quotations from the Bible are from *The Holy Scriptures According to the Masoretic Text* (Philadelphia: Jewish Publication Society, 1961) unless otherwise indicated by an abbreviation that identifies another translation. "NEB," for example, refers to *The New English Bible With Apocrypha*, 2d ed. (New York: Oxford University Press, 1970). A complete list of Bible translations and the abbreviations used to identify them can be found on page 355.

centuries—I censored the text to spare my audience the juicy parts. And so my son's question is answered here: The stories collected in these pages are the ones that I—like so many other shocked Bible readers over the millennia—was tempted to leave out.

The Forbidden Bible

The stories that are retold here will come as a surprise to many readers precisely because, over the centuries, they have been suppressed by rabbis, priests, and ministers uncomfortable with the candor of the biblical storytellers about human conduct, sexual or otherwise. At times, the instruments of censorship have been subtle and even devious, and that's why even regular church- and synagogue-goers may not know that these stories, bold and blunt as they are, can be found in the original text of the Bible.

The Bible as a Banned Book

At certain times and places, some of the more lurid stories in the Bible have been banned outright. For example, the prayer service in Judaism is built around the public reading of the Torah, that is, the first five books of the Hebrew Bible, and selected passages from other books of the Hebrew Bible. Since the typical Jewish congregation was (and is) unfamiliar with the ancient Hebrew in which the Bible is written, the text was translated into the languages spoken by the Jewish people outside of the Holy Land. The Torah is read out loud to the congregation, word by word, in a cycle that lasts an entire year and then begins again—but, long ago, the rabbis set down strict rules that were expressly designed to prevent their congregants from hearing or understanding certain passages of the Holy Scriptures.*

---

*The Hebrew Bible has been explored, explained, and embroidered upon by successive generations of rabbinical sages for more than two thousand years. Much of their work is found in the Talmud, a vast collection of Jewish law, lore, and legend, and a separate accumulation of Bible-inspired commentary known as the Midrash. When I refer to "the rabbis" (or, sometimes, "the sages"), I mean the rabbinical commentators whose work appears in the Talmud or the Midrash. Specific citations to Talmudic and Midrashic sources can be found in the works that are referenced in the endnotes to each chapter.

For example, the rabbinical authorities once decreed that the story of the seduction of Jacob's concubine, Bilhah, by his firstborn son, Reuben (Gen. 35:22), and the frank account of King David's lust for Bathsheba (2 Sam. 11)—a tale that features voyeurism, seduction, adultery, bastardy, and the murder of a loyal and heroic soldier by vile and cowardly means—were permitted to be read aloud in the synagogue in the original Hebrew but were not to be translated from Hebrew into a language that the congregation was more likely to understand. And some stories—including, for example, the rape of King David's daughter, Tamar, by her love-crazed half brother (2 Sam. 13)—were so troubling to the rabbis that these stories were not to be read out loud *or* translated out of biblical Hebrew.[1]

Similarly, an English bishop of the eighteenth century named Porteus produced an index to the Bible that was designed to identify exactly which passages the goodly churchman considered to be suitable for the lay reader. A star was used to mark the sayings of Jesus and the approved portions of the Psalms and the Book of Isaiah, and the numerals 1 and 2 were used to designate other approved chapters and verses of the Holy Writ. Any passage of the Bible *not* marked with one of these symbols was considered by Bishop Porteus to be off-limits to the ordinary Bible reader—and he declared nearly half of the Hebrew Bible (and some of the New Testament) to be too hot to handle. Of course, the so-called Porteusian Index, if used in reverse, was an ideal tool for the curious Bible reader seeking out precisely the stories that the bishop sought to ban.[2]

Some efforts to bowdlerize the Bible are even more blunt. One enterprising and easily offended woman in late eighteenth-century America was so fearful of letting her children read the Bible that she published a version from which she simply omitted "indecent expressions" that she found in the original text. In fact, she blue-penciled so much "bad language" that she ended up cutting out and throwing away nearly half the text that the rest of the world regards as the Revealed Word of God. Like biblical exegetes of all ages, however, she went on to add so many of her own notes and comments that her edition bulked up to six volumes.[3]

The Rewritten Bible

Even in antiquity, some sages and scribes were so appalled by what they found in the Bible that they were moved to rewrite the Holy Scriptures and simply leave out the passages that they found awkward or objectionable. Some of these rewritten texts are found in the earliest translations of the Hebrew Bible into Greek or Aramaic, the language of late antiquity that was probably spoken by Jesus. For example, the pious translators who rendered the Bible into Aramaic felt at liberty to tamper with the original text in an effort to explain away the bloody and baffling tale of God's attempt to stalk and kill Moses (Exod. 4:24–26), and other authors of the ancient world who collected and retold the stories of the Bible simply leave the tale out altogether.[4]

One rewritten version of a biblical narrative actually found its way into the Bible itself. The First and Second Books of Chronicles, the very last books of the Hebrew Bible, are essentially a sanitized version of the court history of King David that appears in its unexpurgated form in the First and Second Books of Samuel. The author of Samuel is admirably honest about David, sparing no detail of the various sexual excesses and crimes of passion that tainted his reign, but the author of the Chronicles insists on cleaning up David's reputation by simply cutting the more lascivious stories. The Book of Samuel, for example, devotes considerable attention to the deadly love triangle between David, Bathsheba, and her husband (2 Sam. 11). To judge from the Book of Chronicles, however, none of it ever happened. "See what Chronicles has made out of David!" exclaimed Julius Wellhausen, an early and important German biblical scholar who allows us to understand that the *real* authors of the Bible were ordinary human beings who were perfectly willing to engage in a cover-up.[5]

"What Is Written" and "What Is Said"

One of the more curious approaches to cleaning up the Bible was adopted by the Masoretes, a succession of rabbinical scholars who sought to preserve an authoritative version of the Hebrew Bible starting as early as the fifth century C.E. Among the helpful notations added to the so-called Masoretic Text are a series of cautions that distinguish between "What is written" (*Kethib*) and "What is said" (*Qere*)—that is, the rabbis identified certain words that were supposed to be read aloud differently than they were actually written in the text.

For example, the Book of Deuteronomy includes a long list of curses that will befall the Israelites if they do not obey the commandments of the Lord. When we read the curse that appears in Deuteronomy 28:30 (NEB)—"A woman will be pledged to you, but another shall ravish her"—the biblical text plainly uses the Hebrew word that indicates sexual intercourse, but the Masoretes instruct us to pronounce the Hebrew word for "recline" in place of the word for "ravish" when reading the text out loud.

"Passages written with unclean expressions," the rabbis of "hoary antiquity" decreed, "are changed to more seemly readings."[6]

The Translator as Censor

Some passages of the Bible are bawdier than we suspect because idiomatic expressions in the text are translated literally in order to conceal their real meaning. The best example is found in the familiar story of Ruth, where the young widow's mother-in-law sends her to the threshing-floor of a wealthy landowner named Boaz. "And it shall be, when he lieth down," says the wily mother-in-law, "thou shalt go in, and uncover his feet, and lay thee down; and he will tell thee what thou shalt do" (Ruth 3:4). The scene is a bit baffling—why, after all, is she uncovering his *feet*?—until we discover what the translators have failed to tell us: the word "feet" (or "legs") in biblical Hebrew is sometimes a euphemism for the male sexual organ.[7] What Naomi is telling Ruth to do to Boaz, we realize now, is to expose his genitalia while he sleeps—and see what happens when he wakes up: "[H]e will tell thee what thou shalt do."

What actually happens between Boaz and Ruth is obscured by yet another untranslated euphemism. Boaz wakes up to find his genitals exposed and lovely young Ruth beside him. "Who art thou?" he asks. "I am Ruth thy handmaid," she replies, "spread therefore thy skirt over thy handmaid" (Ruth 3:9). But, once again, the translator neglects to tell us that "spreading one's skirt" is a biblical euphemism for sexual intercourse: "For a man to spread his 'skirt' over a woman," cracks Bible scholar Marvin H. Pope, "meant more than merely preventing a chill."[8]

Another favorite trick of self-appointed censors is the use of translations that are misleading or intentionally wrong. For example, the Book of Joshua includes a Bible-era cloak-and-dagger story about two spies who are sent into the land of Canaan in advance of the invading army of Israel to scout out the enemy defenses (Josh. 1:1–19). The spies are sheltered by a Canaanite woman named Rahab whom the original text plainly identifies as a harlot, not once but several times. Indeed, the Hebrew words can be read to suggest that the spies are availing themselves of Rahab's professional services when they are interrupted by an enemy patrol.[9] Yet some Sunday school teachers prefer to tell their impressionable young charges that the kindly and courageous Rahab is an "innkeeper," and Bible scholarship has tried to validate the little white lie by pointing out that "the inn and the brothel have been found in one establishment often in the history of mankind."[10]

God himself is sometimes the victim of bland and blurry euphemisms that are left unexplained by embarrassed translators. For example, we are told in Exodus (33:18–23) that Moses, alone among all humankind, is permitted to actually look upon the Almighty, but only from the back; God takes care to cover Moses' eyes "while My glory passeth by." The word used in the Hebrew text and translated as "glory" is *kabod*— but we are not often told that *kabod* also may be translated as "liver" and is sometimes used idiomatically to refer to the male reproductive organ. "The fact that the Lord wants to be seen only from behind," writes Jack Miles in *God: A Biography*, "may suggest that he is concealing his genitalia from Moses."[11]

Does the Bible Mean What It Says?

Finally, when neither outright censorship nor a convenient mistranslation is practical, religious authorities have resorted to the desperate measure of arguing that the Bible does not really mean what it says.

The Song of Songs, for example, is nowadays recognized by scholars for what it is: "The Song clearly deals explicitly with sexual love between a man and a woman."[12] Indeed, it's impossible to read the work and conclude otherwise: "Let him kiss me with kisses of his mouth," goes the very first line, "for thy love is better than wine" (Song of Songs 1:2). Precisely because of its frank sensuality, the rabbis who decided what books belonged in the Bible debated among themselves whether we ought to regard the torrid love poetry of the Song of Songs as divinely inspired, and some of them even argued that the steamy book ought to be withdrawn from the biblical canon once and for all.[13]

Even though the Song of Songs was never actually excluded from the Bible, the clergy of both Judaism and Christianity over the centuries have chosen to ignore the plainly erotic content. Instead, they stubbornly insist that the Song of Songs is merely an elaborate metaphor for "the love relationship between God and Israel," according to Jewish commentators, or "the love relationship between God (Christ) and the Church," according to Christian ones.[14]

Censorship by Silence

But the single most common technique for making sure that we do not know what the Bible actually says about the ragged edges of human behavior is silence. Today, most Bibles are unexpurgated, and most of the translations in common use in the English-speaking world are largely accurate and unabashed, but casual readers rarely find their way to the "forbidden" stories of the Bible because they simply do not know such stories exist and do not bother to look for them.

Indeed, clergy of all faiths and denominations still tend to shun these stories when they mount the pulpit, and Sunday school teachers still prefer the Bible stories where they know they will find endearing Disneyesque animals and simple uplifting moral lessons. That is why even a regular church- or synagogue-goer, for example, will rarely be exposed to the rape of Dinah by a lovesick prince, the mass circumcision that follows her sexual assault, and the slaughter of innocents that is the climax of Genesis 34, which has been accurately described as "the most graphically human story . . . [in] the whole of Genesis."[15]

"I have never heard it given in an Anglican lesson nor mentioned in any sermon,"[16] observes Julian Pitt-Rivers, a British anthropologist who recalls his shock at discovering at a tender age that rape and mass murder are not the only dirty little secrets of the Bible: "[I]ncest, fratricide, filiocide, wife-lending, polygamy, homosexuality and prostitution" were among the revelations for a curious young boy at home alone with the family Bible. "It seemed positively unfair," Pitt-Rivers remarks, "that Adam and Eve should have been cast out of Eden for such a trivial peccadillo as eating an apple off the wrong tree."[17]

So I have attempted in these pages to let the reader see what is actually written in stories that have been suppressed, censored, or merely ignored over the millennia. To be sure, our understanding of the Bible should not end with an open-eyed reading of the stories that are told by the biblical authors with such candor and such passion. But it should certainly begin there.

THE FORGOTTEN BIBLE

Nowadays few of us bother to open the Bible at all. But now and then a modern storyteller will resurrect some of these forbidden texts and make them accessible to a readership that has forgotten what's in the Bible—or never knew in the first place. Andrew Lloyd Webber retells one of the most familiar of Bible stories in his much-performed musical *Joseph and the Amazing Technicolor Dreamcoat*, and yet he feels compelled to footnote his own libretto, so to speak, when he refers to an incident that appears in every version of the Bible but not in the common experience of his audience.

Thus, when Webber shows us the failed seduction of young Joseph by the nymphomaniacal wife of his Egyptian master, the librettist feels obliged to reassure us that he did not just make up the half-comical, half-erotic tale of an embittered seductress who condemns Joseph to prison because he does not succumb to her charms.

"It's all there in chapter thirty-nine," croons the narrator of *Joseph and the Amazing Technicolor Dreamcoat*, "of Gen-e-sis."[18]

Other storytellers may be less scrupulous when they scavenge a plot line from the Scriptures. Mordecai Richler, describing a gang of "hard-core show biz expatriates" at play on Hampstead Heath in *St. Urbain's Horseman*, a novel set in London in the swinging '60s, introduces us to one enterprising television scriptwriter who knew exactly where to find story ideas that would strike the network executives (and the viewers, too) as stunningly original:

> Not only had he plundered the Old Testament for most of his winning *Rawhide* and *Bonanza* plots, but now that his Lilian was obviously in heat again, his hard-bought Jewish education, which

his father had always assured him was priceless, served him splendidly once more. Moey remembered his *David ha'Melech: And it came to pass in the morning, that David wrote a letter to Joab, and sent it by the hand of Uriah. And he wrote in the letter, saying, Set Uriah in the forefront of the hottest battle, and retire ye from him, that he may be smitten, and die.* Amen.[19]

The point of Richler's story, of course, is that we are so little acquainted with what goes on in the Bible that no one in Hollywood will notice if a plot is cribbed from the Book of Samuel. Only rarely will some secular reader happen across one of the forbidden tales of the Bible, parse out the dense and difficult passages of the typical English translation, and wake up to the fact that the Bible is one hot read.

"From start to finish, it is a book of wild, shattering behavior," reports Michael Ventura, a newspaper columnist whose thoroughly modern mind was blown by what he found in the Bible. "Women consort with serpents, brothers kill one another, peoples are massacred, tribes roam deserts, babies are abandoned, murder follows prophecy, prophecy follows murder, dancers call for the heads of prophets." And Ventura comes to the conclusion that any society which elevates the Bible to the stature of Holy Writ is bound to be outrageous. "It is ridiculous," he concludes, "to expect a civilization based on such a book to be other than wild and shattering."[20]

THE LIBERATING BIBLE

The forbidden texts of the Bible deal frankly with sex and violence, but there is much more than mere shock and titillation in these stories of human passion. Buried in the dusty old texts, almost like artifacts in an archaeological dig, are treasures of insight and inspiration that remind us of the loftiest values of Judaism, Christianity, and Islam while, at the same time, allowing us to see the traces of much older spiritual traditions that have been ignored or suppressed by all three faiths.

Indeed, these artifacts of ancient spirituality reveal that the Bible is *not* a work of strict fundamentalism. We have been encouraged to think of God as a divine father who bestowed his blessings on a series of men created in "his" image—but here we will encounter women who are so daring, so powerful, and so resourceful that they outshine even the venerable patriarchs and prophets who are supposedly the moral beacons of the Bible. We are taught that the Bible is a work of strict and highly refined monotheism—but we will find the intriguing remnants of forbidden spirituality, including goddess worship, fertility rituals, and even human sacrifice, all of which were supposedly repudiated by the Children of Israel and expunged from the Judeo-Christian tradition in deference to the One God. Above all, we will be reminded of the humane and compassionate message at the heart of the Bible, both the Hebrew Bible and the New Testament, a message that has often been overlooked over the centuries, and never more so than in our own times.

Today, fundamentalists of all three Bible-based religions claim to find in the Holy Scriptures a divine excuse for repression and much worse. They cite chapter and verse, literally, to condemn abortion, divorce, and homosexuality; they claim to find in the Bible divine justification to take and keep some of the most hotly disputed territory on earth; they feel empowered by the Almighty to pronounce death sentences on those whose words and thoughts offend them. Yet if we look deeply into the forbidden texts of the Bible, we will discover that men and women, clans and tribes, peoples and nations—despite their differences of race and faith—manage to tolerate each other, to share the earth with each other, and to encounter each other in peaceful and loving ways. It's a liberating experience to discover what the Bible *really* says about the politics of sex, for example, as well as the politics of nations.

"A NEED TO TELL AND HEAR STORIES"

The book you are about to read consists of seven surprising and even shocking stories from the Bible. All of the stories are drawn from the portion of Holy Scripture that is known in Christian usage as the Old Testament, that is, the Hebrew Bible, a book that is regarded as sacred by Judaism, Christianity, and Islam. Each story is retold in contemporary English prose, and each one is accompanied by a chapter that explores the "backstory" of the biblical narrative: how and when the story found its way into the Bible; how it has been understood and explained; what it tells us about the lives and beliefs of real men and women who lived in biblical times; and what it can reveal to us about our own troubled world.

The biblical authors were master storytellers, and the Bible survives precisely because its stories are so powerful and so resonant. Indeed, the Bible feeds a primal appetite that is at least as demanding as our hunger for God. "A need to tell and hear stories is essential to the species *Homo sapiens*," writes Reynolds Price in his retelling of tales from the Gospels, *A Palpable God*, "second in necessity apparently after nourishment and before love and shelter."[21]

So, one of my goals in retelling these stories is to tug the sleeve of the reader who does not know or even suspect the richness (and, often, the ribaldry) of biblical narrative. That's why I have attempted to open up and flesh out the stories, to render them in a prose style that will be more familiar and more accessible to the contemporary reader than the compressed language of the original Hebrew—or, for that matter, the sometimes dense and difficult language of the Bible in traditional English translation. Now and then I have taken the liberty of adding scenes, dialogue, and description that are not actually in the original text of these stories as they appear in the Bible, but I have tried to find some plausible source in biblical scholarship or the Bible itself to justify the exercise of poetic license. As we will see later in this book (see chapter sixteen), the tradition of retelling and reinterpreting the stories of the Bible is a long and honorable one, and I have not been shy about following in that tradition.

To assist the reader in distinguishing between the retelling of each story and the real thing, I have reproduced an English translation of the original and complete text of the stories as they actually appear in the Hebrew Bible in text boxes alongside the retold stories. When I quote the original biblical text, I generally use an English translation of the Bible first published by the Jewish Publication Society in 1917, a translation that closely follows the classic King James Version that has long been used in Protestant churches of various denominations. Occasionally I refer to other English translations of the Bible, and I will let you know when I am quoting another version.

As I have suggested here, readers may be startled, perhaps even shocked, and—I hope—entertained *and* enlightened by what is to be found in the neglected and forbidden corners of the Bible. These stories reveal the complexity of the human heart and mind; they show us what human beings really feel and what they really do; and they suggest that a good and righteous life is not always a matter of simple obedience to what we imagine to be the moral strictures of the Bible. In that sense, I hope to take back the Bible from the strict and censorious people who wave it in our faces and to restore it to the worldly man or woman who will appreciate the flesh-and-blood passions that are described in the Holy Scriptures.

Someone very near and dear to me once turned to the stories of Isaac Bashevis Singer as a kind of balm for the suffering that he experienced after a messy love affair ended badly. "I didn't know people like *me* actually did things like *that*," he said of his own misadventures, "until I started to read Singer."

What I know now is that he need only have picked up the Bible to discover what Singer already knew: The Bible is a map of the human heart, and no secret chamber or hidden passage is left out. And it's a map whose creator, whether human or divine, regarded even our most outlandish passions with a kind and compassionate eye. That's why the forbidden tales of the Bible are not merely a rollicking good read; above all, the Bible affirms the essential qualities that make us human in the first place.

CHAPTER TWO

LOT AND HIS DAUGHTERS

"Come, let us make our father drink wine. . . ."
—GENESIS 19:32

A blood-red moon finally rose after midnight, but a distant glow had been visible on the horizon long before, as if something afire were boiling up from the waters of the Dead Sea and spreading across the desert floor. Ever since that terrible morning when the earth shuddered and fire fell from the sky, the air was full of foul-smelling smoke and greasy ash by day, and the moon was stained red by night.

Day and night, the youngest daughter of the man called Lot watched from the mouth of the mountain cave where they had sought shelter. Her sister refused to come out at all; she lingered in the dark corners of the cavern, curled up alone, arms wrapped around her knees, rocking back and forth like a child in a bad temper. A few feet away, their father dozed in his own stony alcove, occasionally lifting himself up only to nibble something from the basket of food or sip from the bottle of wine that they had thought to bring along, then slipping into sleep again.

The younger one was not afraid to venture out of the cave. She skittered up and down the rocky slope, sometimes daring to go as far as a stone's throw from the mouth of the cave, but never so far that she could not scamper back inside if danger threatened. She looked for something green that they might be able to eat, some small animal that they might be able to hunt and kill, and—God willing—a spring that might replenish the skins of water that they had dragged up from the oasis town far below them.

Above all, the younger one looked for the sign of another human being, whether man, woman, or child. She surveyed the jagged peak of the mountain, peered into the cracks of the black and gray rock on the lower slopes, shaded her eyes as she looked out over the empty desert floor, but she saw no one.

"You're foolish, little sister," the older one would insist whenever they spoke of her vigil outside the cave. "No one else is alive but us. And it's a good thing, too, because if anyone *did* find us, he would be like one of those brutes from back home—he would take you, if and how he wishes, and then he would slay you."

Then the older one would fall silent, and begin to rock back and forth again.

"But don't worry, little sister," she would always say. "No one will come—because no one else is alive but us."

The older one was right, of course, about the kind of men who lived in Sodom. Back home, the younger one remembered, the menfolk were brutal to any stranger who was unlucky enough to reach the city gates,

---

And the two angels came to Sodom at even; and Lot sat in the gate of Sodom; and Lot saw them, and rose up to meet them; and he fell down on his face to the earth; and he said: "Behold now, my lords, turn aside, I pray you, into your servant's house, and tarry all night, and wash your feet, and ye shall rise up early, and go on your way." And they said: "Nay; but we will abide in the broad place all night." And he urged them greatly; and they turned in unto him, and entered into his house; and he made them a feast, and did bake unleavened bread, and they did eat.

—GENESIS 19:1–3

and they were not much friendlier to their own neighbors. Toward women, they were like beasts. On the day before they fled to the mountains, Lot's family had learned that lesson once again.

Their father returned to the house after nightfall with two hooded strangers. They had appeared at sunset at the gates to the city, where Lot bowed low to them and begged them to come home with him for a bath, an evening meal, and a bed for the night. At first the strangers refused: "We will spend the night on the street," they said. But Lot begged and pleaded with them, as was his custom when he encountered strangers who might bring him some good fortune, and they finally agreed to follow him home.

"Make welcome our guests," he commanded the women of the household, suddenly stern and imperious. "Wash their feet and make a meal for them!" And then Lot whispered to his wife the same wishful words she had heard many times before from her husband: "Who knows when an ordinary stranger on the road might turn out to be an angel sent from heaven?"

But the neighbors up and down the lane were not so welcoming. Someone had noticed the two strangers following Lot back to his house, and a knot of rowdy young men gathered outside his door. Perhaps they had been drinking, which was hardly surprising in Sodom, but wine alone did not explain their rough manners, which were common enough around town. Bored with the all-too-familiar pleasures readily available to them in Sodom, the townsfolk were aroused by the very presence of strangers: Here was fresh meat! Soon the young men were joined by other curiosity-seekers, young and old, and the crowd began to grow into a mob.

> *But before they lay down, the men of the city, even the men of Sodom, compassed the house round, both young and old, all the people came from every quarter. And they called unto Lot, and said unto him: "Where are the men that came in to thee this night? Bring them out unto us, that we may know them."*
>
> —GENESIS 19:4–5

"Hey, bring them out," someone shouted. "Bring out the strangers and let us have a look at them!"

"Yes, bring them out," another one called in a slurred voice, "so we can bugger them!"

And the rest of the crowd took up the cry, not only the rowdy young men who always seemed to range through the streets in search of excitement but their fathers and uncles, too. To Lot's younger daughter, who peered out from a window on the second floor while her sister cowered in bed, it seemed as if every lout and his brother had gathered outside their house.

Then she saw her father boldly step out of the house and close the door behind him. The crowd fell silent, as if in sheer amazement that Lot would actually leave the safety of his house and expose himself to their shouts, their fists—and worse.

"No, no, my friends," he said to them in a lilting voice, seeking to ingratiate himself with them by a fatherly scolding. "Do not be so wicked!"

"We want to bugger *someone*!" a voice called out from somewhere in the crowd, a voice thick with liquor and dangerous with the threat of sudden violence. His words were greeted with laughter that sounded like the braying of donkeys. "Give them to us!"

What her father said in reply, the younger daughter found hard to believe even though she heard it plainly.

"Look, my friends, I have two daughters in my house," cried Lot, raising both hands in a gesture of prayer. "Both of them virgins!"

And Lot went out unto them to the door, and shut the door after him. And he said: "I pray you, my brethren, do not so wickedly. Behold now, I have two daughters that have not known man; let me, I pray you, bring them out unto you, and do ye to them as is good in your eyes; only unto these men do nothing; forasmuch as they are come under the shadow of my roof."

—GENESIS 19:6–8

> *And they said: "Stand back." And they said: "This one fellow came in to sojourn, and he will needs play the judge; now will we deal worse with thee, than with them." And they pressed sore upon the man, even Lot, and drew near to break the door. But the men put forth their hand, and brought Lot into the house to them, and the door they shut. And they smote the men that were at the door of the house with blindness, both small and great; so that they wearied themselves to find the door."*
>
> —GENESIS 19:9–11

A murmur rolled through the crowd, and the younger daughter shivered.

"I beg you to let me bring them out to you," Lot continued, "and you can do what you want with them . . ."

Yes, that's right, the younger daughter later told her incredulous sister, not once but many times, *that is exactly what our father said.*

". . . do whatever pleases you with my daughters, I beg you," Lot repeated pleadingly, "but do not touch the strangers who have sought shelter under my roof!"

If the prospect of having their way with two young virgins was appealing to the men in the crowd, they gave no sign of it. Indeed, Lot's offer seemed to stir them to an even hotter rage than before.

"Out of our way," one of the men shouted at Lot. "*You* are a stranger, too! And now you set yourself up so high and mighty—you think you can tell us what to do? Out of our way, *stranger!*"

"Or," another man took up, "we'll bugger *you* instead of *them!*"

The crowd surged forward, and Lot's daughter feared that her father would be crushed and dragged away. But then she saw the front door fly open, and the light from the lamps inside the house fall on the faces of the crowd. The two strangers reached out from the doorway, clapped their hands on Lot's shoulders, and yanked him back inside the house so suddenly that he seemed to disappear.

———

The crowd lingered outside the house, calling out and pounding on the door, but she could tell that their bloodlust had begun to ebb. A few men drifted away, laughing and singing bawdily, and the ones who remained were content to pass around flasks from which they occasionally took a long pull. Now and then, Lot's daughter heard the sound of shouting and cursing, but the words were directed from one man in the crowd toward another; they seemed to have forgotten about the strangers—and the young women—inside the house. Now and then, she heard a *thunk* and then a cry of pain—"*Owww!*"—as one of the men, blind drunk, bumped into a wall or a corner of the house. Before long, the stalwarts who lingered outside Lot's house were so drunk that they could not have found the front door if they tried, and even they began to stagger off in one direction or another.

But there was still a quiet commotion in Lot's house, and his youngest daughter positioned herself at the top of the staircase so she could hear the words that her parents were whispering to one another in such urgent tones.

"Who *are* these strangers?" demanded Lot's wife, looking to the corner next to the hearth where the two figures, wrapped in their long cloaks, appeared to sleep. "And why have you brought them here to afflict us?"

"As I have told you, they are angels! They are messengers of the Lord who have come to bestow some gift upon us, which is what I have predicted many times, if you will recall," Lot said solemnly. "I could do no less than welcome them into our home."

"Angels, you say!" His wife laughed bitterly. "Demons, more likely. Or madmen."

"Quiet," Lot pleaded. "Did you not see them pluck me out of the

And the men said unto Lot: "Hast thou here any besides? Son-in-law, and thy sons, and thy daughters, and whomsoever thou hast in the city; bring them out of the place, for we will destroy this place, because the cry of them is waxed great before the Lord; and the Lord hath sent us to destroy it."

—GENESIS 19:12–13

hands of the crowd? Did you not see the light that shone when they opened the door to rescue me? Did you not see how the men in the street were struck blind? They *must* be angels—"

"What I saw," Lot's wife hissed, "is a man who would sacrifice the virtue of his own flesh and blood in order to protect a couple of strangers!"

"Angels, that's what they are," he repeated. "Listen to what they told me: 'Get out of Sodom, you and your family, because God has sent us to destroy this place! Take your wife, your children, take anyone who belongs to you—and flee!' That is what they told me."

"And, of course, you will do what *they* say even though you never do what *I* say, your own wife and the mother of your daughters?" his wife parried. "If, in fact, you are not simply making up another tale."

"I swear, good wife, this is what they told me: The evildoers in Sodom are so many and so vile in the eyes of the Lord that He sent them to destroy the whole place and everyone in it, right down to the last blade of grass."

"Husband, you are mad, too!"

Never before had Lot's daughter seen her father so agitated, and she watched as he paced back and forth, kneading one hand in the other, stopping occasionally to sway back and forth as if in prayer. Then, suddenly, he headed for the door.

"Where are you going, madman?" her mother called. "It's the middle of the night!"

"To fetch our married daughters and their husbands!" her father called. "So they, too, can flee!"

Lot's youngest daughter slept where she sat, leaning against the wall at the top of the stairs, but she was wakened before dawn by the sound of

---

And Lot went out, and spoke unto his sons-in-law, who married his daughters, and said: "Up, get you out of this place; for the Lord will destroy the city." But he seemed unto his sons-in-law as one that jested.

—GENESIS 19:14

her father clambering back into the house. Her mother, too, stirred and rose to approach the old man, who was no less agitated than when he had left an hour or two before.

"What, then?" her mother asked, a mocking tone in her voice. "Where are our daughters and their husbands?"

"They refused to come," he said in a dull voice. "They laughed at me, as you do."

Lot sounded so dispirited that his wife took pity on him for a moment. "Sleep, then," she said in a softer tone, "and we'll talk more of this in the morning."

"Their husbands called me a fool," Lot complained. " 'Up, up and out of Sodom, because God is going to destroy this place,' I told them. And they said: 'Every night there is plenty of food and drink, plenty of singing and dancing in the streets. Everyone in Sodom is happy but you—and only *you* say Sodom will be destroyed.' "

She beckoned him to the bed she had made up near the stove, and he laid his head on the pillow next to her. Lot and his wife slept, and so did their daughters, as if they had forgotten about the strangers who waited out the long night somewhere in their house, neither seen nor heard.

At dawn, an unfamiliar voice awakened them all.

"Arise!" said one of the strangers, hovering over Lot. "Arise, take your wife and your daughters, and flee."

By now, Lot's older daughter was awake, too, and the younger one

---

And when the morning arose, then the angels hastened Lot, saying: "Arise, take thy wife, and thy two daughters that are here; lest thou be swept away in the iniquity of the city." But he lingered; and the men laid hold upon his hand, and upon the hand of his wife, and upon the hand of his two daughters; the Lord being merciful unto him. And they brought him forth, and set him without the city.

—GENESIS 19:15–16

> *And it came to pass, when they had brought them forth abroad, that he said: "Escape for thy life; look not behind thee, neither stay thou in all the Plain; escape to the mountain, lest thou be swept away."*
>
> —GENESIS 19:17

followed her down the short staircase to the room where Lot and his wife now stood before the strangers.

"What is going on here?" the older daughter demanded. "What do these men want?"

The two strangers reached out and took each member of the family by the hand. Their touch was hot, and their fingertips seemed afire with fever. A strange light burned in their eyes.

"The Lord will show his mercy to you, but only to you," one of the men said. "The rest will be destroyed—every man, woman, and child in Sodom, everything, right down to the last blade of grass."

Lot cast a glance in his wife's direction as if to say *I told you so!* She caught his glance and scowled back.

"Come with us now," the other stranger said, "and we will take you to safety before we begin our work."

Lot's wife started to speak, but the two strangers moved abruptly to the door and then into the street, where they disappeared from sight in a silver-gray fog that had settled over Sodom by night. Lot followed in haste, and suddenly he was gone, too. Now Lot's wife seized the two young women by the hand and followed her husband through the doorway. As if in a dream, they all seemed to float down the road in the morning mist, past houses where the carousers still slept, until they found themselves on the outskirts of Sodom, well past the city gates, on the road leading out of town. Here the two strangers stopped and turned to face Lot and his family.

"Keep going until you reach the highest mountain," one of the strangers said, gesturing toward the range of black and gray peaks on the far horizon. "If you stay here, you will be burned into ash along with the others."

"Flee for your life!" the other one commanded. "And do not look back!"

And Lot said unto them: "Oh, not so, my lord; behold now, thy servant hath found grace in thy sight, and thou hast magnified thy mercy, which thou hast shown unto me in saving my life; and I cannot escape to the mountain, lest the evil overtake me, and I die. Behold now, this city is near to flee unto, and it is a little one; oh, let me escape thither—is it not a little one?—and my soul shall live."

—GENESIS 19:18–20

"Why can't we look?" demanded Lot's wife, emboldened by the fact that they were now safely out of Sodom.

"Hellfire and brimstone will rain from the heavens," intoned one of the strangers in a solemn voice, "and all will be destroyed—"

"Right down to the last blade of grass?" Lot's wife interrupted.

"Yes, that's right," the other stranger continued, glancing at Lot and then fixing a stern gaze on his wife, "and you are not permitted to see it happen, or something terrible will happen to you, too!"

"Hasten to the mountain," the first one repeated, "and do not look back."

"The mountain, you say?" asked Lot.

The stranger sighed in exasperation. "Yes, the mountain."

"But, surely," Lot said, "if your servant Lot has found grace in your eyes—and, surely, I am your very humble servant—and if you have stretched your mercy so far that you are willing to save the life of one miserable man—*my* life, you understand—well, then, surely you can stretch your mercy just a bit farther, can't you?"

"What?" the stranger interrupted, now plainly out of sorts and anxious to get started on his work back in Sodom. "What are you talking about?"

"Kind masters, merciful masters," Lot stammered, "it's the *mountain*, which is so far off, and covered with snakes and wild beasts, I'm sure, and a hard climb even if we managed to get there at all. Surely it would be a foolish thing to spare my life here and now, only to have some evil befall me on the way to the mountain—and have me die anyway."

"Perhaps you do not understand," the other stranger said, struggling to control his temper, speaking slowly and clearly as if to a child. "A terrible thing is going to happen to the cities of the plain and everything that lives there, from your ill-mannered neighbors right down to the last blade of grass under your feet—as your wife has already grasped, even if you haven't—and you can only save yourself by *going to the mountain*."

"What is it about the word 'Flee!' that you don't understand?" the first one asked.

"Look," said Lot, bargaining now rather than pleading. "There's a small town not far away from here, just a watering hole and a few palm trees and some miserable hovels, just a *little* place, not a big cesspool of corruption like Sodom. I'm sure the people there are much nicer than the Sodomites who were so rude to you last night. Why don't you let me go *there*? After all, it's a tiny place, not even worthy of being called a town at all, really, don't you see? But it's so handy and close by, and if you could see it within yourselves to spare that little town, then my poor miserable family and I will find a decent place to lay our heads, and we won't have to go all the way into the wilderness and climb the mountain you speak of. So we might actually *survive* all the terrible things you're going to do, which is what you want, isn't it?"

"All right, all right, we'll do it," said the first stranger. "We'll spare the little town you speak of. But you've got to *go*, and you've got to go *right now*—"

"—because," the other one interrupted, "we can't even *start* doing what we came here to do until you're gone!"

"We'll go," Lot conceded at last. "Believe me, we're as good as gone already."

And he said unto him: "See, I have accepted thee concerning this thing also, that I will not overthrow the city of which thou hast spoken. Hasten thou, escape thither; for I cannot do any thing till thou be come thither." Therefore the name of the city was called Zoar.

—GENESIS 19:21–22

The sun was risen upon the earth when Lot came unto Zoar. Then the Lord caused to rain upon Sodom and upon Gomorrah brimstone and fire from the Lord out of heaven; and He overthrew those cities, and all the Plain, and all the inhabitants of the cities, and that which grew upon the ground.

—GENESIS 19:23

The sun was high in a cloudless blue sky by the time Lot and his little band of refugees spotted the oasis and the cluster of low houses that made up the little town, and then, suddenly, the terrible thing began, just as the two strangers had said it would. From somewhere far behind them came a low rumble of thunder, a belch of foul-smelling smoke, and a shudder of the earth itself that seemed to travel under their feet, tossing them up and down like puppets on a string.

Lot's older daughter began to cry.

"Father, what is happening back there?" she asked. "What is happening to our good sisters and their babies?"

"Maybe they have changed their minds," the younger daughter suggested, "and they're following behind us right now."

"Yes, yes," said Lot's wife, no longer sounding so scornful of what the strangers had vowed to do. "Maybe the little one is right. Maybe we should wait here for them to catch up with us—"

"Don't be a fool," Lot commanded, though his quivering voice betrayed his fear. "We do what the angels told us—and flee!"

Lot's wife laughed bitterly. "Angels?" she said. "You still call them angels, these strangers with the blood of your own daughters on their hands?"

Then, as if to silence her, a sharp cracking sound was heard from far away, and a wave of heat rolled up from behind them and enveloped them. The air seemed to thicken and shimmer before their eyes, the stink of sulphur filled their nostrils, and new sounds reached their ears, as if the cries of men and women and babies, suffering and dying, were carried on the hot wind across the plain all the way from Sodom.

"Oh, Momma—" cried the older daughter.

"Hurry!" cried Lot, pulling ahead of his wife and daughters.

> *But his wife looked back from behind him, and she became a pillar of salt. And Abraham got up early in the morning to the place where he had stood before the Lord. And he looked out toward Sodom and Gomorrah, and toward all the land of the Plain, and beheld, and, lo, the smoke of the land went up as the smoke of a furnace. And it came to pass, when God destroyed the cities of the Plain, that God remembered Abraham, and sent Lot out of the midst of the overthrow, when He overthrew the cities in which Lot dwelt.*
>
> —GENESIS 19:26–29

Now they began to walk faster, panting and gasping in the vile air, suddenly so heavy with greasy white ash, and they hastened toward the first house on the outskirts of the little town. They heard another rumble from far behind them and broke into a trot, not stopping until they reached the shelter of the first house.

Lot bent over, hands on his knees, trying to catch his breath. His older daughter simply folded up like a doll and rolled to the ground, weeping quietly. But his wife stood upright and rigid. "Maybe the others are coming right now," she said aloud. "Maybe we can see them on the road—"

"Momma, don't!" cried the younger daughter, but it was too late. Her mother turned and looked. Shading her eyes with one hand, squinting against the terrible light that burned on the far horizon, Lot's wife stared into the distance. What she saw, the rest of them never knew.

Her eyes widened, but she did not speak. Her mouth twisted into a horrible knot, and then, as Lot's younger daughter looked up at a face she barely recognized, the terrible expression began to harden. The hot ash that was drifting down from the sky like silent rain began to cover the crown of her head, the tip of her nose, her arms and shoulders. And then, falling more quickly now, the ash cooled, hardened, and crystallized, until Lot's wife was encased in a shell of opalescent white rock that turned her into a statue of herself. Whether it was the flakes of ash falling on her lips or the tears falling from her eyes, Lot's youngest daughter suddenly tasted salt on her tongue.

"Father!" she shouted, but Lot could barely hear her voice over the hot wind that blew around them from the direction of Sodom. Then, turning to follow his daughter's gaze, Lot beheld what had become of his wife. He nodded slowly, then sighed.

"She should not have looked," their father said. "You heard the angels tell her so, did you not?"

The little town where they found refuge had been spared from hellfire and brimstone, as the strangers promised, but the place was deserted. To Lot's relief, no corpses were to be seen in the tents and low houses that lined the road, but also no townspeople, no livestock, not even a stray dog. Perhaps the townspeople had been exterminated by the angels, or, more likely, they had fled before the sights and sounds coming from the direction of Sodom and Gomorrah. Lot and his daughters trudged along the road, hungry and weary, their eyes burning and their lungs straining for breath, until Lot stopped and held up one hand.

"Let us pause here," Lot said at the threshold of the largest house, "and refresh ourselves."

If the owners of the house had escaped, they left in a hurry. Lot and his daughters found warm food on the plates in the kitchen, clothing in the chests, a well-stocked pantry, and a storehouse behind the house, full of wine and grain and oil in earthenware vessels. They sat down at the table and dined in silence on the food that had been left behind. The two young women ate and drank sparingly, but Lot poured himself generous portions of wine from one of the jars that he found in the storehouse. Then he claimed a large bed that had belonged to the master of the house, wrapped himself in the dusty bedding, and fell into a deep sleep while his daughters searched out some blankets and made up their beds on the floor.

Neither daughter slept soundly. Nightfall came early, if only because the day was turned into twilight by the bilious clouds that boiled up out of Sodom and drifted overhead. All the while, they were afflicted by the stench on the wind that blew from the direction of Sodom, the greasy smoke and the settling ash that was carried along with it, and the occasional rumbles and shocks that could be felt before they were heard.

If one of Lot's daughters succeeded in drifting off to sleep, she would awake with a start at a sound that seemed to come now from the street outside, now from the roof, now from the very next room. Yet if one of them rose and peered out, she found the courtyard of the house and the street beyond utterly empty. And when they found their father in the kitchen the next morning, already swigging a bottle of wine, they discovered that he, too, had been stirred by these ghostly sounds.

"I swear the place is haunted," he said. "We will not stay here another night."

"But where will we go?" his older daughter asked mournfully. "Sodom is destroyed, and everyone with it. Even our poor mother!"

Lot considered for a moment, took another long pull on the bottle, and then nodded.

"The mountain," he announced in a voice that struck his daughters as almost cheerful.

No one spoke of it, but Lot's younger daughter thought to supply the little band of survivors with a few supplies from the house. When at last they trudged out of town, she pulled along a wooden cart loaded with skins full of water, sacks of flour, and a few sealed clay jars, some filled with wine, some with oil. Her sister carried a bundle of blankets and cloaks on her back. Lot led the way, wielding only a long wooden staff that he had found by the threshold of the house.

Once they cleared the last stand of date palms and joined the road out of town, they began to see the aftermath of what had happened on the day their mother was turned into a pillar of salt. Corpses of men, women, and children could be seen here and there along the roadside and in greater numbers at the crossroads. Their packs and carts were broken and overturned, their household goods scattered in the sand. Their animals had fled, and the hot wind was already turning their remains into mummies.

At the crossroads, Lot and his daughters kept their eyes down to avoid even a glimpse in the direction of Sodom, and turned instead toward the low range of ash-gray mountains on the horizon. The highest one, studded with crags and peaks, seemed only a short distance off, but they would have to cross a vast expanse of cracked hardpan and sharp stones before they reached the place of refuge promised to them by the strangers.

Lot's younger daughter soon showed herself to be adept at finding food and water and shelter even in the forbidding reaches of the hill country. She scouted out a cave where they spread their bedding and stored their provisions. She caught small animals in a snare fashioned out of twigs and strips of cloth torn from her own clothing. She found a desert plant that was prickly on the outside but sweet and wet on the inside. As she grew braver, she explored the rocky peaks above the cave, and she found a hidden canyon that offered a stand of date palms and a spring of water deep inside a grotto. It was then she realized that, even if the rest of the world had been blasted into salt ash, they would not die after all.

"We will be all right, sister," the younger one said one day. "We have enough to eat and drink."

"Yes, but what kind of life will we have here?" the older one complained. "We are alone in all the world. Everyone else is dead. Do you know what that means?"

The little sister looked at her quizzically.

"It means that we will never see a man other than our father for as long as we live," the older one said. "We will never marry. We will never bear children. Our father is already an old man and growing older fast, as you can see for yourself. When he dies, we will be alone in this miserable place until *we* grow old and die."

The little one considered her sister's dire prediction. True enough, they had seen no living human being since the morning they rushed out of Sodom. And she, too, had noticed that her father seemed older, grayer, and more feeble as each day passed.

"I wish Momma was here, don't you?" she said at last.

And the first-born said unto the younger: "Our father is old, and there is not a man in the earth to come in unto us after the manner of all the earth. Come, let us make our father drink wine, and we will lie with him, that we may preserve seed of our father."

—GENESIS 19:31–32

"But she isn't," the older one said in a sharp voice that reminded the younger one of their mother. "And that means there is only one solution to the problem."

"What do you mean, sister?"

"We will lie with our father," she announced grimly, "and *he* will give us babies."

"Lie with Father?"

"Don't pretend to be so innocent. You heard what the women used to talk about when you were drawing water from the well. You know how babies are made."

"You want to make a baby with our *father?*" she squealed. "What a horrible thought!"

"We will make babies so we will not be alone when he dies—and so there will be someone left here when *we* die." The older sister seemed angry. "It's the only thing left for us to do."

"If we were back home," the younger one said, "we would have proper husbands to lie with us and give us babies, as our poor dead sisters did with their husbands."

The older sister laughed out loud. "Have you already forgotten what men were like in Sodom? Anyway, they're all gone now, and the only man left is our father."

The younger one thought for a moment and then nodded.

"Tell me what I need to know," she said. "Tell me what I need to do."

The older one had contrived to put aside a couple of jars of wine from the oasis town, and she kept them hidden even when Lot's supply ran out and he began to groan in despair over the lack of something to drink besides water. Now she fetched the wine from its hiding place,

---

And they made their father drink wine that night. And the first-born went in, and lay with her father; and he knew her not when she lay down, nor when she arose.

—GENESIS 19:33

---

and she appeared at his alcove as the sun was setting and the shadows inside the cave were deepening. Soon, she knew, it would be so dark that neither of them would be able to see the other at all.

"Look, Father," she said cheerfully. "Look what I found."

"What is it? I can't see a thing."

"A jar full of wine," she announced. "From the house back in that little town."

"Where the devil did that come from? I *knew* I had another jar somewhere. Have you been hiding it from me, you ungrateful child?"

"Oh, no, how could you think such a thing of me?" she said coquettishly. "I found it among the rocks outside the cave—we must have dropped it on the way up the mountain."

"Well, then, give it to me—"

"Here it is, Father," she said. "Drink your fill."

She hung back in the shadows while her father pulled the stopper and lifted the heavy jar to his lips. He drank greedily, but took care not to spill even a drop of the precious stuff. Then he pushed the stopper back into the mouth of the jar.

"I'll save some for tomorrow," he announced virtuously. "I'll make it last."

"No, father, drink your fill. Actually, the truth is that I found two jars. So you will still have a drink tomorrow."

"Two jars you have hidden?" Lot said. He drank a long draught, belched loudly, and then drank again. Deprived of wine for so long, he seemed to feel the stuff boil up into his head as soon as it touched his lips. His eyes blurred, and his head swam. To his amazement, his daughter seemed to disappear before his eyes, although he could not be sure because the cave itself seemed to tilt crazily and slip into profound darkness as the sun went down. He took another long sip and allowed himself to doze.

Lot's daughter, crouching a few feet away in the darkness, heard the rhythmic sound of his breathing. She sighed, then unfastened her robe and set herself to the task at hand. Her father was heavy and hard to handle, and she was panting with exertion as she struggled to position him. So drunk was her father that when she emerged from the cave some time later, he did not even stir.

———

> *And it came to pass on the morrow, that the first-born said unto the younger: "Behold, I lay yesternight with my father. Let us make him drink wine this night also; and go thou in, and lie with him, that we may preserve seed of our father." And they made their father drink wine that night also. And the younger arose, and lay with him; and he knew not when she lay down, nor when she arose.*
>
> —GENESIS 19:34–35

The younger sister was waiting at the mouth of the cave, watching the reflection of the full moon on the far-distant waters of the Dead Sea, when the older one joined her at last. She half-expected her older sister to look somehow disfigured, somehow tainted, but the moonlight did not reveal any obvious scars. She noticed only that her sister seemed pale and fatigued and vaguely disheveled.

"What happened?" the younger one asked with urgent curiosity. "What did he say?"

"He didn't say anything, thank God," the older one said grimly. "He was too drunk to even notice."

"He didn't notice when you—"

"He did not even know I was there," her older sister interrupted, as if afraid to hear spoken out loud what had happened back in the cave, "and he didn't even know when I left." She paused. "I did what I had to do, and when I was done, I left him fast asleep like a beast."

"Well," the younger one ventured, "that makes it all a little easier, doesn't it?"

"Yes, it does," the older one said. "And tomorrow, little sister, it's your turn."

The younger one was silent.

"But there are some things you'll have to know," the older sister began. "Some things you'll have to *do*."

"You've already told me how to make a baby—"

"Well, as it turns out, there's more you need to know," she said. "At least, when the man is dead drunk on the floor, there's more."

"What do you mean, sister?"

> *Thus were both the daughters of Lot with child by their father.*
> *And the first-born bore a son, and called his name Moab—the*
> *same is the father of the Moabites unto this day. And the*
> *younger, she also bore a son, and called his name Ben-ammi—*
> *the same is the father of the children of Ammon unto this day.*
>
> —GENESIS 19:36–38

Lot's older and now wiser daughter pulled the younger one to her side and began to explain.

If Lot remembered anything of what happened on those two nights on the mountain, he said nothing of it. Even when the bellies of his daughters began to swell, even when it was quite obvious that they had lain with *someone* long after the last man in Sodom had been slain, Lot was silent.

When Lot's daughters gave birth, the older one called her son Moab, which means "from father," and the younger one called her son Ben-ammi, which means "son of my kin." But Lot gave no sign that he understood the message that his daughters intended to send him.

CHAPTER THREE

LIFE AGAINST DEATH

The Sacred Incest of Lot's Daughters

GOOD AND EVIL IN THE STORY OF LOT
A TRAGIC BUFFOON
INCEST IN THE ANCIENT WORLD ✣ SISTER AND WIFE
SEX AS POLITICS ✣ WHAT DID SARAH SEE?
"WHO IS THE THIRD WHO WALKS ALWAYS BESIDE YOU?"
LIFE AGAINST DEATH

Apologists of three religions have tried to explain away the scandalous conduct of Lot and his daughters ever since their tale was first recorded in the Book of Genesis. And yet, curiously enough, Lot's willingness to cast his virgin daughters to a lusty mob and his own incestuous (if unconscious) couplings with his daughters after their flight into the mountains are not regarded by clergy and commentators as his worst offenses as a father, a husband, and a man.

Lot is the hapless nephew of Abraham, the patriarch and "paradigm of the man of faith"[1] on whom God bestows a rich and enduring blessing: "I will make of thee a great nation," God tells Abraham (Gen. 12:2). Lot, by contrast, is something of a schlemiel who tags along after Abraham and relies on his kindly uncle to get him out of trouble. According to one of the oddest passages of the Bible, Abraham—a gentle old man "rich in cattle, in silver, and in gold" (Gen. 13:2)—is shown as a rough-and-ready campaigner who mounts up and rides out at the head of an army to rescue Lot from a powerful king who has taken Lot hostage (Gen. 14:14–16). The last and greatest of Abraham's favors to Lot—an act of audacity that Abraham does not undertake even when God orders him to sacrifice his own son—is the patriarch's plea to

God to spare the righteous of Sodom and Gomorrah (Gen. 18:23), Lot and his family presumably among them.

The jury of biblical exegetes, so to speak, is hung when it comes to the question of whether Lot is righteous at all. One faction insists that Lot, like his Uncle Abe, is "perfect and pious," as one of the sages put it.[2] Christian tradition regards Lot as a "righteous man," in the words of Peter, who likens him to Noah and argues that the rescue of Lot and his family from Sodom is a sign of God's willingness to "deliver the godly out of temptations" (2 Pet. 2:7–9 Scofield KJV). The Koran characterizes Lot, like Mohammed himself, as a prophet sent by Allah to rebuke the wicked.[3] The other faction holds that Lot is not much better than his fellow Sodomites: Lot is described elsewhere in rabbinical literature as "lascivious,"[4] and it is suggested that he chose to settle in Sodom precisely because he was attracted by the ribald goings-on.

The Bible itself is undecided on the moral worthiness of Lot. But it appears that sleeping with his own daughters in a drunken stupor—not once but twice—is the least of his crimes.

GOOD AND EVIL IN THE STORY OF LOT

Lot's righteousness—or lack of it—is the unspoken subtext of a remarkable debate between the patriarch Abraham and the Almighty over the fate of Sodom, where the question takes on life-and-death implications for Lot and his family. Abraham, who will later raise a knife to his son's throat at God's command without a single word of protest, summons up the courage to argue with God over good and evil, a gesture of defiance that may seem bizarre to any Bible reader who is under the impression that God prefers his believers to shut up and do what they are told.

One hot afternoon, as the story is told in Genesis, God* and a

---

*The "personal" name of God, conventionally rendered in English as "YHWH" or "Yahweh," is used in the biblical account of the destruction of Sodom and Gomorrah. Other names are used to refer to the deity elsewhere in the Bible. For the sake of simplicity, I will use "God," "the Lord," and "the Almighty" interchangeably to refer to the deity. The specific words and phrases used in the Hebrew Bible when referring to God are important clues to identifying the various authors to whom the biblical text is attributed, and the reader will find a brief discussion of the authorship of the Bible—and the significance of the names of God—in the appendix, *Who Really Wrote the Bible?*

couple of his angelic sidekicks appear at Abraham's tent "by the tere-binths of Mamre" in the guise of desert travelers, and Abraham hastens to make them welcome by washing their feet and serving them a meal. Since the dietary laws against mixing meat and milk will not go into effect until Moses comes along a few centuries later, the divine guests dig into a distinctly nonkosher meal that includes a veal roast *and* "curd and milk" (Gen. 18:1–8).

God's traveling companions are on their way to destroy Sodom and Gomorrah "because their sin is exceedingly grievous" (Gen. 18:20). God, who lingers behind, feels obliged to confide their mission of mass destruction to Abraham, apparently out of loyalty to the human being with whom he has recently made "an everlasting covenant" (Gen. 17:8 Scofield KJV). The otherwise compliant and uncomplaining Abraham has the chutzpah to argue with the Almighty over his bloodthirsty intentions toward Sodom and Gomorrah, the twin cities of sin and wretched excess.

"Will Thou indeed sweep away the righteous with the wicked?" says Abraham, acting as the self-appointed defender of the Sodomites, among whom his nephew Lot is numbered (Gen. 18:23).

After much carping and cajoling by Abraham, who haggles with the Almighty like a bazaar merchant, God finally concedes that if he finds as few as ten righteous souls in Sodom, then the whole city will be spared (Gen. 18:25–32). (For that reason, some sources suggest, the minyan or prayer quorum required for a Jewish religious service is ten.[5]) But we are forced to conclude that the Sodomites could not scrape together even a minyan, because the angelic messengers proceed to destroy not only Sodom and Gomorrah but several other "cities of the Plain" without mercy to man, woman, or child (Gen. 19:29).

As it turns out, however, Lot and his family *are* spared from the famous "hellfire and brimstone" that sweeps away the rest of the Sodomites, but *not* because they are declared to be righteous by God or anyone else. "[E]ven the righteous in these sin-laden cities, though better than the rest, were far from good," a rabbinical sage would later say.[6] So Lot's good fortune is yet another favor from his uncle—or a favor that God is willing to do for the otherwise undeserving kin-folk of his chosen one, Abraham.[7] "God remembered Abraham," the Bible pauses to tell us, "and sent Lot out of the midst of the overthrow (Gen. 19:29).

A TRAGIC BUFFOON

If Lot is *not* a righteous and upright man, exactly what are his crimes and misdemeanors? Much attention is paid in religious literature to the fine points of the hospitality that Lot extends to the two strangers who show up in Sodom on the eve of destruction. We are asked to believe that, according to the ethical code—and, more important, the etiquette—of the time and place where Lot lived, he did the right thing. "The spectacle of a father offering his virgin daughters to the will and pleasure of a mob that was seeking to despoil his household," offers one apologist, "would not have seemed as shocking to the ancient sense of proprieties as it may seem to us."[8]

Astoundingly, scholars and sages over the centuries have tended to overlook the most obvious and abhorrent conduct of Lot, and they spend much breath and ink in debating whether, for example, Lot ought to be condemned because he procrastinates in leaving Sodom or because he haggles with the angels over the place of refuge. A favorite subject is the comparison of Abraham and Lot as good hosts: Lot is found wanting because Abraham *ran* to meeting the angelic visitors who appeared at his tent while Lot "display[ed] no effort to go in haste" when they showed up in Sodom![9]

Even these supposed failings are excused by most sermonizers and exegetes. Lot's dillydallying before actually leaving Sodom is characterized as the cautious conduct that we might expect "of any home owner," and Lot's slightly ludicrous plea that the little town of Zoar* be spared is motivated not by Lot's desire for a more convenient refuge but by "an understandable concern for small and helpless things."[10] At worst, Lot is criticized as "passive, foppish, [and] foolish."[11]

When it comes to the most grotesque and repulsive of Lot's conduct—his willingness to cast his daughters to the mob—the apologists offer two thin excuses. First, we are told that the ancient laws of hospitality imposed on Lot a sacred obligation to protect his guests, even at the risk of his family and his own life. The fact that the guests turn out to be angels, which is not yet known to Lot at the moment when he

---

Zoar is translated from the Hebrew as "little." The "little town" that is spared at the request of Lot is thereafter called Zoar in the biblical text (Gen. 19:22) because Lot emphasized its small size in his plea to the angels of destruction.

offers his daughters to the mob, is entirely beside the point; a couple of nameless drifters, we are instructed, are no less worthy of Lot's hospitality than a team of heavenly messengers. Second, we are asked to believe that children were regarded as something less precious in biblical times than they are today, more nearly chattel than loved ones, and so a father was at liberty to do with his children (and especially his daughters) exactly as he pleased.

Now, it is true that a strict and perhaps even sacred code of hospitality prevailed among the desert-dwelling nomads of the ancient Near East, as it does among the Bedouins of the contemporary Near East: "As soon as a stranger had touched the tent-rope," explains one contemporary rabbinical scholar, "he could claim guest-right."[12] Survival in the wilderness may depend on the generosity and goodwill of travelers who encounter each other by chance, and it was held to be a solemn duty to shelter a stranger who appeared at one's tent. The Bedouin code of hospitality traditionally requires that strangers be offered food, drink, and a place to sleep for no less than three days even if the host is so poor that he is reduced to starvation by his efforts.[13]

Some anthropologists suggest that the duty of a good host extended even to providing sexual companionship to his guests, a practice that was supposedly observed among certain Bedouin tribes, "the modern-day heirs of Abraham," as recently as the last century.[14] If Lot regarded himself as obliged to extend a similar kind of "hospitality," of course, then the offer of his daughters for the sexual pleasure of the mob may have been even less remarkable in his own eyes, even if it strikes us as still more grotesque than the scene presented in the Bible itself.

It is true, too, that biblical law bestowed upon an Israelite father a considerable degree of authority over his family and especially his children. A father was empowered to mete out punishment to his offspring, to exclude them from his household, or even to sell them into slavery or concubinage as a pledge for a debt.[15] The Book of Deuteronomy authorizes a father to put a rebellious son to death, at least under certain narrow circumstances (Deut. 21:18–21). And, not unlike other times and places (including our own), a male child was valued more highly than a female child in the biblical world and the Bible itself. Only male children inherited property from their father, and a daughter was expected to marry into her husband's family—"and so," as one Bible scholar puts it, "the strength of a house was not measured by the number of its daughters."[16] For all of these reasons, some critics and commentators conclude that Lot simply does not value his daughters highly enough to place their safety above his duties to the strangers who sheltered under his roof.

So we are asked to exonerate and even to praise Lot for offering his daughters to the mob in order to protect his houseguests. Even if surrendering his daughters was "abhorrent to Hebrew morality," as one commentator concedes, we are supposed to regard Lot not as a craven coward but as "a courageous champion of the obligations of hospitality in a situation of extreme embarrassment,"[17] which we are encouraged to see as a higher calling than, say, the physical safety of one's children. Above all, we are urged *not* to render a moral judgment on the conduct of Lot as reported in the Bible—an ironic argument to make in defense of a book that is supposed to be the definitive authority on good and evil.

"The surprising offer of his daughters must not be judged simply by our Western ideas," urged Gerhard von Rad, a distinguished commentator on Genesis. "That Lot intends under no circumstances to violate his hospitality, that his guests were for him more untouchable than his own daughters, must have gripped the ancient reader."[18]

What grips the modern reader, by contrast, is Lot's readiness to allow "the claims of courtesy [to] transcend moral obligations of fatherhood," as one Bible scholar rather delicately puts it.[19] And it is simply not enough to shrug and say that we cannot understand how men and women who lived a few thousand years ago must have felt about *their* children. Even the first readers of these stories could not have failed to recoil at Lot's readiness to consign his daughters to gang rape, if only because, "as any Israelite reader of this text would know,"[20] the crime of rape is flatly condemned in biblical law and harshly punished in biblical legend. (See chapters four and fourteen.) Both the Bible itself and the weight of biblical scholarship confirm that children were regarded by the Israelites as nothing less than "a precious gift from God" and the fulfillment of God's oft-repeated promises to Abraham, Isaac, and Jacob that he would "multiply [their] seed."[21]

The attitude of the biblical author toward Lot is not spoken out loud, but it is hard to miss in an open-eyed reading of the Bible. Lot is depicted as neither a coward nor a champion; rather, he is shown to be a clown: "A tragic buffoon,"[22] in the words of one contemporary Bible scholar; "a laughing stock," "a jester," "a passive fool" according to another.[23] The encounters between Lot and his neighbors, his family, and his angelic rescuers remind us of the pig's bladder, the comic patter, and the blue humor of the vaudeville stage. As I have tried to suggest in my own retelling of the story, Lot's banter with the destroying angels over the fate of the "little town" called Zoar is the stuff of an Abbott and Costello routine, not a morality play.

"[T]he story of Lot and his desperate daughters ought to be told in a Yiddish accent," observes one dramatist who turned the story of Lot and his daughters into a stage play, "ending with: 'So, after all that work what happened? Their kids were *goyim!*' "[24]

When it comes to the forbidden sexual union of father and daughters, however, the biblical storyteller is straight-faced and even solemn. Neither Lot nor his daughters are criticized in the Bible or the religious literature that tries to explain away their sexual misadventures in that mountain cave overlooking a blasted Sodom. For his part, Lot is regarded as wholly innocent of what happens after his daughters ply him with wine and send him into a drunken stupor: "Lot is the victim, rather than the instigator, of this disgraceful affair," says one commentator.[25] And even his daughters, as we shall see, are regarded as heroines rather than seductresses. Incest, the biblical author seems to suggest, is hardly the worst offense against the moral order, especially when survival of the species, the kingship of Israel, and the birth of the Messiah appear to be at stake.

INCEST IN THE ANCIENT WORLD

Ever since Sigmund Freud replaced the Heavenly Father as a source of moral law, we have been taught to regard the taboo against incest as something deep and powerful, ancient and universal, and that is why the scenes of sexual intercourse between Lot and his own daughters are so shocking and unseemly when we encounter the story in the Holy Bible. But the fact is that the biblical world (and, as we shall see, the Bible authors) regarded incest with far less horror than we might suppose by reading the catalog of sexual prohibitions in the Book of Leviticus.

Sexual relations between blood relatives were *not* universally condemned in the faiths and cultures of the ancient Near East. For example, the civilizations of Mesopotamia, the place where Abraham and Lot were born, tolerated incest among gods if not among ordinary human beings. Although a prohibition against sexual intercourse between a father and his daughter is literally chiseled in stone in the Code of Hammurabi, the sacred myths of ancient Mesopotamia depicted the gods in sexual couplings with their own offspring and siblings.[26]

The laws and customs of ancient Egypt, the place to which Abraham and Lot traveled in search of sustenance during a famine, were more evenhanded: Gods and human beings alike were permitted to engage in incestuous marriages under certain circumstances. Since under Egyptian law property descended from a mother to her eldest daughter, rather than from father to son, a father might resort to marrying his own daughter (or a son might marry his sister) in order to prevent the family wealth from falling under the control of an outsider.[27] And a reigning pharaoh might wed his own sister in imitation of the myth of Isis and Osiris, the sibling-lovers with whom the rulers of Egypt identified themselves.[28]

The land of Canaan, located to the west of Mesopotamia and to the north of Egypt, fell within the contesting spheres of influence of both civilizations, and the Israelites who came to live in Canaan encountered a local tradition that imagined the Canaanite god called Baal in sexual union with his sister, Anat. Still, by the time the Israelites conquered and settled in Canaan after the Exodus from Egypt, the laws that are preserved in the Five Books of Moses—the first five books of the Hebrew Bible—plainly and pointedly condemned all forms of incest as practiced by non-Israelites:

"After the doings of the land of Egypt, wherein ye dwelt, shall ye not do," the Bible commands in the Book of Leviticus, "and after the doings of the land of Canaan, whither I bring you, shall ye not do" (Lev. 18:3).

Thus, the Bible specifically forbids sexual intercourse between an Israelite and any blood relative: mother or father, sister or brother, aunt or uncle, children or grandchildren, even in-laws and stepparents. "None of you shall approach to any that is near of kin to him, to uncover their nakedness: I am the Lord," is how the King James Version introduces the whole notion of incest, using a common biblical euphemism for sexual intercourse. And then, lest anyone start looking for loopholes, a veritable catalog of forbidden sexual conduct begins: "The nakedness of thy father, and the nakedness of thy mother, shalt thou not uncover. . . . The nakedness of thy sister. . . . The nakedness of thy father's wife's daughter . . ." and so on (Lev. 18:6–30).

Of course, according to the sequence of events described in the Bible itself, Lot and his daughters were not subject to *any* formal law against incest, since the legal codes found in Exodus, Leviticus, Numbers, and Deuteronomy were not handed down until God revealed them to Moses several centuries later. But modern biblical scholarship generally assumes that much (if not all) of the Bible was compiled and reduced to writing in its present form sometime around 600 B.C.E.* by editors (or "redactors") who drew on sources and traditions of great antiquity, added glosses and even whole new passages of their own, and tacked on new books of more recent authorship. For that reason, the authors and editors who compiled the stories that we find in Genesis were thoroughly familiar with the law codes that appear in Leviticus, and so it seems likely that they regarded incest as a forbidden act when they were retelling the story of Lot and his daughters. (See appendix: Who *Really* Wrote the Bible?)

Yet the very first act of incest reported in the Bible—Lot and his daughters—draws no punishment at all. Even when Reuben, the eldest son of the patriarch Jacob, slips into the bed of his father's concubine, Bilhah, he faces no consequences of any kind until the final illness of his father, when he finds out for the first time that he will be denied the inheritance that is due to him as the firstborn son. "[T]hou shalt not excel," says the dying patriarch to Reuben when the time comes to hand out the blessings and the curses, "because thou wentest up to thy father's bed; then defiledst thou it" (Gen. 35:22, 49:4).

Indeed, at least one biblical commandment—the curious tradition of the so-called levirate marriage—actually *requires* sexual intercourse between a man and the widow of his dead brother (Deut. 25:5–10). We will encounter a torrid example of the levirate tradition in action in the story of Judah and Tamar (see chapter six), and—rather like the story

---

*As used in the dating of historical events, B.C.E. (before the Common Era) is the equivalent of B.C. (before Christ), and C.E. (Common Era) is the equivalent of A.D. (Anno Domini, or Year of Our Lord). B.C.E. and C.E. are favored by many scholars who seek to avoid abbreviations that have specific religious implications, and I use them here for the same reason.

of Lot and his daughters—we will see that the biblical author does not suggest the slightest disapproval of what is otherwise a flagrant violation of the law against incest between a man and his sister-in-law or a father and his daughter-in-law as it appears in Leviticus (Lev. 18:15–16).

Thus the Bible betrays an attitude toward incest that is far more casual than one might expect from the stern pronouncements of Leviticus. And so, when the rabbis declared that the story of Reuben's affair with his father's concubine was not suitable to be read aloud in the synagogue, perhaps they were less concerned about the lurid details of the sexual encounter in Jacob's marriage bed than about the matter-of-fact quality of the narrative and the mildness of the punishment.

Indeed, we might wonder whether the catalog of forbidden sexual partners composed by the censorious authors of Leviticus says something about how commonplace the practice of incest may have been among the Israelites; after all, if incest were not regarded as a fact of life in the biblical world, why would the biblical lawgiver feel a need to go on at such length and in such tantalizing detail?[29]

SISTER AND WIFE

The willingness of a father to turn over his daughters to a mob bent on sexual violence is the single most disturbing moment in the story of Lot, and indeed one of the most alarming incidents in the Bible. But it is not the only story in which an otherwise righteous man is perfectly willing to expose a woman to danger in order to save his own skin; for example, a story in the Book of Judges tells us in stomach-turning detail exactly what would have happened if Lot *had* cast his daughters into the street. (See chapter twelve).

Not once but three times, the Bible depicts a scene in which a patriarch passes his wife off as his sister in order to protect himself from physical violence. For example, when Abraham and Sarah journey to Egypt to escape a famine in Canaan, Abraham insists on masquerading as Sarah's brother out of fear that any man who took a fancy to Sarah would be more likely to slay her spouse than her sibling in order to get Sarah into his bed. In fact, Sarah is recruited for service in the harem of the Pharaoh, and the Egyptian monarch lavishes gifts upon Abraham, the man he believes to be Sarah's brother. Abraham accepts the bounty of Pharaoh without comment, and only the intervention of God himself spares Sarah from actually sleeping with Pharaoh (Gen. 12:10–20).

We find the very same story in two other passages of Genesis. Abraham resorts to the same deception with yet another lusty monarch, Abimelech, King of the Philistines, and with the same results—Sarah ends up in Abimelech's bed but God warns him off at the very last minute (Gen. 20:2–10). Abimelech, like Pharaoh before him, is depicted as horror-stricken at the thought that he might have inadvertently slept with another man's wife, and both monarchs actually scold Abraham for putting them in such moral peril.

When confronted with his act of deception by the indignant Abimelech, Abraham concedes that Sarah is his wife—but insists that she is his half sister, too, as if that fact explained and excused his ruse. "She is . . . the daughter of my father," Abraham riddles, "but not the daughter of my mother" (Gen. 20:12). We cannot be entirely sure whether Abraham's belated claim that Sarah is his half sister is yet another deception, but rabbis and scholars have taken Abraham at his word and concluded on such sparse evidence that marriage between half siblings were permissible under the laws of ancient Israel. And they have argued that half-incestuous marriage was apparently still acceptable as late as the reign of King David, when his daughter, Tamar, proposes marriage as an alternative to rape at the hands of her half brother (see chapter fifteen).

The same ploy is adopted by Isaac, the son of Abraham and Sarah, when he makes his own journey to Abimelech's kingdom in the company of his wife, Rebekah. Like his father, Isaac resorts to the deception of calling Rebekah his sister out of plain cowardice. "[H]e feared to say: 'My wife,' " we are told, " 'lest the men of the place should kill me for Rebekah, because she is fair to look upon' " (Gen. 26:7). But the deception fails when Abimelech happens to look out the window of his palace and sees Isaac "sporting" with Rebekah—the Hebrew word used in the original text (*t'sahak*) suggests "fondling" or what we used to call "petting"[30]—and the good king figures that Rebekah is not really Isaac's sister after all. Abimelech realizes that he has been fooled (again!) and scolds Isaac for putting his own moral standing at risk, just as he once scolded Isaac's father for playing the same dirty trick (Gen. 26:1–10).

Bible scholars and sermonizers have engaged in much subtle

argument to explain away the baffling and cowardly conduct of Abraham and Isaac, which readers have always found "puzzling and disturbing,"[31] even "offensive."[32] Perhaps Sarah was merely adopted by Abraham's father at some undisclosed point in his childhood, they have speculated, and thus she was not a blood relation at all.[33] The boldest explanation, and the one that puts the patriarchs in the best light, is based on a long-forgotten tradition of an ancient people known as the Hurrians who placed such importance on the brother-sister relationship that a man might adopt his wife as his sister at the same time he married her.

Abraham and Isaac adopted the Hurrian tradition of identifying their wives as their sisters, suggests one authoritative Bible scholar, in order to invoke "all the . . . safeguards and privileges" that were available to a man's sister (but not to his wife).[34] By the time the biblical authors and editors assembled the legend and lore of ancient Israel into what we now know as the Bible, it has been suggested, they simply did not know or understand the Hurrian tradition of wife-as-sister. "Tradition had apparently set much store by these incidents," Ephraim Speiser explains, "but the key to them had been lost somewhere in the intervening distances of time and space."[35] Rather than discard the three baffling tales, they tried to explain what Abraham and Isaac were doing in terms that their readers might understand.

The only explanation that made sense to biblical redactors—or, for that matter, makes sense to us—is the one that shows us the otherwise worthy patriarchs as timid souls who are perfectly willing to consign their wives to the beds of powerful men in exchange for their own physical safety and, perhaps, a king's reward.

SEX AS POLITICS

The choice of bed partners as depicted in Holy Scripture is sometimes a matter of politics and diplomacy rather than love or lust. Solomon, for example, is said to have accumulated seven hundred wives (1 Kings 11:3), and it is likely that many of these marriages were meant to seal alliances between an Israelite king at the height of his power and the princes and potentates of the surrounding nations and empires. And even when the Bible reports a sexual encounter that is frankly incestuous, political ambition rather than sexual adventure is sometimes at the heart of the matter, as when Absalom, son of King David, conducts a public orgy with his father's concubines on the palace rooftop.

David's concubines were installed in what can only be called a harem—the kings of Israel, like other monarchs of the ancient Near East, collected wives and concubines in great profusion, and the harem was a symbol of the grandeur and opulence of a king's court. The much-married Solomon, for example, stocked his harem with an additional three hundred concubines. And we are plainly told that Ahaziah, a descendant of David and Solomon, aped the ways of pagan kings by recruiting (or making) eunuchs* to secure the chastity of his wives (2 Kings 9:32), even though a man whose "privy parts" are "crushed or maimed" is regarded with horror by the biblical author known as the Deuteronomist (Deut. 23:2).

A harem guard was essential because the chastity of a king's wife or concubine was another symbol of the monarch's power and potency. Thus, when the rebellious Absalom goes to war against his father, King David, and drives the monarch out of Jerusalem, he chooses a striking (and notably Freudian) gesture to symbolize the assumption of his father's throne: Absalom takes captive the royal concubines who had been left behind by the fleeing monarch, erects a tent on the roof of the royal palace, where he can be seen by all of Jerusalem, and makes love to each of the ten concubines "in the sight of all Israel" (2 Sam. 16:22). The political message was unmistakable: "To lie with a monarch's concubine," one Bible scholar has written, "was tantamount to usurpation of the throne."[36]

Unlike Reuben, who also may have been challenging his father's authority by sleeping with Jacob's concubine, Absalom pays for his sexual defiance with his life—but, then, he would have been subject to execution for his rebellion against the reigning king whether or not he had crowned his palace coup with a public orgy. And David apparently regards the women as tainted by sexual contact with his son, and he spurns them after he regains his throne and his harem: "So they were shut up unto the day of their death, [living] in widowhood" (2 Sam. 20:3).

Of course David could not have been too surprised by Absalom's sexual derring-do. After all, David himself had slept with the wives of

---

*As translated in NEB; some other versions translate as "officers."

his predecessor, King Saul, as a symbol of his kingship (2 Sam. 12:8), thus setting an example for his own randy and rebellious sons. And when Solomon is crowned as king of Israel after the death of David, one of his brothers, Adonijah, ever-so-politely asks permission to sleep with their father's favorite concubine, the delectable but untouched Abishag; Solomon marks the gesture for what it is—a bid for the throne—and sends an assassin to kill his impudent brother (1 Kings 2:12–25).

To engage in sexual relations with the concubine of one's father— an act that we might liken to sleeping with one's stepmother—was a violation of a sexual taboo that had been raised to a divine commandment in the Bible. But the real crime of these daring and ambitious men—David, Absalom, Adonijah, and others whose exploits are recorded in the Holy Bible—was treason rather than incest.

WHAT DOES SARAH SEE?

The disappearance of four words in an early version of the biblical text raises the intriguing if troubling prospect that the Bible also records an incident of incestuous child molestation, a notion so shocking that it may have been literally written out of the Bible by the rabbinical censors. Did Ishmael, the firstborn son of the patriarch Abraham, molest his five-year-old half brother, Isaac?

Abraham and Sarah* are childless, as we read in Genesis, and so Sarah sends her husband to the bed of her own handmaiden, an Egyptian woman named Hagar, to find a fertile womb. When Hagar is impregnated, however, a suddenly jealous Sarah has a change of heart and banishes the handmaiden to the wilderness. An angel rescues Hagar from death by thirst and starvation in the desert and sends her back to Abraham's encampment, where she bears a son named Ishmael (Gen. 16:4–16).

---

*In the early passages of Genesis, Abraham's name is given as Abram, and Sarah's name is given as Sarai. Not until Abram is ninety-nine years old does God give him a new name in honor of the blessing he has bestowed upon Abram and his progeny. "[B]ehold, my covenant is with thee, and thou shalt be a father of many nations." So Abram is dubbed Abraham or "Father of many nations," and Sarai becomes Sarah, or "Princess" (Gen. 17:4–5, 15 KJV). I have used their God-given (and more familiar) names, Abraham and Sarah, throughout this book.

Later, as Ishmael is growing up, God makes a remarkable promise to the ninety-nine-year-old Abraham and his ninety-year-old wife: Sarah will bear a son who will replace Ishmael as the inheritor of Abraham's divine blessing. "I will establish my covenant with him, and with his seed after him," God says of Isaac. "I will make nations out of thee, and kings shall come out of thee" (Gen. 17:19). So remarkable is the news that Sarah laughs out loud—she laughs, almost literally, in God's face—and her son is given the name Isaac, a bit of Hebrew wordplay that means "I laughed" (Gen. 18:12, 21:4).

And now the Bible shows us a deeply enigmatic scene in which we find the fifteen-year-old Ishmael at play with his five-year-old step-brother at a feast in celebration of the fact that Isaac has been weaned (at last!) from the breast. But the festivities are ruined for Sarah because she happens to see Ishmael doing *something* to Isaac, something so disturbing that Sarah promptly demands that Ishmael and his mother be "cast out" in the wilderness a second and final time.

Exactly what does Sarah see, exactly what does Ishmael do, that prompts such anger and outrage in Sarah? All we are told in conventional English translations of the Bible is that Sarah sees Ishmael "mocking" young Isaac—and we are asked to believe that, thanks to a single adolescent taunt by one sibling toward another, Sarah drives mother and son into the desert to die.

Unless, that is, she saw something much worse than mere mockery.

A clue to the mystery of Sarah's murderous rage is to be found in the Hebrew word actually used in the Bible to describe what Ishmael does to Isaac: *t'sahak*. The word is translated as "mocking" by the Shakespearean-era translators who gave us the King James Version of the Bible. A more recent Jewish translation (JPS), derived largely from the King James Version, uses the phrase "making sport." So we are given to understand by these translators that Hagar and Ishmael are condemned to death in the wilderness because a teenager makes fun of his little brother. But the real meaning of *t'sahak* suggests that something else is being hidden in these translations.

One of the meanings of *t'sahak* is "laugh"—a play on Isaac's name—and that's the one on which the translators, old and new, have relied in suggesting that Ishmael merely "mocked" or "laughed at" Isaac. What the translators are reluctant to let us know is that another meaning of *t'sahak* is "fondle," and the original Hebrew text of the Bible may suggest that what Sarah actually saw was some kind of sex play between Ishmael and his little brother.

Indeed, the very same Hebrew word that is used to describe what Ishmael does to Isaac appears only a few lines later in Genesis to describe Isaac fondling Rebekah outside the window of Abimelech, King of the Philistines. What Abimelech saw through his window was enough to tip him off that Rebekah was Isaac's wife rather than his sister—and the translators of the King James Version (KJV) do not hesitate to allow us to understand the sexual overtones of the scene: "Behold, Isaac was *sporting* with Rebekah his wife" (Gen. 26:8).

The mystery of what Sarah saw deepens when we notice that an entire phrase has been dropped from the passage in some versions of the Bible itself. The authoritative version of the Bible in its complete Hebrew text—the so-called Masoretic Text—includes only a truncated description of what Ishmael is doing when Sarah sees him. "Sarah noticed that [Ishmael] was playing." But the early Greek version of the Bible called the Septuagint and the Latin version called the Vulgate, which may have been translated from Hebrew manuscripts even more ancient than the Masoretic Text, give the same verse as "Sarah noticed that [Ishmael] was playing *with her son Isaac.*"

What are we to make of the missing words in the Masoretic Text of the Bible? Some Bible critics have been bold enough to suggest that the biblical text is intended to reveal that Ishmael is engaged in some kind of sex-play with young Isaac, but the pious editors of the Masoretic Text sought to play down the disturbing sexuality of the scene by leaving out the key phrase "with her son Isaac." The Septuagint and the Vulgate, it is suggested, preserve the original, complete and unexpurgated text—and these translations preserve, too, a hint of what Sarah sees.

Indeed, the severity of Sarah's reaction is puzzling and even alarming if Ishmael is only "playing with" Isaac or even if Ishmael is actually "mocking" him. Abraham himself understands that Sarah's decree that Hagar and Ishmael be driven into the desert is a death sentence; we are told that "the thing was very grievous in Abraham's sight on account of his son," and Abraham goes to the trouble of provisioning them with bread and water. Only after God reassures Abraham that Hagar and Ishmael will survive—"[O]f the son of the bondwoman I will make a nation"—does the goodly patriarch actually send them into the wilderness (Gen. 21:11–13).

Still, the very suggestion that the Bible hides an incident of incestuous child molestation is simply too hot for most Bible scholars to handle. The rabbis explained away the whole episode by suggesting that Ishmael liked to play with a bow and arrows, and "was in the habit of aiming his missiles in the direction of Isaac, saying at the same time that he was but jesting."[37] Even when some commentators are willing to concede that "mocking" is not justifiable translation of the Hebrew word, they still insist that the encounter between Ishmael and Isaac is wholly innocent.

"[H]is 'playing' with Isaac need mean no more than that the older boy was trying to amuse his little brother," wrote Ephraim Speiser, one of the most venerated contemporary Bible scholars. "There is nothing in the text to suggest that he was abusing him, a motive deduced by many troubled readers in their effort to account for Sarah's anger."[38]

But we might reach a different conclusion, if only out of regard for the simple human decency of the matriarch Sarah. After all, Hagar and Ishmael nearly perish in the wilderness to which Sarah has condemned them, and only the reappearance of a guardian angel spares their lives (Gen. 21:16). Unless we are supposed to regard Sarah as so jealous of her son's birthright that she would literally kill for him—or as an out-and-out paranoid, as one Bible scholar has suggested[39]—then we might look for a more plausible explanation for her punishing rage than the mockery of an older brother toward his younger sibling.[40] And four missing words that have somehow disappeared from the Masoretic Text of the Bible provide one intriguing explanation for what Sarah sees: Ishmael is taking a liberty with his little brother that his stepmother finds too shocking to tolerate.

"WHO IS THE THIRD WHO WALKS ALWAYS BESIDE YOU?"

Angelology has always been a big business among theologians, who are commonly accused of spending rather too much time counting how many angels can dance on a pinhead. But the very presence of angels in the Hebrew Bible may be seen as the earliest form of Bible censorship by priestly scribes who did not want to encourage their readers to believe that God was in the habit of calling upon mere mortals without the assistance of priests and their elaborate rituals. To discourage ordinary men and women from entertaining the thought that God himself might show up at their door and sit down to supper, the scribes may have systematically inserted angels into the biblical text as intermediaries between God and humankind.

The angels of the Hebrew Bible, as we see in the story of Lot and his daughters, resemble not at all the fat cherubs of Renaissance art or the herald angels of which we sing in Christmas carols. In fact, the angels who appear at the gates of Sodom more closely resemble a couple of drifters who wander into town—and turn out to be mass murderers. And a close reading of the Bible suggests that, in some profoundly mystical and even slightly spooky sense, when we behold an angel in the Bible, we may be encountering God himself in the guise of changeling, trickster, and destroyer.

The mysterious figures who appear at the city gates of Sodom are among the first angels whom we encounter in the Bible; the biblical author describes them first as "messengers" (Gen. 19:1) and later as "men" (Gen. 19:10), neither of which necessarily suggests that they possess any divine powers. We know that they eat and sleep, because Lot—like his uncle Abraham back in Mamre—serves them a meal before they go to bed (Gen. 19:3). We are given to understand that they travel to Sodom by foot, "about forty miles of difficult road."[41] And we know that they exert a certain carnal appeal to ordinary human beings because the lusty men who gather outside Lot's door prefer the two strangers to Lot's virgin daughters as sexual playthings.

"One must think of the heavenly messengers as young men in their prime," explained the stately Bible scholar von Rad, perhaps betraying a certain lustiness of his own, "whose beauty particularly incited evil desire."[42]

So how do we know that the destroyers are angels at all? The Bible refers to them by the Hebrew word that means "messenger" (mal'akh), a term used to refer to all kinds of emissaries, some human, some divine. The English word "angel," as we understand it today, derives from the Greek word angelos, which originally meant only "messenger" and was used to render mal'akh in early Greek translations of the Bible. Only when the Bible was translated into Latin were celestial messengers routinely distinguished from flesh-and-blood ones by the use of the Latin term angelus, from which the English word "angel" is derived.[43]

The mysterious strangers in the story of Lot *are* presented as messengers on a mission from God, armed with celestial powers and ready to carry out their orders. The first clue that they are something more than merely bringers of bad news comes when the townsfolk try to break down the door of Lot's house in order to gang-rape them—the mob is struck with blindness by the strangers (Gen. 19:11), and the Hebrew word used in the original biblical text suggests that the strangers literally dazzle their attackers with a supernatural explosion of light, "a blinding flash emanating from angels."[44]

But the mystery as to the nature of these two messengers only deepens when the biblical storyteller describes the devastation that befalls Sodom and Gomorrah: Is it the angels, or is it God himself, who does the dirty work? At first the two strangers announce themselves as the destroyers of Sodom and Gomorrah. "We will destroy this place," they tell Lot, "because . . . the Lord has sent us to destroy it" (Gen. 19:13). Moments later it is God himself who is depicted as the destroyer: "The Lord rained down fire and brimstone from the skies upon Sodom and Gomorrah" (Gen. 19:24–25 NEB). Characteristically, the biblical author never allows us to know with clarity whether God is acting on his own or empowering his angelic messengers to act on his behalf.

Or perhaps God is doing both at once, appearing interchangeably as a man (or several men) and an angel (or several angels). The same curious phenomenon of God as changeling is found throughout the Hebrew Bible: Is it God, or an angel, or merely a mortal man who wrestles with Jacob by night and is defeated by Jacob at sunrise (Gen. 32:25)? Is an angel of death or the Almighty himself who sets upon Moses in a murderous rage on the road to Egypt (Exod. 4:24–26)? (See chapter eight.) All of these strange encounters between God and man betray a certain nagging anxiety and a deep, almost neurotic conflict that besets the biblical authors whenever a human being draws near to the deity.

The Hebrew Bible is uncomfortable with the depiction of any direct encounter between God and a human being. Indeed, when God appears at all, he usually chooses a manifestation that somehow seems more like a magician's trick or special-effects wizardry than a glorious revelation of the Lord of the Universe: a bush that "burned with fire [but] was not consumed" (Exod. 3:2), a "pillar of cloud by day" or a "pillar of fire by night" (Exod. 13:21), or a disembodied voice heard only by a child in a darkened room (1 Sam 3:8–9). Even Moses, the only human who is said to actually speak with God "face to face, as a man speaketh unto his friend" (Exod. 33:11 KJV), is permitted to *see* God only once and only from behind. "Thou canst not see My face," God admonishes his chosen one, "for man shall not see Me and live" (Exod. 33:20). After his sojourn in the presence of God on Mount Sinai, Moses suffers with something like a case of divine radiation burn—his face shines with a mysterious light and he is forced to wear a veil to avoid scaring the wits out of the Israelites (Exod. 34:29–35).

So angels turn out be a convenient device for a priesthood that wants its followers to regard God as aloof and reclusive, mercurial and sometimes even murderous, so dangerous that only a single man in all of history is permitted to encounter him "face to face." That is why some Bible scholars suggest that the whole notion of a celestial go-between, whether in the guise of a seemingly ordinary human being or a bewinged sword-wielding archangel, is a pious fraud that found its way into the Bible. The scribes who preserved the sacred texts of ancient Israel, it is suggested, took it upon themselves to "[tone] down" the encounters between God and human beings by "interposing an angel" between the Creator and his creatures in the pages of Holy Scripture.[45]

Christianity, of course, is perfectly comfortable with the idea of God manifesting himself in human form and even dying a mortal death by the hands of his own creatures. "[T]he Word was God," declares the Gospel according to John (John 1:1, 14 KJV), "[a]nd the Word became flesh and dwelt among us." One early church father insisted that the figure who calls upon Abraham is the Logos, an earthly incarnation of the Word of God,[46] and the fact that two others accompanied him is seen in Christian tradition as the earliest augury of the Trinity.[47] After his death and entombment, Jesus appears at the side of two disciples on the road to Emmaus, walking and talking with them, but they regard him as merely a fellow traveler on the road—"Are thou only a stranger in Jerusalem?"—until he reveals himself as the resurrected Son of God. And even then, like God at Abraham's tent, Jesus pauses to share a humble meal—a bit of broiled fish and a piece of honeycomb—with his disciples (Luke 24:18, 37, 41–43 KJV).

Still, even the disciples are unnerved by the appearance of the Son of God in the guise of an ordinary man. No one is blinded by celestial light, no herald angels sing, no one's face is set aglow, and yet the manifestation of God is all the more eerie precisely because it is so ordinary: "[T]hey were terrified and affrighted, and supposed that they had seen a spirit," the New Testament says of the disciples who suddenly realize that Jesus is standing among them. "Behold my hands and my feet," Jesus says. "[A] spirit hath not flesh and bones, as ye see me have" (Luke 24:38–39 KJV). The unsettling sensation of seeing God as a creature of flesh and bone is echoed in an emblematic work of our own anxiety-ridden century. "Who is the third who walks always beside you?" muses T. S. Eliot in *The Waste Land*,[48] evoking the subtle and sometimes affrighting experience of Abraham at the terebinths of Mamre and the disciples on the road to Emmaus, all of whom encountered not an angel but God himself as the third man.

Still, the prospect of an unmediated experience of God has always troubled religious authority of all faiths. After all, if God is thought to make a habit of appearing to men and women without going through the proper channels of ritual and prayer, all suitably supervised by rabbi or priest or minister, how can we know whether the guy who claims to have dined on veal roast with the Almighty last night is a prophet or a madman? The high priests of ancient Israel, too, appeared to regard the description of *any* direct encounter between God and humankind as so subversive that the Hebrew scribes may have been compelled to insert an angel or two whenever God himself chose to make a personal appearance.

LIFE AGAINST DEATH

Whether Sodom or Gomorrah were destroyed by God himself, or his angelic host, or, as some scholars have suggested, an eruption of subterranean gases brought on by a random seismic tremor in an area long known for its earthquakes and its bitumen deposits,[49] the story of Lot and his daughters reminds us that God himself is depicted in the Bible as a moody and mercurial deity who is more often the destroyer than the creator of human life. And it is Lot's daughters, seducers of their own father, who defy not only the taboo against incest but also the ill temper and possibly the ill will of the Almighty himself. Lot is a tragic buffoon, but his daughters are heroines.

If there is a single overarching theme in the Bible—a single primal drive that animates the men and women whose lives are chronicled in its pages—it is the affirmation of life and the celebration of child-bearing. The opening passages of Genesis show God as a creator and life-giver: "Be fruitful, and multiply" is the first and oft-repeated command of God to his creatures (Gen. 1:28). So, too, does God promise countless offspring to Abraham. "Look now toward heaven, and count the stars, if thou be able to count them," God says to Abraham. "So shall thy seed be" (Gen. 15:5).

We can readily understand the basic economic rationale that explains the biblical obsession with bearing children. War, disease, famine, and natural disaster put life at terrible risk in biblical times; a family was likely to lose children at an early age, and an abundance of babies increased the odds that enough of them would survive into adulthood to provide labor in the fields, defense against marauders, and support for aging parents. A large family was the social security of the biblical era.

But a brood of healthy children is not merely a source of wealth and status for the men and women whose lives are depicted in the Bible. Children are a flesh-and-blood symbol of divine blessing, and infertility is regarded as an affliction and a punishment. "Give me children," Rachel begs the patriarch Jacob, "or else I die" (Gen. 30:1), and the same urgent plea can be heard on the lips of men and women throughout the Bible. God himself makes the very point by denying children (or sometimes even killing them) when he is displeased and bestowing children as a sign of divine favor: God afflicts Job by permitting Satan to kill his seven sons and three daughters, and blesses Job by giving him a replacement set of children even more beautiful than the first (Job 42:13–15).

So we are reminded that God is the taker as well as the giver of life, and the destruction of Sodom and Gomorrah is hardly the first time that God turns against his own creatures. By the time hellfire rains down on Sodom, God has already judged all of humankind except Noah and his family to be unworthy of life, and he has exterminated everyone and everything on earth except the chosen remnant. "I will blot out man whom I have created from the face of the earth; both man and beast," God tells Noah as he reveals his dark side. "The end of all flesh is come before me" (Gen. 6:7, 13). Nor is the destruction of Sodom and Gomorrah and the other cities of the Plain the last time that God will become a destroyer rather than a creator of human life. "I kill, and I make alive; I have wounded, and I heal," God will later boast to Moses after killing the firstborn of Egypt. "I will make Mine arrows drunk with blood, and My sword shall devour flesh" (Deut. 32:39, 42).

Lot's daughters see with their own eyes what terror God is capable of visiting upon the men, women, and children whom he created in the first place. While Sodom and Gomorrah are blasted into ruins on the far horizon, these two young women are witness to an act of divine violence so arbitrary, so excessive, and so petty that God appears not merely wrathful but slightly demonic: they are forced to watch as the Almighty turns their mother—a woman whose only offense is that she looks back on the smoking ruins of Sodom after being told not to do so—into a pillar of salt, thus providing the enterprising tour guides of the last century or so with something to show the tourists during their excursions to the Dead Sea.

Why does Lot's wife look back? The traditional (and highly sexist) view is that she is so curious about what is happening back in Sodom that she cannot resist the impulse to look and see, to "spy out the mystery of God," as one commentator loftily puts it.[50] Others suggest that she is saddened at the prospect of leaving Sodom, a place that she loves despite (or, perhaps, because of) its sinfulness.[51] Both of these interpretations, of course, encourage us to see her as flawed, whether by idle curiosity or by a longing for the fleshpots of Sodom, and thus somehow deserving of her half-comical, half-tragic fate: Presto change-o, and she is suddenly turned into stone by the Divine Prestidigitator.

A depiction of Lot's wife that I find more comforting, if rather less flattering to God himself, can be found in the rabbinical literature. According to a countertradition among the sages, she despairs of the fate of her other daughters, the ones whose husbands laugh at Lot's warnings and refuse to flee the city, and so she casts a single backward glance toward the doomed city where her innocent children are suffering along with the sinners. "Her mother love," the rabbis speculated, "made her look behind to see if her married daughters were following."[52] And one contemporary Bible scholar, D. Alan Aycock, has compared Lot's wife to other biblical figures whom he calls "suspended heroes"— "Noah in his ark upon Ararat, Isaac tied to the altar below Abraham's knife . . . and Jesus on the cross"[53]—all of whom are innocents who are made to suffer despite their innocence by a deity who is quite capable of random acts of violence.[54]

So we are left with only Lot and his daughters, and it is these two women who stand out as the real (and only) heroes of the tale. Lot's daughters, like his wife, are unnamed in the Bible—a considerable slight in a book whose authors are fairly obsessed with genealogies and the giving and meaning of names—but they show themselves to be bold, intrepid, and resourceful young women who are willing to defy the taboo against incest and the apparent will of God in order to restore life to the blasted and empty place that they behold from their mountain refuge.

Significantly, the elaborate seduction of their father is described without a single disapproving word from the biblical author. Lot's daughters are spared the harsh judgment that is visited upon so many other women in the Bible. Starting with Eve and that damned apple, women have been depicted (and mostly condemned) as the willful and wily seducers of men: Potiphar's wife (Gen. 39:7), Delilah (Judges 16:5), and Salome (Matt. 14:6–8)[55] are only some of the most famous examples. Even the daughter of the patriarch Jacob, a woman who is the apparent victim of rape, is blamed by some of the more misogynistic rabbinical sages for provoking her rapist. (See chapter five.) And a minority tradition in the rabbinical literature reaches a similar conclusion about Lot's daughters: "Lot is a warning example to men to avoid being alone with women, lest [they] should entice them to sin, as did Lot's daughters."[56]

But the vast weight of rabbinical commentary overlooks the manner in which Lot's daughters impregnate themselves and focuses instead on their noble motive: Lot's daughters know that Sodom and Gomorrah and the surrounding cities have been destroyed. They have no reason to believe that anyone besides their father and themselves have survived. They are alone in the empty wilderness of the Judean desert, and they have no prospect of finding a suitable husband. But life must be preserved, as the Bible insistently reminds us, even if God shows himself to be utterly indifferent or even openly hostile to the survival of the creatures on whom he bestowed life in the first place. When Lot's daughters take it upon themselves to bear children and thereby to repopulate the earth, at all costs and by any means necessary, the taboo against incest may be, must be, ignored.*

In fact, according to one tale told by the sages, God himself recognized the purity of Lot's daughters in sleeping with their father and actually assisted them in the seduction by miraculously planting a supply of wine in a nearby cave. "Lot's daughter found the wine with which they made their father drunk," the tale goes. "God caused the wine to be put in that place in order that they should succeed in their plan."[57]

The incestuous seduction of the drunken Lot serves the biblical manifest destiny of humankind in two vital ways. First, the simple act of bearing and rearing children is a fulfillment of the fundamental commandant to "be fruitful and multiply," an act that preserves Lot's bloodline in the face of extinction. If Lot's daughters had not borne his children, his name and line would have ended once and for all in that desert cave along with the other victims of Sodom and Gomorrah. Second, and even more important in the eyes of the biblical authors, the birth of the two boys—sons and grandsons of Lot at the very same time—is a crucial link in the unbroken chain of life that leads directly from Creation to the Messiah.

The Bible tells us, by the way, that the sons of Lot's daughters are the eponymous patriarchs of two nations, Ammon and Moab, that will become the bitter enemies of the Israelites. Located to the east of Canaan in what is now the modern nation of Jordan, Ammon and

---

*The biblical storyteller introduces one troubling contradiction in the account of Lot and his daughters. Since the angelic destroyers have agreed to spare Zoar—and since Lot and his daughters find a temporary refuge there before moving on to the mountains—Lot's daughters know that the whole world has not been destroyed. In my retelling of the story, I have taken the liberty of suggesting that the townspeople of Zoar have fled, and so Lot and his daughters find it empty. Otherwise, they would have encountered other survivors and, thus, potential husbands and fathers. The biblical storyteller is silent on how the sparing of Zoar figures in their conclusion that they are the last people on earth or, at least, the region around Sodom and Gomorrah.

Moab are specifically spared from conquest when God sends the Israelites into the Promised Land under a banner of war. "Be not at enmity with [them]," God says, "because I have given [Moab and Ammon] unto the children of Lot for a possession" (Deut. 2:9, 19). Nevertheless these two nations will become geopolitical rivals of Israel, and the Israelites will meet them repeatedly on the field of battle. "Come, and let us cut her off from being a nation," the prophet Jeremiah rails against Moab, and he vows a similar fate for Ammon: "And it shall become a desolate mound, and her daughters shall be burned with fire" (Jer. 48:2, 49:2).

So some scholars suggest that the story of Lot and his daughters is intended by the biblical authors as a kind of "black propaganda," a scurrilous tale meant to dishonor the hated Ammonites and Moabites: a "product of popular political wit," explains one commentator, "by which Israel tried to repay her occasionally powerful enemies . . . for everything she had suffered at their hands."[58] Elsewhere in the Bible, they point out, we find the Moabites and Ammonites singled out among the many adversaries of Israel as worthy of special contempt: the Bible decrees that the child of an intermarriage between an Israelite and an Edomite or Egyptian might be admitted to the nation of Israel "in the third generation" but the offspring of a marriage with an Ammonite or a Moabite is to be permanently excluded (Deut. 23:4, 8–9).[59]

But the fact is that the Bible reserves a crucial role for these cave-born bastards in spite of their incestuous origins and the future clashes between their descendants and the Israelites. A Moabite woman named Ruth is destined to marry an Israelite man, and their bloodline will lead directly to the birth of David, the greatest of the kings of Israel (Ruth 4:18–22). An Ammonite woman named Naamah will be counted among King Solomon's one thousand wives and concubines—and, fatefully, it is Naamah who will give birth to Solomon's successor on the throne of Israel (1 Kings 14:21). And it is from the House of David and Solomon that the Messiah will come, in both the Jewish and Christian traditions.

So the mountain cave in which Lot and his daughters seek refuge turns out to be the womb of history, and their drunken couplings amount to a sanctified union that will bestow upon the world what the Bible regards as its ultimate savior. Neither the taboo against incest nor

the fear of divine retribution are sufficient to discourage these two audacious young women from doing what needs to be done to preserve their
father's seed. What appears at first to be merely black comedy or black
propaganda is suddenly elevated into a sublime morality tale, a saga of
the struggle of life against death, in which Lot's unnamed daughters are
the unlikely heroes.

CHAPTER FOUR

THE RAPE OF DINAH

"Should one deal with our sister as with a harlot?"

—GENESIS 34:31

A clamor in the distance roused Jacob in the heat of the late afternoon, and he trudged to the door to see what the disturbance was all about. He heard the shrill keening of women's voices, and he saw a small cluster of young women heading toward him, followed by a few of the field hands and, finally, one or two of the older women, who struggled to keep up.

"What is the trouble?" Jacob asked wearily, calling out from the doorway as the young women surged up to the house.

The women murmured and moaned, a few of them wept, but no one spoke.

"Well, then?" Jacob asked.

At last, one of the young women, a slender maiden with black eyes whom Jacob vaguely recognized as one of his daughter's handmaidens, stepped forward and spoke up boldly.

"Our sister—your daughter—has been dishonored," she announced, and then fell abruptly silent as the shrill cries of the women reached a new crescendo.

"Dishonored?" asked Jacob. "What do you mean?"

And Dinah the daughter of Leah, whom she had borne unto Jacob, went out to see the daughters of the land. And Shechem the son of Hamor the Hivite, the prince of the land, saw her; and he took her, and lay with her, and humbled her.

—GENESIS 34:1

"Dishonored," the young woman repeated, "by one of Hamor's people."

Jacob frowned. The Canaanites among whom he had settled were none too friendly toward Jacob and his clan, and Jacob had expended many ingratiating words—not to mention rich gifts of food, wine, cloth, and handiwork—to cultivate the man called Hamor, the local chieftain. Jacob had paid one hundred silver coins to Hamor for the parcel of land on which he built his house and raised up his sheepstocks, but Jacob was uncomfortably aware that he remained a stranger in the land of Canaan.

"Where is Dinah now?" Jacob demanded. "Tell me exactly what happened. And the rest of you—quiet!"

"We went to the well inside the town wall," volunteered the young woman. "We went to see the women from the countryside who come to fill their water jars."

"Yes," Jacob urged her on.

"On the way, we passed some men sitting under an olive tree outside a big house," the girl continued. "They shouted and laughed and mocked us. All of them except one who just stared and said nothing. That one waited, and when we came back, he walked up to Dinah and spoke very rudely to her."

"What do you mean?"

" 'You're a very pretty one,' he said. 'I've never seen such a pretty one as you,' " answered the handmaiden, deepening her voice to mock the man whom she described. " 'I didn't know there was one as pretty as you in the camp of the Israelites.' "

"And then?"

"He put his arm around her shoulders and walked with her toward a

> *And his soul did cleave unto Dinah the daughter of Jacob, and he loved the damsel, and spoke comfortingly unto the damsel.*
>
> —GENESIS 34:3

grove of trees on the other side of the road," she continued. "All the while saying: 'You're a very pretty one.' When they reached the trees, Dinah stumbled and fell down, and he fell, too—right on top of her! They were still for awhile, and then I could see that he was pulling at her robe. . . ."

The young woman paused. For a moment, she seemed bewildered, as if fearing to say aloud what she had seen.

"Go on," Jacob demanded.

"And then he dishonored her."

The young woman stopped again. Should she tell *everything* she'd seen? Should she describe how, afterwards, the young man gently put his arm around Dinah and slowly walked with her? Should she mention how the young man was whispering into Dinah's ear all the while, as if he were comforting her? The handmaiden paused again, staring at the ground in embarrassment.

"Go on!" Jacob commanded once more. The handmaiden looked up, caught his fierce gaze, and spoke plainly to the old man.

"The young man took Dinah, and he forced himself upon her, and he lay with her," said the young woman. "And then he led her to the big house by the side of the road, and when she went inside, we ran back here to tell you what had happened."

"And do you know the man who did this?" Jacob asked. "Do you know his name?"

"We have seen him before on the way to the well, him and his friends." She paused. "The women at the well say his name is Shechem, and he is the prince's son."

The next day, a curious sight could be seen from Jacob's doorway: Hamor, the prince of the land in which Jacob dwelled, was making his way along the road toward the compound where Jacob and his sons had

And Shechem spoke unto his father Hamor, saying: "Get me this damsel to wife." Now Jacob heard that he had defiled Dinah his daughter; and his sons were with his cattle in the field; and Jacob held his peace until they came. And Hamor the father of Shechem went out unto Jacob to speak with him. And the sons of Jacob came in from the field where they heard it; and the men were grieved, and they were very wroth, because he had wrought a vile deed in Israel in lying with Jacob's daughter; which thing ought not to be done. And Hamor spoke with them, saying: "The soul of my son Shechem longeth for your daughter. I pray you give her unto him to wife."

—GENESIS 34:4–6

built their houses and pitched their tents. Hamor was accompanied by an agitated young man in the clothes of a nobleman and a guard of watchful soldiers who wore short swords at their side and carried spears in their hands. But Jacob was reassured by the expression on Hamor's face: the old man seemed friendly enough and perhaps just a bit ill at ease to be approaching Jacob on his own parcel of land.

Jacob walked out of his house to greet the princely visitor and his entourage. Jacob's sons, all twelve of them, were still in the distant meadows where the goats and sheep were fed and watered, and he fretted at how long they had tarried in their encampment. He would have preferred to welcome Hamor with his own strong sons near at hand.

Now Hamor stepped forward to greet Jacob, leaving the young man and his guard a few steps behind. The two men, each a chieftain among his own people, displayed an exaggerated courtesy to one another, as if each one were trying to outdo the other. Hamor introduced the young man as his son, Shechem, and then instructed him to wait outside while the two elders conferred with each other in Jacob's house. Jacob made a show of ordering refreshments to be brought and a meal to be prepared, and wondered to himself when his own sons would return from the pastures.

"My daughter—" Jacob began, not quite knowing how to confront the chieftain with the ugly truth of what had happened.

"An honored guest in my home," Hamor said smoothly, if perhaps too quickly. "We are looking to her every comfort."

Before Jacob could press the point—after all, his daughter was a prisoner or a hostage, not a guest, of the prince—both men paused at the sound of angry shouting outside the door, the sound of scuffling and butting, one sharp cry of pain. Jacob hastened to the doorway and, to his relief, saw that his sons were back—and he saw, too, that someone had intercepted them on the way back from the fields and told them of the indignity that had befallen their sister at Shechem's hands.

Now all of Jacob's sons were lined up in a ragged phalanx in front of his house, long wooden staffs in their hands, and they faced off the men-at-arms who had accompanied Hamor and Shechem to the camp of the Israelites. Simeon and Levi—Dinah's full brothers, all of them the children of Jacob's wife Leah—stood two paces in front of their brothers, menacing Shechem with tentative thrusts of their staffs. Hamor's soldiers had not unsheathed their swords, but both fathers saw the red faces and hot eyes of the young men, and realized that a single gesture might set them to a bloody fight.

"Peace unto you," said Hamor, stepping slowly and deliberately out of Jacob's house.

Jacob followed Hamor, and he, too, addressed them in a soothing voice.

"Our good neighbor and lord Hamor is here to—"

"We have heard why he is here," growled Simeon, daring to interrupt his father. "And we are ready to do what must be done to avenge our sister—"

"I do not know exactly what happened yesterday between my son and your daughter," Hamor began. "Perhaps none of us really know—"

"Let me tell you what your son did to our sister if you truly do not know already." Simeon stared hard at Shechem as he spoke, but Jacob waved him into silence.

"Here is what I came to say," Hamor continued. "My son returned to my house at the end of the day in great excitement, and he described a young woman he had met on the road. He told me that she was more beautiful than any woman he had ever seen. And he said to me: 'Get me this girl for a wife.' So I come to you today, Jacob, and I say in all humility: The soul of my son Shechem longs for your daughter, and I pray you give her to him to be his wife."

"And make ye marriages with us; give your daughters unto us, and take our daughters unto you. And ye shall dwell with us; and the land shall be before you; dwell and trade ye therein, and get you possessions therein."

—GENESIS 34:9–10

And Shechem said unto her father and unto her brethren: "Let me find favour in your eyes, and what ye shall say unto me I will give. Ask me never so much dowry and gift, and I will give according as ye shall say unto me; but give me the damsel to wife."

—GENESIS 34:11–12

Levi laughed bitterly. "So your son defiles our sister," he demanded, "and now he wants to *marry* her?"

Hamor deigned a glance at Levi, and the slightest smirk crossed his face. And then he spoke to Levi's father.

"You are strangers in our land, and you live among us on a plot of ground that was once mine," Hamor said with a delicacy that did not conceal the unspoken barb. "But if your daughter marries my son—if you give your daughters to our men, and you take our daughters for your men—then you will no longer be strangers. You will be one with us."

Jacob did not mistake the meaning of Hamor's invitation, but Levi persisted in taunting the chieftain.

"Perhaps there is something else we can do to your daughters beside marrying them," the young man hissed. "Perhaps your son will have an idea of what I mean."

Hamor once again replied to Levi by addressing himself to Jacob.

"If you marry with us, you can live among us as if you were native-born and not merely strangers," Hamor said. "The land shall be open to you, and you can move freely from place to place, you can sell your crops and your wares, you can buy land wherever you like."

> *And the sons of Jacob answered Shechem and Hamor his father with guile, and spoke, because he had defiled Dinah their sister, and said unto them: "We cannot do this thing, to give our sister to one that is uncircumcised; for that were a reproach unto us."*
>
> —GENESIS 34:13–14

Now Shechem himself spoke up, and Jacob's sons seemed to tense at the very sound of the young man's voice, anxious and urgent.

"Just do me the favor of letting me have your daughter, and I will pay any dowry that you ask," Shechem said to Jacob and his sons. "No matter how great the price, I will pay it—if you will only give her to me to be my wife!"

Simeon stepped forward, face to face with Shechem, who seemed to flinch at the fury in the young man's face.

"So you are willing to pay for what you did to our sister," Simeon shouted, "as if she were a whore?"

But Levi put himself between Simeon and Shechem, a hand on each man's shoulder, and he began to speak slowly, even sweetly.

"What my brother means to say is that we cannot do what you ask, as much as we might want to," said Levi. "We cannot give our sister in marriage to one who is not circumcised—it is the law of our people, and to do otherwise would be unthinkable."

Shechem seemed confused by Levi's words, and he glanced at his father. Simeon, too, was incredulous at what his brother was saying, as if he wondered if his brother had gone suddenly mad.

"Among these people," Hamor explained, "it is the custom of the men to cut off the foreskin."

"Cut off the foreskin?" asked Shechem, incredulous and a bit frightened. "How do you do such a thing?"

"Why, I suppose with a knife," said Hamor with a slight smile. "A sharp one, I hope."

Father and son looked at Jacob, who only nodded solemnly in assent.

> *"Only on this condition will we consent unto you: if ye will be as we are, that every male of you be circumcised; then will we give our daughters unto you, and we will take your daughters to us, and we will dwell with you, and we will become one people."*
>
> —GENESIS 34:15–16

> *"But if ye will not hearken unto us, to be circumcised; then we will take our daughter, and we will be gone." And their words pleased Hamor, and Shechem Hamor's son.*
>
> —GENESIS 34:17–18

"So we will give you our sister for your wife," Levi continued in perfect seriousness, "but only if you are circumcised when you take her to the marriage bed."

Shechem looked dubious and slightly ill, which seemed to amuse Jacob and only encouraged Levi.

"I'll do it," Shechem said grimly.

"Please don't misunderstand me," Levi continued. "Not only you but every man among your people must be circumcised, too. Only then will we give our women to be your wives, and only then will we take your women to be our wives. Only then will we dwell with you throughout the land, and become one people."

If Shechem heard the sniggers among the other sons of Jacob, he did not show any sign of it, but Hamor could not suppress a grin.

Simeon grinned, too, as if he had suddenly understood what game his brother was playing. Now it was Simeon's turn to join in the game.

"But if you refuse to do what we ask," he lectured Shechem, "then we will take our lovely sister—such a pretty one!—and we will be gone."

"Done!" said Shechem in a voice that seemed to quaver, as if fear and longing were struggling within his throat as he spoke.

> *And the young man deferred not to do the thing, because he had delight in Jacob's daughter. And he was honoured above all the house of his father. And Hamor and Shechem his son came unto the gate of their city, and spoke with the men of their city, saying: "These men are peaceable with us; therefore let them dwell in the land, and trade therein; for, behold, the land is large enough for them; let us take their daughters to us for wives, and let us give them our daughters. Only on this condition will the men consent unto us to dwell with us, to become one people, if every male among us be circumcised, as they are circumcised. Shall not their cattle and their substance and all their beasts be ours? Only let us consent unto them, and they will dwell with us."*
>
> —GENESIS 34:19–23

Simeon laughed out loud as Dinah's handmaiden recounted the scene she had witnessed the day before when Hamor and the court physician appeared in the marketplace and addressed the crowd.

" 'You all know of the stranger called Jacob and his people, they are our *friends*,' " the young woman recited, reciting Hamor's words and mimicking his gravelly voice. " 'Let them live with us and move freely around the country—the land is big enough for all of us.' "

"Yes," Simeon urged, "and then what?"

"Well, the prince saw that the crowd was not ready to riot—so far, so good!—and so he said: 'Let us marry their daughters, and let them marry our daughters.' Some of the men in the crowd began to hoot a bit—I suppose they fancy our women, too. And then the prince gave them the bad news: 'But these people will agree to live with us and become one people with us on one condition only: Every man among us must be circumcised like them.' "

"And what happened when they heard?" demanded Levi.

"Oh, they did not like the sound of it at all! They began to grumble, and Hamor's voice was not quite so deep now."

The girl raised her voice to a shrill squeak and mocked the way

> *And unto Hamor and unto Shechem his son hearkened all that went out of the gate of his city; and every male was circumcised, all that went out of the gate of his city.*
>
> —GENESIS 34:24

Hamor pleaded with his people: " 'If we marry with these strangers, their livestock will be ours! Their goods will be ours! All we have to do is consent to be circumcised, here and now.' "

Now all of the brothers were laughing out loud as the young woman brazenly imitated the shocked expressions that she had seen on the faces of Hamor's people, and demonstrated how some of the men in the crowd had covered their private parts with their hands as if to protect themselves from the circumciser's knife. And she pointed out how the prince had taken the precaution of stationing his guards around the crowded marketplace so the menfolk might better understand that they had no real choice in the matter.

"And so," the handmaiden continued, "all of the strong and able-bodied men ended up in perfect agreement with the good prince, and every single one of them was circumcised right then and there."

"Every one?" Simeon asked, betraying a touch of anxiety because, as he knew but did not say, everything depended on it. "Every able-bodied man went under the knife?"

The handmaiden nodded solemnly and then broke into bawdy laughter along with Simeon and Levi and the rest of the brothers.

On the second day after the mass circumcision at the city gate, Simeon and Levi walked with the handmaiden to a distant hilltop where they would not be interrupted or overheard. They listened carefully as she described the lay of the land, the path to take if one wanted to pay a visit to Hamor's big house and the other houses where the menfolk were resting from *their* encounters with the surgeon's knife.

On the third day, Simeon and Levi rose before dawn, strapped on their short swords, and slipped out of the compound in silence. Only the handmaiden saw them go, and then she went back to sleep for an hour or so before her long day of work would begin.

Simeon and Levi knew that every last man in Hamor's town—including Hamor himself, and his son, Shechem—was in his bed, still wrapped tightly with bandages in the place where the surgeon's knife had cut him. A grown man who had just been circumcised is in no condition to be up and out of bed and walking about the town—every step would be another moment of pain. On that, the two brothers were counting.

At the first house they encountered, Simeon and Levi unsheathed their swords and shouldered open the door with a loud crack that awakened only a pair of servant girls who were bedded down on the floor near the stove. The girls looked up, bleary and confused, as Simeon and Levi stalked past them in search of the room where the master of the house slept. As soon as the kitchen girls noticed the swords Simeon and Levi were carrying, they began to wail. And so, when Levi finally found a man with a black beard on a pile of bedding in a back room, the poor soul was already awake and alert as Levi dispatched him with one short blow to the neck.

The same brutal operation was repeated in dwelling after dwelling, tent and shack and house, as Simeon and Levi stalked through the streets of Hamor's town and methodically did their work. They were shepherds, and they knew how to dispatch a living creature swiftly and efficiently. Now they put their expertise to a new use, although they held their victims in somewhat less regard than they would a beast being slaughtered for their table.

Now and then, one of the men of Hamor rose from his bed and seized a staff or a sword in a desperate attempt at self-defense, but two armed men on their feet were always more than a match for some

> *And it came to pass on the third day, when they were in pain, that two of the sons of Jacob, Simeon and Levi, Dinah's brethren, took each man his sword, and came upon the city unawares, and slew all the males.*
>
> —GENESIS 34:25

> *And they slew Hamor and Shechem his son with the edge of the sword, and took Dinah out of Shechem's house, and went forth.*
>
> —GENESIS 34:26.

bedridden soul whose private parts were bloody and bandaged. By sunrise, they had slain all but two of the newly circumcised men in the town, and the last house they visited belonged to Hamor and Shechem, who were awake and astir but unsuspecting, still lingering in their beds and waiting to be called to breakfast by one of the servants.

Hamor half-rose in his bed when he saw Simeon and Levi at the threshold, but they reached him before he could cry out, and a single blow with the cutting edge of a sword across the neck silenced him forever. Shechem appeared behind them, bellowing like a bull, but no one but the servants was left to hear the sound. With another strike of the blade, Shechem, too, was dead.

Blood-spattered and breathing heavily, Simeon and Levi searched the house from room to room until they found Dinah in the richly decorated bedchamber that had been set aside for her until her wedding day. Their sister stared at them with an expression of horror that they had never seen before, not even on the faces of their victims and the bystanders who had witnessed the slaughter.

"Come, sister," said Simeon, taking her by the arm and leading her toward the door of the house, "we are here to take you home."

Jacob fretted and sputtered as he watched the grim parade that headed toward the compound. What would become of them now, he wondered? What vengeance would be visited upon him because of the massacre of Hamor and his people? Hamor and his menfolk might be dead, their wives and children taken captive, but there were still many more Canaanites than Israelites across the land. Surely they would not overlook what had happened.

Simeon and Levi had returned only hours before, leading their weeping sister between them, and their brothers had greeted them with shouts and laughter. But they celebrated only briefly before the bloodied

The sons of Jacob came upon the slain, and spoiled the city, because they had defiled their sister. They took their flocks and their herds and their asses and that which was in the city and that which was in the field; and all their wealth, and all their little ones and their wives, took they captive and spoiled, even all that was in the house.

—GENESIS 34:28–29

And Jacob said to Simeon and Levi: "Ye have troubled me, to make me odious unto the inhabitants of the land, even unto the Canaanites and the Perizzites; and, I being few in number, they will gather themselves together against me and smite me; and I shall be destroyed, I and my house."

—GENESIS 34:30

heroes sent their brothers back to the town with orders to wreak a further vengeance on Hamor's people.

"Take the spoils of the city," Simeon had commanded his willing brothers, "because they have defiled our sister."

Levi had been even more precise. "Take their sheep and their oxen, take everything you find in the city and everything you find in the fields," he instructed them. "Take their wealth, and their little ones, and their wives, too."

Now the brothers were returning from the day of conquest, driving before them a herd of many species—lowing cattle, wailing women, weeping children—and carts loaded high with clothing and bedding, silver vessels and objects of wrought gold, jars of wine and jars of oil, all the spoils of the now-empty city of Hamor.

If Simeon and Levi expected praise from their father, they were disappointed in their moment of glory. The fretful Jacob looked at them—their bloody clothing, their captive women, their spoils—and glowered with anger and fear.

"Do you know what trouble you have caused for me?" Jacob scolded them, pacing back and forth in front of his house. "For all of us? You have made my name *stink* among the people of the land, the Canaanites and Perizzites. Today you have slain a hundred of them, but we are still few and they are many. Did you not realize that they will gather themselves together against *me* and slay *me* because of what *you* have done? I shall be destroyed, me and my house!"

Simeon was silenced by his father's anger, but Levi spoke up for both of them in a voice that sounded like it came from a sulky adolescent rather than a bloodied warrior.

"What would *you* want us to do?" he cried. "Should our sister be treated as a whore?"

And they said: "Should one deal with our sister as with a harlot?"

—GENESIS 34:31

CHAPTER FIVE

"SEE WHAT A SCOURGE IS LAID UPON YOUR HATE"

The Strange Affair of Dinah and Shechem

RAPIST, SEDUCER, OR SUITOR
THE CURIOUS PUNISHMENT FOR THE CRIME OF RAPE
"MY COVENANT SHALL BE IN YOUR FLESH"
"I HAVE LOVED STRANGERS"
TWO BELLIES, ONE SPEAR
THE BIBLICAL COURT OF CONSCIENCE
"FOR THE HONOR OF OUR SISTERS"

One voice alone is not heard in the Bible's account of the rape of Dinah, the voice of Dinah herself. While the menfolk speechify and haggle and plot among themselves and against each other, no one bothers to ask her whether she wants to marry Shechem or see him slain. Dinah's silence, so odd and so provocative, reminds us that the biblical author conceals far more than he reveals in telling us the tale of Dinah and Shechem.

Only a single sentence is offered to explain Dinah's role in the tragic affair: "[S]he went out to see the daughters of the land" (Gen. 34:1). Yet even this sparse bit of intelligence is tantalizing. To the stern rabbinical sages who interpreted and embroidered upon the story of Dinah, the sight of a single woman at liberty in the countryside was distressing and dangerous. Indeed, they could not rid themselves of the notion that a woman is a seducer by nature or, at best, a victim of her own vanity and curiosity. Thus, one ancient rabbinical sage suggested that Dinah ventured out of her father's tent "adorned like a harlot,"[1] and another rabbi speculated that Shechem hired a troupe of gaily clad women to sing, dance, and play in the streets in order to lure Dinah out of Jacob's compound so he could ravish her.

"Had she remained at home, nothing would have happened to her," goes the rabbi's homily. "But she was a woman, and all women like to show themselves in the street."[2]

Contemporary readers, of course, recoil at such misogyny. But the ancient rabbis, no matter how sexist they may appear to us now, were responding to something extraordinary in the text itself. For a woman of the biblical era, young and unwed and living among strangers, to venture out of her father's encampment and seek the companionship of local women is a bold and courageous act: Dinah is defying the strict and narrow protocols that governed the lives of the wives and daughters of the patriarchs. In fact, a feminist Bible critic named Ita Sheres has described Dinah's excursion as an "outing," a word that once meant only a day in the country but now suggests that Dinah engages in something even more daring: "[A] bold act that implied individuality and purpose," as Sheres puts it.[3] Dinah is a woman who kicks over the traces of traditional morality and asserts her own authentic identity.

So daring and dangerous is Dinah's adventure in the eyes of the biblical author that she is made to nearly disappear from her own story. But we can still detect faint echoes of Dinah's voice in the text of Genesis 34. Some readers insist that she is whispering the words of a long-suppressed love story rather than a bloody tale of rape and revenge. Others argue that the real heroes of Dinah's story are the sword-wielding brothers who slaughter a whole people in her name. Long neglected and even suppressed by sermonizers and Sunday school teachers, Genesis 34 takes on new and urgent meanings in our own troubled world, where the distant descendants of Jacob and the modern counterparts of Hamor still encounter each other in the Holy Land.

RAPIST, SEDUCER, OR SUITOR?

None of the Hebrew words and phrases used by the biblical author to describe what Shechem did to Dinah are translated straightforwardly as "rape." The Bible tells us that he "saw her, and he took her, and lay with her," according to the conventional English translation, and then the biblical author adds one more intriguing phrase: "and humbled her" (Gen. 34:2). So we might ask: Does Shechem actually *rape* Dinah? Or is something more subtle going on between the lovestruck young prince and the adventurous daughter of Jacob?

The Hebrew word *innah*, translated in some English-language Bibles as "humbled" (KJV/NEB) is rendered in other translations as "abused"[4] or "defiled" or "dishonored," indicating a "degrading and debasing" experience by which "a girl loses the expectancy of a fully valid marriage," mostly because she is no longer a virgin.[5] The distinguished Bible translator Ephraim Speiser, who wants to let us know that the Hebrew word implies the threat or even the use of physical violence, renders the word as "slept with her by force," which may be an awkward metaphor but certainly suggests the functional equivalent of rape.[6] And feminist Bible scholar Ita Sheres insists on translating the Hebrew text even more forcefully: "[Shechem] *tortured* her."[7]

While none of the English translations of the Bible use the word "rape," some commentators insist that no other meaning can be gleaned from the Hebrew text. According to one Bible critic, the "three-fold repetition" of verbs and "ascending order of violence"—"[He] *took* her, and *lay* with her, and *humbled* her"—"quashes the idea of seduction," and the same critic insists that the Hebrew phrase customarily translated as "[he] lay with her" really ought to be rendered in blunt street slang: "[he] *laid* her."[8]

Still, the very next sentence of the biblical text assures us that Shechem falls promptly, powerfully, and poignantly in love with his victim. Again, the biblical author uses a string of verbs to make the point: "And his soul did *cleave* unto Dinah . . . , and he *loved* the damsel, and *spoke comfortingly* unto the damsel" (Gen. 34:3). After reporting the sexual encounter itself in a single sentence, the narrator turns his attention to the real concern of his story: the ardent courtship of Dinah by Shechem, the elaborate negotiation of a marriage contract, the cunning efforts of her brothers to prevent the marriage from being consummated, and the massacre that crowns their efforts.

So the Bible itself allows the possibility that something other than forcible rape may have taken place. For example, the storyteller later uses the word "defiled" to describe what Shechem does to Dinah: "Now Jacob heard that he had *defiled* Dinah his daughter" (Gen. 34:5). The word "defiled" is used elsewhere in the Bible to describe *forbidden* sexual relations rather than *forcible* ones: the adultery of a straying wife

(Num. 5:12–14), for example, or the consorting of a priest with a harlot (Lev. 21:4–7).[9] A reference to the "defiling" of Jacob's daughter by the smitten young prince might be understood to mean only that the two of them were not married when they made love to each other.

As if to elevate and even sanctify the love that Shechem feels toward Dinah, the biblical writer pauses to point out that Shechem "cleaves" to Dinah. The only other passage in the Hebrew Bible where the word is used in the same sense—"to describe a loving relationship between two human beings"[10]—is the story of Creation in the Book of Genesis, where God creates Adam and Eve, and then blesses the bond between them as an expression of the natural order of human life: "Therefore shall a man leave his father and his mother, and shall *cleave* unto his wife, and they shall be one flesh" (Gen. 2:24). The oblique reference in the story of Dinah and Shechem to the very first man and woman can be read as an endorsement of Shechem's good will toward Dinah, whether he first approached her as a rapist, a seducer, or a suitor.

Some scholars have detected traces of both rape *and* seduction in the biblical text, a seeming contradiction that can be explained by the fact that the oldest strands of the biblical narrative are probably the work of two distinct authors, one known as "the Yahwist" because he (or she) calls the deity by his proper name, "Yahweh," and the other known as "the Elohist" because he calls the deity by the Hebrew word "Elohim," a term that may literally mean "the gods." (See appendix: Who *Really* Wrote the Bible?) The blending of two separate versions of the story of Dinah by the editors or redactors who gathered together the texts that we know as the Bible may explain why one sentence in Genesis 34 emphasizes Shechem's abuse of Dinah while the very next sentence emphasizes his love for her. One Bible scholar has decoded the text of Genesis 34 in a way that suggests the Yahwist was describing a rape, the Elohist was describing a seduction, and the so-called Redactor stitched the two accounts together into the ambiguous narrative that appears in the Bible.[11]

So the biblical account of Dinah and Shechem may preserve *two* separate and starkly different tales or "traditions" from the earliest history of the Israelites. One tradition is a pure and pristine love story—the courtship of Shechem and Dinah and the marriage negotiations that followed between their fathers and families, perhaps leading to a successful marriage and a happy ending. The other tradition is a war story—the armed conflict between the clan of Jacob and the native-dwelling Canaanites whom they sought to displace. According to some scholars, a biblical author conflated the two stories and turned the encounter between Dinah and Shechem from a romantic liaison into a forcible rape in order to justify the slaughter of the Shechemites.[12]

Seduction rather than rape may also be suggested in a passage of the Book of Judith, a work that was excluded from the biblical canon but is included in some Christian Bibles as a part of the Apocrypha (or Deuterocanon, in Catholic usage). Judith appeals to God in the name of her forefather, Simeon, and briefly recalls the massacre of Shechem and his people. Significantly, she credits God for sanctioning the violence against Shechem by bestowing upon Simeon the very sword that he used "to take revenge on the strangers who had loosed the adornment of a virgin to defile her" (Judith 9:2).[13] The same passage as translated in the New American Bible (NAB) is even steamier in describing Dinah's treatment at the hands of Shechem, who is accused of having "immodestly loosened the maiden's girdle, shamefully exposed her thighs, and disgracefully violated her body." Notably, while Judith condemns Shechem for "shaming" and "dishonoring" and "polluting" Dinah, she does not assert that he actually raped her, and some of Judith's phrases—"loos[ing] the adornment of a virgin"—somehow evoke a gentle if insistent seduction rather than a forcible rape.

One striking omission from the biblical text, however, raises even more troubling questions about the intentions, good or ill, of *all* of the characters in the tale. After the encounter between Shechem and Dinah is reported at the very outset of Genesis 34, we are told nothing more about Dinah or her whereabouts until the very end of the biblical text, when we discover for the first time that Dinah had apparently been sojourning in Shechem's house since the day of their first encounter. Is she a prisoner and a hostage of Shechem, as conventional biblical commentary would have us believe? Or, as some scholars have dared to suggest, is she a willing and perhaps even a loving guest of the young man who is so smitten with her?[14]

The Bible does not provide an answer to the mystery of Dinah's whereabouts. If, however, Dinah is held as a hostage in Shechem's house during the marriage negotiations between Hamor and Jacob, then we might begin to see Hamor as even more cynical than his own oily words suggest; his friendly entreaties to Jacob take on a dark and sinister meaning if, in fact, Dinah remains at his son's mercy. And the vengeance that her brothers will wreak on Hamor and his people seems somehow less excessive if, in fact, they concede to Shechem's marriage proposal only under the unspoken threat of further violence to their sister.

Even more intriguing is the notion that Dinah lingers in Shechem's house because she has fallen in love with him. Contemporary scholarship is willing to entertain the notion that Dinah is seeking solace from Shechem, a "kind and loving" man, as Bible critic Ita Sheres puts it, who "recognizes [Dinah] as a person of value."[15] Although the biblical text provides no hard evidence of Dinah's motives, a faint trace of the same idea can be found in the commentary of one ancient rabbi who surmised from the biblical text that Simeon and Levi found it necessary to drag their sister out of Shechem's house after slaying her betrothed. "When a woman is intimate with an uncircumcised person," wrote the sage, betraying what may be a certain degree of sexual jealousy, "she finds it hard to tear herself away."[16]

But if we recall Shechem's fervent protestations of love and his urgent desire to marry Dinah, we may be tempted to speculate that the two of them—young, unwed, and, crucially, each from a different tribe—have fallen so deeply in love with each other that they dare to engage in some kind of forbidden sexual encounter. If Dinah takes up residence in Shechem's house after that first encounter out of choice rather than compulsion, then we might conclude that the two of them are lovers, not rapist and victim.

In fact, some scholars have argued that the rape of Dinah may have been inserted into the biblical text by a priest or a scribe with an ulterior motive. According to the conventional wisdom of modern Bible scholarship, the biblical editors brought a sometimes harsh ideological agenda to the task of collecting and retelling the tales and traditions of the Israelites, a burning distrust of non-Israelites and an explosive hatred of the gods and goddesses they worshipped. For these religious authorities, the prospect of marriage with a non-Israelite and the risk that one of the Chosen People might be lured by a spouse into the worship of some thundering mountain god or lascivious fertility goddess, were a threat to the very survival of Israel. So the anonymous editor of Genesis 34 may have sought to sully the reputation of Shechem—and to provide an excuse for the massacre of his people by Simeon and Levi—by accusing him of a crime of sexual violence.*

Perhaps the real crime of Shechem and Dinah, then, is that they happened to fall in love with each other despite the fact that one was an Israelite and the other was not.+ Perhaps what *really* happened between Shechem and Dinah was more nearly a forbidden romantic liaison than a rape or even a seduction, an expression "of innocent love between two young people who were ready to merge culturally, politically, and religiously,"[17] as one contemporary feminist scholar proposes—or, to put it another way, the story of a man and a woman whose love for one another boldly defies ancient tribal rivalries and ends in catastrophe for both of their families.

"See what a scourge is laid upon your hate," Shakespeare wrote of

---

*Shechem is both the name of a lovestruck prince in Genesis 34 *and* the name of an important place in biblical history. The site of ancient Shechem, located forty-one miles north of Jerusalem, near the modern town of Nablus on the West Bank of the Jordan River, is the first place in Canaan where God appears to Abraham and promises the land to his descendants (Gen. 12:6–7). Shechem was briefly the capital of the northern kingdom of Israel and later an important ritual center for the Samaritans, a people who embrace certain Jewish scriptures and observances but separated themselves from the Israelites in antiquity. Some Bible scholars see in the *character* called Shechem an allegorical figure who symbolizes the *place* called Shechem, and they argue that Genesis 34 is merely an account of the struggle between the Canaanites and the Israelites for sovereignty in the region in ancient times. But the tale of Dinah and Shechem is so rich and so resonant—"the most graphically human story . . . [in] the whole of Genesis," according to British scholar Julian Pitt-Rivers—that it cannot be dismissed as mere allegory.

+Shechem's father, Hamor, is described as a "Hivite" in the Masoretic Text of the Bible, and a "Horite" in the Septuagint, an early Greek translation of the Bible. Some biblical scholars suggest that Hamor and his clan were actually Hurrians, a people of the ancient Near East whose native land was located to the north and west of Canaan. Other scholars have argued that Jacob and his sons were linked to the so-called Habiru, an enigmatic people once believed to be nomadic invaders who ranged across the ancient world. Especially intriguing is the mention of the Habiru in connection with the conquest of the city of Shechem in the Amarna Letters, a cache of Egyptian diplomatic correspondence dating back to the nineteenth century B.C.E. However, recent biblical scholarship no longer identifies the Hebrews with the Habiru, a term that is now understood to refer generally to landless people of various tribes and nations who were reduced to the status of fugitives and refugees, mercenaries and slaves, throughout the ancient Near East.

another pair of star-crossed lovers from rival houses, and the words apply to the Israelites and Hivites as well as the Montagues and Capulets, "That Heaven finds means to kill your joys with love."

THE CURIOUS PUNISHMENT FOR THE CRIME OF RAPE

Even if Shechem *is* a rapist, his proposal of marriage is less bizarre than it may first seem if we consider the curious punishment for the crime of rape under biblical law. According to the Book of Deuteronomy, any man who comes upon an unbetrothed virgin "and lay[s] hold on her, and lie[s] with her," must pay her father fifty shekels—and marry the woman he wronged (Deut. 22:28–29). To avoid adding insult to injury, of course, the rapist is obliged to marry his victim only if the woman and her family are willing.[18] And the Bible decrees that, unlike the husband in an ordinary marriage, the rapist is never permitted to divorce his victim-turned-wife.[19]

The Book of Deuteronomy was probably composed long after the events described in Genesis were supposed to have taken place, but similar laws are found elsewhere in the ancient Near East dating back to the eighteenth century B.C.E. Indeed, the legal codes of nearby Assyria suggest that a man might actually claim a wife by forcing himself upon her,[20] a practice that offends our contemporary sensibilities but suggests that Shechem's motive (if not his method) may have been rather more honorable than the biblical text allows us to understand.

What's more, the law that compelled a rapist to marry his victim can be seen as an entirely positive and even progressive measure, at least in the social context of the world in which Dinah actually lives. A woman in biblical times was expected to remain under the authority of a male at all times: as a child and a virginal young woman, she lived in her father's home until she married; once married, she lived with her husband and, she fervently hoped, bore and raised his children; and, if widowed, she relied on her own male children, who inherited their father's property.[21] No other role was permitted, and a woman like Dinah—not yet married but no longer a virgin—was not entitled to marry, bear or rear children, earn a living, or safely engage in sexual conduct.

So the notion of marriage as a punishment for rape can be seen as a form of reparation. The victim is now "damaged goods" in the eyes of her community and no longer acceptable as a wife and mother to any man *except* her rapist, and thus he is expected to repair the damage he has done to her—and, in a sense, to her family and the tribe at large—by marrying her. Of course, the Bible does not suggest that anyone bothered to ask Dinah whether she wanted to marry Shechem, but neither did they ask whether she wanted to see him dead. And by slaying Shechem, Dinah's vengeful brothers deny Dinah even the possibility of marriage and thus condemn her to a life of solitude and loneliness.[22]

The Bible does not tell us what happened to Dinah after the night of carnage in Shechem's house. All we know is that Dinah is still in Jacob's household when, many years later, the whole clan follows Jacob down to Egypt, where his favorite son, Joseph, now reigns as Pharaoh's chancellor (Gen. 46:15). The ancient literature that attached itself to the Bible imagines one or another grotesque and ironic epilogue to the biblical tale: Perhaps Simeon offered to marry his "defiled" sister, according to one bit of overheated speculation by an ancient rabbinical sage, or maybe Dinah wed an Egyptian high priest and gave birth to the daughter who later marries Joseph, according to another traditional source.[23] But a more likely surmise is that Dinah was shut away in the house of her father or perhaps one of her brothers, a spinster aunt with a dark past and no prospects, and she lived out her life in despair.

"MY COVENANT SHALL BE IN YOUR FLESH"

Shechem's desire to marry Dinah is so ardent that he offers to pay any price—the Hebrew word is *mohar*—in exchange for her hand in marriage. *Mohar*, commonly translated as "dowry" or "bride-price" or sometimes "marriage gift," is mentioned in only three places in the Bible: the story of Dinah; the Book of Exodus, where it is decreed that one who seduces a virgin must marry her and "pay money according to the dowry of virgins" to the father (Exod. 22:15–16); and, finally, the First Book of Samuel, where the payment of a bride-price figures oddly but importantly in David's courtship of the daughter of King Saul.[24] As we shall see, there is strong if curious linkage between the rape of Dinah and the courtship of Saul's daughter: both stories turn the solemn rite of circumcision into a grotesque *mohar* and, at the same time, an elaborate dirty trick.

A *mohar*, as the story of Shechem makes clear, is something of value that is given to the father of the bride by his prospective son-in-law. Fifty shekels is the prescribed bride-price to be paid by one who rapes a virgin and is compelled to marry her (Deut. 22:29), but the Bible is silent on the going price for a bride under ordinary circumstances. Several biblical stories suggest that a man could pay the bride-price for his betrothed in labor or goods rather than in money. When Dinah's own father, Jacob, falls in love with Rachel, the younger and more beautiful daughter of a man named Laban, young Jacob offers to render seven years of labor to his future father-in-law as a bride-price. But Jacob is tricked into serving a second term of labor when the wily Laban slips his older and less comely daughter, Leah, into the marriage bed in place of Rachel (Gen. 29:18–29).

Much later in the Bible, we encounter David, the future king of Israel, as a young war hero who seeks to marry one of the daughters of the reigning king, Saul. Like Jacob, David is tricked into paying an odd bride-price, a bizarre "payment in kind" that was designed by the jealous king to cost David his life.

Saul is already envious and distrustful of David when the young warrior asks him for one of his daughters in marriage. "Saul hath slain his thousands, and David his tens of thousands," the Israelite women sing in praise of David when he returns from a glorious campaign against the Philistines (1 Sam. 18:7). Saul's son, Jonathan, declares his love for David—"[T]he soul of Jonathan was knit with the soul of David" (1 Sam. 18:1)*—and so does Saul's daughter, Michal. To

---

*When Jonathan and Saul are later slain in battle with the Philistines—actually, Saul chooses to take his own life to avoid capture by "these uncircumcised"!—David delivers a famous eulogy in which he declares of Jonathan: "Wonderful was thy love to me, passing the love of women"—a line that has inspired much speculation about David's sexual orientation (2 Sam. 1:26). These words from Holy Scripture were recently invoked in a debate in the Knesset, the national legislature of Israel, over the rights of gay men and women under Israeli law. Yael Dayan, daughter of another war hero of Israel, succeeded in drawing the ire (and raising the blood pressure) of some of her fellow members of the Knesset by "outing" David; she argued, on the strength of David's eulogy of Jonathan, that the two of them were gay lovers.

eliminate the up-and-coming and much beloved David, the crafty old king comes up with a scheme quite as dastardly as the one that Dinah's brothers work on Shechem.

Saul promises Michal's hand in marriage to David, but only if he is able to pay an exceedingly bizarre bride-price—the *mohar* demanded by King Saul is "a hundred foreskins of the Philistines." Sensibly enough, Saul is counting on the Philistines to resist circumcision: "For Saul thought to make David fall by the hand of the Philistines." But Saul did not allow for the young warrior's skill and courage, his sheer determination to marry the king's daughter, and his flair for the flashy gesture in battle. David, ever the overachiever, brings back two hundred foreskins, each one forcibly separated from its former owner, and claims Michal as his wife (1 Sam. 18:22–29).

What is remarkable about both stories is that the sacred ritual of circumcision is treated so lightly and even so perversely, as if it were a cruel joke rather than a solemn sacrament. One could hardly tell from these tales that circumcision—that is, the surgical removal of the foreskin of the penis—was the single most important symbol of identity among the Israelites, and remains so among the Jewish people today. Indeed, circumcision is literally the sign by which the fateful contract between God and Abraham is sealed: God appears to Abraham, promises to make him "the father of a multitude of nations," and, in exchange, extracts a single promise from Abraham on behalf of his offspring—Abraham and all of his descendants will submit to circumcision. (See chapter nine.)

"My covenant shall be in your flesh for an everlasting covenant," God decrees. "And the uncircumcised male who is not circumcised in the flesh of the foreskin, that soul shall be cut off from his people; he hath broken My covenant" (Gen. 17:13–14).

When the biblical author who composed the Book of Samuel called attention to the grotesque bride-price that King Saul demands, he was seeking to show how deep and twisted is Saul's hatred of young David. The point of sending David to retrieve a hundred Philistine foreskins, of course, is to put him in harm's way and, Saul hopes, to let the Philistines rid the jealous king of the pesky young David once and for all. Indeed, the Bible tells us that David's astounding success in his mission is taken by Saul himself as a sign of God's favor toward David and an augury of his own doom.

A different point is made by the biblical author who tells the story of Dinah; this author uses circumcision to underscore the "otherness" of Shechem and his people. Here is a tribe so alien to the Israelites, the storyteller seems to say, that mass circumcision is necessary to purify them before a single daughter of Israel might be betrothed to their prince. Even then, the prospect of "marrying out" is so repugnant to Dinah's brothers that they feel obliged to conduct a massacre to prevent the forbidden union. A fierce irony can be seen in the fact that Simeon and Levi feel free to turn the sacred rite of circumcision into a form of torture and trickery in order to prevent the wedding from taking place at all.

To the contemporary reader (and to a fair number of biblical exegetes), the use of a sacred ritual to render men helpless so they can be more easily slaughtered is not only a dirty trick but a sacrilege. At best, the mass circumcision demanded by Dinah's brothers suggests a kind of rough justice—Shechem and all the menfolk of his tribe are scarified in the very organ that Shechem used to "defile" her in the first place. But the biblical author who retold the tale of Dinah and her brothers was not merely setting up a sadistic joke at the expense of Shechem. Rather, he was reminding his readership of what was regarded by the established religious leadership as an urgent threat to the very survival of the Israelites: the lure of strange gods and strange bedfellows.

"I HAVE LOVED STRANGERS"

Although Genesis 34 purports to describe events of the far-distant past—long before the Israelites were enslaved by Pharaoh, long before they left Egypt under the leadership of Moses, long before they conquered and settled in Canaan—the story of Dinah and Shechem may have found its way into the Holy Scriptures in its current form as late as 400 B.C.E., when the oldest strands of Israelite legend, lore, and law were gathered and woven together into the work that we now know as the Five Books of Moses.

At that moment in the history of Israel, according to the conventional wisdom of contemporary biblical scholarship, the priests and scribes who assembled and edited the Bible were in despair over the unhappy fate of the Israelites. The "united kingdom" of David and

Solomon had fallen into ruin centuries earlier, and the exploits of these great and powerful kings were the stuff of legend. The northern kingdom, known as Israel, had been conquered by the Assyrian empire in 722 B.C.E., and the northern tribes—the famous "Ten Lost Tribes of Israel"—had been dispersed and largely destroyed. The southern kingdom, known as Judah, was conquered by the Babylonian empire in 587–586 B.C.E.; the Temple of Solomon in Jerusalem was razed, and the ruling class of the kingdom was deported to Babylon. A tiny remnant was allowed to return to Jerusalem sometime around 538 B.C.E., when the Babylonian empire was itself conquered by the armies of the Persian emperor. Only after the Babylonian Exile came to an end, and the Israelites straggled back to Canaan, were the holy writings and the traditional lore stitched together into the book that we now know as the Bible, at least according to the consensus of contemporary biblical scholarship.

When the princes and priests of ancient Israel returned to Canaan, they found a land, a culture, and a community in deep crisis. Ritual sacrifices to Yahweh were no longer possible because the Temple had been destroyed, and the land of Canaan was filled with rival clans and tribes that worshipped a pantheon of strange gods and goddesses. Discouraged and disaffected by their long ordeal, the Israelites were tempted to consort with the strangers among them, to marry them and to worship their deities, sometimes by venerating forest groves and "high places," stones and posts, graven images of gold and silver, and sometimes by availing themselves of the sexual services of temple prostitutes or participating in bacchanalian rituals or perhaps even offering human sacrifice. The priests and scribes who collected, compiled, edited, and rewrote the texts that make up much of the Bible were plainly obsessed by the powerful allure of strange gods and strange women, both of which they regarded as a threat to the very existence of the Israelites, and they used the holy texts as a rhetorical weapon to coax, cajole, threaten, extort, or simply scare the Chosen People into shunning their neighbors in Canaan and marrying only their fellow worshippers of Yahweh.

Much rhetorical ammunition could be found in the writings of the prophets, ancient and contemporary, whose visions and oracles were added to the Five Books of Moses to create the heart of the Hebrew Bible as we know it. One can literally open the prophetic books at random and find some hot-eyed and heavy-breathing tract on the subject of pagan worship, or intermarriage, or both. Indeed, the sin of apostasy and the sin of sexual promiscuity are treated as interchangeable by many of the prophets, one serving as a metaphor for the other throughout the Bible. All of the woes of Israel—conquest, dispersion, despoliation, and destruction—are depicted in the prophetic books as just punishments inflicted by God on the Chosen People for their spiritual and carnal infidelities.

"I have loved strangers," boasts a wanton and impudent Israel to an angry and jealous God in the Book of Jeremiah, "and after them will I go" (Jer. 2:25).

"Because of thy filthy lewdness," God thunders back, "thou shalt not be purged from thy filthiness . . . till I have satisfied My fury upon thee" (Ezek. 24:13).

The condemnation of marriage with non-Israelites in the Bible is not merely metaphorical. In one remarkable scene in the Book of Ezra, we see the priest called Ezra—"a ready scribe in the Law of Moses" (Ezra 7:6)—as he returns to Jerusalem from exile in Babylon and discovers, to his horror, that "the holy seed have mingled themselves with the peoples of the lands." After sitting down in the dust, rending his garments and tearing his hair like a man in mourning, Ezra lifts himself up, dusts himself off, and resolves to do something about the "abomination" of intermarriage. So he conducts a public ceremony in which a multitude of Israelite men, abject and weeping, are divorced en masse from the non-Israelite women whom they have taken as wives. "[L]et us make a covenant with out God to put away our foreign wives, and such as are born of them," exhorts the stern priest as he tears asunder an uncounted number of mixed marriages (Ezra 10:3). "Be of good courage, and do it!" (Ezra 10:3–4).

Ezra's words of encouragement—"Be of good courage"—consciously echo the words spoken to Joshua by Moses (Deut. 31:23) and by the Almighty himself (Josh. 1:6) on the very eve of the invasion of Canaan, when the Israelites cross the Jordan River and launch a war of conquest that is intended to rid the Promised Land of its native peoples. (See chapter seven.) According to the Bible, God himself endorses a scorched-earth campaign against the Canaanites that is only slightly less horrific in detail—and far greater in scale—than the fate of the innocent men, women, and children who are made to pay for Shechem's crime, whatever it might have been.

TWO BELLIES, ONE SPEAR

The massacre of Shechem and his people as recounted in the Book of Genesis foreshadows the carnage that is found in subsequent books of the Bible, a kind of "ethnic cleansing" that is intended to purify the Promised Land by obliterating the idol-worshipping men and women whom the Israelites apparently find so beguiling. By the time we reach the heroic saga of the Exodus from Egypt—the stirring national myth of the Israelites and the centerpiece of the Bible itself—we find a biblical atrocity story that is the mirror image of the tale of Dinah and Shechem; it is a tale in which the victim of seduction is an Israelite prince from the tribe of Simeon and the seducer is a Midianite woman. The two stories differ in one basic and crucial way: The patriarch Jacob is distressed and remorseful over the revenge that his hotheaded sons have taken against the people of Shechem, but Moses and God himself specifically sanction the punishment inflicted on the Midianites.

The tale of the Israelite prince and his Midianite lover is set in the wilderness during the wanderings of the Israelites after the Exodus from Egypt. Moses, who is forever caught between a cranky God and the whiny Israelites, confronts yet another incident of backsliding on the part of the Chosen People, who are now "commit[ing] harlotry with the daughters of Moab" and sacrificing at the shrines of their gods (Num. 25:1–9). At the urging of the Almighty, Moses pronounces a death sentence on the Israelites who have strayed into strange shrines or strange beds—some twenty-four thousand Israelites will perish from the plague that God sends down on his Chosen People (Num. 25:9)—and a punitive campaign against the foreigners who have lured them there.

At precisely that moment, one impudent fellow wanders into the camp of the Israelites with his Midianite lady friend in tow. (We are told, by the way, that he is a prince of the tribe of Simeon and thus a direct descendant of Dinah's brother and avenger.) While the rest of the Israelites watch in horror, the prince and the Midianite woman who "beguiled" him brazenly retire to the tent where Moses and the Almighty conduct their tête-à-têtes. A man named Phinehas emerges from the crowd and follows the amorous couple into the tent, where he manages to spear both of them with one thrust of his weapon (Num. 25:7–9, 14). Exactly what the man and woman were *doing* when they were both impaled through the belly with a single spear is left to our imagination, but there is one form of physical encounter between man and woman that nicely explains it.*

The murder of the prince and his lover is enough to halt the plague that is ravaging the camp of the Israelites as a divine punishment for their "harlotry," but the carnage is not over yet. Not content with the extermination of a single temptress, and apparently overlooking the fact that his own wife and in-laws are Midianites, Moses sends Phinehas and his comrades-in-arms on a mission to kill as many of them as possible. All of the Midianite men are slain, and all of the women and children are taken captive—but the decision to spare the women and "their little ones" turns out to be an act of dubious mercy. Moses is surprised and annoyed at his captains for bringing back so many prisoners of war along with the customary plunder and booty, and he coldly utters a command that we are shocked to hear on the lips of the man who brought down the Ten Commandments from Mount Sinai.

"Have ye saved all the women alive?" Moses complains, plainly irritated at the sight of so many potential seducers of Israelite men, so many Midianite mouths to feed. "Now therefore kill every male among the little ones," he continues, "and kill every woman that hath known man by lying with him." Only the virgin girls are allowed to survive, Moses decrees, and they are consigned to his men of war for their own pleasure (Num. 31:15–18).

The slaughter of the Midianites comes as an appalling surprise to most casual Bible readers precisely because the clergy of both Judaism and Christianity have preferred to focus on the kinder and gentler passages of the Holy Scriptures. But the plain fact is that the Bible accommodates both love and hate, mercy and vengeance, life and death, and often in the very same passages. For example, the Book of Leviticus is where we find many of the stern and narrow commandments that are often cited nowadays by fundamentalists of various faiths, including, for example, the biblical decrees against gay sexuality (Lev. 18:22), tattooing (Lev. 19:28), and sorcery (Lev. 19:31, 20:6, 27). The priestly

*An Orthodox rabbi in Israel recently invoked the example of the slain Simeonite prince in condemning contemporary Jews who marry non-Jews. The subtext of the rabbi's remarks was clear enough to his audience, and he was later criticized for indirectly calling for the murder of Jews in mixed marriages. So we can see that the Bible is not a dead letter in the debate over morality in our own world, especially in the land of the Bible!

author of Leviticus broadly condemns *all* of the rites and rituals regarded as sacred by the native dwellers of Canaan: "And ye shall not walk in the customs of the nation which I am casting out before you" (Lev. 20:23). Yet it is also in Leviticus that we find the humane and compassionate credo that has been embraced as the essential moral instruction of the Bible-based faiths:

> And if a stranger sojourn with thee in your land, ye shall not do him wrong. The stranger that sojourneth with you shall be unto you as the home-born among you, for ye were strangers in the land of Egypt: I am the Lord your God (Lev. 19:34).

We have been taught—and we ought to hope and pray—that the ideals of justice, mercy, and loving-kindness are the ones that should be embraced by the faithful of the Bible-based religions. "What is hateful to you, do not unto your neighbor" is how Hillel, a revered Jewish teacher of the first century C.E., summarized the wisdom of the Torah, and Jesus of Nazareth goes even further: "Love your enemies, bless them that curse you, do good to them that hate you" (Matt. 5:44 KJV). Even if history shows that it is more often talked about than practiced, the so-called Golden Rule remains the keystone of the Judeo-Christian tradition: "We have built every idea of moral civilization on it," writes Cynthia Ozick.[25]

Yet we cannot penetrate the inner meanings in the story of Dinah and Shechem unless we discern the fear and loathing of the stranger that burned in the heart of at least some of the pious ghostwriters who fashioned the myth and legend of the Israelites into the book we know as the Bible. The rape of Dinah in the Book of Genesis and the seduction of the Israelite prince in the Book of Numbers are offered as morality tales, not atrocity stories, and they are meant to caution the readers of the Bible against the temptation of strange gods and goddesses and, above all, the men and women who worship them. For the redactors who slipped these two tales into the Bible and put their own spin on them, the real atrocity in each story is not the mass murder of men, women, and children, but the single act of seduction by a stranger that precedes it.

The Biblical Court of Conscience

The Bible can be read as, among many other things, a manual of survival for a nation of outsiders. The patriarch Jacob, like his own father and grandfather and countless generations of their descendants, is "a stranger in a strange land," as Moses puts it, and he embraces a strategy that will turn out to be mostly (if not always) effective for preserving life and limb, identity and destiny, against conquerors, inquisitors, and pogromists. When he rebukes his bloodthirsty sons—"You have made my name stink among the people of the country" (Gen. 34:30 NEB)—Jacob is articulating his preference for diplomacy over war, accommodation over confrontation, going along and getting along rather than fighting back against the powers that be.

"My numbers are few," complains Jacob, a master in the art of realpolitik, and he makes it clear that his concerns about the Canaanites are pragmatic rather than principled: "[I]f they muster against me and attack me, I shall be destroyed, I and my household with me" (Gen. 34:30–31 NEB).

Simeon and Levi, by contrast, are warriors who are driven by a fierce sense of honor rather than a cool assessment of relative military strength. But they also seem to believe that their embattled clan must answer violence with even greater violence if they are to survive as outsiders in the land of Canaan. Their act of revenge anticipates the strategies for survival that have been observed among the Bedouin tribes of the contemporary Near East. If a single Bedouin, man or woman, is set upon by members of a rival tribe, the victim's relations feel obliged to inflict a mighty and memorable punishment on the whole tribe in order to deter future attacks; otherwise, it is believed, the clan (or "blood revenge group," as the Arab word for "clan" can be rendered more literally) will be seen as weak and irresolute, and all members of the clan will be vulnerable to yet more insults and assaults.[26] Like the Bedouins, the sons of Jacob seem to believe that both honor *and* deterrence make it essential to take revenge against Shechem in a way that will literally terrorize the rest of the Canaanites.

The clash between Jacob and his sons—a clash between generations, values, philosophies, and strategies—is expressed in the bitter words that Simeon and Levi speak to Jacob after he rebukes them for the massacre of Shechem. To the patriarch Jacob, the betrothal of

Dinah to the man who "defiled" her is an honorable compromise that will bring the blessings of peace and prosperity. To his sons, it is a peace without honor, a disgraceful sellout, and they utter an accusation that seems to apply even more to Jacob himself than to Shechem or Hamor: "Is our sister to be treated as a whore?"

The "Bible's court of conscience," as one scholar puts it,[27] has weighed the deeds of Simeon and Levi and found them wanting. Jacob himself delivers the verdict on his deathbed, withholding his blessing from Simeon and Levi, declaring them to be unworthy sons and successors precisely because they acted so rashly and so excessively, and denying them any portion of the Promised Land.

> Simeon and Levi are brethren,
> their spades became weapons of violence.
> My soul shall not enter their council,
> my heart shall not join their company,
> for in their anger they killed men,
> wantonly hamstrung oxen.
> A curse be on their anger because it was fierce;
> a curse on their wrath because it was ruthless!
> I will scatter them in Jacob,
> I will disperse them in Israel (Gen. 49:5–7 NEB).

Tradition has approved and embraced Jacob's example. His is the "[s]easoned voice of maturity," and he sagely puts statesmanship above all: "[H]e rebukes such a childish religion which will endanger its own life rather than face realities."[28] Indeed, Jacob's way has characterized a couple of thousand years of Jewish history, and we see his moral and practical example in a long line of revered figures that stretches from Maimonides, a renowned Jewish philosopher who served as the court physician to the vizier of Egypt and, it is said, the crusading Richard the Lion-Hearted, down to Chaim Weizmann, the "George Washington of Zionism," who fought his war for a Jewish homeland in Palestine in the corridors of Whitehall and secured the first modern-day foothold on the soil of the Holy Land in the form of the Balfour Declaration with a pen rather than a sword.

Then, within a single decade of the mid-twentieth century, history appeared to reverse the judgment of the court of conscience. Jacob's way failed the Jewish community in Germany and the rest of Europe during the Holocaust, when the strategies of survival that had worked for a couple of millennia proved worthless against industrialized mass murder. Some were alert enough—and fortunate enough—to escape from Europe in time to avoid the worst excesses of the Holocaust. A heroic few armed themselves and fought back in the ghettos and forests and even in the death camps. But the greater number of European Jews perished, at least in part because they assumed that the Germans were too civilized to murder six million men, women, and children in cold blood—and, later, they assumed that the Western democracies were too civilized to permit it.

The scene that emblemizes the failure of Jacob's way is one that was described to me by a Holocaust survivor who saw it with his own eyes: The venerable rabbi of a shtetl in Poland marched down the street with a Torah in his arms to welcome the storm troopers of the Third Reich because the old man recalled his own experiences during World War I, when the German occupiers turned out to be far more gentle and generous than the Polish peasantry or the Russian overlords who ruled them. The rabbi's assumptions proved to be tragically wrong, and, like millions of his brethren, he paid for his mistake with his life.*

As if prompted by the agonies of the Holocaust, the biblical court of conscience has begun to reconsider the antagonism between Jacob and his sons. A pronounced revisionist strain in postwar biblical scholarship suggests that Simeon and Levi, rather than Jacob, are the "real heroes" of Genesis 34 precisely because they picked up their swords and made war on Shechem to vindicate their sister's defilement. For example, one contemporary biblical critic was moved to point out that two "extra-canonical" books—that is, Bible-era religious writings that were excluded from the Hebrew Bible itself—offer a countertradition that undercuts the "official" version of the massacre of Shechem as reported in the Book of Genesis. The Testament of Levi shows us an angel descending from heaven to hand Levi a sword and shield: "Take

---

*No one who was spared the experience of the Holocaust is qualified to second-guess the character or conduct of the innocents who found themselves in the grip of Nazi Germany and its collaborators. We may speculate on the lessons of history, but we are not entitled to blame the victims of mass murder for the tragic fate that befell them, and it is not my intention to do so.

revenge on Shechem because of Dinah, and I will be with you, for the Lord has sent me." And the Book of Judith, as we have seen, suggests that God himself armed Simeon with divine weaponry.[29] God was on the side of the warriors, the countertradition holds, rather than the peacemaker.

The revisionist approach to the rape of Dinah reaches a crescendo in the work of one Bible critic, Meir Sternberg, who boldly insists that Jacob, "the tale's least sympathetic character," is guilty of "egocentricity" and "cowardice" and even "immorality" because his only stated concern about the massacre of Shechem is wholly self-serving. "[T]he slaughter is reprehensible only in its consequences," writes Sternberg. By contrast, he argues, Simeon and Levi are "the real heroes" of Genesis 34. "Their concern has been selfless and single-minded: to redress the wrong done to their sister and the whole family," Sternberg concludes. "Their idealistic and uncompromising stance makes them the most intricate, colorful, and attractive characters in the story."[30]

Against the background of the Holocaust, of course, the sword-bearing sons of Jacob seem far more compelling to us than their pragmatic and pacifistic father. For the same reason, the resistance fighters who made a heroic last stand against the Nazis in the streets and sewers of the doomed Warsaw ghetto strike us as nobler than their fathers and mothers, sisters and brothers, who boarded the boxcars and rode into Auschwitz, even if the fighters ended up just as dead as the victims of the gas chamber. But the real question, the tough question, is not how to die but how to live, and it is a question that is being asked—and answered—in the streets of Jerusalem and Tel Aviv, Hebron and Nablus in our own times.

The taunting words of Simeon and Levi—"Is our sister to be treated as a whore?"—may be blood-stirring and soul-shaking, especially in the light of recent history, but it turns out to be the wrong question to ask at a time when men and women in what we still call the Holy Land are all too willing to raise a sword against each other because each one persists in regarding the other as a stranger.

"FOR THE HONOR OF OUR SISTERS"

The Bible confirms that *something* convinced the rest of the Canaanites not to revenge themselves upon the Israelites for the slaughter of

Shechem, as Jacob feared they would do. One explanation is found in the passage that follows the story of Dinah in the Book of Genesis: God abruptly orders Jacob and his clan to leave the place where the blood of Shechem and his people was spilled, and to pitch their tents at another site in Canaan. Jacob purifies his household by ordering the removal of any idols and other paraphernalia of idol worship, and then the clan sets off toward its new encampment at a place called Bethel. Jacob's fear that the Canaanites will muster against the Israelites turns out to be unfounded.

"And they journeyed," we are told in Genesis, "and a terror of God was upon the cities that were round about them, and they did not pursue after the sons of Jacob" (Gen. 35:5).

The traditional interpretation of the passage is that the ritual of purification conducted by Jacob and his clan, an act of obeisance to the Almighty, induces God to keep the Canaanites at bay: "a terror of God" is what deterred the Canaanites from revenging themselves for the deaths of their countrymen. But the modern reader might be tempted to conclude that terror of Simeon and Levi had something to do with it— and, for that reason, the way of Jacob's warrior sons threatens to over-shadow Jacob's way in the moral and political calculus of various decision-makers, both Arab and Jew, in the modern Middle East.

Something closer to Simeon and Levi, for example, can be seen in the pioneers of modern political Zionism in the late nineteenth cen-tury, who organized self-defense units in the towns and villages of Russia. "Violence must be answered with violence," declared the mani-festo of one of the early Jewish bands. The leader of another movement appeared to invoke the memory of Dinah when he wrote that armed self-defense was not less than "[a war] for the honor of our sisters, for our national honor, for our future as a nation."[31] The veterans of those early skirmishes served as role models—and, in some instances, as leaders— of the Haganah, the underground army of the Zionist movement in Palestine, which was organized to protect the Jewish community against Arab violence and later prevailed against the armies of seven Arab nations that declared war on Israel as soon as the tiny Jewish state declared its independence in 1948. To the men and women who struggled to create the Jewish homeland, and especially to the survivors of the Holocaust, the destiny of the Jewish people now passed into the hands of what Menachem Begin called "a new specimen of human being . . . completely unknown to the world for over 1800 years, 'the fighting Jew.' "[32]

Over its first half century of statehood, Israel came to rely on the sword to protect and preserve itself against the enmity of its Arab neighbors and, perhaps more crucially, the Arabs who live among Jews in Israel itself and the lands that Israel secured during the Six-Day War. The military prowess of the Israel Defense Forces fundamentally changed the very image of the State of Israel from a David to a Goliath. Only recently has Jacob's way reasserted itself in Israel, and the fighting Jew has been forced to learn once again when and how to sit down and talk.

Significantly, Yitzhak Rabin—a veteran of the Haganah who repeatedly distinguished himself on the battlefield in Israel's struggle for independence and survival—went on to earn a Nobel Peace Prize precisely because of his willingness to make peace with the Palestine Liberation Organization. Rabin commanded the Israel Defense Forces during the Six-Day War, but he will be best remembered for shaking hands with Yasir Arafat. Significantly, Rabin is also an exemplar of "the new Jew"— a soldier and a statesman, a man who knows when to make war and when to make peace, a vigorous hybrid of Jacob and his warrior sons.

But it is equally significant that Rabin was felled not by an Arab but by a fellow Israeli who insisted that he had been called upon by the Almighty to slay the man who made peace with the stranger. The assassination of Rabin demonstrates exactly why the example of Simeon and Levi is so treacherous—all it takes to strike down a towering figure like Rabin is a little man with a loaded gun who had managed to convince himself that God handed it to him and bid him use it. One can almost hear the impudent question that Simeon and Levi put to Jacob—"Is our sister to be treated like a whore?"—on the lips of the assassin who murdered Yitzhak Rabin.

A close reading of Genesis 34 allows us to see that the Bible offers two visions of the stranger and two approaches to dealing with him: one that exhorts us to make war, the other that encourages us to make peace and even, as the story of Dinah and Shechem may secretly suggest, make love. "I have set before thee life and death, the blessing and the curse; therefore choose life," says Moses to the Israelites (Deut. 30:19), as if to suggest that the correct choice is so obvious that only a fool or a miscreant would choose the wrong one. But the Bible is not always so clear and straightforward in its moral instruction, and much mischief has been done over the centuries and millennia precisely because zealots can always find chapter and verse to justify even the most grotesque article of faith or plan of action.

In fact, no matter how excessive the revenge of Simeon and Levi on Shechem may appear to us, the Bible suggests that Jacob's way *and* the warrior's way are appropriate, each in its own time. "To every thing there is a season," we read in a celebrated passage of Ecclesiastes: "A time to love, and a time to hate; a time for war, and a time for peace" (Eccles. 3:1, 8). Tragically, the Bible never tells us with clarity or certainty how and when to choose between them. The enigmatic fragment of Genesis in which Dinah's story appears, like so much of the Bible, can be used to validate either one.

CHAPTER SIX

TAMAR AND JUDAH

*Then he asked the men of her place, saying: "Where is the
harlot, that was at Enaim by the wayside?" And they said:
"There hath been no harlot here."*

—GENESIS 38:21

Tamar reclined against the trunk of an ancient olive tree at a fork in
the road near the village gate. Her face was artfully veiled, and
between her breasts she wore a tiny cloth sack of balsam and myrrh that
she had cadged from one of the village women. Beneath her robe of blue
cotton, the afternoon heat began to raise a fine sweat on her skin. A
scent—of myrrh, of lemons and oranges, of the private places of her
body—suffused her garment like a perfume.

She watched the road with half-closed eyes and waited for the man
called Judah. She had heard that he was on his way to the festival at
Timnah and she counted on catching his eye as he passed by. If her plan
worked, he would not recognize Tamar as his own widowed daughter-
in-law. Instead, Judah would take her for a common whore. And, more
than that, his passion would be aroused and he would seek her favors in
the nearby olive grove.

On that, Tamar thought to herself, everything now depended.

> *And it came to pass at that time, that Judah went down from his brethren, and turned in to a certain Adullamite, whose name was Hirah.*
>
> —GENESIS 38:1

> *And Judah saw there a daughter of a certain Canaanite whose name was Shua; and he took her, and went in unto her.*
>
> —GENESIS 38:2

Judah had wandered into the district a few years before, a lone Israelite among the native people of Canaan. He was seeking to put himself at a distance from his stern father, an Israelite chieftain called Jacob, and a gaggle of brothers who competed for the old man's favor.

The prospect of settling as a stranger among the Canaanites was more agreeable to Judah than staying in the household of his father. Jacob's favorite son, Joseph, had been set upon and killed by some wild beast while tending the old man's flocks—or so the brothers had told Jacob when they returned from the distant hills with Joseph's blood-stained robe. The brothers consoled their father and competed with each other in displaying their grief, but they watched each other with cautious eyes: Would one of them tell the grieving father what had *really* happened in the place where Joseph disappeared?

So Judah decamped from his father's place in the hill country near Hebron and moved into the lowlands where the Canaanites tended their fields and their flocks. Near the Canaanite village of Adullam, Judah and a few of his men pitched their tents in a meadow that belonged to a villager named Hirah. When Hirah and his men approached the Israelite squatters, Judah hailed them with one hand raised in greeting and the other hand on the short sword that he wore on his hip.

And she conceived, and bore a son; and he called his name Er. And she conceived again, and bore a son; and she called his name Onan. And she yet again bore a son, and called his name Shelah. . . .

—GENESIS 38:3–5

As it turned out, Hirah did not seek to drive Judah and his band of Israelites out of the meadow. Indeed, he saw a chance to profit by the encounter. Like all newcomers, Hirah calculated, they would be willing seekers of advice and buyers of land and goods. So Hirah befriended the stranger and offered to sell him houses and fields and livestock, and Judah was soon the master of his own estate: a plot of open land, an orchard of lemon and orange trees, a flock of sheep and another of goats.

Judah built a house, dug a well, raised a wall of rough stone to mark the boundaries of his land. The fields were planted with wheat, and the flocks were allowed to graze in the distant wadis. Before long, a few of Judah's kinfolk heard of his good fortune, and their tents began to blossom like wildflowers around the compound. Judah boldly married a Canaanite woman, the daughter of a neighboring landowner named Shua. And Judah's wife, a shy, soft-spoken woman known as Bathshua—daughter of Shua—gave him three sons.

Soon enough, Judah was a chieftain in his own domain, surrounded by dutiful Israelites who sought his favor and protection even as they had once attended on Jacob. Judah sent gifts to his father's house at Hebron to demonstrate his wealth—a Canaanite weaving, a vessel of worked silver, a ram or a ewe—but Judah preferred to stay within his own walls. He did not want to face his father with the burden of his guilty knowledge about the fate of Joseph, a slave in Egypt—or, perhaps more likely, dead.

As time passed, Judah continued to rely on Hirah's knowledge of the curious dialect spoken by the locals and his willingness to offer advice on their ways in everything from sheepshearing to well-drilling. But Judah learned that he was still at the mercy of the Israelite graybeards who had attached themselves to his compound and constantly reminded him of his duties as the chieftain of his own clan. "The Law decrees . . ." was their tiresome refrain, and they were constantly nudging him in one direction or another.

"The worship of Baal is an abomination in the eyes of the Lord," the elders insisted, and so Judah forbade the Canaanites who lived among them as servants and shepherds to sacrifice to their own gods.

"The Canaanites are fornicators who seduce our young men and turn our young women into whores," they cried, and Judah forbade the Israelites to visit the temple prostitutes who offered their bodies as altars for the worship of Astarte, the goddess of fertility, in the nearby Canaanite towns.

"Your firstborn must marry so that the clan will survive into yet another generation," the old men carped, reminding Judah that a grandson was all the more crucial because his own wife had ceased giving him sons. And so Judah cast about for a wife for his eldest son, the one called Er.

Judah mentioned the matter to Hirah, of course, and soon his old friend appeared at Judah's door with a match to propose.

"I have found a suitable wife for your firstborn son," Hirah said. "A flower of Canaan! And so your son may be assured of a willing woman with a fertile womb."

"Perhaps I should send back to my father's house for a woman of our own people," Judah mused. "That's what the old men say."

"Your father's spies!" Hirah hissed, saying out loud what Judah had always suspected. "If you allow your father to pick a wife for your son, you will put a spy in his bed. Far better that you should choose Tamar—"

"Tamar?" asked Judah. The name meant "date palm," and Judah

And Judah took a wife for Er his first-born, and her name was Tamar.

—GENESIS 38:6

was reminded of the oasis where he and his brothers had struck a bargain with the caravaners who carried Joseph off to Egypt.

"Tamar is the woman I have found to be the bride of your firstborn," Hirah explained. "Her name suits her: she flowers even in the desert, and she will bear the sweetest of fruit."

From the day she arrived in the compound, Tamar was not like the Israelite women among whom she suddenly found herself as the bride of Judah's eldest son. The other young women fell silent when Judah passed the women's tent. Drawing their veils about their faces, they followed him with their eyes, then fell into chatter and giggles when he was out of earshot.

Tamar, by contrast, ignored the chieftain—or seemed to—and continued to speak in a voice that was somehow too loud, too strong. Although a married woman, she was not careful about her veil and boldly allowed her father-in-law to see her uncovered face; sometimes she actually smiled or even laughed in the presence of the menfolk! Some of the young women were outraged by Tamar; some secretly admired her audacity. But if Judah noticed that his daughter-in-law was bolder than the rest—indeed, if Judah noticed the dark-eyed young woman at all—he gave no sign of it.

Not long after her marriage to Er, however, Tamar turned into an object of pity rather than outrage in the eyes of the women. As the wife of Er, who was destined to become the chieftain in his own time, she was to be the mother of many powerful sons. But one day her husband left the compound on some errand that no one bothered to explain to Tamar, and he never came back. Tamar, the Canaanite flower, found herself a childless widow among the Israelites.

No one who actually knew the fate of Judah's firstborn son ever talked about it—Judah himself was silent on the subject—but there was

> *And Er, Judah's first-born, was wicked in the sight of the Lord; and the Lord slew him.*
>
> —GENESIS 38:7

a hint of scandal in the strange disappearance. "He was wicked in the sight of the Lord," was all that the old men were willing to say, "and the Lord slew him."

As if that explained everything! the Israelites complained to one another. Exactly what sin did Er commit to bring down God's wrath upon him? Did he sacrifice to the Canaanite gods and go up in flames along with the sacrificial lamb? Or, more likely, was he discovered in a bed where he did not belong, and did he then suffer the wrath of a vengeful father or husband? Tamar, who knew all too well that her husband did not burn very hot in bed, did not think much of either explanation. Perhaps, she thought to herself, he fell under a blow from one of the sullen young men of Canaan who did not share Hirah's affection for the strangers among them.

Judah called Tamar into his presence only once after Er's death. She noted that her father-in-law never actually looked at her, averting his eyes as if out of embarrassment, but the three old men who hovered behind his chair studied her with brazen curiosity and open disdain.

"You will not be forgotten," Judah announced brusquely. "My second-born son will do what he is obliged to do."

"I am sorry, Father," she said, "but I do not understand."

"Quiet, girl!" one of the old men hissed.

"Of course you don't understand, poor benighted heathen that you are," another of the old men began. "The Law decrees—"

Now the third old man interrupted, noisily clearing his throat and speaking in a rumbling drone that sounded like distant thunder to Tamar.

"Onan will come unto you in your tent, and lie with you, and perform the duty of a husband's brother," the graybeard said, using the stilted Hebrew phrases of the Law to describe the fate that awaited the widowed Tamar. "Though you will never marry Onan, the child of your

---

And Judah said unto Onan: "Go in unto thy brother's wife, and perform the duty of a husband's brother unto her, and raise up seed to thy brother."

—GENESIS 38:8

> *And Onan knew that the seed would not be his; and it came to pass, when he went in unto his brother's wife, that he spilled it on the ground, lest he should give seed to his brother.*
>
> —GENESIS 38:9

union with him will be regarded as the true son of your dead husband, and the child will take the name of your dead husband and his inheritance, too."

"And so," said the first old man in a voice that sounded almost cheerful by comparison, "you may remain among us and raise the child."

"Enough," Judah said, allowing himself one oblique glance at her veiled face. "You may go, daughter."

The old men watched as Tamar backed out of the house and then put their heads together behind Judah's back.

"Now let us pray," one of them intoned, "that the second-born is more fruitful than the firstborn."

"For her sake," another one said, "as well as ours."

Onan glowered at Tamar from the shadows of the tent where his father had delivered him. Freshly bathed, anointed with fragrant oil, and draped in bridal robes, she now reclined on a mound of weavings on the floor—the very same bedding on which she had once submitted to the attentions of his older brother.

"Go to her," Judah had instructed his second-born son, "and take your brother's place between her legs." And when Onan grimaced at the suggestion, Judah laughed out loud: "It won't be so bad, I promise you."

Now, as Onan hesitated, he noticed that his brother's robe, familiar and haunting, still hung from one of the ropes of the tent.

"Are you ready?" he croaked.

Tamar nodded at him but did not speak.

"Well," he said, lingering near the opening of the tent, "I am not."

Tamar was lovely enough—Onan had not failed to notice the glittering dark eyes above her veil even when Er was alive—and the thought of bedding his brother's widow was tantalizing precisely because it would have been forbidden under any other circumstances. But Judah had explained the solemn consequences of a moment of pleasure with Tamar, and Onan could not rid himself of the thought that he was about to do himself out of his own good fortune.

The death of his older brother had been a stroke of luck, Onan had thought at first. Er had been so arrogant, so lazy, always lording it over his brothers simply because he had been fortunate enough to be born first. Now Er was dead, and it was Onan who stood to inherit Judah's lands and houses and flocks as the eldest son. *He* would be the next chieftain, and Judah's place would someday be his own.

Unless, that is, Onan performed his duty in Tamar's tent and succeeded in impregnating Tamar with a son. The birthright of his dead brother would pass not to Onan but to the baby whom he sired with his brother's widow, and the bawling little bastard would grow up to regard his own real father as a mere servant!

"Damn!" Onan said out loud.

"Master?" called Tamar. If she feared him, she did not show it.

"What do you want?"

"Come to me now," Tamar said sweetly, "and I will help you. . . ."

Onan stared at her in the half-light of summer twilight, and he noticed that Tamar had removed her veil and her robes. He made out the shape of her breast, the curve of her hip, the slender legs. At last he approached, crouched at her side, and reached out to touch her.

Tamar said nothing. She tried to anticipate what her brother-in-law desired of her, but Onan pushed her delicate hand aside and handled her crudely and brusquely, almost in anger. Onan poked and probed Tamar's body with a kind of brutal curiosity, and then, quite to Tamar's amazement, he reached under his cloak and fingered himself urgently.

Onan saw the look of astonishment on her face.

"If you want me to do my duty," he admonished her, "then leave me be!" A moment later: "Enough! On your back! Let me—"

Tamar shivered ever so slightly as he entered her, a spasm of tension rather than pleasure, and she felt breathless under the deadweight of his body. But she encouraged him with a tender hand at the back of his neck and the same sweet words that she had once whispered into his brother's ears.

Tamar consoled herself with the single thought that she held with perfect clarity even as Onan labored over her: A son would restore Tamar to her rightful standing in the compound of the Israelites. A son of her own would ensure her a place in Judah's house, a seat at his table, an opportunity to survive and even to prosper. A son, she told herself, was life itself.

Onan was nearly breathless with pleasure, but he cautioned himself against yielding to the impulse to spend himself between Tamar's legs.

"Ah!" he began to groan. "Ah, ah—"

"Yes, yes, yes—" coaxed Tamar.

Summoned away from her body by the cawing of his mind, Onan drew back and pulled himself out. Then—in a terrible moment that caught both of them by surprise—he spent himself in three shuddering spasms, and spilled his seed on the floor of the tent in an arc of wasted passion.

"No!" shouted Tamar as she grasped what he had done—but it was too late. She began to weep, and her tears were hot and angry. "You pig—"

Onan, flushed red with shame, could think of nothing else to do but slap her across the face to silence her. But the weak, glancing blow stopped only her tears, not her words.

"You pig," she repeated.

Tamar rose, gathering her robe around her waist to cover her nakedness, and backed away from him. She dressed hastily in a dark corner of the tent as Onan watched. At last he got up, walked to the opening of the tent, then paused at the threshold and stared out into the compound.

"Whore," he spat out, although Tamar was already too far off to hear him.

As if Tamar had wished it upon him, a fever seized Onan the very next day and did not let him go. The compound fell into that strange silence

And the thing which he did was evil in the sight of the Lord; and He slew him also.

—GENESIS 38:10

that always marked the onset of illness. Was it the plague? Who else would fall ill and die? And exactly what offerings and sacrifices were necessary in order to preserve the health of the others? Even the children seemed to disappear into the tents and the houses around the compound, as if to avoid disturbing the ailing young man with the sound of play, and Judah himself was not to be seen for seven days.

At last, the word was passed from Judah's house: Onan, too, was dead.

Now the whispers that spread from tent to tent were more pointed: the hand of the God of Israel, the deity that the Israelites knew as Yahweh, had struck down two of Judah's sons. What evil had Onan done that the vengeful god of the Israelites would take his life? And did Tamar play a role in the death of the two men who went to her bed?

Judah summoned Tamar into his house a second time. The elders of the clan were there, but so was Hirah. Judah spoke quietly: The house of Judah again would do its duty to Tamar. Shelah, his youngest son, would be sent to her tent as soon as he was deemed old enough. Until then, she would return to her own village and wait.

"Take her to her father," Judah instructed Hirah.

"And remind him," one of the old men added, "that she must live in a manner that is worthy of a woman who is both widowed and betrothed."

Judah watched his old friend and his daughter-in-law stoop to cross the threshold of his house, and suddenly he was taken with a peculiar sensation. Their dialect, their manner of dress, their rites of worship, all of their Canaanite ways suddenly struck him as alien and mysterious and terribly dangerous. And Tamar, so fierce and so dark, struck him as a creature more nearly like a spider than a woman. Judah vowed to himself: God forbid that his third son, his last son, should fall into her tainted bed.

"Let her remain a widow in her father's house," he said to the gray-

---

Then said Judah to Tamar his daughter-in-law: "Remain a widow in thy father's house, till Shelah my son be grown up." For he said: "Lest he also die, like his brethren."

—GENESIS 38:11

And Tamar went and dwelt in her father's house.

—GENESIS 38:11

And in the process of time Shua's daughter, the wife of Judah, died; and Judah was comforted, and went up unto his sheep-shearers to Timnah, he and his friend Hirah the Adullamite. And it was told Tamar, saying: "Behold, thy father-in-law goeth up to Timnah to shear his sheep."

—GENESIS 38:12

beards, using the old phrases of the Hebrew tongue, "lest Shelah die like his brothers."

A year passed, and Shelah's beard began to grow—or so Tamar learned from the gossip of the kinfolk who passed through her father's village—but she was not summoned to the compound of the Israelites. Every morning and every night she brushed out her long black hair, as if to prepare herself for her betrothed, and then one day she noticed that a few strands of silver had appeared at her temples. On that day, Tamar vowed to wait no longer for what was owed to her: a son and a place in the house of Judah.

Not long after, one of the men of her village who tended the flocks of the Israelites brought word that Judah's wife had been laid to rest. Bathshua had given him no more children after Shelah, and, more recently, her belly had grown hard and round with some foul growth. She lingered a long while, then died at last, and Judah observed the Israelite ritual of mourning even though Bathshua had been a Canaanite like Tamar.

"And now that he is finished with one of our women," said the shepherd to Tamar's father, "he is rushing off to Timnah with his good friend Hirah to carouse with a few more."

Tamar listened in silence to the coarse talk as she worked with needle and thread over a long blue cloak.

"Perhaps he will find another one," Tamar's father said, "to become his wife."

"Oh, he will find plenty of women at Timnah," the shepherd said with a leer, "but no wife."

At Timnah, as Tamar knew, the shepherds—and not a few of the rich landowners who hired them—gathered with their flocks for the sheepshearing, and when the wool was gathered and the hard work was done, they fell into a celebration that lasted for days on end. The wine merchants and the whores were always there, too, and the men freely availed themselves of their goods and services. Hirah, Tamar thought to herself, knew how to console the grief-stricken Judah in a livelier way than the sour old graybeards would have allowed.

"And when will you go back to the Hebrews?" Tamar's father asked the shepherd.

"Not soon," the man said. "Judah leaves for Timnah in three days and he won't be back until the new moon. Until then, I will stay here and drink with my own people for a change."

Tamar continued to slip the needle deftly through the thick blue fabric on her lap. As she worked, an intricate pattern appeared beneath her fingers in delicate silver thread, as if by magic.

As Judah trudged along the road to Timnah with Hirah at his side, he spotted a figure in the distance, a woman in a blue robe who leaned

And she put off from her the garments of her widowhood, and covered herself with her veil, and wrapped herself, and sat in the entrance of Enaim, which is by the way to Timnah; for she saw that Shelah was grown up, and she was not given unto him to wife. When Judah saw her, he thought her to be a harlot; for she had covered her face.

—GENESIS 38:14–15

against an olive tree at the crossroads. The heat of the afternoon and the tedious rhythm of their footfalls had lulled him into a kind of half sleep. Even Hirah had fallen into silence as the sun rose directly overhead. And so the beguiling woman by the side of the road seemed to appear as if in a dream.

Only when he approached the crossroads did Judah see that the figure was a slender young woman with long black hair, veiled like a married woman but dressed like a common whore. As he drew closer still, Judah caught the scent of the woman, saw the strong muscles of her calf and thigh as she reclined in the shade of the tree, and imagined in his stupor that her dark eyes sparkled with a light of their own.

"Hirah, my good friend, I believe I'll rest my feet for awhile," said Judah to his companion as they approached the fork in the road, "and I will catch up with you later on."

"We must keep going if we are to reach Timnah by nightfall—" Hirah scolded Judah gently. Then he caught the hungry look on Judah's face. He laughed out loud and slapped Judah on the back.

"Be patient, my friend," said Hirah, "and you will soon be able to comfort yourself with seven women at once."

But Judah had already turned aside and was striding toward the veiled woman. Hirah stopped, shrugged, and called out to Judah.

"I will wait for you around the bend," Hirah shouted. "Do not tarry too long."

As Judah approached, the young woman remained frozen and silent, her arms wrapped around her knees and her head slightly inclined toward the ground. If she were not dressed like a common whore, Judah would have thought she was terrified of the strange man who strode up to her so boldly.

"Woman," Judah said gruffly, "let me lie with you."

And he turned unto her by the way, and said: "Come, I pray thee, let me come in unto thee." For he knew not that she was his daughter-in-law. And she said: "What will you give me, that thou mayest come in unto me?"

—GENESIS 38:16

> *And he said: "I will send thee a kid of the goats from the flock."*
> —GENESIS 38:17

The young woman did not answer, and Judah wondered for a moment if he had been mistaken in taking her for a harlot. But now he felt a fluttery ache in the pit of his stomach, a vague but insistent hunger that he could not ignore. Of course she was a whore! The alluring garment that she wore, the scent of strong perfume that rose from her skin, and the pendant that hung between her breasts belonged to no decent woman.

"Let me lie with you," Judah demanded again.

When the young woman finally looked up at Judah's face, she spoke in a clear and certain voice. "What you will give me, then," she asked, "to lie with me?"

Judah was surprised at her bluntness—and surprised, too, to realize that he was haggling with a whore like a coarse field hand. What would the graybeards say? And yet Judah felt almost giddy as he imagined the moment of pleasure that he knew he would not deny himself, no matter what price she asked.

"A kid from my flock," he said.

An extravagant offer, Judah thought to himself, since he knew that the price of a whore was no more than a loaf of bread or its equivalent in copper coins. But he wanted to impress the young woman with his wealth and generosity, even if she was only a common harlot. Judah calculated that the woman would be more ardent if she knew that he was a rich and powerful man. Anyway, it was Hirah who carried his purse on the road to Timnah, and Judah had no coins to give her.

"And where is the little beast?" she demanded. Her voice was bolder now, more commanding, as she sensed how urgently he desired to satisfy himself with her body. "I don't see it."

"Do you take me for a herdsman?" he asked, irritated and impatient. "I leave it to others to tend my flocks. But I will pick out a fat kid when I return to my house, and I will send it to you."

"How do I know that you will not take your pleasure now," she taunted, "and then forget about me?"

> *And she said: "Wilt thou give me a pledge, till thou send it?"*
> *And he said: "What pledge shall I give thee?" And she said:*
> *"Thy signet and thy cord, and thy staff that is in thy hand."*
>
> —GENESIS 38:17–18

"What?" Judah asked, suddenly irritable. "Do you take me for a cheat?"

Tamar studied Judah's face—his hooded brown eyes, his swarthy skin, his bristling black beard, and his fleshy cheeks now flushed red. She could see that he was angry, but so needful that she no longer doubted that she could get what she needed from him.

"Give me a pledge until you send the kid," Tamar said playfully, "and I will give you what you want."

"A pledge?" Judah was frankly baffled. "Are you jesting?"

"Something of value," Tamar explained, moving her shoulders so that her breasts swayed slightly under the fabric of her robe, "that I may keep until you send me what you have promised."

The proposition was ludicrous, even laughable, but Judah did not laugh. "And what can I pledge?" he asked impatiently.

"Give me your seal," Tamar said.

Judah reached up and touched the cylinder of carved quartz that hung around his neck on a cord.

"Your seal," she repeated, "and your staff, too. Give them to me as a pledge for the kid—and then I will spread my legs for you."

If Judah had paused long enough to think about it, he would have realized how risky and foolhardy it would be to hand over his seal to a common whore. The tiny cylinder was the device that Judah used to imprint his name on the clay tablet and papyrus scrolls that Hirah sometimes prepared to confirm the purchase of a new plot of land or the sale of a season's harvest of wool; it was the very symbol of identity and authority. And the long trek to Timnah and back would seem longer still without a walking staff. But Judah was thinking only of the scent that rose from the young woman's body—he was thinking only of the shadowy place between her legs—as he stood over her in the heat and the dust.

> *And he gave them to her, and came in unto her, and she conceived by him.*
>
> —GENESIS 38:18

"Done," Judah said, letting the leather-laced walking staff fall to the ground next to the young woman. Then he pulled the cord over his head and cast it down at her feet. "Let's go, then."

Tamar reached for the cord and held the seal in a closed fist. Then she rose to her feet and led Judah deeper into the olive grove on the hillside overlooking the crossroads. She reclined on the ground beneath one very old tree and drew up the hem of her robe to reveal her ankle, her knee, her thigh—and then she paused and waited.

Judah, biting his lower lip and breathing hard through his nose, lowered himself to the hard-packed soil. He reached out to touch her so tentatively that Tamar wondered for one anxious moment if Judah knew perfectly well that she was no harlot.

"Master!" she cried out when she felt his fingers on her flesh. Her purpose had nothing to do with getting pleasure, but she was suddenly aware of a strange hunger of her own. "Oh, master—"

Judah touched her with a tenderness that took her by surprise. As she yielded to his insistent caresses, Tamar thought to herself: sorry that the sons did not learn what the father clearly knows.

"Are you ready now, master?" she whispered at last.

He lowered himself over her body and began to probe with short, strong, rhythmic motions. Once, twice, three times, on and on. And then, as she responded to him with equal urgency, her veil fell aside and her face was revealed. Would he recognize her now? Tamar wondered. Would he draw back or—as Tamar imagined in a kind of wild reverie—would he persist even though he recognized her? And would he persist with even greater fervor *because* he recognized her?

And when they had spent themselves in each other's arms, after he rolled to the earth next to her and Tamar hastily fixed the veil across her face once again, her thoughts took wing like prayers: *Take hold,* she instructed the seed that was about to plant itself within her womb.

Judah lay beside her for another long moment, cradling her briefly

> *And she arose, and went away, and put off her veil from her, and put on the garments of her widowhood.*
>
> —GENESIS 38:19

> *And Judah sent the kid of the goats by the hand of his friend the Adullamite, to receive the pledge from the woman's hand; but he found her not.*
>
> —GENESIS 38:20

with one strong arm. Then he rose to his feet and looked back down at her.

"My seal and my staff," he mused aloud. "I will be taken for a beggar on the road."

"Then you must send me a kid as you promised," she said, "and be sure it is a healthy and strong one."

Tamar reclined against the trunk of the ancient tree and watched as Judah hurried away, walking upright because he had no staff on which to lean, and she folded her arms on her belly.

Judah returned from Timnah in high spirits. The flock had flourished, the yield of wool was plentiful and of good quality, and Hirah had led him down the alleys and lanes of lantern-lit tents to sample the strongest red wine, the fattest cuts of mutton, and the most willing women. And now Judah could be seen striding with such a quick step through the compound that the graybeards could not keep up with him.

"He mourns no longer," said one of the Canaanites who served Judah at table.

Still, Judah had not forgotten the young woman at the crossroads, and he began to afflict himself with the thought that she might appear at the door of his house to demand what was owed her. What a scandal she would make, not only among the chattering women in the compound but especially among the old graybeards. Knowing that it would cost him little to honor his pledge, he summoned Hirah to his chamber.

"You remember the woman at the crossroads near Enaim?" Judah asked in a low voice.

"The whore to whom you gave your staff and your seal?" Hirah taunted. "Yes, friend, I have not forgotten what a foolish old goat you have become."

"She was not a common whore," Judah protested. "She was a temple prostitute."

Hirah laughed out loud. "What do you know of the temple women, my Hebrew friend? And did you make an offering to Baal before you worshipped between her legs? No, Judah ben Jacob, make no mistake— she was a whore, and that's all. Only now it is the whore who keeps your signet."

"Listen, now, and do what I say," Judah said earnestly. "Take a kid from the flock. Pick one with some meat on the bones. Then take it to the harlot at Enaim, and bring back my seal and my staff."

"Of course," Hirah smirked. "I will send one of my men—"

"No!" Judah said. "I want you to go, old friend."

"Me?" Hirah was astounded. "You expect me to go in search of some whore with a kid on my back?"

"Your men would make light of the whole business," Judah complained, "and soon the women's tent would be buzzing. I need *you* to go. Do you understand?"

Hirah nodded and grinned. The sly twist of his mouth told Judah that he understood all too well.

Then he asked the men of her place, saying: "Where is the harlot, that was at Enaim by the wayside?" And they said: "There hath been no harlot here."

—GENESIS 38:21

*And he returned to Judah, and said: "I have not found her;
and also the men of the place said: There hath been no harlot
here." And Judah said: "Let her take it, lest we be put to
shame; behold, I sent this kid, and thou hast not found her."*

—GENESIS 38:22–23

Toward sunset on the second day after Hirah's departure, Judah heard
the commotion that always attended the arrival of a visitor to the compound. Judah cautioned himself against hurrying from the house to
meet Hirah, and he waited instead by the threshold.

Even from a distance, Judah saw that Hirah carried something
around his neck like a dark shawl. To his disappointment, he saw that it
was the same kid that Hirah had selected from the flock to redeem
Judah's pledge.

"Why do you return with *that*," he demanded, "instead of my seal
and my staff?"

"I asked after the woman at Enaim, but I could not find her."

"Whom did you ask?"

"Who else would know the whereabouts of a temple prostitute?"
Hirah taunted. "The men of Enaim, of course—I asked where I might
find the temple prostitute who sits by the fork in the road, and they said:
'There is no temple prostitute here.' "

Judah's throat closed. Of course, he knew perfectly well that the
woman who held his seal and his staff as a pledge was a common whore,
not a temple prostitute, and he worried that Hirah had asked after the
wrong woman.

"But what if the woman," Judah ventured, "was not actually a
temple prostitute—"

Hirah laughed out loud. "So you admit it, then?"

"Curse you, Hirah," Judah muttered, "to jest with me about something like this."

"Do not worry, friend," Hirah said. "The woman—whether she is a
temple prostitute or a common whore—is long gone, and your seal and
your staff are gone with her. Forget about them."

"It was," Judah said, "a matter of honor."

"You have honored your word, haven't you?"

Judah allowed himself to be consoled. "You're right," he said. "I sent the kid, and what more can I do? Let her keep the pledge, then, and no one can say that I do not keep my word."

"And now you must give me something to drink," Hirah complained, "or I will have a few stories of my own to tell."

Judah led his friend into the house and waved over one of the servants. Good riddance to the whore, he thought to himself. Tomorrow he would ask Hirah to arrange for the artisans in the village to fashion him a new seal and a new staff. And what if it cost him more than the price of the kid to replace the missing pledge? The fact was that the harlot was gone, and along with her the prospect of scandal in the house of Judah.

Now and then, Judah thought of the harlot by the side of the road, but mostly he attended to the flocks and the crops, the petitions of his beseeching cousins, the repair of his houses and walls. Only Hirah knew what had happened at the crossroads, Judah kept telling himself, and his secret was safe with his old friend. And, since no one dared speak of the incident in Judah's presence, he did not suspect that the compound and the women's tent had fairly hummed with speculation for at least a week after Hirah had returned with a kid over his shoulder.

Eventually, the whispered stories of what had prompted Judah to send Hirah to Enaim in the first place were replaced by a new and much more urgent scandal. One of the old women had trekked to the village of Tamar's father for a wedding, and she returned to Judah's compound with the most remarkable news. Tamar was carrying a child.

"Young Shelah must have slipped into her bed," she cackled as the rest tittered, "and done his duty after all."

Of course, it could not have been Shelah. No one had ever told him

And it came to pass about three months after, that it was told Judah, saying: "Tamar thy daughter-in-law hath played the harlot; and moreover, behold, she is with child by harlotry."

—GENESIS 38:24

of Judah's vow—and, truth be told, Judah was still fearful of the warning that could be heard in the crude jokes that his cronies uttered to each other when Tamar's name was mentioned.

"She has killed off two of Judah's sons," they would say to each other. "Why risk the last one?"

Word of Tamar's predicament finally reached Judah in the form of a whispered denunciation by the mother of a young woman who fancied Shelah for her own son-in-law.

"Tamar has played the harlot in her own father's house," she whispered to one of the graybeards, "and now she carries someone's bastard in her belly."

"And what am I to do about it?" Judah complained when the story was repeated to him.

"Burn her," said one of the old men. "That's what the Law decrees for adulteresses."

"You want me to put Tamar to the fire?" Judah asked. "Are you serious?"

"The Law decrees it—" the old man began.

"Let the woman be," Judah said, almost pleading. Judah found himself repulsed at the prospect of putting her lovely young flesh to the flames. And, as Judah now realized, no one would expect him to send Shelah to her bed any longer. "Let her stay in her father's house," he concluded, "and raise the bastard."

"Bring her out, so that she may be burned," one old man threatened, "or else you will be laughed at."

Judah understood that a threat to his authority could not be safely ignored. What's more, he did not relish the thought of the gossip that would persist for as long as Tamar and her bastard lived in the nearby village.

"All right, then," Judah relented. "Summon her to my house."

So it happened that Tamar was brought from her father's house and escorted to Judah's compound by the elders and a half-dozen young men

---

And Judah said: "Bring her forth, and let her be burnt."
—GENESIS 38:24

whom they had pressed into service. Everyone along the way could see that the story was plainly true: Tamar's belly was big, and she carried low—a son, to be sure, but *whose* son?

Tamar was accompanied by her mother, who walked at her side, keening and moaning without pause, and one or two of her menfolk, who had been permitted to come along on the condition that they left their staffs and swords behind. Her father—or so it was whispered among the Israelites—had refused to enter the compound of the Israelites and submit to the indignity of a trial before Judah.

The old woman hung her head as they walked through the compound, but the shrill noise she made carried all the way to Judah's door. The men from Tamar's village cast cautious glances to the left and right as they passed the gauntlet of Israelites who had gathered to see the scandalous sight of Tamar, pregnant and doomed. But Tamar, wearing the black robes of mourning, held her head upright and stared straight ahead. A chill winter wind swept the robe around her ankles, but she did not shiver or comfort herself with folded arms.

At last, the procession entered the courtyard before Judah's house, and Tamar was left under guard outside the door while the elders pushed into the room where Judah awaited them on a chair with arm-rests and a high back. One old woman, then a few younger men, and finally a small crowd of onlookers pushed into the room after them, and the graybeards did nothing to discourage them. An audience, they felt, would force Judah's hand if he showed signs of timidity.

"The harlot stands outside," one of the old men said, "and the evidence of her adultery is plain to see."

"What will you do?" another one demanded, and Judah heard a few murmurs and titters from the crowd that surged around him.

"What does Tamar say?" Judah asked.

The elder snorted. "She says nothing," he said, "because there is nothing to say. So burn her!"

Though it was chilly inside the house, Judah suddenly felt slightly feverish. A fine sweat appeared on his brow, and his skin prickled beneath his woolen robe. With a quick swipe of his right hand, he brushed the sweat from his forehead, then wiped his hand on his sleeve.

"Say the words," one of the old men encouraged in a low whisper. "The Law decrees it—"

At that moment, there was a commotion at the back of the room, and the crowd parted slightly to reveal the figure of Tamar's mother and one of the menfolk from her village. The mother, casting her eyes down and wearing a look of misery and confusion, stumbled forward. Behind her, a young man held a bundle in his outstretched arms, but Judah could not see what was wrapped in the bulky gray blankets.

"Go away, woman," one of the elders hissed. "You have no business here."

Judah raised one hand to silence the old man, and he did the same to the crowd with a single black look. The Canaanite woman took three more steps in utter silence and then fell to her knees, pressing her forehead to the floor. The young man carefully lowered the bundle to the floor in front of Judah's chair, and he, too, fell to his knees.

"I beg you to listen, master!" the old woman cried out in a desperate screech.

"Yes?" Judah encouraged her. "What do you want to say?"

"My daughter sends me with a message."

"Go on."

The old woman raised her head slightly but stayed on her knees.

"Tamar bids me say these words to you: 'The father of my child is the man to whom these things belong.'"

And then Judah rose from his chair and knelt in front of the old woman. He reached out and drew open the folds of the woolen blanket to reveal a cylinder of carved quartz on a length of worn rawhide and a leather-wrapped walking staff.

For one crazy moment, Judah wondered exactly how the old woman had gotten her hands on the pledge that he had given to the harlot by the side of the road. And then, a moment later, he understood.

"Whose seal is it?" demanded one of the graybeards. "Whose seal? Whose staff?"

When she was brought forth, she sent to her father-in-law, saying: "By the man, whose these are, am I with child." And she said: "Discern, I pray thee, whose are these, the signet, and the cords, and the staff."

—GENESIS 38:25

> *Judah acknowledged them, and said: "She is more righteous than I; forasmuch as I gave her not to Shelah my son."*
>
> —GENESIS 38:26

"Tell us," called a harsh woman's voice from the crowd, "and he'll burn, too!"

The old woman did not speak, and it was Judah's voice that was heard in the cold room.

"No one will burn today," he said, amazing himself no less than the others. "Tamar is right, and I am wrong—I should have sent Shelah to her bed."

The room fell silent, and even the querulous old men waited to hear Judah's words.

"The seal and the staff are mine," Judah said, "and so is the child."

CHAPTER SEVEN

THE WOMAN WHO WILLED HERSELF INTO HISTORY

Tamar as the Harlot by the Side of the Road

"SAVE ALIVE NOTHING THAT BREATHETH"
THE SACRED WHORE
"A BAG OF MYRRH BETWEEN MY BREASTS"
"GIVE ME CHILDREN OR ELSE I DIE"
THE STRANGE TRADITION OF THE LEVIRATE "MARRIAGE"
THE RED THREAD

The narrator of Genesis 38—or, more likely, some pious editor who came along later and tried to cool down and clean up the story[1]— hastens to reassure us that Judah did not sleep with his daughter-in-law a second time: "And he knew her again no more" (Gen. 38:26). But Tamar does not disappear from the biblical narrative. Rather, she gives birth to twin boys, Perez and Zerah, and the Bible carefully notes that Perez is the progenitor of a long line of celebrated figures, including David, Solomon, and, according to the New Testament, Jesus of Nazareth. So Tamar, the willful young woman who plays the harlot in order to seduce her own father-in-law, is the great-great-grandmother of kings, prophets, and the Christian Messiah.

Still, the figure of Tamar—a Canaanite, a seducer and sexual trickster, a young woman who refuses to submit to the authority of the stern patriarchy under which she lives—has been nearly written out of the biblical tradition over the centuries precisely because her sexual adventure on the road to Enaim is so audacious, provocative, and titillating. When forced to confront her story in the Holy Scriptures, clergy and scholars have struggled to explain away the sexual encounter between Tamar and her father-in-law, a coupling that is specifically prohibited elsewhere in the Bible (Lev. 18:15) and one so close to incest that it is still capable of shocking us.

A favored explanation in the rabbinical tradition is that the tale of Tamar and Judah, which pops up in Genesis in the middle of the story of Joseph in Egypt, is intended to be contrasted with the episode that immediately follows it: the failed seduction of Joseph by the wife of Potiphar, the Egyptian overlord to whom Joseph has been sold as a slave. As Judah is succumbing to Tamar's charms at a roadside in Canaan, the righteous young Joseph is turning away the hot overtures ("Lie with me!") of Potiphar's wife in an Egyptian palace with chilly indignation: "How then can I do this great wickedness, and sin against God?" (Gen. 39:7-9).

Joseph, the rabbis encourage us to believe, illustrates how a goodly man is supposed to react to the sexual allure of a forbidden woman; he just says "No!" even if it means an open-ended stay in Pharaoh's dungeon. Judah, by contrast, is supposed to be a sorry example of weak flesh and a failed spirit. And yet this facile explanation falls under its own weight: Joseph leads his people into the place where they will be enslaved and nearly destroyed, but the coupling of the virile Judah and the fecund Tamar will bring forth the greatest kings of ancient Israel and ultimately the Messiah.

Tamar is a woman who demonstrates how an Israelite and a Canaanite can transcend the bitter and often bloody antagonism between these rival claimants to what we still like to call the Holy Land. She allows us to glimpse the deadly peril that confronted women of the biblical era who did not submit to the mastery of a male, whether father or husband. Above all, Tamar is a woman whose will is so strong, whose passion burns so bright, that she writes herself into history through an act of illicit physical love.

"SAVE ALIVE NOTHING THAT BREATHETH"

That Tamar is a Canaanite may have been even more embarrassing to the rabbinical authorities than the fact that Judah sleeps with her and fathers a pair of sons by her. One of the great themes of the Hebrew Bible, as we have already seen, is the outright condemnation of marriage outside the Twelve Tribes of Israel, and the Canaanites are the most strictly forbidden of all prospective lovers and spouses: "[N]either shalt thou make marriages with them: thy daughter thou shalt not give unto his son, nor his daughter shalt thou take unto thy son" (Deut. 7:3).*

The fear and hatred with which the Canaanites are regarded throughout the Bible lead us to another of its awkward and mostly overlooked features. We are told in the Book of Genesis that Canaan is promised by God to Abraham and his descendants, but we discover in the Book of Exodus that Canaan is not an empty paradise "flowing with milk and honey." When the Israelites, after fleeing Egypt and spending forty hard years in the wilderness under the troubled leadership of Moses (see chapter nine), finally cross the Jordan River into "the Promised Land," the place is teeming with tribes and clans that had lived there long before the Exodus: "The Hittite, the Amorite, and the Canaanite, the Perizzite, the Hivite, and the Jebusite," among others (Josh. 12:7).

God's solution is to declare a war of conquest—we might easily use the terms "ethnic cleansing" and even "genocide"—against the native dwellers of the Promised Land. The slaughter of Midianites that we encountered in the Book of Numbers is only an augury of the bloodthirsty campaign in Canaan itself. According to the rules of war set forth in Deuteronomy, the invading Israelites are obliged to "proclaim peace" to a besieged city, and if the city-dwellers respond with "an answer of peace" then their lives are to be spared and they are to be permitted to live as "tributaries" to the Israelites. But these rules of engagement apply only to the "far off" cities. An entirely different strategy is decreed for the cities within the Promised Land itself, the cities of the Canaanites and the other peoples who dwelled in Canaan before the Exodus.

---

*The events described in Genesis 38 supposedly take place *before* the enslavement of the Israelites under Pharaoh, the Exodus from Egypt, and the conquest of Canaan, at a time when Jacob and his sons are only sojourners in Canaan. According to the chronology of the Bible itself, the Book of Deuteronomy and its laws against intermarriage are unknown to Judah because they would not be handed down until centuries later. But, as we have already seen, Genesis was probably edited by redactors working sometime after 400 B.C.E., and the biblical author who retold the story of Judah and Tamar was intimately familiar with the laws of Deuteronomy. Biblical scholarship suggests that Genesis 38 describes the landscape of Canaan and the circumstances of the Israelites at a much later date than the text itself indicates, long after the Exodus from Egypt and the conquest of Canaan, when the troubled coexistence of Israelites and Canaanites in the Promised Land was not only a fact of history but an unavoidable reality of daily life.

[O]f the cities of these peoples, that the Lord thy God giveth thee for an inheritance, thou shalt save alive nothing that breatheth, but thou shalt utterly destroy them (Deut 20:10–18).

God takes credit for the early victories of the Israelites over their enemies on the field of battle: "I gave them into your hand, and ye possessed their land; and I destroyed them from before you" (Josh. 24:8). But the Promised Land is *not* cleansed of its native population, and the Bible explains that God eventually withdraws his favor from the Israelites because they are so tempted to "forsake the Lord, and serve strange gods" (Josh. 24:20). So Canaan turns out to be a place where men and women of different tribes and different faiths live side by side—not unlike our own country or, for that matter, the Holy Land in our own times—and the Israelites are forced to make some kind of peace with the tribes whom they did not defeat in war. The Promised Land is divided up among the tribes of Israel, we are told in the Bible, but the various native-dwelling tribes (including the Canaanites) remain on the land, living and working among the conquering Israelites as a kind of disempowered working class or even as slaves.

[T]he Canaanites were resolved to dwell in that land. And it came to pass, when the children of Israel were waxen strong, that they put the Canaanites to taskwork, but did not utterly drive them out (Josh. 17:12–13).

Why is the Bible so bloodthirsty toward the Canaanites and the others who dwelled in the Promised Land? The obvious geopolitical fact is that the Israelites hope to remove these peoples from their homeland—or at least to rule over them—out of an entirely amoral impulse toward the conquest of Canaan and the establishment of national sovereignty for the Israelites. Even the Almighty recognizes a certain injustice in the displacement and exploitation of the Canaanites:

And I gave you a land where thou hadst not laboured, and cities which ye built not, and ye dwell therein; of vineyards and oliveyards which ye planted not do ye eat (Josh. 24:13).

But as we have already discerned beneath the surface of the story of Dinah and Shechem, other, even darker reasons explain the fear and loathing of the Canaanites that we find throughout the Bible. The Canaanites must be destroyed, the Bible says, so that they will not teach the Israelites "all their abominations, which they have done unto their gods, and so yet sin against the Lord your God" (Deut. 20:18). Such "abominations" included not only the making of idols (and the bacchanalian abandon with which the idols were worshipped) but also the tantalizing (and thus sternly forbidden) rite of sexual intercourse with sacred prostitutes as an act of goddess worship. Ironically, when God announces that he will no longer assist the Israelites on the field of battle because of their infidelities, the Almighty is fully aware that the temptations facing his Chosen People will be all the more alluring. "I will not drive them out before you," God says of the Canaanites, "but they shall be unto you as snares, and their gods shall be a trap unto you" (Judg. 2:3).

The Canaanites, then, turn out to be both the strategic and the religious rivals of the Israelites. That is why we find stories throughout the Bible that are meant to ridicule the Canaanites and to depict them as unworthy of lordship over their own land. An often-ignored incident in the story of Noah (Gen. 9:22–24), for example, shows one of Noah's sons, Ham, as a coarse and irreverent brute who dares to peek at his father's naked body when the old man is lolling around in a drunken stupor and then boasts about it to his brothers, who are too respectful of their father to look at his nakedness. Ham, we are pointedly told by the biblical storyteller, is "father of Canaan."*

When it turns out that the Canaanites and the other peoples of the Promised Land cannot be exterminated, the Israelites are sternly warned against intermarriage with strangers in general and the Canaanites above all, and they are threatened with divine punishment if they consort with non-Israelites:

[T]hou shalt make no covenant with them, nor show mercy unto them; neither shalt thou make marriages with them: thy

---

*At least one contemporary Bible critic has proposed that Ham's encounter with his father is an incident of incestuous homosexuality and not merely filial disrespect.

daughter thou shalt not give unto his son, nor his daughter shalt thou take unto thy son. For he will turn away thy son from following Me, that they may serve other gods; so will the anger of the Lord be kindled against you, and He will destroy thee quickly (Deut. 7:2–4).

Now there's a certain stinging irony to the decree against intermarriage that figures so prominently in the Bible. A long list of Israelites did, in fact, marry outside the Twelve Tribes, and some of the most inspiring stories of the Bible feature successful intermarriages. Jacob's celebrated favorite son, Joseph, marries the daughter of an Egyptian high priest (Gen. 46:20). Moses marries a Midianite woman, Zipporah, who plays a crucial role in the history of the Israelites by taking on God himself to spare her husband's life (Exod. 4:24–26). Ruth, a Moabite woman who seduces and then weds an Israelite man, is (like Tamar) a direct ancestress of King David and, therefore, of the Messiah. David himself falls in love with Bathsheba, who was married to a Hittite and may well have been a non-Israelite (2 Sam. 11:3).[2] Their son, Solomon, manages to collect some seven hundred wives of his own, including a fair number of idol-worshiping foreigners. "[K]ing Solomon loved many strange women," the Bible is forced to concede, "[and] his wives turned away his heart after other gods" (1 Kings 11:1, 4 KJV). So the Bible is deeply conflicted on the subject of marriage with non-Israelites, flatly condemning intermarriage in theory but not always in practice.

As we saw in chapter five, the bitter and often bloodthirsty hatred of the stranger that we find in certain passages of the Bible can be traced to the priests and scribes who compiled and edited much of the Bible sometime after the series of foreign invasions dispersed and nearly destroyed the Israelites. As these editors, or redactors, labored over texts that described the events of the long-distant past, they saw around them an endangered remnant of the Israelite people, the pitiable survivors of a once-glorious monarchy who now lived at the mercy of foreign conquerors and rival claimants to the land of Canaan itself. To these pious men, intermarriage with non-Israelites was a threat as profound as conquest or exile, and it is likely that they insinuated their xenophobia into the ancient texts.

Still, the redactors of the Bible were forced to deal with facts of recent history—and a rich body of legend and lore—that plainly depicted intermarriage by some of the greatest prophets and kings of Israel. So the Bible is forced to accommodate two very different traditions, one that tolerates and even celebrates marriage with non-Israelites, and one that bitterly condemns and forbids it. Thus, on one hand, the fact that Moses married Zipporah, a Midianite woman, was apparently deemed too fundamental to ignore and too crucial in the history of Israel to condemn; Zipporah is depicted in the Book of Exodus as a heroic woman who literally saves the life of Moses when God himself seeks to kill him. On the other hand, readers are reminded that God disapproves of such couplings when it comes to ordinary Israelites. As we have already seen, the redactors included the gruesome and slightly leering account of the Israelite prince who is impaled along with his Midianite lover as a punishment for the crime of making love (Num. 25:1–9, 17).

So, too, does the story of Tamar and Judah present a puzzling and contradictory moral example, at least according to the unambiguous legal boilerplate of the Bible itself. Even if Tamar *had* been an Israelite, her elaborate conspiracy to seduce her father-in-law by playing the harlot would be a shocking violation of the biblical commandment that is intended to keep men from sleeping with their daughters-in-law. But the fact that she is a Canaanite makes her not only an incestuous seducer but a stranger, and the Bible is sometimes even harsher on strangers than it is on those who merely indulge in forbidden sexual practices.*

---

*One contemporary scholar has argued that we ought to regard Tamar as an Israelite, pointing out that Genesis 38 does not plainly state that Tamar is a Canaanite. According to the revisionist interpretation, the real lesson of Tamar is that Judah's three "half-breed" sons—the offspring of his marriage to a woman who *is* plainly identified as a Canaanite—are doomed by the Almighty and unable to father any children. Only when Tamar is mated with Judah himself, a full-blooded Israelite, are healthy male offspring born. The "purity of Israelite blood" is the whole point of Genesis 38, according to the revisionist reading, and the Talmud includes a story that starts with the same premise and reaches a similar conclusion: Judah's wife, a Canaanite woman, plots to keep her sons from impregnating Tamar precisely because "she was not a Canaanitish woman." But the scholarly consensus, and the sense of the text itself, suggests that Tamar is a beguiling outsider and not an Israelite.

The Sacred Whore

The biblical authors were fairly obsessed with the alluring but forbidden figure of the harlot, and the Bible is studded with references to literal and metaphorical prostitution. The prophet Hosea, for example, reports that he was called upon by God to go out and marry a whore, which he apparently did with alacrity and perhaps even some enthusiasm, although he insists that the point of his illicit union was to rebuke his fellow Israelites for their spiritual faithlessness in worshipping strange gods.

> Go, take unto thee a wife of harlotry and children of harlotry;
> for the land doth commit great harlotry (Hos. 1:2).

The Bible allows us to understand that prostitution was common enough in ancient Israel, if only because harlotry among the women of Israel is condemned in such strong terms: "Profane not thy daughter, to make her a harlot, lest the land fall into harlotry, and the land become full of lewdness" (Lev. 19:29). Priests are specifically prohibited from marrying a prostitute, and death by burning—the punishment prescribed for Tamar—is decreed for any daughter of a priest who turns to prostitution (Lev. 21:7, 9, 14).

The story of Tamar confirms that there were at least two kinds of prostitutes whom an Israelite man might have encountered in ancient Canaan: a common whore (*zonah*, according to the original Hebrew) and a temple or "cultic" prostitute (*qedeshah*),[3] whose sexual practices were sanctified among the Canaanites as a form of worship of the goddesses of fertility. Tamar is described by the biblical narrator as a common prostitute (*zonah*) when we are first told how she disguises herself as a harlot to seduce her father-in-law. But when Judah sends his Canaanite crony, Hirah, in search of the woman who is holding his seal and staff, Hirah refers to the woman by the Hebrew word for a sacred temple prostitute (*qedeshah*) rather than a common whore.

The Hebrew term *qedeshah*, translated as "sacred" or "cult" or "temple" prostitute, actually means "a consecrated woman" and was understood to refer to a woman who literally made herself available to all comers at a place of pagan worship—perhaps a temple of Ishtar, the Babylonian goddess of love, or Astarte, the Canaanite goddess of fertility; "divine intercourse" was understood to be a form of prayer that would be rewarded with "abundant harvests and an increase of cattle."[4] Such titillating notions were encouraged by the chronicles of the Greek historian Herodotus, who reports that even the wealthy matrons of Babylon were legally obliged to serve as sacred prostitutes at least once: "Such of the women as are tall and beautiful are soon released," he writes with a leer, "but the ugly ones have to stay a long time before they can fulfill the law."[5]

More recent and discerning historians who have studied ancient texts and other archaeological evidence from sites throughout the Near East suggest that a *qedeshah* was actually a midwife, a wet-nurse, a singer, and perhaps a sorceress rather than a prostitute. "Tragically," observes Bible critic Mayer I. Gruber, "scholarship suffered from scholars being unable to imagine any cultic role for women in antiquity that did not involve sexual intercourse."[6] According to the revisionists in Bible studies, "divine intercourse"—if it actually took place at all— was less likely to have been the "whole-scale debauchery" depicted by the biblical prophets than an occasional act of ritual sexual union between a priest and a priestess on a seasonal holy day or perhaps in time of plague, drought, or famine.[7] Thus, as used by the biblical author in Genesis 38, *qedeshah* may not be intended as a technical term for a cult prostitute but rather as a "poetic synonym" for a "common or garden harlot."[8]

To the modern reader, the reference to Tamar as a sacred prostitute rather than a common whore may suggest that the biblical author was trying to dignify and elevate Judah's dealings with the woman. We might imagine that a visit to a temple prostitute was perceived as something loftier than buying the sexual services of a whore, especially in the eyes of his Canaanite friend. We are tempted to conclude that the biblical storyteller was trying to put the best face on Judah's dalliance with the harlot by the side of the road.

Of course, there is nothing sacred about the roadside transaction between Judah and Tamar: it is a bargain of the oldest and most secular kind, sex for money, and the repartee between Tamar and Judah shows us a whore haggling with a trick over the terms of payment. Indeed, the pledge that Judah gives to Tamar—his staff and his seal*—is simply a form of collateral to secure his promise to pay her for the services that she has rendered, "a kind of Near Eastern equivalent . . . of a person's major credit cards," in the words of contemporary Bible scholar Robert Alter.[9]

But if the reference to Tamar as a sacred harlot strikes us as an effort to pretty up Judah's encounter with her, the very opposite would have been true for the Bible reader of two thousand years ago. Any trafficking by an Israelite with a sacred harlot was not merely a sexual indiscretion but an act of apostasy—an outrage against divine law and a capital offense among the Israelites. When Hirah uses the word for a temple prostitute to refer to Tamar, he is suggesting that Judah had done exactly what the Bible condemns as the worst offense imaginable, worshipping a pagan goddess by engaging in sexual intercourse with that deity's sacred harlot.

Indeed, one scholar suggests that the casual use of the term for a sacred prostitute in Genesis 38 is the best evidence that the story itself originated with the Canaanites rather than the Israelites.[10] And, as we shall see (see chapter eleven), some Bible readers go so far as to suggest that Tamar was actually the priestess of a Canaanite fertility cult who was seeking to lure Judah's sons away from the God of their fathers. But the very fact that the story of Tamar and Judah earned its way into Holy Scripture, and survived the efforts of later religious authorities to rewrite the history of Israel, tells us something important and surprising about the degree of tolerance toward sexual adventure that prevailed among at least some of the biblical authors and editors.

---

*Judah's seal, described in the text of Genesis 38 as "thy signet and thy cord," is something that a man in biblical times might wear around his neck on a rope cord or a chain. The seal itself was a small cylinder of fired clay or carved stone in which were inscribed the letters of the man's name or other symbols to indicate his identity. At a time when legal documents consisted of clay tablets, the cylindrical seal was rolled over the wet clay in order to imprint the bearer's name or symbol on the document; later, when papyrus scrolls were in common use, the seal was pressed into a ball of wet clay (a *bulla*) that was attached to a string wrapped around the scroll.

"A BAG OF MYRRH BETWEEN MY BREASTS"

The story of Tamar suggests that there was nothing unusual about encountering and even patronizing a prostitute in the Holy Land in the days of the patriarchs. Other passages of the Bible confirm that prostitution was so commonplace that the price of a harlot's services might be as little as a loaf of bread (Prov. 6:26), and that one might encounter a prostitute along the road (Prov. 7:11–12) or even at holy sites where pilgrims congregated (Hos. 4:14). Indeed, it's possible that Judah recognizes Tamar as a prostitute simply because he sees her sitting at a crossroads, a place where harlots may have typically plied their trade in biblical times.

> Thou hast built thy lofty place at every head of the way, and
> hast made thy beauty an abomination, and hast opened thy feet
> to every one that passed by, and multiplied thy harlotries
> (Ezek. 16:25).

And yet the story of Tamar provokes a tantalizing question. Exactly how does Judah know that Tamar is a harlot in search of business? And we might wonder: Is he really fooled by Tamar's disguise?

We are told only that Tamar wears a veil, an essential plot device that conceals her identity from her father-in-law. But, according to current scholarship on the folkways of the ancient Near East, only married women—*not* prostitutes—were veiled in public.[11] If we believe that Judah is tricked into thinking that Tamar is a harlot, we know that she had to adopt some other adornment or costume to signify that she is a prostitute and thereby to arouse Judah's sexual appetite.

A pendant or some other decoration on her face and around her neck might have been the way a prostitute of biblical times announced her availability as a paid sexual partner. For example, the prophet Hosea calls on his adulterous wife to "put away her harlotries from her face, and her adulteries from between her breasts, lest I strip her naked" (Hos. 2:4), which suggests to some commentators that a harlot was identifiable by "the badges of her profession, something on her face, something between her breasts." So we might imagine that Tamar wears makeup or perhaps a nose-ring, and hangs some object around her neck that Judah would identify as the markings of a harlot.[12]

The Song of Songs, a book of erotic love poetry that somehow found its way into Holy Writ, suggests what woman might wear around her neck as a symbol of sexual availability: "My beloved is unto me as a bag of myrrh, / That lieth betwixt my breasts" (Song of Songs 1:13). And the Talmud confirms that "wanton women" would put a mixture of balsam and myrrh in their shoes "so that its scent would arouse passion in young men."[13]

All we really know with certainty, of course, is that Judah decides that the woman whom he sees on the road to Timnah is sexually desirable—and sexually available. He is a widower who has just completed the long period of mourning for his dead wife, and he is needful of sexual companionship; indeed, the spare text of Genesis 38 is fairly aglow with sexual tension at the moment of their encounter. We might surmise that a harlot's disguise is only a thin excuse, perhaps devised by Tamar and perhaps by the biblical storyteller, to justify the blunt sexual proposition that Judah makes to Tamar.

"Will you have sex with me?" is how Judah's proposition can be understood in plain English, although most translations use more decorous and euphemistic language: "Let me lie with you" (NEB) or "Let me come in unto thee" (JPS).

We might even imagine that Judah actually recognizes Tamar behind the veil, that he had longed for her even when she was wed to his son, that he seizes the opportunity to act on his longings. Perhaps the harlot's disguise is merely a game that each of them plays by prior arrangement or by tacit consent, whether to provide "plausible deniability" for their love affair or to titillate each other. If so, the story of Judah and Tamar can be read not as a cautionary tale but as an erotic love story that somehow slipped into the pages of the Holy Bible.

"GIVE ME CHILDREN OR ELSE I DIE"

The theme of woman as a seducer is as ancient as Eve, and Judah's words to Tamar evoke the image of a black widow who mates and then kills, a metaphor that sums up the fear that some men feel toward a powerful woman:

> "Remain a widow in thy father's house, till Shelah my son be grown up"; for he said: "Lest he also die, like his brethren" (Gen. 38:11).

The story of Tamar may trouble contemporary readers who are uncomfortable with a heroine whose weapon of choice is her own sexuality, whether because they are put off by the lurid roadside coupling or because they are offended by the depiction of Tamar as a seducer who tricks a powerful man into giving her children. To some, the tale is scandalous because it is so sexually explicit; to others, it is "sexist." Yet if we understand what is actually at stake for Tamar when she entices Judah to make love to her, the story takes on both heightened drama and urgent meaning: Tamar *must* conceive a male child, and she will go to the extreme of seduction in the guise of a whore in order to do it. Why is Tamar so desperate? And why are Judah and the rest of his clan so tolerant of her act of incest and seduction?

The answer lies in the plight of women in biblical times. A woman was defined by her ability to produce children, and a childless woman was seen as someone cursed by God. Over and over again in the Bible, we encounter women for whom childlessness was a matter of life and death. The matriarchs of the Israelites—Sarah, Rebekah, and Rachel—are only the most prominent examples. "Give me children," cries Rachel to Jacob, "or else I die" (Gen. 30:1).

The urgency is explained by the fact that a woman's identity, her social status, and even her livelihood were utterly dependent on the men to whom she was related: first her father, then her husband, and later her sons. A woman was forced to rely on her children for support if her husband died because a widow generally did not inherit property from her deceased husband in the ancient Near East; under biblical law, a man's estate passed directly to his children (Deut. 21:16–17) or his other blood relations (Num. 27:8–11). A childless widow like Tamar, then, had no acceptable and comfortable place in the community where she lived; she could not safely engage in sexual conduct, bear or rear children, or earn a living outside these narrow confines.[14]

In fact, if a woman like Tamar dared to engage in a sexual relationship at all, she was regarded as so threatening to the social and moral order of biblical society that she simply had to be obliterated. An unmarried woman who slept with a man faced a death sentence under the stern law of the Bible (Deut. 22:21), and so did the wife who strayed outside the marriage bed (Lev. 20:10). It's significant that the stoning of an unmarried woman who engaged in forbidden sexual activity was supposed to take place "by her father's house," as if to make the point that a woman without an approved male protector—whether father, husband, or adult son—was simply too dangerous to be allowed to live at all.

For Tamar, a Canaanite woman who has married into her husband's tribe, the crisis of childlessness is even more dire. An outsider *must* bear children in order to earn a place in her husband's family, and if she is widowed before she has produced a child, then she is likely to remain a stranger in the eyes of her husband's clan.[15] For that reason, Tamar finds herself in terrible peril. She could not inherit her husband's property, she could not rely on the inheritance of her children, and she could not comfortably return to the house of her father, except perhaps as a lonely spinster to be shut away and ignored. The childless and widowed Tamar is a "misfit" who simply does not belong anywhere.[16]

So Tamar's sexual ambush of Judah on the road to Timnah was the act of a courageous and resourceful woman who refused to accept passively the fate that the patriarchy of ancient Israel decreed for a childless widow. She was not merely a seducer who tricked her father-in-law into giving her children by playing the harlot. Rather, she was a woman who stood up for her legal rights in the only manner available to a woman of her time and place.

THE STRANGE TRADITION OF THE LEVIRATE "MARRIAGE"

To understand the story of Tamar, we must look back to a curious tradition of the biblical era called *yibbum*[17] in Hebrew but more commonly known in English as the "levirate marriage." As we shall see, the phrase itself is yet another fussy euphemism. A levirate marriage is not really a marriage at all; rather, it is a form of approved sexual intercourse outside of marriage, a process that we might liken to "stud service" rendered by a brother-in-law to his widowed sister-in-law.

Levir is the Latin word for "brother-in-law," and the so-called levi-rate marriage was a custom that obliged a man to impregnate his dead brother's widow if the brother died without a male heir. The child born of a levirate "marriage" was not considered to be the offspring of his bio-logical father. Rather, the child was named after the dead brother, and—crucially—inherited the property of the dead brother.[18] Thus, the levirate tradition assures that Tamar, if successfully impregnated, will earn a position within the household of her dead husband's family.[19]

Although the Bible also speaks of the custom of *marriage* between a widow and her brother-in-law,[20] the essential responsibility of the brother-in-law is to implant his seed in her womb. And, in fact, Genesis 38 does not tell us that Tamar married Onan, or Shelah, or Judah, or anyone else. All we know is that Judah "knew her again no more," but he recognized her children as his rightful heirs (Gen. 38:26).

The story of Tamar depicts a young widow who is so insistent on her rights under the levirate tradition that she turns to her father-in-law to impregnate her when her brothers-in-law are not up to the task. But even her choice of mates is not quite so shocking when we consider it in the context of the biblical era; the levirate duty might be fulfilled by men in the family other than the brother-in-law.[21] The Book of Ruth, for example, depicts the elaborate plan of the widowed young woman to place herself under the protection of an even more distant relative of her dead husband than either brother-in-law or father-in-law. But there is always a distinction between impregnation, which is the woman's right according to the levirate tradition, and marriage, which has little or nothing to do with it.

"Marriage may come," writes one scholar. "It is perhaps to be desired, at least by the widow. But within the scope of the levirate custom, at least for this story, Tamar can expect only conception of a child."[22]

Tamar is not alone in regarding the duty of the levirate as something nearly sacred. The Book of Deuteronomy decrees that a man who refuses to do his duty to his dead brother's widow is worthy of contempt and humiliation. The wronged woman is specifically empowered to "spit in his face" and, curiously, remove one of his sandals (Deut. 25:9), a ritual whose significance is the subject of much debate among scholars.[23] But an even more dire fate is imposed on Onan, who spills his seed on the ground rather than impregnate the widowed Tamar as the law requires.

"Yahweh," a Bible scholar has cracked, is "the God who kills levirate dodgers."[24]

Onan's name has come to be associated with masturbation, but only because of an intentional misreading of the Bible story by sermonizers of Victorian England who were obsessed with the imagined evils of masturbation. Anxious to find at least some faint biblical authority for condemning it, the moral guardians of the nineteenth century seized upon Onan as a cautionary example of what can go wrong when one engages in "self-abuse."[25]

But what is actually depicted in Genesis 38 has nothing to do with masturbation. Onan is engaging in a form of coitus interruptus to avoid impregnating Tamar, and he is condemned to death because of his dereliction of duty. Spilling one's seed on the ground, especially in an effort to avoid the duty of the levirate, is a capital offense in a culture that valued, above all else, childbearing and the preservation of a man's name through his offspring. Indeed, the rebuke that a widow is to deliver to the reluctant brother-in-law is specified in the Bible: "My husband's brother refuseth to raise up unto his brother a name in Israel" (Deut. 25:7).

To the modern reader, the fact that Onan spills his seed on the ground suggests that he is motivated by feelings of guilt, embarrassment, or moral restraint. When we consider the real purpose of the levirate marriage, however, we realize that Onan is acting out of pure greed. He knows that he stands to lose a portion of his own inheritance by providing an heir to his dead brother, and so refuses to bring the sexual encounter to a climax that might actually produce a child.

Even if clergy over the centuries have shunned the story of Tamar when writing their sermons, the biblical storyteller makes it clear that we are intended to see Tamar as a courageous woman who risked death by fire in order to claim what was hers by right. Onan, the "levirate dodger," is killed by divine wrath because he would not make love to her, but Judah suffers no punishment at all for sleeping with daughter-in-law under lurid circumstances precisely because he is fulfilling the duty that his son neglected. If any blame is attached to Judah, it is only that he delayed in putting a man in Tamar's bed to carry out the strange tradition of the levirate marriage.

"She is more righteous than I," declares Judah, explicitly acknowledging his own defiance of the levirate custom, "forasmuch as I gave her not to Shelah my son" (Gen. 38:26).

THE RED THREAD

The story of Tamar and Judah as told in Genesis 38 does not end with the sublime moment when Judah acknowledges that he is the father of the babies in her womb. The biblical storyteller goes on to tell an odd incident about the birth of the infants, and if the encounter between Tamar and Judah sometimes reads like an erotic fairy tale with a trick ending, the birth scene ends with an even odder twist.

As it turns out, the pregnant Tamar is carrying not one but two babies. During labor, we are told, one of the infants thrusts his hand out of Tamar's womb. The midwife, mindful of the primacy of the firstborn son, ties a red thread around the tiny hand so that she can identify the infant who was truly the first to emerge from the womb, in case the hand is withdrawn during labor.

> And it came to pass, when she travailed, that one put out a hand; and the midwife took and bound upon his hand a scarlet thread, saying: "This came out first" (Gen. 38:28).

And, sure enough, the tiny hand disappears from sight, and the other baby—the one *without* the red thread around his hand—is delivered first.

That child is named Perez—the Hebrew word means "breach"—because he "broke forth" from his mother's womb ahead of his brother. Zerah, the baby with the red thread around his hand, is delivered next. Technically, Zerah is the firstborn son and the one who is entitled to inherit his father's name and estate, but it is the second-born infant, Perez, who is named in the Bible as the ancestor of David, the glorious king who establishes Jerusalem as the capital of a united Israel; and Solomon, who builds the temple in the Holy City; and, ultimately, the Messiah of the New Testament. (See chapter fifteen.)

So the story of Judah and Tamar embodies one of the persistent but sometimes overlooked themes of the Bible: the usurpation of the first-born son by a younger brother. Abraham's firstborn son, Ishmael, is cast aside in favor of his younger half brother, Isaac (Gen. 17:15–22); Isaac's second-born son, Jacob, resorts to outright fraud to steal the blessing of the firstborn from his older brother, Esau (Gen. 27:1–30); among Jacob's twelve sons, it is his fourth-born, Judah, who bestowed his name upon the Jewish people and whose line prevailed in the history of Israel. So, too, in Genesis 38, we see that the second-born, Perez, prevails over his twin brother, not to mention all three of Judah's sons by his Canaanite wife.

We are reminded by all of these stories that biblical history is not always shaped by the hand of God. Rather, the destiny of the Israelites is more often served by willful men and women who act on their own initiative and impulse, often in daring and even shocking ways, to make sure that their seed will survive and their descendants will inherit the blessing promised by the Almighty in such ambiguous terms to the Chosen People. And none of the men and women in these stories displays more chutzpah than Tamar herself.

Of course, Tamar can be likened to other women of the Bible who are depicted as sexually adventurous and yet utterly righteous. Like Tamar, Lot's daughters and Ruth the Moabite woman deploy themselves in bed in order to secure children for themselves and survival for their distant descendents. And Tamar is linked in a curious way to another Canaanite woman who acts valiantly to preserve and serve the Israelites and their destiny: Rahab, the original hooker with a heart of gold, whose life is saved by a red thread like the one that figures in the birth of Tamar's children.

The story of Rahab is told in the Book of Joshua, which chronicles the conquest of Canaan by the Israelites after the Exodus from Egypt. Before the Israelites launch their attack, two unnamed spies are sent to infiltrate the town of Jericho and report on its defenses. But the spies pause in their dangerous mission to avail themselves of the services of a local prostitute (*zonah*) named Rahab, and they are interrupted when a patrol sent by the King of Jericho shows up at her house. The good-hearted Rahab conceals the spies and then allows them to escape. To reward her, the spies promise that Rahab and her family will be spared when the Israelite army returns in force, and they instruct her to hang a red thread in her window as a signal to the conquering army of Israel (Josh. 2:1–19).

To emphasize the similarities between Tamar, the feigned Canaanite harlot, and Rahab, the authentic one, the sages elaborated upon the biblical text by imagining that Tamar's sons, Perez and Zerah, are the two unnamed spies in the Book of Joshua—and by suggesting that the red thread that is hung in Rahab's window as a signal to the conquering army was the very same one that the midwife wrapped around Zerah's hand. And the New Testament, too, suggests a direct linkage between Tamar and Rahab: The genealogy of Jesus of Nazareth, as given in the Gospel of Matthew, identifies four women from the Hebrew Bible as his direct ancestresses: Tamar, Rahab, Ruth, and Bathsheba (Matt. 1:5–7). Notably, all four of these women are non-Israelites who married Israelite men, and all four engaged in sexually questionable conduct, including acts of prostitution and seduction.

Still, Tamar was so troubling to the stern rabbinical authorities who studied and explained the Bible that they sought to attribute the whole steamy episode to the hand of the Almighty. The rabbis imagined Tamar to be a descendant of the high priest Shem, son of Noah; she has been given the gift of prophecy by "the holy spirit" and knows with certainty that she is destined to be "the mother of the royal line of David, and the ancestress of Isaiah." When she plays the harlot to ensnare Judah, the goodly man ignores her, but "God [sends] the angel that is appointed over the passion of love" to compel Judah to turn back and place himself in Tamar's embrace.

Later, according to rabbinical tales, Tamar is summoned to a celestial court of justice, where her fate is to be determined by a jury consisting of a ghostly Isaac, an aging Jacob, and Judah himself. At first, Tamar declines to defend herself out of fear of incriminating Judah, and so Judah declares the pregnant Tamar to be guilty and worthy of burning.

At the last moment, to save herself, Tamar searches for the pledges that would prove her innocence—Judah's seal and staff—but cannot find them; an evil angel has hidden them in order to prevent the birth of David. So God sends the angel Michael to place the crucial evidence before the jury. Confronted with the truth, Judah confesses not only to fathering Tamar's child but also to selling Joseph into slavery—and, moved by the spirit of confession, his brother Reuben volunteers a mea culpa for sneaking into the bed of his father's concubine, Bilhah!

"It is better that I should perish in a fire that can be extinguished than I should be cast into hell fire," Judah is made to declare by the rabbinical storytellers, who also tell us that Judah later married the wronged woman. "Now, then, I acknowledge that Tamar is innocent."

"Ye are both innocent!" a heavenly voice is heard to say. "It was the will of God that it should happen!"[26]

The tale as told by the rabbis betrays a certain unmistakable anxiety about a flesh-and-blood woman who simply refuses to shut up and go away. But their version of the story turns the intrepid Tamar into a marionette whose strings are worked by the divine puppeteer. What makes her so remarkable and so memorable—and so appealing to the contemporary reader—is the fact that Tamar will *not* be manipulated or intimidated or ignored.

The sheer willfulness of Tamar was celebrated by Thomas Mann, who retold the story a millennia or so later in *Joseph the Provider*, one volume in the novel *Joseph and His Brothers*, which he based on the biblical tales. Mann imagines Tamar as a young Canaanite woman, "gifted with the soul-and-body charm and mystery of Astarte," who sits at the feet of the Hebrew patriarch Jacob and learns from him that God has chosen the Israelites as his people and has promised them "the hero who one day should be awoken out of the chosen seed . . . [t]he prince of peace and the anointed." Tamar resolves that *she* will be the one to bear a son to carry on Judah's name and line; hers would be the "womb of salvation," the place where the "chosen seed" would be planted, where it would grow and flourish.

"Tamar had made up her mind, cost what it might, by dint of her womanhood to squeeze herself into the history of the world,"[27] writes Mann in *Joseph the Provider*. "She played the temptress and whored by the way, that she might not be shut out; she abased herself recklessly to be exalted."[28]

Even in the spare and measured words of Genesis 38 itself, the willful and indomitable Tamar is not less than the savior who ensures the survival of the Jewish people and, ultimately, the birth of a savior. The very word "Jew" (*Yehudi*) is specifically and directly derived from "Judah" (*Yehuda*)—and, among the Twelve Tribes of Israel, it is the tribe of Judah that survived and, through the House of David, supplied the Israelites with its greatest kings and the line that would ultimately produce a savior. But the tribe is facing early extinction precisely because none of Judah's sons is able to implant a son in Tamar's womb, and the Jewish people would have perished then and there if not for Tamar's courage and determination. By playing the harlot, she saves the tribe of Judah—and thus the Jewish people—from obliteration.

Thus the story of Tamar and Judah suggests an urgent and crucial truth that has never been more pertinent than it is now. God instructed the Israelites to drive out or kill the Canaanites, but the Israelites were forced by the circumstances of history to live side by side with them; today, the struggle of Arab and Jew to find a way to live with one another on the same bloody ground where Judah and Tamar first met is no less momentous than it was three thousand years ago. To be sure, the Bible offers abundant and bloody examples of war and terror practiced on each other by Israelite and non-Israelite. But the story of Tamar, like other shining examples in the Bible, suggest that these ancient enemies did, and can, find a way to live in peace with one another.

CHAPTER EIGHT

ZIPPORAH AND MOSES

The Lord met him, and sought to kill him.

—EXODUS 4:24

The flames in the fire-pit threw shadows against the walls of the tent where Zipporah's husband and baby slept. But Zipporah lay wide awake on the pile of bedding that all three of them shared, gazing at the ghostly figures that seemed to dance and leap across the taut fabric.

Only that morning, Zipporah had stood in the family compound in the hills of Midian and bidden farewell to her father and six sisters. Father, a priest of the Midianites, had been no less stern and solemn than if he were presiding over some ritual offering to the ever-demanding gods, although Zipporah had detected a slight hoarseness in his voice that betrayed some sorrow. Her sisters wept openly, and she heard the keening sound of their voices for a long time after she turned, her infant son in her arms, and followed her husband down the rocky path that pointed in the direction of Egypt.

Now she found herself alone with her husband and baby at a sparse oasis far from her home. They had trekked from sunrise to sundown, her husband driving a pair of pack-asses ahead of them. The moon had already risen when they came to a muddy watering hole and a couple of strangled palms that served as a lodging place for travelers on the caravan route through the desert. On the far side of the pool were a cold fire, a pile of camel droppings, the shards of a shattered wine jar—all

And it came to pass on the way at the lodging-place, that the Lord met him, and sought to kill him. Then Zipporah took a flint, and cut off the foreskin of her son, and cast it at his feet; and she said: "Surely a bridegroom of blood art thou to me." So He let him alone. Then she said: "A bridegroom of blood in regard of the circumcision."

—EXODUS 4:24–26

signs that someone else had recently paused here—but not a living soul could be seen. At odd moments, a gust of wind would howl through the oasis, stirring up little whirlwinds of sand; then it was still and quiet again.

Zipporah gathered a few sticks of wood, built a cooking fire, and prepared a pot of porridge while her husband watered and tied up the asses, unpacked and raised their tent. Then he joined her and the baby at the firepit for a hasty evening meal. They ate without speaking, as if silenced by the terrible dangers of the journey they had undertaken. Now and then, when the baby fretted, Zipporah loosened her cloak and gave him a breast to quiet him down. With the fire still burning in the pit, a faint candle in the vast darkness of the desert, they retreated to their tent for the night. Soon she heard the rhythmic breathing of her slumbering husband and baby, one loud and one faint.

The shadows on the tent wall caught Zipporah's eye and forbade her to sleep. She thought of the tales that she had heard as a child from a woman of her father's clan, a crone who told fearsome stories in a voice that hissed like a serpent. The stories came back to her now—of gods who demanded unspeakable pleasures from young women who had not yet known a man, demons who set their mouths upon the mouths of innocents and sucked the life out of them while they slept, fat and foul-smelling creatures who oozed up from muddy pools and swallowed strong men right down to their feet.

Zipporah shuddered as if in the grip of a fever, then pulled a corner of the bedding around her shoulders to warm herself against the cold desert air.

———

Zipporah glanced at her husband as he slept, one arm curled around the slumbering infant. He was a kind man, but a strangely quiet one who seemed to hold a great many secrets in his heart.

He had the bearing of a prince, although his rough hands and his muscled arms and legs clearly belonged to a shepherd whose flock grazed on the steepest and rockiest of mountainsides. He spoke in the refined language of a prince, but he did not speak very often because it took so much effort to suppress his stammer. His name sounded faintly like a name from far-off Egypt, but he insisted that he was not an Egyptian. Yet, plainly enough, he was a stranger among the Midianites, and when their first son was born, he insisted on naming the infant Gershom, a word that meant "a stranger there" in her husband's native tongue.

She recalled the day when she first encountered her husband, a day that seemed very far off to her now. Zipporah and her sisters had driven their father's flock to a well, some distance from their father's compound, where they customarily drew water for the sheep and filled the water jars for the household. They began to fill the watering troughs. When the troughs were full, two boisterous young shepherds appeared over the rise of the hill, driving their flocks before them, and one of them pushed Jethro's seven daughters aside.

"We'll water ourselves and our beasts first," said the bolder of the two shepherds to Zipporah with a laugh and a leer. "But don't run away—we'll have some pleasure with *you* when we're done."

Zipporah and her sisters had seen them before—the tall, gangly, pimple-faced one who never spoke, and the short, thick, pig-nosed one who taunted them and touched them in insulting ways. And, as before, Jethro's daughters began to move away from the well in order to put some distance between themselves and their tormentors. Sometimes they were forced to wait all day in the cleft of some nearby wadi, out of sight of the shepherds, listening to the sounds of the short one's braying laughter, until the young men tired of their game and moved off.

But on that memorable day, as Zipporah summoned her sisters away from the well, a stranger's voice was suddenly heard from a shady spot under an outcropping of rock, and a man bearing a stout wooden staff stepped out of the shadows.

"Stand back," the man shouted at the two shepherds without a trace of the stammer that Zipporah would later hear in quieter moments, "and let the maidens finish watering their flocks."

All of them—Jethro's daughters *and* the bullying shepherds—looked up in surprise.

What they saw was a young man whose tattered and dusty clothing did not conceal his strength, a man who stood as proud and erect as a prince of Egypt even if it was quite obvious that he had been traveling alone through rough country like a fugitive on the run. He drove off the shepherds with a single threatening gesture of his staff raised high in a clenched fist. Then, as the flock watered at the troughs, he drew more water from the well, pulling up one bucketful after another with his strong arms. When Jethro's daughters returned to their father's house, they were giggling to each other about the stranger who had rescued them from their old tormentors.

"How is it," Jethro asked, "that you have come back so soon today?"

"An Egyptian chased away the shepherds who always bother us at the well," said the youngest of Jethro's daughters.

"He even drew water for us—" said another.

"And watered the flock," a third one interrupted.

Jethro nodded, pulled at his long beard, and then looked sharply at Zipporah, his eldest daughter.

"Where is he then?" asked Jethro. "Why did you leave the man? Ask him in to break bread."

So it was that the stranger came to Jethro's house, broke bread with the priest and his seven daughters, and accepted Jethro's offer to stay with them and tend his flocks. The man had few words for any of the young women, but he accompanied Jethro on long walks into the countryside, and Jethro learned a great deal about him: how he had been born the son of an Israelite slave in Egypt but raised in the court of Pharaoh himself, how he had witnessed the beating of a slave by one of Pharaoh's taskmasters, how he had struck down the taskmaster and then fled to the wilderness of Midian to escape the wrath of Pharaoh and the certain punishment that would be inflicted upon him.

Jethro offered the stranger a safe refuge in the land of Midian and, not much later, the hand of his eldest daughter in marriage. Only then did Zipporah learn the name of the stranger, the man who would be her husband and the father of her children. He was called Moses.

———

A sudden noise from just outside the tent, a hiss and a rattle like a serpent arching to strike, interrupted Zipporah's thoughts and sent a chill through her body. She sat up with a start, her heart racing.

"Moses!" she whispered, but her husband did not stir, and the baby only snuffled and then fell silent again.

She heard the rustle of flesh against cloth as someone or something moved against the fabric of the tent, and she imagined that she saw an odd bulge that moved slowly but steadily toward the tent opening. A wheezing noise reached her ears—the sound of labored breathing—but it came from neither her husband nor her baby. A stench that reminded her of the greasy smoke that poured from the altar when her father sacrificed a bloody hunk of flesh to the gods wafted into the tent.

"Husband!" she said again, and again he did not stir.

Now she recalled the strange tale that her husband had told her when he first announced that he must return to Egypt and asked her to accompany him. Moses had been tending Jethro's flocks on a mountainside in the wilderness when he saw a strange sight, a bush that burned with fire but did not burn up. Then he heard a voice that seemed to come out of the bush, a voice that announced itself as "the God of your fathers," a god whose name was Yahweh, a god who demanded that Moses go back to the place where his own people were enslaved, the place where he had killed the Egyptian taskmaster, the place where Pharaoh sought his life.

"Come, I will send you to Pharaoh," the voice said from within the burning bush, "and you shall free My people, the Israelites, from Egypt."

Zipporah would have laughed at her husband's tale if he had not told it to her in such a plainspoken and quiet voice. She noticed that his stammer disappeared and she marked the urgency in his voice when he asked her to return with him to Egypt. Without allowing herself to think much about the implications of her husband's tale—Was Moses truly called by the God of Israel? Was he jesting? Was he mad?— she agreed to undertake the long, difficult, and perilous journey from the sheltered wilderness of Midian to the land of the Egyptians and the mighty Pharaoh.

Now she could no longer drive the mounting terror from her breast. The spirits and demons of her own people were so familiar to Zipporah that they had lost the power to frighten her, but her husband was a stranger whose curious ways seemed grotesque and dangerous, too. Among her own people, for example, a man was circumcised when he reached his thirteenth year, when he was old enough to take a bride and strong enough to endure the circumciser's knife. But Moses insisted that a son must be circumcised on the eighth day after his birth, when the child was still frail and vulnerable to every sort of peril. "This is what the God of my fathers demands," he told Zipporah's father on one of their long walks, and Jethro later complained to Zipporah: "What a barbaric people to circumcise so young!"

And there the whole matter had been left by her father and her husband, but now Zipporah found herself seized with anxiety at the thought that her infant son lay beside her with his foreskin intact on that tiny bit of flesh between his fat little thighs. Perhaps she had been wrong to allow her father to argue with Moses over the matter of the circumcision; perhaps she had placed all of them in terrible danger by allowing her son to remain uncircumcised. After all, what might the strange and demanding god of the Israelites do to them if they defied his commandments?

A sound that Zipporah could not recognize now reached her ears, a sound that might have been water running over stones or the night wind in the branches of a palm. Her eyes were drawn to the opening of the tent, and there she saw a silvery mist reaching into the tent, moving over the ground like a morning fog except that it glowed with a light that resembled the glare of the full moon. Pouring into the tent, swelling like a freshening stream, the mist surrounded the bedding on which Zipporah, Moses, and Gershom lay as if on an island of clouds in a quicksilver lake.

"How pretty," Zipporah thought to herself, suddenly calm and even enchanted by the sight and sound. She wanted to wake her husband, not out of fear but to show him what she beheld, but the mist filled her throat and prevented her from speaking.

Now a figure seemed to rise up out of the swirling mist, and Zipporah beheld the shape of a man, or something like a man, and yet not a man at all. The figure began to swell up like a corpse that had been in water too long—and then she saw its mouth open wide to reveal two rows of yellowed and twisted donkey teeth in which she saw bits of flesh and bone, eyeballs, fingertips, fragments that could be recognized as bloody pieces of lung and scalp and kidney. Zipporah watched in silent terror as the mouth slowly closed around her sleeping husband, drawing into that vast maw his head and his feet, his arms and his legs, his chest and his thighs, until only a single organ of his body was still visible, the organ with which Moses had first implanted a seed in her womb.

Zipporah awoke from the nightmare with a start. Her eyes burned, her head ached. She shuddered as she remembered the enormous jaws that had closed around her husband's body—and then, to her immense relief, she looked around the tent and saw that her husband was still asleep next to her, and her baby was still safely nested in the crook of his arm. Perhaps I do have a fever, Zipporah thought to herself, and she snuggled comfortably under a fold of the bedding.

Then Zipporah heard a snigger from someone standing inside the tent, someone standing so near to her that she could hear his breathing, and she knew that she was no longer dreaming.

His laughter reminded Zipporah of the pig-nosed shepherd who had tormented her and her sisters when they watered their flock at the well, and the mad thought occurred to her that it was the young bully who was in the tent with them now.

"Who are you?" she said, choking out the words. "What do you want?"

The intruder did not speak. Zipporah glanced around the tent to see if she might find something to use as a weapon—her husband's new walking staff, perhaps, or a spare tent stake, but neither was within sight or reach. On the tent floor were the supplies she had used to prepare their evening meal—a water jug, a pouch of milled flour, a tiny jar of oil, a little bundle of kindling, a flint stone that she had used to strike a spark and start the cooking fire.

Then, suddenly, something moved quickly through the still air in the tent. Zipporah felt the slightest breeze but still saw only a shadow. But now Moses awoke with a start, sat up awkwardly, and raised his arms as if to defend himself against a blow. The baby tumbled out of his arm and rolled to the ground, crying out in surprise and indignation. Zipporah sensed rather than saw the attack on her husband—somehow, without quite knowing why, she realized that the intruder, whoever or whatever it was, had come to kill him.

At that moment, Zipporah dived to the floor where the cooking supplies were neatly arranged and snatched the flint stone in her right hand. She felt the jagged edge of the stone with one finger—was it sharp enough, she wondered, to cut the attacker? Would a blow or even a knife-cut be enough to stop him? Or would something else be needed, some more potent magic, to stave off the ghostly figure in the shadows? She wished she had something longer or sharper at hand—a long-bladed knife like the one Jethro used to slit the throats of the bleating sheep that were led to the sacrificial altar, or even the short, sharp blade that was used to circumcise a young Midianite man before his marriage to a virgin bride. But the flint stone was all she had now, and she would inflict as much damage on the attacker, draw as much blood, as the jagged edge would allow.

As Zipporah raised the stone and looked around for the attacker, she heard two anguishing noises: her husband's strangled cry, as if the attacker were already on top of him, and the sharper cry of their infant son, who lay helplessly on his back, arms and legs flailing, shrieking in panic. A strange image from her fever dream suddenly formed in Zipporah's mind at the sound of her baby's desperate cry—the image of her husband swallowed up in the mouth of the demon, the whole of his body captured between ravening jaws except one crucial limb—and then she recalled the angry words that her husband and her father had exchanged over the circumcision of Zipporah's newborn son.

Now Zipporah burned with the urgent knowledge that Moses and not her father must have been right. The god that Moses worshipped, the god that had summoned Moses and sent him on the road to Egypt, demanded the flesh and blood of the firstborn sons of his Chosen People—and yet their own child was alive and intact! The intruder in the tent—angel or devil or perhaps God himself—was bent on punishing Zipporah's husband and son for disregarding what Moses had always insisted was a holy ritual. Zipporah did not understand *why* the tiny foreskin of an infant boy, a bit of flesh not bigger than the tip of her little finger, was so important to the deity that Moses called all-powerful, all-knowing, and all-seeing, but she realized that it no longer mattered why. All that mattered now, Zipporah told herself in that moment, was to confront the attacker and turn him away.

Zipporah crawled to her baby's side, pulled off the swaddling, and fumbled to find the tiniest and most delicate part of his small body. The baby fell silent for a moment, so that all that Zipporah heard were the muffled gasps of her husband on the bedding behind her. She bit her lower lip, squinted in the darkness, and then pressed the edge of the flint against the flesh, timidly at first but then with greater force when she realized that the edge was not sharp enough to cut quickly or smoothly. Her baby gasped and then cried out angrily, but Zipporah persisted. Then, suddenly, she saw that she held a bit of flesh in her hands—and that her hands were stained with blood.

So much blood, she thought to herself, from such a tiny bit of flesh.

Zipporah stood and turned, but she saw that the intruder had not broken off the attack on her husband, whose desperate cries seemed quieter now, as if the attacker were choking off the last breath of life in his body. Amid the bedding on the tent floor, now in even greater disarray, Zipporah saw flailing limbs, but she could not make out in the shadowy darkness whether they belonged to the attacker or Moses or both. But Zipporah realized that her husband's all-powerful God had not yet noticed the blood ritual that she had just performed. Or, if he had noticed, he did not seem to care.

Zipporah still held the bloody foreskin delicately between her thumb and first finger, and now she stepped forward and thrust the flesh toward the legs that flexed and kicked as Moses struggled against the attack. She drew the foreskin down one leg and then another, painting a bright red smear of fresh blood on each limb, just as she had seen her father anoint an arm, a hand, a face with the blood of a freshly sacrificed lamb. Zipporah could not be sure whether the blood-smeared legs belonged to Moses or his attacker, but she figured with a kind of crazed logic that if the cutting of flesh and the shedding of blood were what the attacker wanted, the sight of blood might be enough to call his attention to the fact that the child had been circumcised, flesh had been cut, blood had been shed.

Then Zipporah was called back to her baby by his staccato cries, each one punctuated with a gasp. She saw that his face was slightly blue, but the fresh wound that she had just inflicted was no longer bleeding. Quickly, and with far greater deftness than she had just displayed with the flint, Zipporah swaddled him tightly, lifted him into her arms, bared one breast, and gave him to suck. The infant sighed, snorted, snuggled into his mother's bosom, and suckled rhythmically on her teat. Within a moment or two, he was fast asleep.

Zipporah looked up at the scene of the struggle, and she saw that the flailing of limbs atop the bedding had ceased. All was perfectly quiet and still inside the tent. Moses was lying on his back, his arms splayed out, his clothing disheveled, but his breathing was deep and steady. Zipporah watched the steady rise and fall of his chest—he was asleep and alone. The intruder, whoever or whatever he had been, if he had truly been there at all, was gone.

Gershom stirred briefly in her arms, she gave him the other breast, and soon he slept again. Zipporah gazed at her infant son, whose swaddling showed a tiny spot of red from the blood of the circumcision, and then at her husband, whose exposed legs were painted with crude stripes of blood that was now turning brown and crusty.

"Surely a bridegroom of blood art thou unto me," Zipporah said aloud, mimicking the solemn words and phrases of the priestly incantations that her father recited at the sacrificial altar. And then, as if to explain herself, she added: "A bridegroom of blood on account of the circumcision."

The slumbering Moses did not hear her words, nor was Zipporah sure that he would understand them if he did.

CHAPTER NINE

THE BRIDEGROOM OF BLOOD

Zipporah as the Goddess-Rescuer of Moses

WHO IS DOING WHAT TO WHOM?
THE MAN GOD BEFRIENDED
THE CULT OF THE GODDESS-RESCUER
THE BLOOD OF A VIRGIN BRIDE
FIRSTLINGS ✧ "I WILL SLAY THY SON"

For mystery, mayhem, and sheer baffling weirdness, nothing else in the Bible quite compares with the story of Zipporah and the "Bridegroom of Blood" in Exodus 4:24–26. Like some grotesque insect preserved in biblical amber, the spare three lines of text in Exodus that describe God's night attack on Moses—and the blood ritual that Zipporah uses to defend her husband and son—suggest that the faith of the ancient Israelites was far stranger and richer than the biblical authors are willing to let on.

The enigmatic text of Exodus 4:24–26 has distressed Bible readers and scholars—and excited their imaginations—for at least three millennia. No other passage in the Bible has been tortured into such odd and even scandalous readings by otherwise pious hands. Yet no other passage has been quite so resistant to the biblical code-breakers. The original Hebrew text is especially difficult to decipher because only two of the players in the scene are identified by name. The Bible tells us that it is Zipporah and Yahweh who encounter each other by night at the lodging place, but Moses is not named at all. Nor are we allowed to see with clarity who is doing what to whom—or why. So our reading of Exodus 4:24–26 must begin with a litany of troubling questions:

Is it Moses whom God attacks, or his firstborn son, Gershom, or perhaps his second-born son, Eliezer?

Is God himself on the attack, or is it one of his minions—the Destroyer, the Angel of Death, or Satan? Or is the attacker actually a pagan deity or a demon from the pantheon of Egypt or the Midianites?

To whose sexual organ does Zipporah apply the sharpened flint in the ritual of circumcision—her son's? Moses'? or God's?

Does she use the foreskin to smear blood on someone's *legs*, as the biblical text states, or is the word used euphemistically to refer to someone's *genitals*, as it is elsewhere in the Bible? And if we are to understand that "legs" actually means "genitals," we must ask: *Whose* genitals are painted with blood?

And what does Zipporah mean when she utters the mystical phrase: "Surely a bridegroom of blood art thou to me"?

More than a few exegetes, ancient and modern, amateur and professional, have broken their analytical lances on the armor of Exodus 4:24–26. Two ancient Jewish authors of the Roman world, Josephus and Philo of Alexandria, were so baffled by God's night attack on Moses that each of them simply left the story out when he retold the life of Moses[1]—and, for that matter, so did Cecil B. DeMille in *The Ten Commandments* two thousand years later. One contemporary biblical scholar surveyed the battlefield of biblical exegesis that is the study of Exodus 4:24–26, a landscape littered with discredited theories and deflated arguments, and simply admitted defeat: "The original gist of the story," he declared, "is now lost beyond recall."[2]

What we *do* know is that the text of Exodus 4:24–26 is an old and primitive fragment of folklore that somehow found its way into the Book of Exodus in spite of its faintly blasphemous depiction of the Almighty as a night stalker who is appeased only by a woman's blood offering. The passage does not seem to fit into the biblical narrative that comes before and after the incident at the lodging place,[3] and the notion that God would seek to kill the very man he had just selected and anointed as his personal emissary is at odds with the intimate relationship between God and Moses that is depicted in Exodus and elsewhere in the Bible. At least one scholar claims to detect in the Bridegroom of Blood (and other passages of the Bible) the echoes of "an anti-Moses tradition"—the faint "murmuring and accusations" of ancient dissenters—that somehow survived the censor's blade and quill.[4] Still, the story was apparently too memorable to be left out entirely, and yet too shocking to be told clearly and straightforwardly by the priests and scribes.

So the enigmatic text, a mere seventy words in English translation, may be regarded as a window—tiny, cracked, and dirty—through which we glimpse some of the earliest stirrings of spirituality in the ancient Near East and the most primitive ritual practices of the people who would become the Israelites. The bloody and baffling tale is a crack in the wall erected around the Bible by the priests and scribes, a crack through which we can glimpse, in the words of the archaeologist who first peered into the tomb of Tutankhamen, "wonderful things."

WHO IS DOING WHAT TO WHOM?

The tale of the Bridegroom of Blood has prompted hot conjecture among otherwise sensible Bible readers not only because of what is revealed in the biblical text but also because of what is concealed. Although we are eyewitnesses to the bloody encounter between God and Zipporah, the text is so encrypted, so heavy with secret meanings, that we must suspect that some early biblical author or editor felt obliged to blur the picture. Before we can begin to decipher the deeper meanings of the text, we must first try to figure out exactly who is doing what to whom in Exodus 4:24–26.

The original Hebrew text of the Bible states plainly that it is Yahweh who "met him and sought to kill him" (Exod. 4:24), but the object of Yahweh's attack is never actually named in that text. Moses is commonly understood to be the intended victim, although some sources insist instead that one of his two sons was the target rather than Moses himself.[5] But the notion of the Almighty stalking and seeking to kill the very man he had just anointed as his prophet was so unsettling to the sages and scribes that the earliest translators of the Bible insisted on interposing a celestial hit man between Yahweh and his victim— "the Angel of the Lord," "the Angel of Death," or sometimes "the Destroyer" appear in place of Yahweh in the account of the night attack in some early Aramaic and Greek translations of the Bible.[6] The

Talmud preserves an especially bizarre tradition that Zipporah was alerted to the urgent need to perform a circumcision by an angel who descended from heaven and swallowed the whole of Moses' body *except* his uncircumcised sexual organ, thus calling Zipporah's attention to the problem at hand![7]

Indeed, a few of the sages recoiled against the notion of *any* divine assault, even a vicarious one, against the man destined to become the greatest prophet in the history of Israel. So they suggested that it was Satan who sought to kill Moses by swallowing him alive: "Satan appeared to him in the guise of a serpent, and swallowed Moses down to his extremities," goes one version of the story as retold in rabbinic literature. "As soon as [Zipporah] sprinkled the blood of the circumcision on her husband's feet, a heavenly voice was heard to cry out to the serpent, commanding him, 'Spew him out!' "[8] Later, the renowned Jewish sage known as Rashi, an eleventh-century rationalist who was plainly uncomfortable with such pious fairy tales, insisted that the divine attack on Moses ought to be understood as nothing more than a metaphor for a life-threatening illness that Zipporah manages to cure by performing the ritual of circumcision.[9] Similarly, contemporary Bible critics tend to throw up their hands at the Bridegroom of Blood and ascribe the whole confounding mess to "the mysterious saving power of circumcision which it is the purpose of this story to celebrate."[10]

A deeper mystery is the nature and purpose of the bloody ritual that Zipporah uses to stave off the night attack. The Bible tells us that she is somehow moved to perform a hasty circumcision on her infant son using the only tool at hand, a crude flint knife or perhaps just a flint stone of the kind used to start fires. Then Zipporah does *something* with the bloody foreskin, although the Bible does not tell us exactly what. One common but misleading English translation tells us that she "cast it at his feet" (JPS), but a more accurate translation of the biblical Hebrew reveals that she "touched his legs" (New JPS) with the bloody foreskin.[11] Even this translation, however, is misleading because it fails to disclose that "legs" is sometimes used by the biblical authors as a euphemism for the male sexual organ. "Just where the 'blood(y) husband' was dabbed with the son's prepuce we can only surmise," cracks the high-spirited Bible scholar Marvin Pope, "but the best guess seems the area where foreskins are located."[12] Thus, the most candid reading of Exodus 4:25 is that Zipporah uses her son's foreskin to smear the fresh blood of his circumcision on *someone*'s genitals. Still, the original Hebrew text of the Bible does not tell us *whose* genitals are painted with blood by Zipporah—it might be Moses, or her son, or perhaps God himself.*

Even the words that Zipporah speaks out loud at the climax of her encounter with Yahweh—"Surely a bridegroom of blood [*hattan damim*] art thou to me"—are suggestive, provocative, and yet profoundly enigmatic. The biblical author does not identify the person to whom these words are addressed—it might be God, Moses, or Gershom—nor does the author explain why Zipporah speaks them out loud. All we know is the phrase seems to be a bit of potent verbal magic, an incantation that brings the blood ritual to a successful conclusion and somehow persuades God to break off his attack.

One of the words that Zipporah speaks out loud—*hattan*—means "bridegroom," among other things, in biblical Hebrew, but *hattan* may be related to an Arabic word that refers specifically to the rite of circumcision.[13] Some tribes of the Arabic world in biblical times (including, it is thought, the Midianites) required an adolescent male to undergo circumcision in preparation for marriage—a practice that has survived among the contemporary Bedouins—and so Zipporah's words may preserve a long-forgotten linkage between marriage and circumcision in the ancient Near East.[14] Indeed, the same tradition may be at work in the ill-fated betrothal of Dinah and Shechem, a tale in which a suitor is required to undergo circumcision before he is permitted to marry. When Zipporah declares Moses to be a "bridegroom of blood" (or a "bloody husband," as the phrase is rendered in some English translations), she may be saying out loud what many a bride thought to herself in biblical Canaan!

---

*According to the original Hebrew text of the Bible, we know that Zipporah cast the foreskin of her son "at *his* feet" but we are not told who "he" is. The translators of the Revised Standard Version, an updated translation based on the King James Version, boldly inserted the name of Moses into the biblical text in an effort to clarify Exodus 4:25: "Then Zipporah took a flint and cut off her son's foreskin, and touched Moses' feet with it."

THE MAN GOD BEFRIENDED

The deepest mystery of all in the Bridegroom of Blood, of course, is *why* God would seek to kill Moses so soon after befriending him, anointing him as a prophet, arming him with the power to perform works of divine magic, and sending him on the crucial mission to liberate the Israelites from slavery in Egypt.

The story is especially troubling precisely because Moses is such a commanding figure on the biblical landscape. By tradition, he is the author of the first five books of the Bible, including the one in which the night attack itself is described. He is depicted in the Bible as the liberator and the lawgiver of the Israelites, a potent and deadly miracle-worker, a fierce military commander, and the role model of the Messiah in both Jewish and Christian theology. Moses is the only human being in the Bible to whom God reveals himself in all of his glory, the only human being to whom God speaks "face to face." The Book of Deuteronomy hails Moses as the greatest prophet in the history of Israel, past, present, and future. Yet the tale of the Bridegroom of Blood reminds us that if Moses is the only man whom God befriended, he is also the only man whom God stalked with intent to kill.

Some commentators, both Jewish and Christian, argued that God seeks to kill Moses because he is angered by Moses' apparent lack of enthusiasm for his divine mission. They claimed to discern in the biblical text evidence that Moses delayed in hitting the road,[15] took his own sweet time in journeying toward Egypt,[16] and—of course—insisted on schlepping his Midianite wife and their young children to Egypt along with him.[17] But the blood-soaked text of Exodus 4:24–26 has convinced most Bible critics that *foreskins* (or the lack of them), rather than Moses' bad attitude, are what drives God into a homicidal frenzy.

Circumcision, it is sometimes argued, was first adopted as a ritual practice by the ancients because they somehow discerned that it was hygienic and healthful. Herodotus, for example, reports that the Egyptians engaged in circumcision "for the sake of cleanliness, considering it better to be clean than comely."[18] Others suggest that circumcision was arbitrarily chosen by primitive peoples as a physical sign that marked a young man's coming of age, his formal initiation into the clan or tribe, and his eligibility for marriage.[19] But the Bible itself presents circumcision as an unmistakable and ineradicable symbol of a man's adherence to the covenant between God and Abraham: "My covenant," says God to Abraham, "shall be in your flesh. . . ." (Gen. 17:13).

The traditional explanation of the Bridegroom of Blood is that Yahweh seeks to kill Moses because he has violated the single most important clause of the covenant between God and Abraham by failing to circumcise his firstborn son, Gershom. "And he that is eight days old shall be circumcised among you, every male throughout your generations," God has already decreed to Abraham. "And the uncircumcised male who is not circumcised in the flesh of his foreskin, that soul shall be cut off from his people" (Gen. 17:12, 14). One early Aramaic translation of the Bible places the blame on Jethro,* the father of Zipporah and a priest of the Midianites, who supposedly circumcised their male children only at the onset of puberty or in preparation for marriage. "The husband wanted to circumcise," Zipporah is made to say in a bit of explanatory dialogue that does not appear in the original text of the Bible, "but the father-in-law would not permit him."[20+]

Other traditional sources speculated that God waxes so wroth because *Moses* is not circumcised.[21] Zipporah performs the ritual of circumcision on her infant in place of her husband, they speculate, because the risk of infection while traveling under such primitive circumstances makes it too dangerous to perform the procedure on Moses himself. Rather preposterously, it is suggested that God will not accept an uncircumcised man as the liberator of the Chosen People—but, at the same time, the Almighty is content with a vicarious circumcision by means of Gershom rather than the real thing.[22]

---

*Zipporah's father is identified as "Reuel" in the first passage where he is named (Exod. 2:18) and "Jethro" a few lines later (Exod. 3:1). The Bible uses yet a third name, "Hobab," to identify a man who is described as Moses' father-in-law in Judges 4:11 and as his brother-in-law in Numbers 10:29. From such ambiguities and contradictions, scholars have detected the hand of more than one author at work in the Bible. (See appendix: Who *Really* Wrote the Bible?)

+An ancient tradition holds that Moses and his Midianite father-in-law struck a deal about how the children of the mixed marriage would be raised: half of the offspring would be raised as Israelites, half as Midianites. Thus, according to the rabbinical tale, the firstborn son of Moses and Zipporah, Gershom, was duly circumcised, and the second-born, Eliezer, was not. For that reason, some sages speculated that it was the failure to circumcise Eliezer that prompted the night attack, and that Eliezer was the intended victim. The Bible suggests but does not state that both Gershom and Eliezer were present during the night attack, and I have followed the text of Exodus 4:24–26 in mentioning only one of the two sons in my retelling of the tale.

Now it is true that the Bible nowhere reports that Moses was circumcised, but the rabbis were so horrified at the thought that the Lawgiver might possess a foreskin that they came up with a number of ingenious arguments to prove otherwise. Moses had been duly circumcised as an infant by his Israelite family before he was cast adrift on the Nile. Or he was circumcised in his youth along with the other young men of Pharaoh's court, where the rite of circumcision was routinely practiced. Or perhaps Moses was *born* circumcised, a minor miracle that has been attributed to other biblical figures, ranging from Adam to Noah to Jacob, whose circumcisions are not mentioned in the Bible.[23]

The conventional wisdom about the night attack is reassuring and even comforting because it appears to solve the mystery of Exodus 4:24–26 with the clarity and certainty of a fast game of Clue. God is angry because *someone* is not properly circumcised, either Moses or his son, and the quick-witted Zipporah succeeds in calming down the Almighty by performing a hasty circumcision just in the nick of time. She tosses the foreskin at someone's feet (or genitals)—or, more likely, she uses it to smear blood on those body parts—so that God will not fail to notice that she has corrected the oversight. God is mollified and breaks off his attack. When Zipporah, weary and perhaps slightly in shock, rebukes her Israelite husband for putting her through such a strange ordeal by uttering those baffling words—"Surely a bridegroom of blood art thou to me"—she is saying, in effect, "I never suspected when I agreed to take an Israelite as a husband that things would turn out to be such a bloody mess!"

But the official explanation does not make much sense to any reader who pays attention to what the Bible actually says about God and his weirdly intimate relationship with Moses. From their very first encounter at the burning bush, God knows that Moses is not exactly fired with enthusiasm for the long journey to Egypt: Moses plainly tells him so, and God is reduced to wheedling and cajoling the reluctant prophet into taking the job. When Moses tries to beg off by telling God that he is "slow of speech, and of a slow tongue"—a phrase that is traditionally interpreted to mean that Moses suffered from a severe speech impediment[24]—God is quick to accommodate his special needs by naming his brother, Aaron, as his spokesperson (Exod. 4:10, 14–15). Not once during their long tête-à-tête does Yahweh bring up the subject of circumcision, nor does he even hint that the lack of it might bear on Moses' suitability for the role of liberator and wonder-worker.

Clearly, if circumcision was such a touchy subject, the Almighty did not have to wait until Moses was already on the road to Egypt before doing something about it. God has already demonstrated that he sees exactly what is going on in far-off Egypt. "I have surely seen the afflic- tion of My people that are in Egypt," says God to Moses during the first of their many summit conferences. God has already made it clear that he sees what will happen in the distant future, too: "And I know that the king of Egypt will not give you leave to go, except by a mighty hand" (Exod. 3:7, 19). Surely the all-seeing and all-knowing Yahweh is able to see and know the intimate anatomy of Moses and his sons, which is so much closer at hand, and to say and do something about their foreskins, if these really mattered to him.

Indeed, we might wonder whether it was some priestly redactor, rather than God, who cared so passionately about circumcision. The fact is that circumcision was not a uniquely Israelite ritual in the era of the Exodus; it was practiced by the Egyptians and many of the native- dwelling peoples of Canaan, too. So a circumcised sexual organ could not have served to readily distinguish the Israelites from their neighbors in their early history. Among the peoples of Canaan, the Bible identifies only the Philistines and the unfortunate kinsmen of Hamor, prince of the Hivites, as uncircumcised. (See chapter five.) And the Bible tells us that the Israelite children born during the Exodus are not circumcised at all until Joshua leads them out of the wilderness and into the Promised Land, where he pauses to make a set of flint knives and conduct a mass circumcision at God's command, thereby creating a new landmark known, appropriately enough, as the Hill of Foreskins (Josh. 5:2-6)!

Some Bible critics argue that the sanctity of circumcision is a rela- tively late addition to the biblical text, one that reflects the special con- cerns of the priests and scribes who assembled and edited the Bible sometime after the end of the Babylonian Exile. By the fifth century B.C.E. and after, some scholars suggest, circumcision may have fallen out of favor among the other peoples of Canaan, and so the ritual took on new importance in distinguishing the Israelites from the seductive pagan-worshippers whom the priests feared so much.[25] Indeed, one scholar proposes that the story of the Bridegroom of Blood was "rescued from oblivion" and inserted into the Book of Exodus at a late date pre- cisely because the text appears to be so ancient and thus so authentic; the biblical redactor may have believed that the "new-fangled Priestly notion" of circumcision as a ritual of supreme importance would be given "an aura of antiquity" by an incident that appeared to come from the distant past.[26]

But it is not enough to conclude that circumcision is the alpha and the omega of the Bridegroom of Blood. Even if the story is an ancient fragment that was inserted belatedly into the Bible by a scribe with a hidden agenda, the fragment itself may preserve a tradition that predates—and explains—the ritual of circumcision. Surely something more is needed to explain what is really at stake in the *mano a mano* between Zipporah and the Almighty. As Zipporah seems to understand, and as the biblical authors may be trying to conceal, even the God of Abraham appears to demand the flesh and blood of his Chosen People, and anyone who dares to deny him is at risk of his life.

THE CULT OF THE GODDESS-RESCUER

The text of Exodus 4:24–26 is a kind of Freudian slip by the biblical author that allows the cosmic id to assert itself against a censorious celestial superego. Thus, what we find in these three lines may be a distorted remnant of long-lost and long-forbidden traditions about God— or the gods—once embraced by the Israelites or their brethren. Once liberated from the literal meaning of the biblical text, as we shall see, the conjectures and imaginings of biblical exegetes begin to resemble something out of a fever dream, if not the writings of the Marquis de Sade.

The night attack has been so alarming to sages and scholars, even in our own day, that every effort has been made to blame the divine assault and its bloody consequences on some deity other than the one we know as Yahweh. Some sources suggest that the story itself was borrowed from the Midianites, a Bedouin-like tribe of desert-dwellers who were contemporaries of the Israelites, and then transplanted into the Bible at some later date. Others suggest that Zipporah's encounter with God is patterned after an incident that first appeared in the myths and legends of ancient Egypt or Mesopotamia. We are invited to imagine that the deity who attacks Moses is not *really* Yahweh, the God of Abraham, Isaac, and Jacob, but rather some vengeful Midianite demon, and that the woman who rescues Moses is not Zipporah but an incarnation of the

Egyptian goddess Isis. These pagan images were painted out of the scene, it has been suggested, and painted over with the names and images of Yahweh and Zipporah by the biblical writers who gave us the biography of Moses as it appears in the Book of Exodus.

For example, an intriguing clue to the secret meaning of the Bridegroom of Blood is found in the ruins of a third-century synagogue at Dura-Europos in what is now Syria. Archaeologists who excavated the synagogue in the 1930s came upon a mural that depicts the familiar Sunday school story of Moses among the bulrushes—but the ancient muralist included a detail that the author of Exodus omits. A naked goddess, wearing only a golden pendant around her neck and attended by three demigoddesses, is watching over baby Moses.[27] Some Bible scholars are encouraged by such intriguing evidence to suggest that Zipporah may be a stand-in for a goddess-rescuer who appeared in some long-lost folktale but was written out of the story by the priests and scribes who could not tolerate the presence of a pagan goddess in Holy Scripture—and especially not a goddess who confronts and prevails over the Almighty.

The Bible confirms the provocative but mostly overlooked fact that Moses depends on women, again and again, to preserve his life against various deadly perils, human and divine. We tend to think of Moses as a potent figure, a prophet who is privileged to encounter God face to face because he is so nearly godlike himself. Yet an attentive reading of the Bible reveals that Moses is a flawed prophet, a man who cycles between assertion and passivity, strength and frailty, courage and fear, good cheer and deep depression. Above all, he is a man who survives long enough to play the divinely appointed role of liberator and lawgiver only because of the heroic efforts of what one mythologist called "the shadowy women who surround [him]."[28]

As an infant, Moses is spared from Pharaoh's death sentence on the firstborn of the Israelites by two courageous midwives who refuse to carry out Pharaoh's decree (Exod. 1:15–17). Moses' mother fashions an ark out of bulrushes and sets him adrift in the river, thus saving his life while appearing to comply with Pharaoh's order that all male infants of the Israelites be "cast into the river" (Exod. 1:22, 2:3). His sister watches over the boat from afar to make sure that he is rescued (Exod. 2:4), and it is Pharaoh's daughter who draws him out of the river and raises him as her adopted son (Exod. 2:5–6). Then the "shadowy women" join in an unspoken but fateful conspiracy when his sister con-trives to secure a job for their mother as a wet-nurse in the household of the Egyptian princess so that Moses' authentic Jewish mother will be able to suckle him as he grows up in the court of Pharaoh (Exod. 2:7–9).

The pantheon of the ancient Near East and the classical world is filled with goddesses who, like the women in the life of Moses, inter-vene on behalf of imperiled heroes; they range from Ishtar, the Mesopotamian goddess who was imagined to take each reigning king of Babylon as her bridegroom, to Athena and her celebrated efforts on behalf of Odysseus.[29] Perhaps Zipporah, who steps between God and Moses at the moment of greatest danger, was patterned after one of these pagan goddesses by a Bible-era storyteller who knew a good yarn when he (or she) saw one. In fact, the life of Moses—and especially the tale of the Bridegroom of Blood—suggests a specific linkage to one pagan goddess-rescuer in particular, the deity of ancient Egypt known as Isis.

Isis achieved a kind of superstar status in the ancient world, and both her exploits and her image were copied in one form or another by cultures far beyond Egypt. She came to be seen as a kind of universal divine matriarch. "Mother of the Gods," "mother of all living," and "all-mother" are some of the names applied to Isis, and the influence of Isis-worship has been traced as far as the *mater ecclesia,* "Mother of the Church," a mystical doctrine of the early Christian church that is "rooted in Syrian soil." Indeed, ancient Syria was fertile soil for goddess worship, and the protectress who watches over Moses in the murals at Dura-Europos reminds us of Isis.

Isis found acolytes and worshippers in the nearby land of Canaan[30]—a fact that encourages some Bible critics to detect the traces of Isis in the sacred texts of the Israelites who lived there. Several of the crucial events in the life of Moses as told in the Hebrew Bible, and especially the baffling tale of the Bridegroom of Blood, can be understood as faint echoes of the cult of Isis as it was celebrated not only in Egyptian mythology but throughout the ancient Near East.

According to Egyptian lore, Isis is the wife and sister of the divine ruler Osiris, who is treacherously slain by his jealous brother, Seth. In one version of the Isis myth, Seth tricks Osiris into lying down inside a wooden chest, then seals the chest and casts it into the Nile—an image that evokes the baby Moses afloat in his little boat of reeds. The heartbroken Isis searches tirelessly for the chest containing the remains of her dead brother-husband-lover, but when she finds it at last, Seth manages to dismember the body and scatter the pieces. Isis tracks down the remains of Osiris and finds all but one crucial body part—his penis.

Now Isis engages in a magic ritual that is as thoroughly and weirdly erotic as the one Zipporah uses to stave off the night attack by the Almighty. Isis reassembles the pieces of her dead lover, using a wooden likeness of a male sexual organ in place of the missing one, and breathes life back into Osiris by waving her wings over the reassembled corpse. Then she engages in sexual intercourse with Osiris and succeeds in impregnating herself with a son who will be called Horus. By the traditions of ancient Egypt, the reigning pharaoh was seen as an incarnation of Horus, his immediate predecessor on the throne as Osiris, and both his mother and his wife were seen as Isis.[31] "His sister was his guard," goes an ancient ode to Isis and Osiris, and the ode continues with words that could be used to describe Zipporah and the night attack at the lodging place:

> She who drives off the foes,
> Who stops the deeds of the disturber
> By the power of her mighty utterance.[32]

The decisive clue to the linkages between Isis and Zipporah, according to feminist Bible critic Ilana Pardes, is the fact that Isis is a winged goddess who is often depicted in Egyptian hieroglyphics as a hawk or a kite hovering over the sexual organ of the dead body of Osiris. "We have here a violent persecutor, a wife saving her husband, a penis undergoing treatment . . . and above all, wings!" argues Pardes. "Zipporah means 'bird' in Hebrew, and I venture to suggest that this name discloses her affiliation with Isis."[33]

To see the traces of Isis or some other goddess-rescuer in the depiction of Zipporah in the Bridegroom of Blood is doubly surprising because the biblical authors are plainly ill at ease at the notion of any woman—even a kosher Israelite woman!—encountering and confronting the Almighty. The Bible depicts the matriarch Sarah laughing out loud when she overhears God's promise to Abraham that she will bear a child in old age. God pauses to scold her for her lack of decorum, but insists on making all of his deals directly with Abraham

(Gen. 18:12–15). Later, after Moses has led the Israelites out of Egypt, his sister and brother audaciously claim the right to prophesy just like their kid brother—"Hath the Lord indeed spoken only with Moses?" complain Miriam and Aaron, "hath he not spoken also with us?"—and God promptly punishes Miriam (although not Aaron!) for her impudence by afflicting her with a vile disease: "[B]ehold, Miriam was leprous, as white as snow"* (Num. 12:2, 10). But Zipporah, unlike Miriam but very much like Isis, is unafraid and unbowed when the Almighty goes on the attack, and like Isis she saves the life of her husband and son in the very teeth of divine rage and blood lust.

Only the most daring of Bible critics argue that the figure of Zipporah in the Hebrew Bible was somehow inspired by an Egyptian goddess, but no open-eyed reader will fail to notice that *something* strange is happening in the cracks and corners of the biblical text. Perhaps the Bridegroom of Blood is, as Pardes insists, an intriguing remnant of "a repressed pagan past" that surfaces in the biblical text despite the best efforts of the priestly censors to conceal it from our eyes.[34] Certainly the incident at the lodging place calls into question some of our most familiar and cherished assumptions about God and how he was worshipped by his Chosen People. "We do not know what the faith of the Patriarchs was," Harold Bloom points out in *The Book of J* after musing over the Bridegroom of Blood, "or what Moses believed."[35] The text prompts so many provocative but unanswered questions that we begin to wonder if we really know who the deity called Yahweh is, what he is capable of doing, or what he wants from us.

THE BLOOD OF A VIRGIN BRIDE

By far the most lurid interpretation of the Bridegroom of Blood—and, in fact, the single most grotesque reading of *any* biblical text by an otherwise sober Bible scholar—is one that claims to discern a distorted

---

*Miriam and Aaron also "spoke against Moses because of the Cushite woman whom he had married" (Num. 12:1). The Book of Exodus makes it clear that Moses marries a Midianite woman named Zipporah, but the Book of Numbers suggests that he also has a Cushite (that is, Ethiopian) wife. One rabbinical tradition suggests that Moses traveled to Ethiopia before he showed up at Jethro's house in Midian and was already married to a "woman of color" when he met Zipporah.

version of a long-lost tradition among the nomadic tribes of the ancient Near East, a divine droit du seigneur by which the deity enjoys the right to deflower a virgin bride on her wedding night. According to a turn-of-the-century Protestant theologian named Hugo Gressmann, the night attack described in Exodus 4:24–26 actually takes place on the wedding night of Moses and Zipporah. God seeks to kill Moses, Gressmann proposed, to prevent him from sleeping with Zipporah before the Almighty avails himself of his right to her virginal blood. So the resourceful and intrepid Zipporah works an elaborate deception on God: she hastily circumcises her husband with a handy flint stone, and she uses his bloody foreskin to smear blood on the sexual organ of the divine attacker.

"[God's genitals] became smeared with blood, quite as if he had just had intercourse with her, and his organ had thereby become covered with her virginal blood," suggested the good professor, bringing a touch of Grand Guignol to the churchly art of biblical exegesis. "And when the gullible deity perceived this, he believed that he had received his due, and so he withdrew and left Moses in peace."[36]

To conjure up such a remarkable scene, of course, Gressmann was forced to overlook the facts that are strongly implied or plainly reported in the biblical text itself: Moses and Zipporah are already married, according to the Bible, and their newborn son is with them at the lodging place. Still, on the strength of their own inventive reading of Exodus 4:24–26—if not much else—Gressmann and his successors in the world of biblical scholarship[37] argued that circumcision of bridegrooms evolved as a ritual substitute for the offering of the bride's virginity to the Almighty: "Surely a bridegroom of blood art thou to me" was supposedly a magical incantation addressed to God by every bride by way of her newly circumcised groom on their wedding night.

In fact, another testosterone-charged turn-of-the-century Bible scholar read the same mysterious text and reached an even more prurient conclusion of his own. "[I]t was customary among the ancient Semites for maidens to offer their virginity to the first passing stranger who to them seemed to be the embodiment of the god," suggested one of Gressmann's contemporaries, "and thus received his due of the virginal blood," a custom that he claimed to discern in the biblical accounts of the encounters of Jacob, Judah, and Moses with "strange maidens" whom they will ultimately take to bed, whether as wives or lovers.[38]

Gressmann did not go so far as to suggest that the Israelite god we know by the name Yahweh was actually the would-be rapist of Zipporah. Rather, he theorized that Exodus 4:24–26 preserves a tale first told by the Midianites about one of their own deities or demons and later transplanted into the Hebrew Bible by some rather daring scribe who changed the names (and many of the crucial details) to protect the not-so-innocent. But there is no real evidence, scriptural or otherwise, to justify the febrile conjectures of Gressmann and his colleagues about the sexual demands of "the god or demon or whoever conceals himself behind the letters JHWH," as one skeptical scholar put it, and their work has been dismissed by more recent (and more restrained) Bible critics as "phantastic, not to say ridiculous." The notion that the Almighty was so addled by his own sexual impulses that he could be fooled into thinking that he had just slept with Zipporah simply because his genitals were covered with blood strikes some readers as disgusting or downright blasphemous—and others as merely imbecilic.

"He must be a very silly god who can be cheated so easily," wrote contemporary Bible scholar Hans Kosmala. "Some logicality must be ascribed even to demons."[39]

Still, the heavy-breathing and hot-eyed theologians of the last century were hardly the only ones to let their imaginations run wild while reading Exodus 4:24–26, nor were they the only ones to detect primitive and even pagan traditions buried deep inside the biblical text. Beneath the surface of the biblical text, we begin to make out the features of the shadowy figure that Zipporah faces off against on that terrible night at the lodging place, and what we see is a fearsome deity who demands not merely faith, obedience, and good works from his worshippers but the sacrifice of human flesh and blood: "[A]n uncanny, bloodthirsty demon who walks by night and shuns the light of day," argued Sigmund Freud.[40]

We see, too, a tantalizing suggestion of the real meaning of the blood ritual that Zipporah conducts in her remarkable encounter with the Almighty. Perhaps, as we shall see, something is being feigned on that night, but it is something even more disturbing than sexual intercourse between God and Zipporah.

FIRSTLINGS

Another symbolic meaning, even more primal and authentic, can be detected in the rite of circumcision performed by Zipporah to stave off God's attack, one that enables us to decode an even more shocking revelation in the otherwise baffling text of Exodus 4:24–26. For Zipporah, as for the peoples of the ancient Near East, circumcision is a kind of child sacrifice in miniature, a way of offering human flesh and human blood to appease the deity without actually taking the life of a loved one.

The Bible depicts the sacrifice of living creatures as the central and crucial feature of worship among the Israelites, but they were hardly the first people to regard sacrifice as an essential rite. Indeed, the sacrifice of plants, animals, and human beings to the gods appears to be a spontaneous and universal impulse in humankind. Among so-called primitive peoples, around the world and in every age, the bounty of nature and life itself were seen as the handiwork of the gods, something that belonged to them by right. Unless the creator was appeased in some manner, the living things that he or she had created were "taboo"—that is, forbidden to ordinary human beings. Sacrifice, then, originated as a kind of bargain with the gods, an offering of the first fruits of the harvest, the "firstlings" of the herds and flocks, even a firstborn child, so that the rest of the bounty of life could safely be used and consumed by mere mortals.

We see exactly the same impulse at work in the opening pages of the Bible, where Cain and Abel, the sons of Adam and Eve, are inspired to make "an offering unto the Lord" in the form of fruit from Cain's harvest and a sheep from Abel's flock. Their spontaneous ritual of sacrifice is "the very first recorded act of worship,"[41] and—rather ominously—God appears to prefer flesh (Gen. 4:3–5). His appetite whetted, God later makes a formal claim on the firstlings of the Chosen People. "Sanctify unto Me all the first-born," God commands the Israelites in the Book of Exodus, "whatsoever openeth the womb among the children of Israel, both of man and of beast, it is Mine" (Exod. 13:2).

Since children, no less than crops and livestock, were regarded as a gift of the gods, they were not exempt from sacrifice, at least in principle, in various places around the world and throughout history. In fact, even though human sacrifice is condemned in the Holy Scriptures as an "abomination," the Bible reports that children were the victims of ritual sacrifice in and around Canaan until relatively late in biblical history. "[E]ven their sons and their daughters do they burn in the fire to their gods," says the biblical author known as the Deuteronomist about the Canaanites (Deut. 12:31). The biblical authors concede that some Israelites dared to engage in child sacrifice and other "enchantments" under the influence of their pagan neighbors in Canaan (2 Kings 17). At least two of the kings of Judah are said to have made their sons "pass through the fire, according to the abominations of heathen" (2 Kings 16:3, 21:6), and the biblical chronicler specifically blames the conquest and destruction of the northern kingdom of Israel on the persistence of child sacrifice among the Israelites: "And the Lord rejected all the seed of Israel, and afflicted them, and delivered them into the hands of spoilers" (2 Kings 17:20). The Bible seems to find corroboration in recent archaeological evidence that "human sacrifice was more in vogue [in Canaan] than elsewhere" in the ancient Near East.[42]

In fact, the Bible appears to concede that human sacrifice, even if "abominable," is still effective. When the king of Moab finds his walled city under siege by the armies of Israel, as recorded in Second Kings, he resorts to the desperate measure of sacrificing his eldest son "for a burnt offering" to the Moabite god called Chemosh on a parapet where the Israelites will be able to see the ritual. What happens next is rather puzzling, perhaps intentionally so: "And there came great wrath upon Israel, and they departed from him, and returned to their own land" (2 Kings 3:27). The traditional interpretation is that the pious Israelites were so sickened by the sight of human sacrifice that they withdrew in disgust, but literary scholar Northrop Frye ventured another reading: "The last sentence reads like a somewhat clumsy editorial effort," he urged, "to conceal the fact that in the original story the maneuver worked and the Israelites were in fact driven off."[43]

Still, the Israelites, like other peoples of the ancient world, came up with some ingenious ways to please a demanding god with a hunger for firstlings. God's command to "sanctify" the firstborn as announced in Exodus, for example, was understood to mean only that a firstborn son must be dedicated to the priesthood, and a child could be redeemed from temple service by paying a bounty to the priests. More primitive peoples came up with cruder compromises: the hair of a newborn might be cut and burned on the sacrificial altar instead of the child himself.[44] Such rituals of surrogate sacrifice were so prevalent in ancient and primitive cultures that some historians question whether human sacrifice was *ever* a common practice in the ancient Near East. In any case, it appears that animals had mostly replaced human beings as sacrificial offerings by the time of the biblical patriarchs.[45]

But the most ingenious compromise between bloodthirsty gods and the ancient clans and tribes who worshipped them was one that permitted fathers and mothers to engage in the ritual of cutting human flesh and shedding human blood as an offering to the gods without actually taking the life of the sacrificial victim. Circumcision, an act of human sacrifice in miniature, probably replaced the actual sacrifice of children in many cultures around the world at some distant and unknowable point in human history. "Here, quite manifestly," concludes one Bible scholar with a distinctly anthropological bent of mind, "we have the origin of the rite of circumcision."[46]

The notion of circumcision as a surrogate for child sacrifice begins to explain even the most bizarre and baffling details of Exodus 4:24–26. An angry and vengeful Yahweh seeks to kill the father of a firstborn son—or perhaps the child himself—because Yahweh has been denied the offering of flesh and blood to which he is entitled by divine decree. When Zipporah cuts off the foreskin of her son, her firstling, she is safely mimicking the sacrifice of the child himself—she is "sanctifying" the baby who "opened the womb of Israel" precisely as God had commanded. Only through the mock sacrifice in the form of a circumcision is God appeased, and only then does he break off his attack.

Even the most grotesque aspect of the ritual that Zipporah performs—touching the "legs" (or, more likely, the genitals) of God, Moses, or Gershom with the bloody foreskin—makes sense only if we regard the circumcision of her son as a blood sacrifice. The smearing of blood is a dramatic and effective way of demonstrating that the sacrifice of a living creature has taken place. The Bible specifically instructs the Israelite priests who carry out the ritual sacrifice of animals to make a big show of dipping their fingers into the blood of the slaughtered beast and splashing it around the altar (Lev. 3:8). In fact God himself specifies that the anointing of body parts with sacrificial blood is to be the climax of the ceremony by which Aaron, the brother of Moses, and his sons are later consecrated as high priests of the Israelites:

"Then shalt thou kill the ram, and take of its blood, and put it upon the tip of the right ear of Aaron, and upon the tip of the right ear of his sons, and upon the thumb of their right hand, and upon the great toe of their right foot, and dash the blood against the altar round about" (Exod. 29:20).

Zipporah, daughter of a priest and wife of a prophet, is clearly a priestess and a prophetess in her own right. She appears to understand that Yahweh is angry because her Israelite husband has neglected the commandment of his own faith that his firstborn son must be "sanctified" unto the Almighty. She seems to know that God will be appeased only if the sacrificial knife touches human flesh and draws human blood. And so Zipporah uses the only tool at hand—a crude flint knife or perhaps just a flint stone—to circumcise her newborn son. To make sure that God sees what she has done, she uses the newly cut foreskin to anoint her husband's or her son's body (if not God's!) with blood, just as the priests of Yahweh will later be instructed to do by the Almighty himself. God sees what Zipporah has done—and God is pleased.

"I WILL SLAY THY SON"

The notion that God might demand the sacrifice of a child, even in a surrogate form, seems to contradict the fundamental teachings of the Hebrew Bible, which repeatedly and explicitly condemns the practice of human sacrifice by the Canaanites and the occasional renegade Israelite who falls under their evil influence. The prophet Jeremiah reports that God is angered and repulsed by the spilling of "the blood of innocents" in sacrifice to the Canaanite god known as Baal—a form of worship "which I commanded not, nor spoke it, neither came it into My mind" (Jer. 19:4–5). The prophet Micah ponders the question of child sacrifice—"Shall I give my firstborn for my transgression, the fruit of my body for the sin of my soul?"—and his answer to the rhetorical question sums up the credo that we have come to regard as the essential teaching of the Judeo-Christian tradition:

It hath been told thee, O man, what is good,
And what the Lord doth require of thee:

Only to do justly, and to love mercy,
and to walk humbly with thy God (Mic. 6:7–8).

Yet, long before Jeremiah and Micah, long before the tale of the Bridegroom of Blood, the Bible records an incident even more horrific than the night attack on Moses—an incident in which child sacrifice is precisely what God seeks of his Chosen People, and under the most appalling circumstances.

According to the Book of Genesis, God promises Abraham and Sarah that a son will be born to them in their extreme old age. "And I will bless [Sarah]," God says, "and moreover I will give thee a son of her" (Gen. 17:15), and he delivers on his promise by causing ninety-year-old Sarah to conceive and give birth to Isaac. Then, in a moment of divine perversity that has shocked Bible readers over the last couple of millennia, God abruptly orders Abraham to sacrifice young Isaac on an altar of fire. "Take now thy son, thine only son, whom thou lovest, even Isaac," says God, as if to taunt Abraham with the full horror of what he is demanding, "and offer him . . . for a burnt-offering . . ." (Gen. 22:2).

Perhaps even more perversely, Abraham complies with the divine command to sacrifice his own son without a single word of protest. Abraham, we should not forget, is the same man who has boldly confronted God over his plan to destroy the vile and despicable Sodomites, the man who has haggled at length with the Almighty to spare the ten righteous ones who might be killed along with the sinners. But when it comes to the life of his own son, Abraham falls silent. Meekly and wordlessly, Abraham sets off toward the killing ground with his sweetly befuddled son in tow. "Behold the fire and the wood," asks the unsuspecting Isaac, and his words tug at the heartstrings of any flesh-and-blood father, "but where is the lamb for a burnt-offering?" (Gen. 22:7). Only at the very last possible moment—when Isaac is bound on the altar, the wood for the sacrificial fire is laid beneath him, and Abraham holds the slaughtering knife over his son's throat—does God call the whole thing off.

"Lay not thy hand upon the lad," says "an angel of the Lord" just in the nick of time, "for now I know that thou art a God-fearing man, seeing that thou hast not withheld thy son, thine only son, from Me" (Gen. 22:12).

The more apologetic theologians have struggled to explain away the Binding of Isaac, as the passage is known in Jewish tradition, as a test of faith by a compassionate and merciful God who never really intended to permit the sacrifice of a child at the hands of his own father. God is praised by some apologists for miraculously providing a ram to replace Isaac on the altar at the last moment. "The story," they insist, "opens the age-long warfare of Israel against the abominations of child sacrifice."[47] The terror visited upon Abraham, Sarah, and Isaac by the Almighty during the ordeal—and the prospect of what would have happened to Isaac if his father had *failed* the "test of faith" by refusing to slay his son—is mostly ignored in the more pious readings of the Binding of Isaac.

But the pious readings are neither convincing nor reassuring. What kind of sadist, we might ask, would miraculously bestow a child on a yearnful old couple, then demand that the child be slaughtered by his own father—and wait until the blade is about to draw blood before saying, as it were, "Just kidding"? And what kind of father would be willing to challenge the Almighty with great passion and audacity in defense of Sodom and Gomorrah, the twin cities of evil and perversion, but remain silent and compliant when instructed to cut the throat and burn the body of his own innocent son? The Binding of Isaac, so heartrending and so perplexing, readily explains why one of the many names by which God is called in the Bible is "the Fear of Isaac" (Gen. 31:42).

"The whole of Jewish history might have turned out differently," a young rabbi once told me, "if Abraham had just said 'No.'"

The most troubling detail in the Binding of Isaac is often overlooked. God spares Isaac, but nowhere does the Almighty come out and say that human sacrifice is wrong or even that it is unnecessary. By his abject compliance with God's bloodthirsty demand, Abraham neatly extricates himself from the Catch-22 in which God has placed him: precisely because Abraham is willing to slaughter his son, he is not called upon to actually do it. But God does not rule out the possibility that he might ask the same thing again of Abraham—or someone else. According to Islamic tradition, the beast that God provides to Abraham as a replacement for Isaac is the very same ram that Abel offered up in the first recorded ritual of sacrifice[48]—and so we are reminded that God seems to savor flesh and blood.

"We cannot evade the fact that the core of the narrative actually seems to assume the possibility that God would demand human sacrifice," Nahum Sarna, a distinguished commentator on Genesis, has written with uncommon candor. "God does not denounce human sacrifice as such."[49]

God's troubling indifference toward child sacrifice in the Binding of Isaac sheds an ominous light on the events of Exodus, including not only the night attack on Moses but the whole plan of liberation that God confides to Moses at their very first encounter. God tells Moses that nine of the ten plagues that he intends to send down on Egypt— frogs, vermin, boils, and so on—will not be enough to convince Pharaoh that he must let the Israelites go. Remarkably, God reveals that Pharaoh will defy the first nine plagues not because these "signs and wonders" are too puny to frighten him but rather because God himself will "harden his heart" (Exod. 4:21)! Thanks to God's rather mischievous meddling with Pharaoh's mind and heart, a tenth plague will be needed to break the will of the Egyptian monarch:

> "And thou shalt say unto Pharaoh: Thus saith the Lord: Israel is
> My son, My first-born. And I have said unto thee: Let My son
> go, that he may serve Me; and thou hast refused to let him go.
> Behold, I will slay thy son, thy first-born" (Exod. 4:22–23).

The fact that *two* firstlings are mentioned in God's threat to Pharaoh—the firstborn of the Lord and the firstborn of Egypt—provides an intriguing clue to the night attack on Moses at the lodging place, which takes place *before* the tenth plague is visited upon Egypt. "The destroyer who will strike the first born of Egypt is already on his way," one Bible critic has proposed by way of explaining the night attack at the lodging place, "and he is endangering the first born son of Moses himself!"[50] In other words, God is sometimes so impulsive in his moments of rage, so wild and unpredictable, that he is capable of striking anyone who gets in his way; once God starts killing, he cannot stop. The same horrific notion can be found in the Talmud itself: "[O]nce the destroyer has been given permission to destroy," the rabbis warn, "he no longer distinguishes between the righteous and wicked."[51]

Even though he survives the night attack at the lodging place, Moses (along with the rest of the Israelites) finds himself at risk of death once again on the fateful night when God descends on Egypt to carry out the tenth and final plague, the slaying of the firstborn of Egypt. At midnight, the Bible tells us, God himself (and *not* an angel of death, as advertised in sermons and Sunday school stories) rampages through Egypt and slays every firstborn child, "from the first-born of Pharaoh that sitteth upon his throne, even unto the first-born of the maid-servant that is behind the mill" (Exod. 11:5). Yet God seems to know himself well enough to realize that he is not likely to distinguish between the Egyptians and the Chosen People once he has begun to kill. So the Almighty decrees that a lamb must be sacrificed by every Israelite household at dusk, and its blood must be smeared on the doorposts and lintels of every Israelite house, as a sign to him: "[A]nd when I see the blood," God agrees, "I will pass over you, and there shall no plague be upon you to destroy you, when I smite the land of Egypt" (Exod. 12:13).

So the night attack at the lodging place seems to prefigure the midnight plague on the firstborn of Egypt, and the bloody foreskin that Zipporah uses to stave off the divine assault on Moses is seen again in the lamb's blood that is smeared on the lintels of the Israelite houses in Egypt.* Intriguingly, the Midrash suggests a direct link between the rite of circumcision and the blood ritual that stays the hand of God when he seeks to kill: "two bloods" were used to mark the doorposts of the Israelites, the Midrash suggests, the blood of the sacrificial lamb and the blood of circumcision. "[A]nd when the Holy One passed over to plague the Egyptians, He saw the blood of the circumcision-covenant on the lintels of their houses mingle with the blood of the paschal lamb, and He was filled with compassion for Israel."[52]

The rabbis, as we have already noted, preserved one pious fairy tale in which it was Satan rather than the Almighty who stalked and sought to kill Moses at the lodging place, a convenient if implausible way of shifting the culpability for the night attack from God to the same dark angel on whom Jews and Christians have long heaped the blame for the

---

*These are not the only episodes in the Bible in which God attacks one of his Chosen People by night. God manifests himself as man or angel and sets upon Jacob on the night before Jacob's encounter with his estranged brother, Esau. God and Jacob struggle with each other all night long, and God wounds "the hollow of Jacob's thigh," which we might understand to mean his groin or even his genitals. But Jacob prevails and extracts a blessing from the Almighty (Gen. 32:25–30).

evil that we do to each other. How else to explain what one scholar characterizes as God's "un-Israelite behavior" at the lodging place?[53] But Satan—who does not appear in the Bible until the Book of Job, and even then only as a friendly servitor of God—was falsely accused. Despite the long and ardent efforts of pious censors, the Bible plainly states that God himself, not Satan or even an angelic destroyer, is capable of killing even the innocent and faithful among humankind.

"The early stage of Israelite religion knows no Satan," wrote Martin Buber, one of the towering moral philosophers of the twentieth century, in his musings on Exodus 4:24–26. "[I]f a power attacks a man and threatens him, it is proper to recognize YHVH in it or behind it, no matter how nocturnally dread and cruel it may be. . . ."[54]

And then Buber added one more crucial observation: ". . . *and it is proper to withstand Him*. . . ."[55]

Here we find what may be the real and urgent lesson of the Bridegroom of Blood: Zipporah stood up to God and faced him off and thereby saved the life of her husband and her child. Moses and his son are fortunate indeed that she did not follow Abraham's example of silence and compliance; as we shall soon see, God does not *always* intervene to prevent a child sacrifice, even when he is given plenty of opportunity to do so. So the exploits of Zipporah in the face of divine wrath, so troubling and so mysterious, allow us to glimpse the innermost meaning of Exodus 4:24–26: Perhaps it is Abraham who failed the test of faith after all, and Zipporah who passed it.

CHAPTER TEN

JEPHTHAH AND HIS DAUGHTER

"The Lord shall be witness between us; surely according to thy word so will we do."

—JUDGES 11:10

T he young woman put aside her needle and glanced at her father as he worked a sharpening stone up and down the length of his battle sword and then tested the sharpness of the blade with a thickly calloused thumb.

She had seen her father at the same work many times before— honing the blade of his long sword, oiling his leathern scabbard and leather-bound wooden shield, sharpening a spearhead and fitting it to a freshly cut length of oak. As she grew up, she came to understand that the sight of the long sword signaled the fact that her father had hired himself out yet again as mercenary in the service of some wealthy lord who was willing to pay a price to rid himself of bandits or nomads or soldiers of fortune who fought for some rival chieftain. Weeks or even months would pass before her father returned with the coins and the occasional booty that provided a livelihood for the two of them.

If, that is, he returned at all. At least a few of the men who served with her father would be left behind in a shallow grave somewhere in the distant lands where they went to fight—one or two if the fighting went well, many more if it went badly. So far, her father had been spared such a fate, but she realized that God might not always watch over him with such care.

Now the young woman turned back to her own handiwork, deftly working the needle along the collar piece of a long blue gown and leaving behind a pattern of entwined doves and branches in white thread. But she continued to ponder what her father had told her about the campaign on which he would embark at first light. This time he would fight as a general rather than a mercenary, and he would lead an army of his own—the army of Israel—into battle against the king of Ammon.

"As God is my judge," he had told his daughter in a voice that sang out in pride, "if I return at all, I will return as a chieftain—and you will live out your life as befits the daughter of a chieftain."

The man's name was Jephthah, and the young woman is remembered as Seila. She was still young, but not too young to understand what burned in her father's heart as he told her of the battle to come—the bitter hurt, the anger and defiance, the banked embers of vengeance that were ready to burst into flames. Seila had been raised by her father in that little house in the dusty border town of Mizpah, and the memories he shared with her were almost like fairy tales, except that they were peopled with his own flesh and blood.

Jephthah's father had been a rich and powerful lord with a grand house in the district of Gilead. But Jephthah never knew his mother. He saw her only once from a distance as the great man's entourage passed through the poorer streets of Gilead one fresh morning. Jephthah's father pointed out the gaunt woman with greasy hair and a gaudily painted face who stood lazily at a crossroads, calling out now and then to passersby. Jephthah was too far away to make out her

> *Now Jephthah the Gileadite was a mighty man of valour, and he was the son of a harlot; and Gilead begot Jephthah.*
>
> —JUDGES 11:1

features or the words that she spoke. But his father's voice was clear enough: "That pitiful wretch is your mother," said Jephthah's father. "So count yourself lucky that you ended up in my house and not hers."

But Seila knew that her father did not count himself lucky at all. His father had a wife, a plump and proper woman from a highborn family, who had given him an assortment of sleek young sons. As Jephthah grew older, his father was content to let his stepmother take charge of him along with the rest of the children—and she saw no good reason to keep Jephthah around the house when the very sight of him disgusted her. She contrived to move him to a room in one of the outbuildings where the stable hands and the house servants bedded down; she made sure that he was otherwise occupied when guests arrived for a banquet; she dressed him in plain clothes even as she ordered up richly embroidered garb for her own sons; she found tasks that took him away from the estate at mealtimes. If Jephthah's father noticed how his wife had banished his firstborn son, he said nothing; if he cared one way or the other, he gave no sign of it.

By the time he was sixteen, Jephthah had learned to content himself with the companionship of the stable boys, who taught him skills that would turn out to be useful and even profitable for a young man who grew up poor in a rich man's household. Once Jephthah learned to ride a horse, to fashion a weapon out of iron, to wield his weapon in a fight, he no longer cast yearnful glances at his father, no longer spoke sweetly to his stepmother in the vain hope that she would regard him as a son rather than a bastard. Then, one day, he rode into the courtyard of the great house and saw his half brothers sitting on low stools, their clothing rent and ashes on their head. Jephthah wondered for a moment who had died, and when he realized that it was his father, he was unmoved.

> *And Gilead's wife bore him sons; and when his wife's sons grew up, they drove out Jephthah, and said unto him: "Thou shalt not inherit our father's house; for thou art the son of another woman."*
>
> —JUDGES 11:2

Still, Jephthah understood all too well what his father's death would mean for him. When the thirty days of mourning had passed, Jephthah boldly presented himself at the door of the house and demanded his share of the rich estate his father had left behind. Jephthah was turned away like a whining beggar by his arrogant half brothers, who taunted Jephthah with the fact that *his* mother was not their father's wife. "You will inherit nothing of our father's estate," one of them declared, "because you are the son of that *other* woman."

Afire with anger and indignation, Jephthah took his complaint to the elders of Gilead, who finally agreed to consider the rival claims of the rich man's sons. One day, Jephthah, his half brothers, and the gray-bearded elders of Gilead gathered in the house of the dead man, and Jephthah poured his bile into words of great passion. The elders stroked their beards and nodded their heads and even smiled now and then at Jephthah's plea for justice—the *other* woman's son had a surprising gift for the well-chosen and well-spoken word—and then, as if Jephthah had not spoken at all, the elders of Gilead pronounced judgment wholly in favor of his half brothers and briskly ordered him not to bother them again. Then they rose, bestowed one final patronizing smile on Jephthah, and rushed out of the house as if afraid that the eloquent young man might let his dagger speak for him.

Indeed, one or two of Jephthah's comrades, who were precisely the rough sort that one might imagine to be the friends of a bastard who had been thrown out of his own home, urged Jephthah to pay another visit to his father's house by night. "Slit one of their throats," they said, "and even the fatheads who have taken away your father's legacy will understand your message!" Jephthah briefly considered the proposition but decided that an outlaw was even worse off than a disinherited son. So Jephthah and a few of his cohorts fled from Gilead and made their way to a town on the frontier between Israel and Ammon, a place

> *Then Jephthah fled from his brethren, and dwelt in the land of Tob; and there were gathered vain fellows to Jephthah, and they went out with him.*
>
> —JUDGES 11:3

where a man whose wits were as sharp as his sword might make a living as a soldier of fortune when there were rich men to serve—or a bandit when there were rich men to rob.

Exactly who Jephthah's mother had been—and why she was not his father's wife—was a puzzle to young Seila, one that her father never bothered to explain. Only when Seila was older, after she had been befriended by the young women of Mizpah who became her constant companions during Jephthah's long absences, did she learn the word that described Jephthah's mother, a word that her father never once uttered within her hearing.

"Your grandmother," one of the girls explained, "was a harlot."

So it was that Jephthah came to Mizpah in the land of Tob, and so it was that Seila was born in the little house on the outskirts of town. "My one and only child," Jephthah would say as hot tears welled up in his eyes, "flesh of my flesh, blood of my blood!"

Jephthah raised Seila on his own, and they lived together in a rough-plastered house with a small courtyard where she kept a goat for milk and a few chickens for eggs. Now and then, a woman would appear at the doorway with a bundle of clothing and bedding, a sure sign that Jephthah was ready to pack up his weapons and make off with his cohorts to some distant battlefield. For weeks and sometimes even months, Seila found herself in the not-so-gentle care of a hired nursemaid until the happy day when her father appeared at the threshold with a bag of silver coins that would feed them until the next call to arms. Jephthah was an accomplished and courageous fighter, much in demand in those unsettled days in Canaan, and Seila was consigned so often to so many different women with so many unfamiliar names that she came to recall them as one woman with no name at all.

As she grew up, Seila wondered to herself if one of those nameless women had been her mother. But Jephthah told his daughter nothing about the woman who had given birth to her, always turning away even her most pointed and insistent questions with the same phrase. "It's the two of us against the world," he would say. Seila understood that he intended to comfort her, but he succeeded only in provoking her curiosity. Eventually she stopped asking, but she did not stop wondering about her mother's name, her origins, her whereabouts. Perhaps she had been a harlot, too. Perhaps she had fallen ill and died in childbirth. Perhaps she had run away with one of the battle-scarred old soldiers who could be seen up and down the streets of Mizpah. Yet, no matter how colorful or exotic the stories Seila told herself, her mother always remained nameless, faceless, voiceless, a ghost who haunted a young girl's dreams.

When Seila was old enough to care for herself while her father was away, she ventured beyond the little courtyard of their house, beyond the well in the town square, beyond even the gates on the outskirts of Mizpah. On one of her long walks into the countryside, she found a cleft in the dusty brown hills where a spring bubbled up and an old oak spread its branches. To that hidden place in the hills Seila returned again and again, at first alone and later in the company of one or two young women whom she counted as worthy of knowing her secrets.

Sitting cross-legged beneath the tree, listening to the whispers that seemed to be coming from the highest bough as the wind stirred the leafy canopy, Seila imagined that one day she might look up and see her mother sitting high above her head in the crook of a swaying branch. She imagined the sound of a woman's voice, and she wondered how her own name would sound on her mother's lips.

One day, when Seila was milking the goat in the courtyard, she heard a commotion in the distance, and she peered over the wall of the enclosure to see what was prompting the laughters and catcalls. Shading her eyes from the sun with one hand, she saw a parade of she-asses making their way slowly down the road in a little cloud of dust. Alongside the donkeys ran a few ragged children who whistled and hooted at the riders. At the head of the parade was a soldier on horseback, thoroughly ill at ease and watching the children with real apprehension. Two more soldiers bearing long spears rode at the rear. Between the mounted

---

And it came to pass after a while, that the children of Ammon made war against Israel.

—JUDGES 11:4

---

soldiers rode seven old men perched awkwardly on the she-asses, each man wearing plush robes of a kind not often seen in Mizpah.

To her amazement, the procession drew up directly in front of Jephthah's house, and the old man on the first ass—a gangly fellow with a long, silvery, two-pointed beard—dismounted with an indelicacy that confirmed he was not accustomed to donkey-riding. Seila noticed that his robe had been dragged along in the dust, and the embroidered hem was blackened with dirt. At last, he stood up and addressed Seila without deigning to look at her.

"Is this the house of Jephthah?" he demanded as he peered past Seila and studied the little house beyond the courtyard.

"Yes, my lord."

"Ask the mighty man of valor if he will receive us," the old man instructed. "Tell him the elders of Gilead have come to call on him."

Seila stared at the man for a long moment—she remembered the elders of Gilead and their evil decree—and then she hastened back into the house to summon her father, who was sleeping off a late night of drinking and singing. Jephthah appeared at the doorway, stretched his arms above his head, rubbed his eyes, coughed, and then spat into the dust. When he caught sight of the old man at the gate, he laughed out loud.

"So what brings you all the way to Mizpah, old man?" Jephthah demanded. "Have you changed your mind about the inheritance you and my brothers have stolen from me?"

The elder of Mizpah ignored Jephthah's question and began to

And the children of Israel again did that which was evil in the sight of the Lord, and served the Baalim, and the Ashtaroth . . . and the gods of Moab, and the gods of the children of Ammon . . . ; and they forsook the Lord, and served Him not. And the anger of the Lord was kindled against Israel, and He gave them over into the hand of the Philistines, and into the hand of the children of Ammon. And they oppressed and crushed the children of Israel. . . .

—JUDGES 10:6–8

> *And the children of Israel cried unto the Lord, saying: "We have sinned against Thee, in that we have forsaken our God, and have served the Baalim."*
>
> —JUDGES 10:10

speak in a booming voice, as if he were addressing a multitude instead of just one man. The children of Israel had sinned against the Almighty by worshipping the strange gods of the Canaanites, the old man said, and the Almighty was so angered by their evil ways that he had put it in the mind of the King of Ammon to send an army across the Jordan River to oppress and crush his Chosen People.

"And the children of Israel cried unto the Lord," the old man continued, "saying: 'We have sinned against Thee, we have forsaken our God, and we have served the Baalim.' "

"Yes, yes," Jephthah said dryly. He had already heard about the advance guard of the Ammonites that had crossed the Jordan River to probe the defenses of Canaan. He had already heard of the sorry showing by the ragtag militia of Israelites when they encountered the professional soldiery of the Ammonite king. The old soldiers of Mizpah had laughed among themselves at the militiamen who had broken and run, the rich men who had packed themselves and their finery out of Gilead at the first word of the approaching army. Now the trembling lords and their soundly thrashed army were huddling together in their tents within sight of Mizpah.

"I am sorry that the Ammonites have scared you out of your houses," Jephthah continued, "but what does all this have to do with me?"

The old man frowned briefly at Jephthah and then continued to shout out his grandiloquent words.

"And the Lord said unto the children of Israel: 'Did I not save you from the Egyptians and the Amalekites and the Philistines? Yet ye have forsaken Me and served other gods, and so I will save you no more! Go and cry unto the gods which ye have chosen—let *them* save you in the time of your distress!' "

Seila studied the old man's face, now contorted with anger, and she felt suddenly giddy. If the pious old graybeard who had cheated

And the Lord said unto the children of Israel: "Did not I save you from the Egyptians, and from . . . the children of Ammon, and from the Philistines? The . . . Amalekites . . . did oppress you; and ye cried unto Me, and I saved you out of their hand. Yet ye have forsaken Me, and served other gods; wherefore I will save you no more. Go and cry unto the gods which ye have chosen; let them save you in the time of your distress."

—JUDGES 10:11–14

And the children of Israel said unto the Lord: "We have sinned; do Thou unto us whatsoever seemeth good unto Thee; only deliver us, we pray Thee, this day." And they put away the strange gods from among them, and served the Lord; and His soul was grieved for the misery of Israel.

—JUDGES 10:15–16

Jephthah of his legacy only knew what strange gods were worshipped in Mizpah and its environs, and in what strange ways!

"So the children of Israel put away the strange gods from among them, and served the Lord, and His soul was grieved for the misery of Israel," the old man went on. "And the people said to one another: 'What man is he that will take up the fight against the children of Ammon? *He* shall be our chieftain and *he* shall rule over all of Gilead.' "

Seila noticed a cruel smile play across her father's lips. Now Jephthah understood why they had come to him, but he did not spare them the effort of saying it out loud. After a long moment of awkward silence, the elder of Gilead raised his hands toward heaven in a gesture of prayer and cried out to Jephthah.

"Come and be the general of our army, so that we may fight the children of Ammon!"

Jephthah fixed a stern gaze on the old man, who had suddenly fallen

> *Then the children of Ammon were gathered together, and encamped in Gilead. And the children of Israel assembled themselves together, and encamped in Mizpah. And the people, the princes of Gilead, said one to another: "What man is he that will begin to fight against the children of Ammon? he shall be head over all the inhabitants of Gilead."*
>
> —JUDGES 10:17–18

> *And it was so, that when the children of Ammon made war against Israel, the elders of Gilead went to fetch Jephthah out of the land of Tob. And they said unto Jephthah: "Come and be our chief, that we may fight with the children of Ammon." And Jephthah said unto the elders of Gilead: "Did not ye hate me, and drive me out of my father's house? and why are ye come unto me now when ye are in distress?"*
>
> —JUDGES 11:5–7

silent but who kept his hands in the air. The old man turned awkwardly and looked over his shoulder, as if to plead for assistance from the others, but they said nothing. At last, it was Jephthah who spoke.

Now a second old man stepped forward from the rank of the elders who had watched the first one's performance in obvious discomfort.

"Yes, Jephthah, we are in desperate trouble—all of Israel is in trouble—and that is why we have come to you now," the second one said with both candor and calculation. "We want you to come back to Gilead. We will make you a general, and you will lead our army into battle with the Ammonites. And if you prevail over them in battle, we will make you not only general of our army but chieftain over Gilead. . . ."

The old man paused so that Jephthah would not miss his meaning.

". . . chieftain over all of Gilead," he repeated, "and every man who lives there."

Seila saw that her father did not mistake the meaning of the man's words. A generalship was one inducement, but she had often heard her father say to his comrades that generals who are fortunate enough to prevail in war are quickly forgotten in peace. But a chieftain would rule in war *and* peace, and he would wield his authority over civilians as well as soldiers. Among the cowering civilians of Gilead, of course, were Jephthah's half brothers.

"If you bring me back home to lead your army in battle against the Ammonites," Jephthah said slowly, as if to make sure he would not be misunderstood, "and if the Lord delivers them to me, then—and only then—will I be your chieftain."

The elders clasped their hands, nodded, beamed. The one whose words had won over Jephthah stepped forward and seized his right hand.

"The Lord shall be witness to the words we have spoken to each other," the elder said solemnly. "Surely we will do exactly as you say."

And the elders of Gilead said unto Jephthah: "Therefore are we returned to thee now, that thou mayest go with us, and fight with the children of Ammon, and thou shalt be our head over all the inhabitants of Gilead."

—JUDGES 11:8

And Jephthah said unto the elders of Gilead: "If ye bring me back home to fight with the children of Ammon, and the Lord deliver them before me, I will be your head."

—JUDGES 11:9

And the elders of Gilead said unto Jephthah: "The Lord shall be witness between us; surely according to thy word so will we do."

—JUDGES 11:10

So Seila's father made ready to go to war yet again. By morning, his armor and weapons were loaded atop a single ass, and Jephthah mounted another animal to ride alongside the elders of Gilead toward the encampment on the approaches to Mizpah. Once more he embraced his daughter, holding her perhaps a moment longer than on other partings, and he whispered yet again the words that he had already spoken to Seila several times during the long night: "If I return at all, I will return as a chieftain—and you will live out your life as befits the daughter of a chieftain."

As it turned out, the frightened throngs of Gileadites who camped outside Mizpah made a better bargain with Jephthah than the elders had offered the day before. The richest of the townsfolk, now refugees from their houses and estates back in Gilead, did not wait for Jephthah to meet and defeat the armies of Ammon before acclaiming him both general *and* chieftain, and the elders did not debate the point. Jephthah, after all, was the only man who was willing and able to turn the militia into an army and then, God willing, lead the army to victory over the invaders. Just the sight of Jephthah—strong, self-assured, sturdy, and reassuringly battle-scarred—inspired confidence in the militia *and* the cowering civilians whom they were supposed to defend and avenge.

Jephthah was promptly installed in a pavilion suitable to his new rank—the question of who would take possession of his father's estate in Gilead was left for another day—and his cohorts set to the task of drilling the rank and file of the army of Israel. Day by day, the lines filled out with new recruits. The elders congratulated themselves on their decision to draft Jephthah as commander: he had certainly risen to

> *Then Jephthah went with the elders of Gilead, and the people made him head and chief over them; and Jephthah spoke all his words before the Lord in Mizpah.*
>
> —JUDGES 11:11

> *And Jephthah sent messengers unto the king of the children of Ammon, saying: "What has thou to do with me, that thou art come unto me to fight against my land?" And the king of the children of Ammon answered unto the messengers of Jephthah: "Because Israel took away my land, when he came up out of Egypt, from the Arnon even unto the Jabbok, and unto the Jordan; now therefore restore those cities peaceably."*
>
> —JUDGES 11:12–13

> *And Jephthah sent messengers again unto the king of the children of Ammon; and he said unto him: "Thus saith Jephthah: Israel took not away the land of Moab, nor the land of the children of Ammon."*
>
> —JUDGES 11:14–15

the task, bastard and mercenary though he was, and the soldiers of Israel might actually stand a chance against the professional army of the King of Ammon.

But as the days passed the elders noticed that Jephthah himself did not seem to be in much of a hurry to field his troops against the Ammonites. Instead, the new-minted chieftain summoned scribes to his tent and spent long hours drafting a diplomatic letter that he dispatched by messenger under a flag of truce across enemy lines to the king of Ammon himself. "What have thou to do with *me*, that thou art come unto *me* to fight against my land?" Jephthah wrote to the king of Ammon, turning himself from chieftain to king and the plight of Israel into a matter of personal honor.

To the amazement of the elders, the mighty king and conqueror deigned to write back to Jephthah. "Because Israel took away my land when he came up out of Egypt," the king of Ammon parried. "Now, therefore, restore those cities peaceably."

Jephthah, it seemed, preferred to use words rather than arms—and a great many words at that—to turn back the Ammonite invaders. Much

"Wilt not thou possess that which Chemosh thy god giveth thee to possess? So whomsoever the Lord our God hath dispossessed from before us, them will we possess. . . . I therefore have not sinned against thee, but thou doest me wrong to war against me; the Lord, the Judge, be judge this day between the children of Israel and the children of Ammon." Howbeit the king of the children of Ammon hearkened not unto the words of Jephthah which he sent him.

—JUDGES 11:24, 27–28

ink and parchment were squandered on his long letters, which harked all the way back to the Exodus from Egypt, recited the names and deeds of monarchs long dead, and even invoked the authority of the pagan god of the Ammonites rather than the Almighty.

"Will you not be content to possess the lands that Chemosh thy god gave to you," Jephthah proposed, "and we will possess the lands that the Lord our God has given to us?"

To the elders, the words of Jephthah to the king of Ammon seemed to be a plea rather than a threat, and the enemy king did not bother to reply. Everyone—the elders no less than the king of Ammon—waited to see if Jephthah would actually take up arms and go to war.

As the sun rose over the tents of the Israelites the next day, the soldier who stood the night watch was roughly awakened by Jephthah himself. No longer was Jephthah draped in his chieftain's robes. Instead, he was wearing his poor and battle-pitted leather armor. He had strapped his double-edged sword to his side, and he carried his long spear in his right hand. The sentry cringed slightly, fully expecting a blow or at least a reprimand for sleeping at his post, but Jephthah gave him only a sharp look.

"Take your place in the ranks," Jephthah said curtly to the sentry before moving on, "because today we march."

Even before the drums and trumpets summoned the other soldiers to the drill field, word began to buzz through the encampment: Jephthah

Then the spirit of the Lord came upon Jephthah, and he passed over Gilead and Manasseh, and passed over Mizpeh of Gilead, and from Mizpeh of Gilead he passed over unto the children of Ammon.

—JUDGES 11:29

was ready to fight! The elders of Gilead, hastily gathered on a rise overlooking the drill field, gladdened at the sight of soldiers stepping briskly into line and forming up into long phalanxes that bristled with spear points. Jephthah could be seen moving from column to column, consulting with his lieutenants, calling out by name to this man or that. When he finally joined the elders, they saw not only a new firmness in the set of his jaw but also an unmistakable light shining in his eyes. Suddenly, Jephthah seemed to have run out of words, but a fiery resolve communicated itself even without words. He saluted the elders, signaled to his lieutenants to set the columns of men in motion, and strode off to lead them into battle against the army of the king of Ammon.

"Well, I am relieved to see that Jephthah is no longer content to sit in his tent and write letters to the enemy," said one of the elders. "I wonder what put the will to fight in him at last."

"Surely," one of the others answered, "the spirit of the Lord is upon Jephthah."

Jephthah marched in silence at the head of the army, but his trusted cohorts from Mizpah, following a step or two behind him, were full of chatter.

"We could have used another week of drilling," one of them muttered.

"And another thousand men under arms," said the other. "As it is, we are badly outnumbered—and we are fielding raw yokels against seasoned troops."

"It will be a miracle if a tenth of them survive in battle," said the first one, "and a greater miracle still if we win."

Jephthah looked back over his shoulder without breaking step and

> *And Jephthah vowed a vow unto the Lord, and said: "If Thou wilt indeed deliver the children of Ammon into my hand, then it shall be, that whatsoever cometh forth of the doors of my house to meet me, when I return in peace from the children of Ammon, it shall be the Lord's, and I will offer it up for a burnt-offering."*
>
> —JUDGES 11:30–31

silenced their words with a single glance. The two old soldiers, so accustomed to trading easy banter with Jephthah on the way to a fight, were struck by the chilly light in his eyes and the unfamiliar sternness of his expression.

"If it takes a miracle," Jephthah said, "then God will give us one."

On any other day, they would have laughed out loud at Jephthah's sanctimonious words, but something in his tone of voice warned them that they dare not laugh today.

"If you will deliver the children of Ammon into my hands," Jephthah continued in a low voice that was not addressed to anyone within sight, casting his eyes heavenward, "then I vow, when I return in victory from the battlefield, whatsoever comes forth out of my house to greet me will belong to the Lord, and I will offer it up on the altar as a burnt offering."

The two old soldiers who walked behind Jephthah exchanged a brief glance, but they said nothing.

Seila occupied herself with her customary tasks during the weeks and months of Jephthah's long campaign, but word of his exploits reached her through the young women who accompanied her on weekly excursions into the countryside. As they walked through the dusty streets of Mizpah, Seila was greeted by acquaintances and strangers alike with marked warmth but also a certain deference—after all, she was the daughter of the man in whose sure hands the fate of all Israel was now held, the daughter of the heroic fighter whose victories mounted with each new battle.

> *So Jephthah passed over unto the children of Ammon to fight against them; and the Lord delivered them into his hand. And he smote them from Aroer until thou come to Minnith, even twenty cities, and unto Abel-cheramim, with a very great slaughter. So the children of Ammon were subdued before the children of Israel.*
>
> —JUDGES 11:32–33

"Jephthah fights like one possessed," the townsfolk reassured one another, and Seila heard the phrase countless times as her father and his army engaged the Ammonites across the breadth of Israel. Word of each victory was a cause for celebration in the place where the young women gathered on their excursions, the secret cleft in the hill where Seila had found the spring and the spreading oak. Indeed, Seila and her companions often told each other that it was their song and dance, their rites and rituals, that assured victory to Jephthah as he rode into battle again and again.

Twenty battles were fought by Jephthah, or so went the rumors that flashed through Mizpah like brushfire, and twenty cities of Israel were liberated from occupation by the king of Ammon. As the Ammonites were driven out of each city, another knot of refugees would pack up their belongings and move out of Mizpah. Soon enough, thanks to Jephthah's successes over the king of Ammon in the field, the encampment outside Mizpah dwindled and then disappeared, and Mizpah itself began to resemble the sleepy backwater it had been before Jephthah was called to service.

Then, one day, a clutch of young women appeared at Jephthah's house in a frenzy of giggles and squeals, literally dancing up to the doorway and pounding on ribboned tambourines to call Seila forth.

"Word comes that your father is on the road back to Mizpah," one of the young women said, and then all of them gathered to embrace her, some laughing, some weeping. "Your father returns in victory tonight!"

———

Seila spent the long afternoon tending to chores, but not much was accomplished. She started to sweep the floor, but then she thought to assemble the ingredients for a sweet loaf, and when she knelt by the pantry, it occurred to her to tidy up the courtyard, and then she hastened back into the house to pick up the broom—and still her father did not come home.

The other young women had lingered at the house until the sun began to set, begging and then demanding to be allowed to join her in greeting Jephthah in the traditional manner—a line of dancing maidens, waving ribbons and pounding timbrels, is what the hero ought to encounter when he returned from war! Indeed, Seila's companions insisted that the victory belonged to them, at least in part, because they had been so earnest and so devoted in devising prayers on behalf of Jephthah and sending them forth in such imaginative ways during their excursions to the great oak.

But Seila refused to share the moment of glory with even these intimate friends, and she sensed that her father would want it precisely that way. "Flesh of my flesh, blood of my blood," her father always said, "it's the two of us against the world." So Seila shushed her friends, urged them out of the house and down the road before they could spoil the sublime encounter between Jephthah and Seila, the conquering hero and his beloved daughter, his one and only child. From her friends she took a pair of timbrels, each one gaily decorated with long ribbons of many colors. But it would be Seila alone who danced out of the house and welcomed Jephthah in his moment of greatest glory.

The sun was nearly gone, and the sky had taken on shades of fire and quicksilver, when Seila heard the sound of a horse clip-clopping up to the gate. She crept to the window, peered out, and saw her father slowly and wearily dismount. Even in the half-light she could see that he had been injured, and he moved with an awkward gait. Still, she saw what she imagined to be an aura of golden light around his head, and he seemed longer and leaner than when he had left so many weeks ago.

With a squeal of delight, Seila seized a timbrel in each hand, butted open the door of the house with one hip, and skittered into the courtyard. Then she stopped, straightened up, raised one timbrel high above

> *And Jephthah came to Mizpah unto his house, and, behold, his daughter came out to meet him with timbrels and with dances; and she was his only child; beside her he had neither son nor daughter.*
>
> —JUDGES 11:34

> *And it came to pass, when he saw her, that he rent his clothes, and said: "Alas, my daughter! thou hast brought me very low, and thou art become my troubler; for I have opened my mouth unto the Lord, and I cannot go back."*
>
> —JUDGES 11:35

her head and held the other at arm's length along her leg. Slowly, solemnly, but with a tautness that bespoke her passion, Seila set up a rhythm of clanging timbrels, intoned a sinuous melody in a high ululating voice, and danced slowly and solemnly across the courtyard toward the gate where her father now stood.

Seila performed the same dance that she and the other young women had danced so many times before in a circle around the great oak, but now she felt as if she were floating three inches off the ground. At last, as she reached the place where her precious father stood, she suddenly bowed low, rattling the timbrels all the while, and finally lifted her eyes to behold him at his moment of triumph.

She gasped. Jephthah was staring at her with an expression of unspeakable sadness and horror.

"My daughter—" he croaked, and then all at once he threw himself down in the dust of the roadway. With one clenched fist he began to beat his breast, and with the other he pulled at his tunic as if to rend his clothing from top to bottom. "My one and only child!"

Seila rushed to his side and threw herself to the ground next to him. "Father!" she cried. "What is wrong?"

"Alas, my daughter!" he said, gasping and wheezing. "You have brought me low!"

Seila felt suddenly breathless. She had the thought that somehow her father had learned of the goings-on beneath the ancient oak where she gathered with her companions every seventh day. Had someone spied out Seila and her companions and reported back to the elders? Was her father brought low by what his own daughter had done in that secret cleft in the hills?

"What troubles you so?" Seila pleaded, weeping openly and hanging on his neck. "Tell me, Father."

Jephthah drew away from Seila and wrapped his arms around his own shoulders as if to comfort himself.

"I have opened my mouth," Jephthah said, "and I cannot go back."

"I don't understand," she said, still weeping, still fearful of what words her father had spoken—and to whom.

Jephthah looked at his beloved daughter, his one and only child, but he found that he had no more words to speak.

Long afterward, the townsfolk of Mizpah still spoke of the death of Seila by her father's hand. They described the crude altar he erected in the courtyard of his house, and how he escorted the compliant and uncomplaining young woman from the house, how he laid her—ever so gently—on the rough stones of the altar, how he dispatched her quickly and mercifully with a sure stroke of his dagger, the same one he had used in battle so many times before to slay a wounded but still-dangerous enemy. And they praised Seila as a heroic woman whose fidelity to the Almighty and loyalty to Israel allowed her to see the necessity and even the sanctity of her death.

"My father, you have opened your mouth and made a vow to the

And she said unto him: "My father, thou hast opened thy mouth unto the Lord; do unto me according to that which hath proceeded out of thy mouth; forasmuch as the Lord hath taken vengeance for thee of thine enemies, even of the children of Ammon."

—JUDGES 11:36

> *And she said unto her father: "Let this thing be done for me: let*
> *me alone two months, that I may depart and go down upon the*
> *mountains, and bewail my virginity, I and my companions."*
> *And he said: "Go." And he sent her away for two months, and*
> *she departed, she and her companions, and bewailed her vir-*
> *ginity upon the mountains. And it came to pass at the end of*
> *two months, that she returned unto her father, who did with*
> *her according to his vow which he had vowed; and she had not*
> *known man.*
>
> —JUDGES 11:37–39

Lord, so do to me what you have vowed to do," Seila was said to have reassured her father in a clear and certain voice in the moments before her death, "because the Lord has taken vengeance against your enemies, just as you asked, and delivered the children of Ammon into your hands."

Of course, none of the pious gossips actually saw the sacrifice of Seila with their own eyes or heard her final words to her father, and the unlikely little congregation that witnessed her death—the comrades who fought alongside Jephthah in battle and the young women who danced with Seila around the ancient oak—never spoke of it to anyone except themselves, soldier to soldier and maiden to maiden. But the townsfolk found it comforting to tell themselves that Seila did not cry out, did not plead for her life, did not struggle against the blade in her father's hand, did not groan in misery as her blood spilled over the stones of the altar and the flames turned her beautiful young body into charred meat. "Do to me what you have vowed to do" were Seila's words to Jephthah, at least according to the story that was repeated, generation after generation, by the children of Israel.

A whispered rumor held that Seila begged her father for a single favor before he carried out his vow to the Lord: "Let one thing be done for me, and one thing only," she is said to have asked. "Let me alone for two months that I may leave our house and go to the mountains and bewail my virginity, I and my companions." Said the trusting Jephthah: "Go."

> *And it was a custom in Israel, that the daughters of Israel went yearly to lament the daughter of Jephthah the Gileadite four days in a year.*
>
> —JUDGES 11:39–40

The rumormongers insisted that Seila did not run away and hide from her father, as one might have expected. But before she returned to lay her neck upon the altar, Seila and the young women who were her companions sought out some hidden place, worshipped strange gods in strange ways—and, some say, when they bewailed Seila's virginity, did so in a manner that would have merited burning even if Jephthah had not made his remarkable vow on the eve of battle with the Ammonites.

When two months had passed, Seila reappeared at the door of her father's house in Mizpah. Then and there, her life ended, all according to Jephthah's solemn vow to the Almighty. Eventually, the men and women who knew Seila by name followed her to the grave, and her name was forgotten. But her father's remarkable vow, and the way that he fulfilled the vow, were still recalled among the children of Israel. Indeed, it was a tradition among the daughters of Israel to go to the mountains each year and spend four days in remembrance of the daughter of Jephthah, recalling her life and lamenting her death in a manner that befitted the daughter of a chieftain.

CHAPTER ELEVEN

A GODDESS OF ISRAEL

The Forbidden Cult of Jephthah's Daughter

THE SINS OF THE FATHER ✢ THE SILENCE OF GOD
"THIS GLORIOUS AND AWFUL NAME"
LOOPHOLES ✢ "WOULD A DOG BE SACRIFICED TO ME?"
WOMEN WHO BEWAIL THEIR VIRGINITY
CHILDREN OF HARLOTRY
A GODDESS OF ISRAEL ✢ A CROWN OF FLOWERS

The oddest assortment of rogues, outlaws, and lowlifes in all of the Bible are found in the Book of Judges: seducers and harlots, assassins and mercenaries, rapists and torturers. Yet we also find heroes and heroines, martyrs and saviors, and among them is a beguiling young woman whose strange life—and even stranger death—are preserved in a few intriguing lines of text. The Bible asks us to regard Jephthah's daughter as an accidental but willing victim of human sacrifice, and yet we might wonder whether Jephthah's daughter and her companions did something so shocking to the biblical authors that they dressed up her death in the trappings of sacrifice but dared not speak her name at all.

The Book of Judges is a history of the troubled era that followed the conquest of Canaan by the Israelites, a period of crisis and chaos in which "there was no king in Israel, and every man did that which was right in his own eyes" (Judg. 21:25). But "[c]haos affords opportunity to certain men and women of low birth and mean circumstances,"[1] as one scholar points out, and so it is that a dispossessed and despised soldier of fortune named Jephthah finds a way to reclaim his legacy and restore himself to a position of privilege and power. Or so he thinks.

Jephthah is the bastard son of a wealthy man—or at least he is treated like one by his half brothers. The Bible plainly tells us that his mother was a common whore, a *zonah*, although some fussier commentators argue that we ought to regard her as the divorced wife of Jephthah's father,[2] and the rabbis rather delicately describe her as "a woman of another tribe."[3] Whore or not, Jephthah's mother was "his father's 'other woman,'"[4] and his half brothers find that reason enough to reject Jephthah's claim to a share of their father's legacy. The law codes in the Bible (and elsewhere in the ancient Near East) do not justify the disinheritance of Jephthah: a son was entitled to inherit from his father whether his mother was a wife, a concubine, or a harlot.[5] To Jephthah, then, the galling rejection by his brothers—and the ratification of their deed by the elders of Gilead—is not merely an injustice or a violation of law, but "an act of violence."[6]

So Jephthah, angry and estranged, reinvents himself as a kind of Bible-era gun-for-hire, a mercenary whose base of operations is a remote town on the border between Israel and Ammon. Somehow Jephthah sires a daughter, an only child, and the Bible suggests that the two of them live together in a tender but lonely bond—we are told nothing about the woman who gives birth to Jephthah's only child. Like many adults who grew up in broken homes, Jephthah cherishes his own child above all else—and yet he puts her at risk when he is given an opportunity to redeem himself in battle. "[T]here is something excessive about him which disposes him to tragedy," one scholar observes,[7] and so we are not really surprised when he utters the rash vow that will ultimately deprive him of his precious daughter.

The Bible does not tell us the name of Jephthah's daughter—a fact that takes on special significance in a book whose authors regard names and naming as something sacred. One ancient storyteller dubbed her "Seila," a name that I have chosen to use in retelling her story here, but the stinging irony—and the deepest mystery—of Jephthah and his daughter is that her tragic fate is only dimly remembered and her real name is entirely forgotten. And yet, as we shall see, the Bible preserves some intriguing clues about what Jephthah's daughter and her companions were really doing when they took to the hills of ancient Canaan to "bewail [her] virginity," and these clues suggest that she may have been a young woman quite unlike the willing martyr that the Bible makes her out to be.

THE SINS OF THE FATHER

The Bible itself and many of its pious readers over the centuries place the blame for the death of Jephthah's daughter on Jephthah alone, and they regard his vow to sacrifice "whatsoever cometh forth of the doors of my house to meet me" (Judg. 11:31) as impulsive, shortsighted, even vain and downright stupid—but essentially innocent. Possessed by the spirit of God, distracted by the prospect of the crucial battle to come, charged up with adrenaline and perhaps a certain blood lust, Jephthah does not pause to reason out the ways in which his vow might go wrong. How he could have overlooked the possibility that his daughter would be the first one to greet him on his return from battle is hard to understand in hindsight, but the apologists have tried their best to explain it away. One ingenious argument for Jephthah's innocence, if not his gift for abstract reasoning, points out that a typical Bible-era house was built around a courtyard where livestock was kept,[8] and holds that Jephthah is not an utter fool when he anticipates that a stray chicken or a curious goat would be the first one to encounter him on his victorious homecoming.

But Jephthah's vow can be understood in more troubling ways. The Bible tells us plainly enough that the women of Israel traditionally celebrate a victory on the battlefield "with timbrels and with dances," the very phrase that appears in the story of Jephthah. Miriam leads such a celebration after the defeat of Pharaoh's army at the Red Sea (Exod. 16:30), and King Saul is greeted in the same manner when he returns from battle with the Philistines after David's famous sword-and-slingshot duel with Goliath: "[T]he women came out of all the cities of Israel, singing and dancing, to meet king Saul, with timbrels, with joy, and with three-stringed instruments" (1 Sam 18:6). As a combat veteran who lives alone with his beloved daughter, Jephthah might have expected and even hoped for such a greeting.

That is why more than one contemporary Bible critic insists that Jephthah knows exactly what he is doing when he makes his vow. Mindful of Miriam's example, they suggest, Jephthah thoroughly expects to be greeted by his daughter, "who in the patriarchal society would have been more expendable than a man."[9] Perhaps Jephthah, who has already bartered his soldierly services for high office, is perfectly willing to offer up his daughter as a way of inducing the Almighty to grant him victory in the battle that will determine if he will live in glory in Gilead or die in shame in Mizpah. "[A] bribe under the table" is how one scholar describes Jephthah's words on the eve of battle. "The vow is not impulsive; it is shrewd and calculating."[10] And so, when he appears to blame his daughter for falling victim to his vow—"Alas, my daughter! thou hast brought me very low, and thou art become my troubler" (Judg. 11:35)—the guilt-ridden Jephthah may be desperately trying to comfort himself by shifting some measure of guilt to his wholly innocent child.

Still, even if we are willing to blame Jephthah for making the deadly vow, whether on impulse or by calculation, an awkward question remains: Why does God allow Jephthah to carry out his bloody vow? What is God doing while Jephthah's daughter and her companions bewail her virginity during the remarkable stay of execution granted by her father? Where is God when she is being led to the altar and burned as an offering?

The Silence of God

At least one ancient source insisted that God is horrified at the sight of Jephthah's sacrifice of his daughter. "He rose and slaughtered her before the Holy One, blessed be He," goes a rabbinical version of the story of Jephthah in which God is depicted as mouthing the words found in the writings of the prophet Jeremiah (Jer. 19:5). "The Holy Spirit cried out: 'They have put their children to fire . . . which I never commanded, never decreed, and which never came out of My mind.' "[11]

For some Bible readers, then, Jephthah's vow is "an act of unfaithfulness, an attempt to manipulate YHWH, who has already freely bestowed upon Jephthah the gift of the spirit."[12] But God cannot be acquitted quite so easily as the author of Jephthah's vow—or at least an accomplice of Jephthah in both the making and the fulfillment of the vow. After all, the Bible tells us that "the spirit of God" comes over Jephthah *before* he utters the vow that will eventually result in the death of his daughter. "One could more plausibly argue," insists contemporary Bible scholar J. Cheryl Exum, "that Jephthah made his vow under the influence of YHWH."[13]

Indeed, the Bible tells us that "the spirit of God" is not always benign. Saul, who is chosen by God to be the very first king of Israel, is cast into despair and even madness when the Almighty abruptly withdraws his favor and replaces it with affliction. "Now the spirit of the Lord departed from Saul," the Bible tells us, "and an evil spirit from the Lord terrified him" (1 Sam. 16:14). At first the soothing sounds of a harp played by a young shepherd named David are enough to drive off the evil spirit (1 Sam. 16:23)—ironically, it is David whom God has chosen to replace Saul on the throne—but the "evil spirit from the Lord" is relentless:

> And it came to pass on the morrow, that an evil spirit from God came mightily upon Saul, and he raved in the midst of the house; and David played with his hand, as he did day by day; and Saul had his spear in his hand. And Saul cast the spear; for he said: "I will smite David even to the wall" (1 Sam. 18:10–11).

So it is tempting to regard the "spirit of God" that possesses Jephthah as something dark and distorting. However, even if the spirit of God plays no role at all in the making of Jephthah's vow, the Almighty does nothing to prevent Jephthah from carrying it out—God remains pointedly aloof.

As the Bible reveals, sometimes the Almighty expresses his will, however indistinctly and indirectly, by simply clamming up. When Saul confronts the armies of the Philistines, for example, he desperately seeks advice and assurance from the Almighty—and the sure sign of God's disfavor is silence. "And when Saul inquired of the Lord," the Bible reports, "the Lord answered him not, neither by dreams, nor by Urim,* nor by prophets" (1 Sam. 28:6). So, too, does God fall uncharacteristically silent in the face of Jephthah's vow and the long preparations for the sacrifice of his daughter, all of which affords the Lord plenty of time to consider whether or not to commute her death

---

*"Urim" and "Thummim" are profoundly mysterious objects of unknown description that were somehow used by the high priest of the ancient Israelites to communicate with God. The Bible simply does not reveal what the Urim and Thummim were or how they were used, although scholars speculate that they were inscribed with holy words and used for divination by drawing of lots (Exod. 28:15–20, Lev. 8:8).

sentence. "The source of the tragic in the story of Jephthah is not divine enmity," observes one Bible critic, "but divine silence."[14]

One theologically correct understanding of God's silence in the story of Jephthah's daughter is that the Almighty disapproves of Jephthah's vow and punishes him by allowing his daughter to die on the altar, an explanation that is supposed to acquit God of any culpability in her death but does not offer much comfort to Jephthah's daughter. A less devout but somehow more convincing interpretation of God's silence is offered by the Israeli author Amos Oz, who imagines Jephthah begging in vain for a sign that God wants him to disregard his vow and spare his daughter. "I have not withheld my only daughter from you," Jephthah is made to plead to the Almighty in Oz's short story *Upon This Evil Earth*. "Grant me a sign, for surely you are tempting your servant."[15]

God has already complied with countless such pleas and demands from his people ever since he first befriended Abraham. Only a few pages earlier in the Book of Judges, for example, the Almighty recruits an Israelite named Gideon to do battle on behalf of the Chosen People—"The Lord is with thee, thou mighty man of valour," says an angel who calls on Gideon as he sits under a terebinth—but the reluctant Gideon insists on a sign that it is really God who has called him to service. The angel offers a flashy display of "fire out of the rock," but not until God himself appears is Gideon convinced. "Peace be unto thee; fear not," says the Almighty to Gideon, "thou shalt not die" (Judg. 6:11, 20, 23).

But when it comes to the making and keeping of Jephthah's vow, God falls wholly and ominously silent, and thus condemns Jephthah's daughter to death. So the story of Jephthah reveals that silence is one of the mysterious ways in which God works, his wonders to perform. "Did the Lord desire her for himself?" muses Bible scholar Cynthia Baker,[16] as if to suggest that the whole sordid enterprise is a device by which the Almighty satisfies his own appetite for the martyrdom of Jephthah's daughter. Or is God testing Jephthah, just as he will later test Job, by granting him victory in battle and then waiting to see if the father is really willing to slay his only child in defiance of the words attributed to the Almighty by his own prophets?

"THIS GLORIOUS AND AWFUL NAME"

At the heart of the story of Jephthah and his daughter is the notion that he *must* do exactly what he has vowed to do. The biblical author never entertains the thought that Jephthah might renounce his words or that Jephthah's daughter might refuse to comply with them. "I have opened my mouth unto the Lord, and I cannot go back," Jephthah declares, and his daughter does not argue the point: "[D]o unto me according to that which hath proceeded out of thy mouth" (Judg. 11:35–36). So we are reminded of one of the more curious articles of faith among the Israelites: they regard words and even letters not only with reverence but with fear and awe.

Of course, the Israelites are forced to rely on words alone to express the power as well as the glory of the Almighty. "Thou shalt not make unto thee a graven image," goes the second of the Ten Commandments, "nor any manner of likeness, of any thing that is in heaven above, or that is in the earth beneath" (Exod. 20:4). Thus, for example, the Israelites regarded the four Hebrew letters that spell the proper name of God—conventionally rendered in English as YHWH—to be so powerful (and therefore so dangerous) that no one but the high priest was permitted to speak "this glorious and awful name" (Deut. 28:58)—and even he was permitted to do so only on the holiest day of the year, Yom Kippur, and only in the confines of the Temple at Jerusalem. By the second century B.C.E. even the high priest was forbidden to utter the Holy Name, and anyone who dared to defy the strict decree was doomed to an unspeakable fate, both here and in the "world to come."[17]

Indeed, the rabbinical writings preserve the cautionary tale of an otherwise exemplary rabbi and his family who were martyred by the Romans during the persecutions under the emperor Hadrian. The rabbi was "executed by burning, his wife slain, and his daughter placed in a brothel" by the Roman authorities, who intended to make an example out of the rabbi precisely because of his piety—but the sages offered a much different explanation. The rabbi suffered his fate, they insisted, because he dared to pronounce the Holy Name, even though he did so "not for profane purposes or for personal ends, but rather in a spirit of reverence, and in order to study and to understand the ways of God," and his wife shared his fate "because she did not rebuke him for it."[18]

So, too, does the Bible regard the words of one who makes a vow to the Almighty as sacred. "When a man voweth a vow unto the Lord," Moses decrees in the Bible, "he shall not break his word; he shall do according to all that proceedeth out of his mouth" (Num. 30:3) because "the Lord thy God will surely require it of thee" (Deut. 23:22–24).* For the ancient Israelites, then, God himself regarded a man's word as his bond, and a vow was something more than a mere promise; rather, it amounted to "the creation of a reality even before its fulfillment in practice."[19] The biblical author expects his readers to understand and accept the fact that Jephthah's rash words cannot be ignored or defied even though they amount to a death sentence by a father on his own child.

As if to echo and underscore the life-and-death consequences of Jephthah's vow, the story of Jephthah in the Book of Judges ends on a blackly comic note that reminds us, once again, of the deadly power of a simple word spoken aloud. The tribe of Ephraim, we are told, complains to Jephthah that its men-at-arms were not invited to join the other Israelites in the war against the Ammonites, and the Ephraimites threaten that they will "burn thy house with fire" (Judg. 12:1). Once again, Jephthah tries to talk his way out of a fight by arguing that his call to arms was ignored by the Ephraimites—"[W]hen I called you," he protests, "ye saved me not out of their hands" (Judg. 12:2)—but the tribes end up in a bloody civil war. And here the Bible describes a curious ploy that Jephthah uses to identify the Ephraimites when they try to cross the Jordan River back into their tribal land.

According to Judges, any man who tries to cross the Jordan River is challenged by the soldiers of Jephthah's army to say the Hebrew word *shibboleth*, which happens to mean either "ear of corn" or "flood."[20] Thanks to a quirk in the dialect spoken by the Ephraimites, they are unable to pronounce the "sh" sound in *shibboleth*, and so they answer the challenge by pronouncing the password as "sibboleth," thus betraying themselves as Ephraimites. Any man who cannot pronounce the word correctly is seized and slain, and the Bible reports that forty-

---

*According to the Bible, the vow of an unmarried woman who still lives in her father's household is binding only if her father witnesses the vow and does not exercise his right to veto it. The husband performs the same role in the case of a married woman who makes a vow. "But the vow of a widow, or of her that is divorced . . . shall stand against her" (Num. 30:3–10).

two thousand Ephraimites die at the hands of Jephthah's soldiers, all because they mispronounced a single word."*

LOOPHOLES

The sages ask us to believe that Jephthah's daughter is not merely resigned to her fate but positively eager to repose herself on the altar and expose her neck to her father's blade. According to the rabbinical writings, she is delighted at the opportunity to give her life in exchange for the victory of Israel against the pagan invaders. Indeed, her only anxiety is that she will not be acceptable as a sacrificial offering and that her father's vow would be in vain. Once reassured by God himself that her sacrifice will suffice, Jephthah's daughter turns around and comforts her father!

"Why dost thou grieve for my death, since the people was delivered?" she is depicted as saying in one rabbinical tale. "Dost thou not remember what happened in the days of our forefathers, when the forefather offered his son as a burnt offering, and the son did not refuse but consented gladly . . . ?"[21]

The burnt offering to which Jephthah's daughter refers, of course, is the sacrifice of Isaac by his father, Abraham. Indeed, the Hebrew word used by the biblical author to describe Jephthah's daughter as his "only" (or "beloved") child is the same one that God uses to describe Isaac when calling on Abraham to offer him as a sacrifice.[22] But the allusion to Abraham and Isaac is darkly ironic on the lips of Jephthah's doomed daughter: God stays Abraham's hand at the last moment and provides a ram to be sacrificed in place of his son, but no such deus ex machina appears in the story of Jephthah and his daughter. What's more, Abraham had several wives and an abundance of children (Gen. 25:1–5), but Jephthah's wife is dead or gone, and his daughter is his one and only child.[23] So the story of Jephthah and his daughter is "a grim

---

*The tactic adopted by Jephthah, as it turns out, is clever but not uncommon. "I am told that in World War II," reports Bible scholar Robert G. Boling in his commentary on the Book of Judges in the Anchor Bible series, "the Dutch underground was able to screen out German spies by making them pronounce the Dutch city name Scheveningen, which only the Dutch can do properly."

inversion of the Abraham-Isaac narrative,"[24] a bargain with God that makes Jephthah a chieftain over Israel but reduces him to an even greater loneliness and despair than he must have felt on the day he was driven out of his father's house.

Other sages were more troubled by God's inexplicable willingness to let Jephthah's daughter die in defiance of biblical law that ought to have spared her. To be sure, a vow was sacred, but a vow could be annulled if it violated some other commandment. Some rabbis insisted that the whole sorry affair could have been—and should have been— taken to a rabbinical court, a *bet din*, where the judges would be empowered to literally "interpret it out of existence."[25] Indeed, the rabbis imagined a spirited but learned disputation between Jephthah and his daughter over the finer points of the biblical law—and the law is on her side.

According to a tale told by the rabbis, the daughter points out to Jephthah that a sacrifice must be selected "from the herd or from the flock," and not from one's own family (Lev. 1:2). She argues that Jephthah is entitled to make a cash payment equivalent to the value of the sacrificial victim in place of the sacrifice (Lev. 27:2–8). She invokes the patriarch Jacob, who "vowed a vow" to give a tenth of all of his possessions to the Almighty but whose vow does not extend to the sacrifice of his own children (Gen. 28:22), and she conjures up Hannah, the mother of the prophet Samuel, who "vowed a vow" to give her son to the Lord but meant only that he would be dedicated to service and not sacrificed (1 Sam. 1:11). The rabbis who put these arguments in the mouth of Jephthah's daughter were convinced that Jephthah's vow need not have been fulfilled at all.

"The vow is ridiculous and retroactively void," one ancient rabbi opines, "for a human being is not meant for ritual sacrifice."[26]

The sages imagined that Jephthah's daughter, unable to convince her father to disregard his vow, begs for a stay of execution so that she can bring an appeal to a rabbinical court, where her learned arguments might find a more sympathetic audience. "Perhaps one of [the judges] will find a loophole out of your words," she is made to say to her stubborn father. Jephthah consents, and his daughter spends the last two months of her young life going from rabbi to rabbi, rather than "bewailing her virginity with her companions" as the Bible itself tells us. But the rabbinical tale ends in the precisely same bloody way as the biblical text: "They did not find a loophole," and Jephthah's daughter goes meekly to her death as a burnt offering.[27]

"WOULD A DOG BE SACRIFICED TO ME?"

The most glaring flaw in Jephthah's vow is, of course, the possibility that a human being might be the first to greet him and thus end up on the sacrificial altar. As we have already seen, the prophets stoutly insist that God does not require or even permit human sacrifice of any kind. (See chapter nine.) What's more, the handbook of ritual sacrifice that we find in the Book of Exodus "loftily ignore[s]" the sacrifice of a female of *any* species, human or animal.[28] Yet the story of Jephthah and his daughter, perhaps more plainly than any other passage in the Bible, reveals that the biblical authors were neither surprised nor shocked by the notion that God would countenance the sacrifice of a child by her own father.

According to one ancient source, God is not especially concerned that Jephthah's daughter might be the first one to emerge from his house and greet him on his return from battle. According to an anonymous author of the first century C.E. known only as Pseudo-Philo, whose *Biblical Antiquities* is a kind of "rewritten Bible" in which familiar stories are fleshed out and dressed up, God is angered by Jephthah's vow as soon as he hears it—but *not* because Jephthah put his own daughter's life at risk by coming up with such an impulsive and foolish proposition. Rather, God is insulted and aggrieved precisely because a creature less worthy of sacrifice than a young woman might end up on the altar as a burnt offering. Jephthah's virginal daughter is perfectly acceptable to God as a victim of sacrifice, according to Pseudo-Philo, but what if something else beats her to the door?

"And God was very angry and said 'Behold, Jephthah has vowed that he would offer to me whatever meets him first on the way.' " God is made to complain: "If a dog should meet Jephthah first, would a dog be sacrificed to me?"[29]

To punish Jephthah for putting God at risk of suffering the indignity of a canine offering, God decrees a terrible fate for Jephthah's blameless daughter, whom Pseudo-Philo calls Seila: "Now shall the vow of Jephthah be visited on his first-born, his own offspring."[30] To make sure that his will is done, God beclouds the minds of the judges who hear Seila's otherwise compelling appeal, and so none of them is moved by her lawyering to spare her life. "I have closed the mouths of the sages of my people in this generation," God confesses, abruptly adopting Jephthah's vow as his own, "that *my* vow be fulfilled."[31] To distract his readers from what appears to be God's cold-blooded indifference to Seila herself, Pseudo-Philo puts a few tender words in the mouth of the Almighty. "I know her to be wiser than her father, and all the wise men," God says, "and now her soul shall be accepted at her request, and her death shall be very precious before my face all the time."[32]

Pseudo-Philo goes to the trouble of naming Jephthah's daughter, and he follows the example of the Bible by selecting a name that reflects her destiny: "Seila" means "she who is demanded," as if to confirm that God himself demanded her life. Her father's name, too, seems to comment on his grotesque role in the death of his own child: "Jephthah" is an abbreviated form of the Hebrew phrase "God opens [the womb],"[33] which recalls God's claim on the "firstlings" of the Israelites. "Sanctify unto Me all the first-born," says God to his Chosen People after liberating them from slavery in Egypt, "whatsoever openeth the womb among the children of Israel, both of man and of beast, it is Mine" (Exod. 13:2). For Seila, sanctification means sacrifice, and we are reminded once again in the story of Jephthah that God prefers flesh and blood on the altar of sacrifice.

WOMEN WHO BEWAIL THEIR VIRGINITY

What exactly are Jephthah and her companions *doing* during those two months at large in the mountains of Canaan? The Bible tells us nothing more than what we read in Judges: Jephthah's daughter "bewails her virginity" with her companions, and they commemorate her every year thereafter (Judg. 11:39–40), but no such ritual is mentioned anywhere else in the Bible.[34] Still, even the spare and oblique words of the biblical text are enough to provoke the imagination, and somewhere beneath the imperfectly sanitized tale told by the priests and scribes we can make out dimly something strange and tantalizing, a forbidden tradition that somehow escaped the censor's pen.

At least one excitable exegete speculates that Jephthah's daughter and her companions were acolytes of a "sex cult" in which "Israelite women were dedicated to the deity (presumably Baal) by an act of ritual defloration."[35] Another proposes that they belonged to a pagan fertility cult "based on the ancient and primitive custom of annually bewailing the dead or ousted spirit of fertility during the dry or winter season."[36] No less an authority than Northrop Frye allows that Jephthah's daughter herself became "the center of a local female cult, doubtless originally on the principle . . . that virgin goddesses, like Artemis, are often the protectors of childbirth."[37] A great many scholarly readers of the Bible discern in Jephthah's daughter the features of other figures from Greek myth: Persephone, who is abducted by the king of the underworld to become his wife but is permitted to return to the surface of the earth to visit her mother, the goddess Ceres, at seasonal intervals; or Iphigenia, a virgin who is selected for sacrifice to Diana but is spared so that she can spend her life in service to the goddess. But all of them agree that some faint trace of a forbidden and forgotten ritual is preserved in the biblical account of Jephthah's daughter.

"It may well be that there was a local pagan cult of a Persephone-like goddess whose origins had been forgotten, and the story of Jephthah's daughter was invented to account for the existence of the cult (as well as to justify its existence),"[38] speculates one contemporary Bible critic. Another scholar entertains an even more startling scenario: Judges may be "the literature of a feminist intelligentsia" in ancient Israel, a collection of stories that "gave them the courage to live marginally, in a fashion resembling witches in New England."[39]

The Bible offers at least one intriguing clue to the mystery of what Jephthah's daughter and her companions are actually doing when they take to the hills to "[bewail] her virginity," although the real meaning of the biblical text is concealed and distorted by a common mistranslation of a single crucial word. The word—*betulum*—that is usually translated in English as "virginity" does not refer to virginity at all but rather to "the stage of a young woman's life when she is capable of having children," perhaps signaled by the onset of puberty and a young woman's menarche or first menstruation. In other words, Jephthah's daughter is *not* bemoaning the fact that she will die without engaging in sexual intercourse with a man; rather, she is sorrowing over the fact that she "will be cut off from her people before she has become a mother in Israel, before she has progeny, her posterity."[40]

Perhaps the rituals performed by Jephthah's daughter and her companions on a remote hilltop can be regarded as nothing more startling than a rite of passage and a celebration of puberty that was generally observed by the women of ancient Israel. Only because Jephthah's daughter is forced to celebrate her coming of age under the threat of death does the observance described in the Bible seem so ominous. Only because Jephthah's daughter goes to her death does the same observance later become a yearly ritual of remembrance. That is why some Bible critics reject any suggestion that Jephthah's daughter was the priestess of a pagan "sex cult" and urge us to regard the rites and rituals of Seila and her companions as something wholesome and essentially secular—"a countermovement of resolution and repair [that] serves to ameliorate her tragedy," as one contemporary Bible critic puts it.[41]

But there is another way to understand and appreciate the secret observances of Jephthah's daughter and her companions in their wilderness sanctuary. We do not need to dress her up in the alluring costume of a sex cultist, but neither do we have to strip away the rich trappings that are suggested even by the spare lines of text in the Bible. Rather we can begin to see Jephthah's daughter as someone who recognizes, responds to, and satisfies a deep and undeniable longing among the people of ancient Israel that is left unfulfilled by a male deity.

CHILDREN OF HARLOTRY

What makes the faith of ancient Israel as depicted in the Bible so revolutionary—and so unique among the religions of the ancient Near East—is the insistence that Yahweh is not merely the *supreme* god but the *only* god. "Thou shalt have no other gods before me," goes the very first of the Ten Commandments, "for I the Lord thy God am a jealous God" (Exod. 20:3, 5). Although the commandment itself can be understood in more than one way, as we shall see, the conventional reading of the First Commandment is that all other deities—and the ancient Near East fairly teemed with gods and goddesses—are not merely an "abomination" but a delusion, too. The One God, we are intended to believe, is the One and Only God. And the rivals of the Almighty are not gods at all—"no-gods" is the term Jeremiah uses to describe the objects of pagan worship (Jer. 2:11, 5:7).

Of course, strange gods and goddesses abound in the Bible itself, and the biblical authors readily concede that the Israelites are fatally attracted to the pagan deities worshipped by the Canaanites and other pagans throughout the ancient Near East. In fact, the Book of Judges is one long and despairing cycle of sin and redemption: the Israelites have done "that which was evil in the sight of the Lord" (Judg. 2:11) by lapsing into the worship of pagan gods and goddesses; God is angered by their faithlessness and abandons them to their enemies; the Israelites confess their sin and beg for forgiveness; God relents in his anger and "raise[s] them up a saviour" (Judg. 3:15); the Israelites enjoy a short interval of peace and freedom before taking up the worship of pagan gods—and then the whole sorry cycle starts all over again.

The infidelities of the Chosen People provide a convenient excuse to explain why God does not keep his oft-repeated promise to grant them sovereignty in the land of Canaan. That is supposed to be God's end of the deal in the covenant the Almighty makes with Abraham and renews with Moses: "For ye are to pass over the Jordan to go in to possess the land which the Lord your God giveth you" (Deut. 11:31). Long before they actually reach Canaan, however, the Israelites are warned that they will find a tantalizing array of gods and goddesses, and the Lord sternly orders the Israelites to obliterate all signs of pagan worship in the Promised Land:

> Ye shall surely destroy all the places, wherein the nations that ye are to dispossess served their gods, upon the high mountains, and upon the hills, and under every leafy tree. And ye shall break down their altars, and dash in pieces their pillars, and burn their Asherim with fire; and ye shall hew down the graven images of their gods; and ye shall destroy their name out of that place (Deut. 12:2–3).

But the awkward fact of biblical history is that the Israelites do *not* dispossess all of the native-dwelling nations of the land of Canaan, and they do *not* obliterate the shrines and altars where the Canaanites worship their gods and goddesses. So the author of Judges is forced to explain why God's promise has not been fulfilled—and he points to the apostasy of the Israelites as the reason. The early passages of Judges are devoted to a curious sort of historical revisionism, a battle list that specifies the defeats rather than the victories of the armies of Israel: "And the children of Benjamin did not drive out the Jebusites that inhabited Jerusalem. . . . And Ephraim drove not out the Canaanites that dwelt in Gezer. . . . Zebulun drove not out the inhabitants of Kitron, nor the inhabitants of Nahalol. . . ." and so on (Judg. 1:21, 29, 30). God denies the Israelites complete possession of the Promised Land precisely because they succumb to the temptation of pagan worship: "And they forsook the Lord, and served Baal and the Ashtaroth" (Judg. 2:13), that is, the gods and goddesses venerated by the Canaanites.

"I will never break My covenant with you," God allows, "but . . . I will not drive them out from before you; but they shall be unto you as snares, and their gods shall be a trap unto you" (Judg. 2:1–3).

The Bible itself, with its beguiling catalog of the places and paraphernalia of pagan worship, allows us to understand the powerful seduction that the gods and goddesses worked on the Israelites. As the Bible concedes, the Israelites turn to Baal, to Ashtaroth, to Asherah. Baal is a storm and fertility god, one of the principal deities in the pantheon of the Canaanites and a descendant of their supreme god, El; Ashtaroth is the Hebrew rendering of Astarte, the Canaanite fertility goddess who is one of Baal's consorts; and Asherah is the consort of the supreme god El and thus the mother of all the lesser gods, although the biblical authors sometimes pair her up with Baal, too (Judg. 3:7).

According to the Bible, the altars and shrines of these pagan gods and goddess were sited on hilltops and mountaintops, the "high places" that figure so importantly in the biblical accounts of where and how the Israelites and their neighbors worshipped. Rituals were apparently conducted under the boughs of sacred oaks and around stone columns placed upright in the ground, a faintly druidical practice that was never completely eradicated by the priests and prophets of early Israel. The Canaanite goddess known as Asherah was depicted and venerated in the form of living trees or carved wooden poles, the so-called Asherim of biblical usage. Pagan gods and goddesses were depicted in statues and figurines crafted of precious metals as well as wood, clay, and stone, including the *teraphim* or household idols that figure in the stories of the patriarchs—these are the "graven images" that are specifically condemned in the Ten Commandments and yet have been found in remarkable profusion by archaeologists in the Holy Land.

The worship of idols, by the way, was probably *not* the crude and almost childlike practice that the Bible and earlier Bible scholarship suggest. According to pious tradition, the ancients were gullible and deluded souls who regarded idols as living embodiments of their gods, caring for and even feeding the statues and figurines as if they were alive. The Bible itself attributes these notions to idol-worshippers—and scoffs at them. "[T]he work of men's hands, wood and stone," is how the Deuteronomist describes the objects of pagan worship, "which neither see, nor hear, nor eat, nor smell" (Deut. 4:28). But according to recent archaeological evidence, the ancient pagans understood that idols were man-made artifacts rather than living gods, and they regarded an idol as a source of inspiration and comfort rather than a Pinocchio that might come to life if they prayed hard enough. Thus the graven images of antiquity may have been similar in function to the icons and other ritual objects that can be found in places of worship in our own day.[42]

If we believe the testimony of the prophets as recorded in the Bible, the worship of pagan gods and goddesses is the occasion for displays of sexual depravity, whether in the form of bacchanalian orgies or of more discreet visits to the sacred prostitutes, male and female, who supposedly ply their trade at the temples of pagan gods and goddesses. (See chapter seven.) Although contemporary scholars question whether sacred prostitution was ever as common as the Bible suggests, the prophets are plainly obsessed with the interplay between sex and the worship of pagan deities, and something more than a metaphor is found in the words of Jeremiah: "Upon every high hill, and under every leafy tree, thou didst recline, playing the harlot" (Jer. 2:20).

Even the greatest kings of Israel were apparently susceptible to the temptation of goddess worship. King Solomon, who built the first temple at Jerusalem and whom the Bible regards as both mighty and wise, is plainly described as an apostate, too. "God gave Solomon wisdom and understanding exceeding much, and largeness of heart," we are told at first (1 Kings 5:9). But the love-smitten old king is seduced into idol worship by his several hundred foreign wives: Solomon "turned away his heart after other gods," "went after Ashtoreth," and raised up a "high place" where he conducted pagan rituals. "I will surely rend the kingdom from thee," God vows, although the Almighty defers the punishment to a later generation out of solicitude for David, whose many sins of the flesh did not include paganism (1 Kings 11:5–11).

Now the priestly editors who collected the sacred texts and rendered them into the book we now know as the Bible insist on drawing bright lines between the worship of Yahweh, which is presented as the only acceptable act of faith in ancient Israel, and the worship of pagan gods and goddesses, which is routinely condemned in the Bible as an "abomination." Although the Bible confirms that the Israelites repeatedly and obsessively turned to the forbidden deities, the biblical authors always insist that the Israelites are committing apostasy—and suffer grievous punishment from on high—whenever they indulge in the forbidden pleasures of pagan worship.

The worship of pagan goddesses is made out to be the sin that finally turns God against the Chosen People once and for all. Even though God stayed his hand against Solomon, the Bible is full of outrage toward a long-reigning king of Judah named Manasseh who first took the throne at the age of twelve and proceeded to do "that which was evil in the sight of the Lord, after the abominations of the nations." The biblical author condemns Manasseh for offering his own son as a human sacrifice, practicing the black arts of soothsaying, and divination by ghosts and spirits. But his worst offense by far is held to be the erection of a graven image of the goddess Asherah in the Temple at Jerusalem. Although Manasseh himself is damned for the shedding of "innocent blood," the crime of idolatry brings divine punishment on the guilty and innocent alike.

"Behold, I will bring such evil upon Jerusalem and Judah," God vows, "that whosoever heareth of it, both his ears shall tingle" (2 Kings 21:12, 16).

Still, the line between piety and apostasy—the boundary between the worship of the God of Abraham, Isaac, and Jacob, and the worship of the gods and goddesses of the Canaanites—cannot be drawn with such clarity or certainty. The Bible itself seems to suggest that the faith of ancient Israel appears to owe much to the pagan beliefs and practices of its neighbors. In fact, some of the holiest moments in the lives of the patriarchs and matriarchs bear a curious and telling resemblance to the very practices that are so heatedly condemned by the biblical authors.

For example, God chooses a tree—not unlike the trees that are regarded as sacred by pagan cults—as the place where he will appear to Abraham, first at Shechem (Gen. 12:6) and later at those famous "terebinths of Mamre" (Gen. 18:1). Rachel steals her father's household idols when she returns with her sister, Leah, and their husband, Jacob, to Canaan*—and such "detestable things" are not wholly banned in Israel until the reign of the reformer-king, Josiah (2 Kings 23:24). When Jacob struggles with (and defeats) an angel of God—or perhaps it is God himself—he commemorates his victory by taking the stone he had used as a pillow, setting it upright in the ground, and anointing it with oil. "And this stone, which I have set up for a pillar, shall be God's house," declares the patriarch (Gen. 28:22). According to some scholarly speculation, both Tamar, Judah's seductive daughter-in-law, and Rahab, the good-hearted harlot who shelters the Israelite spies, may have been priestesses of Canaanite fertility cults whose allure proved to be irresistible to Israelite men.[43] (See chapter seven.)

Until the Book of Deuteronomy was belatedly and rather mysteriously discovered during the reign of King Josiah in 622 B.C.E.—and the worship of Yahweh was restricted to the Temple at Jerusalem by King Josiah in hasty compliance with the newly discovered laws of Deuteronomy (2 Kings 23:1–3)—the Israelites felt free to offer sacrifices at a number of "legitimate" altars and sanctuaries that had been erected throughout the land of Judah and Samaria. "The sanctity here was linked with the site itself and its natural features, such as a sacred tree, a sacred spring or the like," wrote the venerable Bible scholar Martin Noth, who pointed out that "a natural rock formation" might be used as "an altar for the presentation or burning of offerings."[44]

So, despite the best efforts of the priests and scribes who were its censors and guardians, the Bible betrays the fingerprints of deities that may have preceded or coexisted with Yahweh. The Bible refers to God as Elohim, a plural form of the Hebrew word for "god," and the Almighty uses the plural when announcing the creation of humankind in Genesis: "Let us make man in our image, after our likeness" (Gen. 1:26). Biblical scholarship holds that these are grammatical rather than theological eccentricities, as Ephraim Speiser insisted,[45] but we are left to wonder whether even the ancient Israelites regarded Yahweh as

---

*The Bible tells us that Rachel hides the stolen *teraphim* in a camel-saddle and then dissuades her father from searching the saddle by sitting on it and telling him that she is menstruating. "Let not my lord be angry that I cannot rise up before thee," she says, "for the manner of women is upon me" (Gen. 31:35).

merely one god among many until the priestly redactors cleaned up the sacred texts and imposed the strict theology that we find in the Bible.

Certainly the Israelites saw some relationship between the god (*el*) called Yahweh and the supreme god whom the Canaanites called El— and perhaps, at some early moment in their history, the Israelites saw the two gods as one and the same. Abraham, for example, encounters a Canaanite king and high priest who blesses him in the name of El Elyon—"God Most High, Maker of heaven and earth"—and Abraham seems to identify and embrace the deity as his own (Gen. 14:19). Later, when God discloses to Moses that his personal name is actually Yahweh, the Almighty explains: "I appeared unto Abraham, unto Isaac and unto Jacob, as El Shaddai"—a phrase that is conventionally translated as "God Almighty" but one that also harkens back to the all-mighty god of Canaan (Exod. 6:3).

Modern scholarship has detected in the Bible certain distinct influences of the pagan civilizations that surrounded ancient Israel. Genesis echoes the creation myth recorded in a Mesopotamian text called the *Enuma Elish*. A tale very like the story of Noah and the Ark is told in a still more ancient Sumero-Babylonian saga, the Epic of Gilgamesh. Certain passages found in the Book of Proverbs—"Eat thou not the bread of him that hath an evil eye. . . ." (Prov. 23:6)—appear to have been copies almost verbatim from ancient Egyptian texts.[46] Even the famous curses and blessings that are found in the Book of Deuteronomy, a relatively late addition to the biblical canon, resemble the legal boilerplate that can be found in contracts and treaties throughout the ancient world. The notion that the faith of ancient Israel was something entirely new and unique is betrayed by the hard evidence in the Bible that many of the laws, rituals, and beliefs were borrowed from other cultures and civilizations.

Some passages of the Bible are simply so weird, so fundamentally at odds with the cosmology of the rest of Holy Writ, that they present themselves as wild atavisms of some far older and long-suppressed faith that existed in ancient Israel before the biblical authors created the Bible. The night attack on Moses in Exodus is one example, and the sudden appearance of the "sons of God" in Genesis is another: "And it came to pass . . . that the sons of God saw the daughters of men that they were fair, and they took them wives, whomsoever they chose. . . . and they bore children to them, the same were the mighty men that were of old, the men of renown" (Gen. 6:1–3, 4). Bible scholars of several faiths have struggled to explain away the unsettling fact that the Bible conjures up a randy gang of demigods who are fathered by the Almighty himself and go on to sire a race of giants on earth, the so-called Nephilim. But even the most cautious exegetes are forced to concede that the Hebrew phrase translated as "the sons of God" can also be rendered "the sons of the *gods*" and appears to refer to "lesser deities or godlings,"[47] a reading that cannot be squared with the fundamental credo of monotheism in the Hebrew Bible: "Hear O Israel, the Lord our God, the Lord is One" (Deut. 6:4).

In fact, the Book of Judges itself contains more than one intriguing reference to the rivalry between God and the pagan deities of the Canaanites, a rivalry that is frequently expressed in terms of sexual adventure. When God scolds the Israelites for their apostasy, he shows himself to be "sick and tired" of the faithlessness of Israel in precisely the same tone that a man or woman might use to address an unfaithful spouse who returns home once too often from a romantic fling. "Go and cry unto the gods which ye have chosen," a hurt and angry God blurts out to his Chosen People in the story of Jephthah. "[L]et them save you in the time of your distress" (Judg. 10:14). And the same sense of sexual betrayal is frequently used by the biblical authors to characterize the relationship between God and Israel. By the time we reach the prophetic books of the Bible, the sexual imagery is explicit. "Plead with your mother," God scolds the Israelites, likening them to the bastard children of his faithless wife, the nation of Israel. "For she is not My wife, neither am I her husband" (Hos. 2:4). And the prophet Ezekiel works himself into a frenzy of reproach in which sexual infidelity, idol worship, and child sacrifice are conflated into one vile sin. "Wherefore, O harlot," he addresses Jerusalem, "hear the word of the Lord!"

> Because thy filthiness was poured out, and thy nakedness uncovered through thy harlotries with thy lovers; and because of all the idols of thy abominations, and for the blood of thy children, that thou didst give unto them; therefore behold, I will gather all thy lovers, unto whom thou has been pleasant, and all them that thou hast loved, with all them that thou has hated; I will even gather them against thee from every side, and

will uncover thy nakedness unto them, that they may see all thy nakedness (Ezek. 16:35–37).

The biblical authors favor the stinging imagery of a cuckolded husband to convey the sense of betrayal that God feels toward his Chosen People—but something else is going on here, something shocking and revealing. When God bitterly turns away the Israelites and sends them back to "the gods which ye have chosen," he appears to concede that these pagan gods and goddesses may, in fact, be able to do some good for the Chosen People. Jephthah, too, tacitly confirms not only the existence of rival deities but also their authority when he invokes a pagan god named Chemosh in his parlays with the king of Ammon: "Wilt thou not possess that which Chemosh thy god giveth thee to possess?" (Judg. 11:24).

The conventional wisdom is that the references to rival gods in the Bible are intended by God *and* the biblical authors to be merely ironic or patronizing or both—the One God is taunting the Israelites to seek the favor of the illusory gods that the Almighty knows to be powerless because they do not really exist at all, and Jephthah is only flattering the god worshipped by the deluded Ammonites in an effort to make peace through diplomacy. But so many gods and goddesses show up in so many surprising places in the Bible—and the Israelites find them so alluring, so seductive—that we may be tempted to believe that the Israelites did not always regard Yahweh as the One and Only God.

As Jephthah's story reaches its tragic climax, as his daughter goes up in flames on the altar of El Shaddai, we might imagine that she is being punished for doing something that the pious authors of the Bible simply refuse to speak aloud.

A GODDESS OF ISRAEL

Another curious feature of the Hebrew Bible is the absence of a female counterpart to God, a deity who is supposedly above and beyond mere gender but is always described in words that unmistakably suggest his masculinity. "The God of Judaism is undoubtedly a father-symbol and a father-image," as one scholar pointed out, "possibly the greatest such symbol and image conceived by man."[48]

Virtually every other people in the ancient Near East—and, in fact, throughout the world—imagined that gods came in pairs, male and female, just like human beings, and their sacred writings describe courtships, marriages, childbearing and child-rearing, and a fantastic variety of sexual encounters among their deities. The Israelites alone are told that *their* God is a bachelor and a loner who lacks father or mother, brothers or sisters, friends or lovers. A female consort to the Almighty—"the divine woman who appears in different forms throughout the world, yet remains basically the same everywhere"[49]—is nowhere in be found in the Bible, or at least not in plain sight.

Although the Bible itself seems to allow no place for her, a celestial consort to the Almighty *can* be found in the writings of the ancient rabbis, the secret books of the medieval savants who studied the mystical tradition called Kabbalah, and the rich folklore of the Jewish people. A figure known as the Shekinah came to embody and symbolize the feminine qualities of God—"the loving, rejoicing, motherly, suffering, mourning, and, in general, emotion-charged aspect of deity."[50] By the thirteenth century, when Kabbalah was in full flower, the Shekinah—sometimes called the Matronit, the Lady, or the Queen—"emerged as a distinct female deity, possessing a will and desire of her own, acting independently of the traditional but somewhat shrunk masculine God, often confronting and occasionally opposing him and playing a greater role than He in the affairs of Her children, the people of Israel."[51]

Did the Shekinah suddenly and spontaneously appear in Jewish folklore and rabbinical literature long after the Bible was a closed book? Or can the Almighty's consort be regarded as a remnant of a long and unbroken tradition of goddess worship that reaches all the way back to the ancient Near East? At least one iconoclastic scholar, anthropologist Raphael Patai, argues that the Israelites experienced the same goddess-hunger that can be found in peoples and cultures around the world in every age—and Patai insists, too, that the worship of a female deity by the Israelites was not an act of apostasy but rather "an integral part of the religion of the Hebrews."[52]

The pioneers of feminist Bible criticism—a movement in biblical scholarship that has refreshed and even revolutionized the study of the

Bible over the last twenty years or so—argue that a "submerged goddess" can be detected in the Bible itself and that "goddess functions"[53] are performed by various women depicted in the biblical text. But Patai goes even further. The Israelites did not merely adopt the deities of their neighbors, a common enough practice in the ancient world; rather, Patai suggests, they borrowed various aspects of the Canaanite goddesses and used them to conjure up a female deity that they embraced as their very own. Not until the coming of King Josiah was the goddess of Israel driven underground.

"[T]he goddess to whom the Hebrews clung with such tenacity down to the days of Josiah, and to whom they returned with such remorse following the destruction of the Jerusalem Temple," writes Patai, "was, whatever the prophets had to say about her, no foreign seductress, but a Hebrew goddess, the best divine mother the people had had to that time."[54]

A poignant story told by the rabbis captures the intimate attachment that the Jewish people felt toward the Shekinah throughout the centuries of exile from the Promised Land—and suggests, too, that the human longing for a female counterpart to the Heavenly Father is fundamental and undeniable. According to one rabbinical tradition, God stayed behind in Jerusalem even after the Temple was destroyed by the legions of Rome and the Jewish people were forcibly dispersed throughout the ancient world. But the Shekinah, a tender and loving mother to the children of Israel, insisted on accompanying them into exile and succored them during the long years of oppression in the lands of the Diaspora.

Still more pointed is the mystical tradition in Judaism that imagines the Shekinah, as queen and consort of God, engaging in sexual intercourse with the Almighty in joyous celebration of the Sabbath. The Kabbalists who espoused the idea of divine sexuality were careful to insist that the mating of God and the Shekinah was only a mystical and not a carnal encounter. But the same notion found a more literal expression in the Jewish tradition that a husband and wife ought to engage in "conjugal union" on the Sabbath, a day of rest, study, and prayer on which every act is sanctified, including the act of sexual intercourse.[55]

Only the dimmest shadow of the Shekinah can be detected in contemporary Judaism, but at least one ritual contains an ember of the old passions that she once kindled in the hearts and souls of the people who

venerated her over the millennia. At the beginning of the Friday evening prayer service in most synagogues, the congregation turns away
from the ark where the Torah scrolls are kept and faces the door of the
sanctuary while singing a hymn that was borrowed from the mystics
who studied the Kabbalah. "Come O bride!" the congregation sings in
greeting the unseen figure who is imagined to be the Sabbath Queen
and the bride of the Almighty. Although few worshippers realize the
origins or meanings of the ritual, it is one last echo of a tradition that
may reach all the way back to Jephthah's daughter.

A CROWN OF FLOWERS

Jephthah's daughter, as she appears in the *Biblical Antiquities* of the
ancient author known as Pseudo-Philo, embodies precisely the same
qualities that are ascribed to the Shekinah: she is "loving, rejoicing,
motherly, suffering, mourning, and . . . emotion-charged." According to
Pseudo-Philo, Seila and her companions seek out a place for their ritual
observances that resembles the "high mountains" and "leafy trees" that
are described as the sites of pagan worship by the biblical authors. Seila
is made to address her words of lamentation to the beasts of the forest
and the forest itself. So we might wonder if the "rewritten Bible" of
Pseudo-Philo offers a clue to the mystery of where Jephthah and her
companions go and what they do to "bewail [her] virginity."

Now Pseudo-Philo did not dare suggest that Seila is a goddess-
worshipper, much less a goddess. Indeed, Seila is made to seem even more
sanctimonious in *Biblical Antiquities* than she appears in the rabbinical literature or the Bible itself. According to Pseudo-Philo, Seila absolves her
father of any guilt in her death. "May my words go forth in the heavens,"
says Seila, "that a father did not subdue by force his daughter whom he
has devoted to sacrifice."[56] Although she seems to understand that her
father's vow is legally flawed, Seila does not engage him in a debate over
the fine points of the law, nor does she appeal to the rabbinical courts;
rather, she encourages her father to do exactly what he has promised to
do. "And now do not annul everything you have vowed," she instructs
him, "but carry it out."

Pseudo-Philo imagines that God himself, who holds himself aloof from Jephthah, hears and responds to Jephthah's daughter as she laments her fate on a holy mountain by night. The Almighty declines to call off the sacrifice, but he praises the young woman who will be the burnt offering for her righteousness and sanctity. "Let her life be given," God says. "[H]er death will be precious before me always, and she will go away and fall into the bosom of her mothers"[57]—a phrase that puts a distinctly feminist spin on the familiar biblical euphemism for death. In fact, the phrase is found nowhere else in the literature of that era,[58] and the attitude of Pseudo-Philo toward women in general and Seila in particular prompts some scholars to wonder out loud whether the author of *Biblical Antiquities* was a woman.[59]

Indeed, when Seila asks her father for a stay of execution so that she and her companions may "bewail [her] virginity," Pseudo-Philo put words in her mouth that seem distinctly at odds with what we have come to expect from the sternly monotheistic (and seemingly masculine) authors of the Bible. For Seila and her companions, not unlike the pagans of the ancient world, the flora and fauna of the wilderness are not merely sacred but sentient, and she seeks out the very same hilltop groves where strange gods and goddesses are worshiped. "[Grant] . . . that I may go into the mountains and stay in the hills and walk among the rocks, I and my virgin companions," she implores her father. "And the trees of the field will weep for me, and the beasts of the field will lament over me." Once we reach the sacred mountaintop in the company of Seila and her friends, she addresses her first words to the landscape itself. "Hear, you mountains, my lamentations . . . ," she implores. "You trees, bow down your branches and weep over my youth."[60]

When Seila speaks her own eulogy in the company of her fellow mourners, however, she no longer thinks to address God, or her father, or even the wilderness and the wild animals around her. Rather, she addresses her absent and missing mother—"O Mother, in vain have you borne your only-begotten daughter!"[61]—and she alludes to the ritual adornments that have been prepared by the various women in her life in anticipation of her coming of age. "[T]he white robe that my mother has woven," "the crown of flowers that my nurse plaited for me," "the coverlet that she wove of hyacinth and purple."[62]

The highest calling for a woman in ancient Israel was marriage and childbearing, and Seila bewails the fact that she will be denied the rites and rituals that accompany them. "I have not retrieved my wedding garlands," she cries. "I have not been clothed in splendor, according to my nobility. And I have not used the sweet-smelling ointment, and my soul has not rejoiced in the oil of anointing that has been prepared for me."[63]

Seila's lament reaches a climax of sorrow when she declares that all of the handiwork of the women who cherish her—and her own mortal remains—are condemned to Sheol, a Hebrew word that refers to the abode of the dead:

> Sheol has become my bridal chamber, though my people
>   [dwell] on earth.
> And may all the blend of oil that you have prepared for me be
>   poured out,
> and the white robe that my mother has woven, the moth will
>   eat it.
> And the crown of flowers that my nurse plaited for me for the
>   festival, may it wither up,
> and the coverlet that she wove of hyacinth and purple in my
>   nobility, may the worm devour it.
> And may my virgin companions tell of me in sorrow and weep
>   for me through the days.[64]

The story of Seila as imagined by Pseudo-Philo probably dates back to the first century C.E., an era when the sacred texts of the Bible had already been cleaned up and canonized, and so we cannot really know whether *Biblical Antiquities* preserves some thread of a forbidden tradition that the priestly censors left out of the Bible. Even the scholars who are willing to speculate that Jephthah's daughter and her companions belonged to a "sex cult" dare not suggest that they were goddess-worshippers. Indeed, the sheer enthusiasm that Seila displays for her fate prompts some exegetes to see her as "a paradigm for later Jewish and Christian martyrology"[65] or even a Christ figure in her own right. "The only other biblical character who is sacrificed by a patriarch for the good of his people," one Bible critic points out, "is Jesus."[66]

Still, it is tempting to imagine another way to tell the story of Jephthah's daughter. Perhaps she was offered up by her father on the altar of some deity other than Yahweh, one of those many forbidden gods and goddesses who so troubled the biblical authors precisely because they hungered for the charred flesh of children. Or perhaps Seila herself and her companions were the ones who defied the First Commandment, "Thou shalt have no other God before Me." If so, we can begin to imagine that her death was not the result of a rash vow to Yahweh, but rather of a death sentence pronounced on an apostate in the name of Yahweh. Either one of these imagined endings might have prompted the biblical authors to turn Jephthah's daughter from a goddess-worshipper into a pious martyr. And either one is reason enough to explain why they dared not write her name into the pages of the Bible.

CHAPTER TWELVE

THE TRAVELER AND HIS CONCUBINE

"Behold, here is my daughter a virgin, and his concubine; I will bring them out now, and humble ye them, and do with them what seemeth good unto you. . . ."

—JUDGES 19:24

In the days when no king ruled in Israel, and every man did what was right in his own eyes, a man from the tribe of Levi found himself at odds with the young woman from Bethlehem who was his concubine.

Who knows how such ugliness starts between a man and a woman? They exchanged bitter words, but the Levite went too far when he shouted "Harlot!" in her face. Not an unusual story, of course; who could have predicted how badly it would turn out in the end? Perhaps if there had been a king in Israel, the whole sordid affair might have ended when it was still just an ugly incident and not yet a bloody civil war.

The woman slammed the door of the Levite's house in the hill-country of Ephraim and headed back to her father's house in the land of Judah. At first, the Levite was sure that she would see her own foolishness and turn back; he waited patiently for the sound of her footfall at the gate. Then, as days turned into a week, he began to fret—what fate had befallen her on the lawless roads between here and Bethlehem? At last, word reached him that she was back in the household of her father, and when the weeks turned into months—*four* months, to be exact—he realized that she was not coming back, at least not on her own.

What stung the Levite's pride most of all was the fact that his concubine apparently did not miss him as much as he missed her. After a

> *And it came to pass in those days, when there was no king in Israel, that there was a certain Levite sojourning on the farther side of the hill-country of Ephraim, who took to him a concubine out of Beth-lehem in Judah. And his concubine played the harlot against him, and went away from him unto her father's house to Beth-lehem in Judah, and was there the space of four months.*
>
> —JUDGES 19:1–2

> *And her husband arose, and went after her, to speak kindly unto her, to bring her back, having his servant with him, and a couple of asses; and she brought him into her father's house; and when the father of the damsel saw him, he rejoiced to meet him.*
>
> —JUDGES 19:3

few more sleepless and fretful nights alone in his bed, the man worked up enough righteous indignation of his own to send him out the door and down the road after her. He took along two asses, one for him to ride and the other to fetch her back home, and a manservant just in case of trouble on the road. Even though one donkey was riderless on the way down to Bethlehem, the servant walked along behind him—but, then, he was accustomed to walking. To the Levite's relief, no danger befell them as they made their way down from the hill-country.

As the Levite traveler and his servant approached Bethlehem, the man wondered about the reception he would receive when he appeared at his father-in-law's door. He knew full well what a sharp tongue was hidden inside the lovely mouth of his concubine, and he began to worry that she had poisoned her father's mind against him with *her* version of what had gone so wrong between husband and wife. What if she told her father that he had accused her of playing the harlot against him? What if her father, outraged and indignant, set upon him and drove him off with blows?

But the Levite need not have fretted. His father-in-law seemed very

And his father-in-law, the damsel's father, retained him; and he abode with him three days; so they did eat and drink, and lodged there.

—JUDGES 19:4

And it came to pass on the fourth day, that they arose early in the morning, and he rose up to depart; and the damsel's father said unto his son-in-law: "Stay thy heart with a morsel of bread, and afterward ye shall go your way." So they sat down, and did eat and drink, both of them together; and the damsel's father said unto the man: "Be content, I pray thee, and tarry all night, and let thy heart be merry."

—JUDGES 19:5–6

glad indeed to see him—and even gladder when he saw the second ass that was intended to carry his daughter back to the place where she belonged now that she was all grown up and married off.

The man lingered at his father-in-law's house for three full days, and he was treated to rich meals, an abundance of good wine, and much music and dancing. But the young woman refused to show herself. Instead she sulked in a back room of her father's house, and the Levite found himself growing angry again. Why had he bothered to come in the first place? he asked himself. Let the wretched woman stay with her father! And so he announced that he would return to his own home in the morning, whether or not she wanted to come along, and he ordered his servant to prepare the donkeys for the journey. The next day, he rose at dawn, but the woman was still nowhere to be seen.

"Have a morsel of bread with me before you go," her father urged him. "You cannot travel such a distance on an empty stomach!"

So the Levite traveler delayed his departure and sat down at the table for what turned out to be yet another sumptuous meal that lasted until the sun was high overhead. His father-in-law poured cup after cup

And the man rose up to depart; but his father-in-law urged him, and he lodged there again.

—JUDGES 19:7

And he arose early in the morning on the fifth day to depart; and the damsel's father said: "Stay thy heart, I pray thee, and tarry yet until the day declineth"; and they did eat, both of them. And when the man rose up to depart, he, and his concubine, and his servant, his father-in-law, the damsel's father, said unto him: "Behold, now the day draweth toward evening; tarry, I pray you, all night; behold the day groweth to an end; lodge here, that thy heart may be merry; and tomorrow get you early on your way, that thou mayest go home." But the man would not tarry that night, but he rose up and departed.

—JUDGES 19:8–10

of wine, and insisted on one last dance by the slave-girl with the fetching smile who had entertained them over the last three days.

"Too late to start on your journey now," his father-in-law said. "Why not spend the night and enjoy yourself? Then you can get off to a fresh start tomorrow."

So he lingered one more night, and rose early on the fifth day, but again the woman did not show herself. Again, his father-in-law pleaded with him to dine before hitting the road—and again he tarried.

Then, quite to his surprise—and his father-in-law's obvious relief—the woman appeared in the doorway of the house, dressed in a long cloak and bearing a bundle on her head, all ready for the journey back home. His father-in-law abruptly ceased his entreaties and instead seized the bundle from his daughter's head, making himself useful by lashing the baggage to one of the donkeys.

"On your way, then, the two of you," prattled the father-in-law, not

> *[He] came over against Jebus—the same is Jerusalem; and there were with him a couple of asses saddled; his concubine also was with him. When they were by Jebus—the day was far spent—the servant said unto his master: "Come, I pray thee, and let us turn aside into this city of the Jebusites, and lodge in it." And his master said unto him: "We will not turn aside into the city of a foreigner, that is not of the children of Israel; but we will pass over to Gibeah." And he said unto his servant: "Come and let us draw near to one of these places; and we will lodge in Gibeah, or in Ramah."*
>
> —JUDGES 19:10–13

bothering to offer his son-in-law another night of hospitality, "and Godspeed!"

The sky was already gray when they left Bethlehem, and the clouds only grew more threatening as they made their way along the road. By the time they reached the outskirts of Jerusalem, the weather was wild and stormy, and the servant looked longingly at the little clusters of houses on the hills around them. Of course, the place was not yet called Jerusalem—the Israelites had not managed to drive out the Jebusites from their impregnable hilltop settlement, and the place still belonged to them. But the servant's misery was greater than his fear of strangers, and he pulled at his master's sleeve.

"Master," pleaded the servant, "let's spend the night here among the Jebusites."

"No, not here," said the Levite. "Not in a town full of strangers!"

"But the storm—" the servant began to protest.

"We will go to a place where we are sure to find a friendly welcome and a warm bed—Gibeah is not far off, or perhaps Ramah," the Levite insisted, naming places along the road where he knew he would find himself among fellow Israelites. "I couldn't sleep knowing I was alone among strangers who might slaughter us in our beds!"

Looking back on that terrible night, the Levite often wished that he

> *So they passed on and went their way; and the sun went down*
> *upon them near to Gibeah, which belongeth to Benjamin. And*
> *they turned aside thither, to go in to lodge in Gibeah; and he*
> *went in, and sat him down in the broad place of the city; for*
> *there was no man that took them into his house to lodge.*
>
> —JUDGES 19:14–15

had consented to stay among strangers in Jerusalem. As it turned out, the Jebusites could not have been less welcoming than the Israelites in whose town they bedded down.

The concubine would certainly have felt the same way, if she were asked her opinion—and if she were able to offer one.

The sun was setting just as the party of travelers—the Levite and his concubine, their servant and the two donkeys—reached the town of Gibeah in the land that belonged to the tribe of Benjamin. They trudged through the streets, chilled and hungry and soaking wet, but no one opened a door to them. At last, they sat themselves down in the town square and waited for some good-hearted soul to offer them food and lodging. But not a single Benjaminite offered to take them into his house for the night.

At last, the empty streets of Gibeah echoed with the footfalls of an old man crossing the town square on his way back from a long day in the fields outside town. The old man's birthplace was in the hill-country of Ephraim, but now he lived among the Benjaminites in Gibeah. He walked with his head down to keep the rain out of his face, and when he glanced up, he saw the travelers in the middle of the square.

"Where are you going?" he asked in a friendly way. "And where do you come from?"

"We are coming from Bethlehem in Judah, and we are heading toward my home in the hill-country of Ephraim," the Levite explained. "We stopped here to find shelter from the storm, but no one has offered us a place to stay."

And, behold, there came an old man from his work out of the field at even; now the man was of the hill-country of Ephraim, and he sojourned in Gibeah; but the men of the place were Benjaminites. And he lifted up his eyes, and saw the wayfaring man in the broad place of the city; and the old man said: "Wither goest thou? and whence comest thou?" And he said unto him: "We are passing from Beth-lehem in Judah unto the farther side of the hill-country of Ephraim; . . . and there is no man that taketh me into his house. Yet there is both straw and provender for our asses; and there is bread and wine also for me, and for thy handmaid, and for the young man that is with thy servants; there is no want of any thing."

—JUDGES 19:16–19

And the old man said: "Peace be unto thee; howsoever let all thy wants lie upon me; only lodge not in the broad place." So he brought him into his house, and gave the asses fodder; and they washed their feet, and did eat and drink.

—JUDGES 19:20–21

Then, lest the old man think him to be a beggar and a vagrant, the traveler continued:

"I have straw and fodder for the asses, food and wine for myself and the girl and the young man," he said. "We have all we need, sir, except a roof over our heads."

"I am a man of Ephraim, too!" the old man said with real warmth. "You are welcome under my roof—I will give you food and drink—but you must not spend the night in the street, I beg you!"

So the Levite traveler and his party followed the old man as he led them to his home. As hospitality requires, the old man put out straw in the courtyard for the asses, set out bowls of water so his guests could wash their feet, and ordered his daughter to lay out food and drink for a late supper. The concubine ate sparingly and in silence, then followed

> *As they were making their hearts merry, behold, the men of the*
> *city, certain base fellows, beset the house round about, beating*
> *at the door; and they spoke to the master of the house, the old*
> *man, saying: "Bring forth the man that came into thy house,*
> *that we may know him."*
>
> —JUDGES 19:22

the old man's daughter to a back room and promptly went to sleep on a pile of bedding in the corner. The servant slept on a pile of straw in a storeroom at the back of the house. But the traveler and the old man stayed up late into the night, laughing and drinking, sharing stories of the good country where the tribe of Ephraim dwelled, and bemoaning their misfortune in ending up among the Benjaminites.

"At least for you and your woman," said the old man from the land of Ephraim, seeking to comfort the Levite after his ungracious reception in the streets of Gibeah, "it is only for one night."

The two of them were still trading stories and sipping wine when they heard sudden noises in the alley outside the old man's house—a shout, a scuffle of feet, a thud. The Levite traveler looked at his host in alarm, but the old man only laughed and reached for the wine jar. Then they heard the sound of urgent whispering right outside the door, and even the old man seemed suddenly alert.

"Hey in there!" someone shouted from outside the front door, pounding on the wooden door with a fist. "Open up!"

"What do you want?" the old man called out, his quavering voice betraying his fear. "It's late. Go home. Leave us alone!"

Then suddenly the noise seemed to come from all directions at once, as if a gang of men had surrounded the little house and were trying to force their way in through every window. A few moments later, the pounding and shouting stopped just as suddenly as it had started, and now a voice was heard again at the front door.

"Bring out the man who is inside there with you," a hoarse voice shouted on the other side of the door. "Bring him out!"

> *And the man, the master of the house, went out unto them,*
> *and said unto them: "Nay, my brethren, I pray you, do not so*
> *wickedly; seeing that this man is come into my house, do not this*
> *wanton deed."*
>
> —JUDGES 19:23

"Yes, bring him out," a second man said with unmistakable menace, "so that we may get to *know* him—" and his words incited harsh laughter from the crowd.

The traveler looked at his host. "What do they mean?" he asked, although he already feared the worst.

The old man only confirmed his fears. "Around here," the old man said, "the sons of hell among these foul Benjaminites like to 'know' a man the way a man knows a woman."

"What will we do?" the traveler asked, looking in vain around the room for a place to hide.

The old man did not answer. He sat for a few moments in silence, then struggled to his feet and staggered toward the front door, still a bit tipsy but sobering up fast. He leaned up to the door and shouted loudly so the men outside would be able to hear him plainly enough.

"No, my brothers," the old man said, his words slightly slurred on his tongue. "Do not do such a wicked thing—"

"Bring him out!" came the shout from outside.

"You can see he is my guest!" the old man continued in a pleading tone. "Do not treat a guest in such a wanton way!"

The crowd answered with a fresh flurry of shouting and pounding, and the old man feared that they would simply break down the door and have their way with him *and* his guest. He glanced toward the curtained opening to the room where his daughter and the traveler's concubine had gone to sleep. Surely they were awake now, he thought to himself—who could sleep through all that commotion? And then quite a different thought forced its way into his wine-soaked brain.

"Hey!" he shouted to the men outside. "I have a daughter—a virgin!"

> *"Behold, here is my daughter a virgin, and his concubine; I will bring them out now, and humble ye them, and do with them what seemeth good unto you; but unto this man do not so wanton a thing."*
>
> —JUDGES 19:24

The Levite turned and stared at the old man.

"And my guest is traveling with a very pretty young woman!" the old man continued. "They're both here right now!"

The noise outside stopped suddenly. The traveler, too, listened in amazement.

"I will bring them out to you now," the old man continued. "Do whatever you want with them—whatever strikes your fancy—but leave the two of us alone!"

At first, the traveler bristled at the old man's words. What right did *he* have to offer up the concubine to the mob? The old man's own daughter—well, that was one thing. But the concubine belonged to *him*, the Levite thought to himself, and no one had asked *him* whether she might be thrown to the mob like a piece of raw meat to a pack of dogs! But he said nothing, waiting to see whether the old man's offer would satisfy the men outside the door. But it only seemed to incite the crowd outside the door to an even louder chorus of catcalls and whistles.

"It's no good," the old man said miserably. "It's not a woman these sons of hell want!"

The Levite, however, was not ready to give up on the idea, which began to seem quite compelling as he contemplated what the mob intended to do to him. After all, he told himself, the concubine was such an annoyance, such a burden, and she had caused him so much grief over the last few months. Why should he put himself at risk of the mob's vile appetites in order to spare her?

So the Levite rose from the corner where he had been huddling in fear, stalked into the room where the concubine, too, was cowering, and manhandled her to the door. When the old man saw what the traveler

[S]o the man laid hold on his concubine, and brought her forth unto them; and they knew her, and abused her all the night until the morning; and when the day began to spring, they let her go.

—JUDGES 19:25

Then came the woman in the dawning of the day, and fell down at the door of the man's house where her lord was, till it was light. And her lord rose up in the morning, and opened the doors of the house, and went out to go his way; and, behold, the woman his concubine was fallen down at the door of the house, with her hands upon the threshold. And he said unto her: "Up, and let us be going"; but none answered.

—JUDGES 19:26–28

intended to do, he lifted the stout length of wood that barred the threshold and opened the door just wide enough for the traveler to shove his concubine into the street.

The young woman hissed and scratched as she tried to brace herself in the doorway, but now a half dozen of the men outside seized her by the hair, by the wrist, by the ankle. Pushed from behind and pulled forward at the same time, the young woman tumbled into the street to the jeers of the crowd. Then the old man and the traveler shouldered the door closed again, dropped the bolt of wood in place, and fell to the floor in exhaustion. Outside, the crowd fell suddenly and ominously silent, at least for one long moment, and then new and even more terrible sounds began to reach the ears of the old man and his honored guest as they sat with their backs against the door.

That is where they stayed all night long, the old man and the traveler, each one mute, each one avoiding the other one's eyes, each one listening to the terrible sounds from the street, the sounds that a gang of men make when they take turns raping a woman over and over again, doing exactly what they please to her, until the sun began to come up.

At first light, the Levite looked over and saw the old man was asleep—or at least he was pretending to sleep. Then he heard a soft thud as if someone had let a sack of flour fall against the door. A moment later, he heard the sound of voices fading into the distance as the men hastened away from the old man's house. The traveler waited a long time to be sure that they were finally gone, then cautiously opened the door of the house.

The young woman was sprawled in front of the house. Her two arms were outstretched, her hands were reaching toward the door, but she was still and silent. She seemed almost at rest, as if she were merely asleep, and the mad thought occurred to him that it had all been a bad dream. Yes, of course, a dream! Somehow, despite everything he had heard during the long night, the Levite traveler succeeded in convincing himself that it was so.

"Up!" the man said out loud, addressing the woman as he crossed the threshold, stepped over her body, and headed toward the courtyard where the two asses were tied up. "Up," he said briskly, "and let us be going!"

No one heard, and no one answered.

The donkey she had ridden from her father's house carried the mutilated corpse of the concubine back to the hill-country of Ephraim. By

[T]hen he took her up upon the ass; and the man rose up, and got him unto his place. And when he was come into his house, he took a knife, and laid hold on his concubine, and divided her, limb by limb, into twelve pieces, and sent her throughout all the borders of Israel. And it was so, that all that saw it said: "Such a thing hath not happened nor has been seen from the day that the children of Israel came up out of the land of Egypt unto this day; consider it, take counsel, and speak."

—JUDGES 19:28–30

the time the traveler and his servant reached home with their gruesome baggage, the Levite had worked himself up into a pious frenzy at the way the Benjaminite sons of hell back in Gibeah had abused her beautiful young body—and he had devised a plan to punish them for what they had done.

The servant laid out her battered and bloody corpse, the face unrecognizable and the private parts unspeakably insulted, on the table in the Levite's house. As the servant watched in amazement, the Levite himself took a sharp knife that he used for butchering and cut the young woman's body into twelve pieces, limb by limb. He wrapped each piece of the corpse tightly in linen and cord, and then he dispatched the twelve grisly packages by messenger to all of Israel—all the tribes except Benjamin, of course, against whom he now hoped to incite a war of revenge, a war that would cleanse all of Israel, a holy war.

"Such a thing hath not been seen from the day the children of Israel came up out of the land of Egypt unto this very day," went the Levite's message. "Consider it, and speak."

CHAPTER THIRTEEN

GOD AND GYNO-SADISM

Heroines and Martyrs in the Book of Judges

FOUR HUNDRED VIRGINS
"ALL UNTRUTHFUL, AND ONE A KLEPTOMANIAC"
GOD, GIBEAH, AND GYNO-SADISM
"BETWEEN HER LEGS HE KNELT, HE FELL, HE LAY"
BLACK PROPAGANDA

The Book of Judges is a grab bag of tall tales about the time of troubles that followed the conquest of Canaan, a place where the Israelites were beset by bitter enemies, riven by tribal hatred, and lured into apostasy by strange gods and goddesses. The tale of Samson and his catastrophic seduction by Delilah (Judg. 13–16) is perhaps the single most familiar story in Judges, one that has escaped the confines of the Sunday school classroom and spread into the popular culture. And Samson is emblematic of the plight of the nation of Israel, whose people were equally susceptible to seduction and brought down calamity on their own heads.

But the tale of Samson and Delilah is hardly the most lurid of the atrocity stories that we find in the Book of Judges, an escalating cycle of sin and scandal that reaches a bloody climax of mass rape and mass murder in the account of the Levite traveler and his concubine. Indeed, the biblical author is eager to show us by gruesome example how badly ordinary people behave when they enjoy too much liberty, and the essential message of Judges is repeated throughout the book like a mantra. "In those days there was no king in Israel," the author writes. "Every man did that which was right in his own eyes" (Judg. 21:25).

The moral chaos that prevailed in ancient Israel before the crowning of a king, as depicted in Judges, begins with sexual violence, escalates into civil war, and ends with genocide. Throughout the Book of Judges, the victims of these excesses are often wholly innocent women. We have now encountered two of them: Jephthah's daughter, a doomed young woman who achieves a certain tragic grandeur in death (see chapter ten), and the Levite's concubine, a woman of whom we know nothing at all except that she is gang-raped to death, then dismembered and scattered among the tribes of Israel. Significantly, the biblical author takes care to specify the tribe of the men who abuse her, and even the town where she dies—Gibeah—but *her* name is never mentioned. So her story has come to be called the Gibeah Outrage in a kind of reverential shorthand.

"Oh miserable men, who destroy your own species through those pleasures intended to reproduce it," cried Rousseau in his own horror-soaked retelling of the tale, "how is it that this dying beauty doesn't freeze your fierce lusts?"[1]

The tale of the Levite traveler and his concubine bears a striking resemblance to a Bible story that we have already encountered: the tale of Lot and his daughters, who are saved from a gang of Sodomites by a pair of helpful angels. The old man who hosts the Levite and his concubine in Gibeah, just like Lot back in Sodom, offers a couple of young women to the lusty mob for their pleasure in order to spare his guest (and himself) from their unwanted attentions. From what we recall about the intervention of the angels in Sodom, we do not really expect the young women in Gibeah to be cast into the arms of the mob—*something*, angelic or human, will spare them at the very last moment.

But no angelic rescuers appear at the doorway in a burst of celestial light to drive off the attackers, and the concubine finds herself at the mercy of mere mortals. As the author of Judges reminds us, mere mortals are not very well-behaved in the absence of some higher authority, human or divine, to check their worst impulses. And no such authority is to be found during those tumultuous years before the Almighty anoints a king to rule over the Israelites. God, who is not much seen *or* heard in Judges, "plays out with ironic detachment his role as a god of convenience."[2] Even the judges who rule over the unruly Israelites are flawed and ineffectual. As both Jephthah's daughter and the Levite's concubine discover, *everyone* is at risk when "every man [does] that which [is] right in his own eyes."

The Book of Judges offers a few glimpses of glory, but even these moments are odd and off-putting. Here in Judges, for example, we find an exceedingly strange account of the exploits of a man named Ehud, an Israelite assassin who tricks his way into the palace of a Moabite king. "I have a message from God unto thee," says Ehud—and then disembowels the monarch with a dagger while he sits in his royal privy! The blade is driven so deep into the king's fat belly that Ehud cannot draw it out, but the odor of the king's spilled bowels fools the courtiers outside the door into thinking that he is still using the privy, thus allowing Ehud an opportunity to make a safe getaway (Judg. 3:12–30).

Here, too, we find the saga of quite a different sort of assassin, a valiant woman who can be seen as the mirror image of the abused and murdered concubine, a Bible-era guerrilla fighter whose heroism somehow redeems the sorry spectacle of the Gibeah Outrage. But by the end of the Book of Judges, we are so sullied and unsettled that we are ready for a king, *any* king, who will bring these wild and dangerous people under control. And that of course is the motive of the biblical author who told these shocking and sorrowful stories in the first place.

FOUR HUNDRED VIRGINS

The Gibeah Outrage does not end with the gang rape of the concubine. Her death and dismemberment, it turns out, are only the first of a series of atrocities that build to a gruesome climax in the final chapters of Judges. The grisly packages of human flesh that the Levite sends to the tribes of Israel prompt a civil war among the tribes and a war of genocide against the tribe of Benjamin. Abruptly, the death of the concubine ceases to be a matter of personal grief and turns into a political cause célèbre. At the end of the harrowing saga, the very survival of the tribe of Benjamin is at risk, and only another outrage allows the Benjaminites to survive at all.

The author of Judges is much concerned with tribal rivalries, but the Levite himself belongs to a tribe that possesses no territory of its own in Canaan. A Levite is *always* a sojourner on the land of another tribe, and so he is a neutral in the rivalry among the tribes of Israel. The

Levites are descendants of Jacob's son, Levi, and—as we have already seen—Jacob denied Levi a deathbed blessing because of Levi's role in the slaughter of innocents at Shechem. (See chapter five.) That is why the tribe of Levi does not enjoy any "portion or inheritance" in the Promised Land (Deut. 18:1), and the role of the Levites is to "minister in the name of the Lord" (Deut. 18:5) to their fellow Israelites.

So the Levites are scattered throughout Israel as a tribe of landless priests who depend on the offerings of the other Israelites for a livelihood. "The first-fruits of thy corn, of thy wine, and of thine oil, and the first of the fleece of thy sheep, shalt thou give him," decrees Moses, himself a Levite and a priest (Deut. 18:4). In fact, the ritual sacrifice of animals, which is described in such exacting detail by the priestly authors of Leviticus and other biblical texts, can be understood as a way to feed and clothe the Levite priests who have no other way to earn a living. And the duties of the priesthood at the altar of sacrifice, which amount to sanctified butchery of animals, allow us to understand why a Levite might be good at cutting a body into pieces!

> And this shall be the priests' due from the people, from them that offer a sacrifice, whether it be ox or sheep, that they should give unto the priest the shoulders, and the two cheeks, and the maw (Deut. 18:3).

Summoned by the Levite's bizarre call to arms in the form of the butchered concubine, the tribes assemble at Mizpah to decide what to do about the "filthy outrage" of the Benjaminites in Gibeah (Judg. 20:6 NEB). If we take the biblical author at his word, some four hundred thousand foot soldiers show up at Mizpah and listen to the Levite's distinctly self-serving version of what happened back in Gibeah. "[T]he men of Gibeah rose against me," the Levite says, conveniently leaving out some of the more awkward details of what actually happened. "[M]e they thought to have slain, and my concubine they forced, and she is dead" (Judg. 20:5).

The assembly resolves to punish the men of Gibeah—and the tribe of Benjamin as a whole—for their "wickedness" and "wantonness." First, they make a sacred vow to the Almighty that no Israelite will allow his daughter to marry a Benjaminite. Then an ultimatum is delivered to the Benjaminites: "[D]eliver up the men, the base fellows that are in Gibeah, that we may put them to death, and put away evil from Israel" (Judg. 20:13). The Benjaminites defy the ultimatum and muster an army of their own, some twenty-six thousand men-at-arms who join the seven hundred men of Gibeah on the field of battle. All of the men in the contingent from Gibeah are left-handed—an ironic play on the name of the tribe, Benjamin, which means "son of my right hand"—and all are able to strike a blow with deadly accuracy using only a stone and a slingshot, the weapon that will soon be made famous in the hands of the future king, David (Judg. 20:16).

On the eve of battle, the Israelites are stricken with sudden doubt over the wisdom of making war on a fellow tribe. So they gather at Bethel and ask God to designate the tribe that will strike the first blow, as if to confirm whether they should fight at all. "Who shall go up for us first to battle against the children of Benjamin?" the Israelites ask. "Judah first," says God. In fact, the Israelites suffer dire losses in two successive battles with the Benjaminites; after each defeat, they lament over their losses to the Almighty—and the Almighty urges them back into the fight. Only when the armies meet for a third time does God finally promise the high priest of the Israelites to "deliver [Benjamin] into thy hand" (Judg. 20:28).

Even then, the victory is based on guile and deceit rather than superior courage in battle: the Israelites feign a retreat to draw the Benjaminites into a deadly ambush. Victorious at last, the Israelites chase down and kill the fleeing soldiers, burn the Benjaminite towns and murder the townsfolk, and even pause to slaughter their cattle. Of the tribe of Benjamin, only six hundred survivors manage to find a place of refuge in a natural redoubt called the Rock of Rimmon.

Now the triumphant Israelites suddenly wake up to the fact that they have condemned the tribe of Benjamin to extinction. Only a few hundred Benjaminite men have survived the battles and the general slaughter that followed; all of the Benjaminite women have been put to the sword; and the other tribes of Israel have already vowed not to permit their daughters to marry a Benjaminite. So the tribe is doomed to extermination, and the Israelites are stricken with remorse. "O Lord, the God of Israel, why is this come to pass," they weep, "that there should be to-day one tribe lacking in Israel?" (Judg. 21:3).

A solution is devised, but it is so bloodthirsty, so bizarre, that the mind simply boggles at the very notion that it is described in the pages of Holy Writ. The Israelites conveniently recall that *two* vows had been made at the assembly of tribes at Mizpah. The first vow, as we have seen, is that none of the participants in the assembly will give his daughter in marriage to a Benjaminite. The second vow is that any Israelite who fails to participate in the assembly will be put to death. Now it occurs to the Israelites that the townsfolk of a place called Jabesh-gilead did not bother to show up at Mizpah. These circumstances provide a way to secure wives for the surviving Benjaminites and to preserve the tribe from extinction.

First, the Bible tells us, an expeditionary force consisting of the twelve thousand "valiantest" soldiers of Israel is dispatched to the unfortunate village of Jabesh-gilead, where every single male—adult, child, and infant—and every single woman "that hath lain by man" is put to the sword. Only four hundred young virgins are spared—and they are promptly turned over to the soldiers who are holed up at the Rock of Rimmon to serve as brood mares for a new generation of Benjaminites. Suddenly, the victorious Israelites find it within themselves to forgive the tribe that they had tried to exterminate, and they take it upon themselves to round up enough virgins, willing or not, to repopulate the tribe of Benjamin.

You mean *that*'s in the Bible?

Yes, dear reader, *that*'s in the Bible.

But wait—it gets worse.

Four hundred virgins, no matter how fecund, are simply not sufficient to provide bedmates to the six hundred surviving Benjaminites at the Rock of Rimmon, and so the remorseful Israelites are compelled to look farther afield for suitable women. Someone points out that a harvest festival is held every year in the vineyards of Shiloh, and the festival is the occasion for singing and dancing by the maidens of the district. And so the surviving Benjaminite soldiers are promptly dispatched to Shiloh. "Go and lie in wait in the vineyards, and see . . . if the daughters of Shiloh come out to dance," the soldiers are told by their former enemies, "then come ye out of the vineyards, and catch you every man his wife" (Judg. 21:20–21).

By such brutal means, we are told, the endangered species of Benjaminites is saved from extinction, the unity of Israel is restored, and all is made well again. "The children of Israel departed," says the author of

Judges, "every man to his tribe and to his family" (Judg. 21:24). Again we are reminded of the story of Lot, where the earnest desire of Lot's daughters to repopulate a God-blasted landscape leads to seduction and incest; here, abduction and rape are the means to repopulate the ravaged tribe of Benjamin. Both Genesis 19 and Judges 19 are disturbing examples of how moral order, always precarious in the Bible, "is turned upside down [when] one lives in an age governed by human selfishness."[3]

After the orgy of violence that follows the gang rape and murder of the concubine—mass murder, mass abduction, mass rape—the traditional reference to the incident of the traveler and his concubine as the Gibeah Outrage seems almost ironic. Only one woman is cast to a mob of rapists at Gibeah, but six hundred women share the same fate at the Rock of Rimmon. The real outrage is that tens of thousands of men, women, and children are slain—and hundreds of young women are sexually enslaved—as the cycle of sin and despair in Israel achieves a kind of moral fission.

"ALL UNTRUTHFUL, AND ONE A KLEPTOMANIAC"

The outrages against women that take up so much of the Book of Judges explain why even the earliest feminist Bible critics tended to regard the Holy Scriptures as hopelessly tainted by the sexism of the stern patriarchy that created the Bible in the first place. More than a century ago, pioneering feminist Elizabeth Cady Stanton published a collection of biblical commentary titled *The Woman's Bible*, in which she complained that the Bible had long been used to enslave and oppress woman. Nothing before or since has exceeded her flat condemnation of the Bible as a rhetorical weapon directed at women.

"Whatever the Bible may be made to do in Hebrew or Greek," wrote Stanton, "in plain English it does not exalt and dignify woman." She declared herself unimpressed by most, if not all, of the women in the Bible. "In fact the wives of the patriarchs, all untruthful, and one a kleptomaniac," she cracked, "but illustrate the law, that the cardinal virtues are seldom found in the oppressed classes,"[4] and she summed up what she saw as the sorry role assigned to women by Holy Writ:

The Bible teaches that woman brought sin and death into the world, that she precipitated the fall of the race, that she was arraigned before the judgment seat of Heaven, tried, condemned and sentenced. Marriage for her was to be a condition of bondage, maternity a period of suffering and anguish, and in silence and subjection, she was to play the role of a dependent on man's bounty for all her material wants, and for all the information she might desire on the vital questions of the hour, she was commanded to ask her husband at home.[5]

Some contemporary feminist Bible scholars still feel the same way. For example, they are troubled by the fact that the women depicted in the Bible resort so often to guile and deception to achieve otherwise praiseworthy ends. The deceit practiced on various men by Rebekah, Tamar, Ruth, Rahab, and others strikes Bible scholar Carole Fontaine as "morally ambivalent," especially when the trickery is based on sexual allure or actual seduction. Rebekah connives with her son, Jacob, to trick her husband into bestowing the blessing of the firstborn on the younger son by cooking up a savory stew. Tamar seduces her father-in-law by dressing up as a harlot. Ruth, at the urging of her mother-in-law, carries out an elaborate seduction of a rich landowner on his threshing floor. And Rahab, a good-hearted hooker, conspires with a pair of Israelite spies to turn away the soldiers of the Canaanite king.

" '[W]oman the Provider,' associated with food, drink, and shelter," writes Fontaine, "turns deceiver, thereby rendering the familiar nurturing figure suddenly dangerous to unsuspecting males who fall into her 'snares.' "[6]

Of course, the use of deceit and seduction by these biblical women can be understood and explained even by critics who are put off by such depictions. To be fair—and perfectly frank—the fact is that women in the biblical era did not have any weapons *other* than trickery to work their will in the real world. A woman in ancient Israel was far more likely to be a wife, a concubine, a handmaid, or a harlot than, say, a queen or a prophetess; and, in any case, the Bible was interpreted to forbid the use of weaponry by women (Deut. 22:5). No matter what their standing, women were always under the domination of a male figure, first a father, then a husband, and sometimes a son. Except when summoned to bed by a man, they were confined to the women's tent and the company of other women. So it should not surprise us that the biblical women who assert themselves at all are compelled to use the offer of food, shelter, or sexual gratification—the only tools available "to those who lack power to achieve their ends in other ways."[7]

Sexism in the Bible, then, is sometimes strictly in the eye of the beholder. Bible critic Esther Fuchs, for example, reads the account of God's visit to Abraham at the terebinths of Mamre, where Sarah laughs out loud when she overhears the divine promise that she will yet bear a son in old age, and concludes that Sarah is depicted by the biblical author as "confined, passive, cowardly, deceptive, and unfaithful."[8] Yet the very same passage strikes novelist Joseph Heller as worthy of celebration: Sarah's laughter is an act of audacity and courage by a woman of "generous, high-spirited good nature." "Old Sarah's fun—she laughed and lied to God," King David is made to say in Heller's *God Knows*, "and I still get a big treat out of that."[9]

What is often overlooked in these debates is the fact that the Bible—and the culture that the Bible defines and describes—treated women with greater care and respect than they generally enjoyed elsewhere in the ancient Near East. Daughters of Israel, for example, are entitled to inherit property under certain limited circumstances (Num. 27:3–8); a man is not permitted to sell his wife into slavery (Deut. 21:14); a daughter who is sold into servititude is entitled to her freedom if her master violates her rights under biblical law (Exod. 21:7–11); and, as we have seen, a childless widow is entitled to the extraordinary benefits of a levirate "marriage" (Deut. 25:5–10). (See chapter seven.) Such grudging allowances may not much impress some contemporary readers, but the fact that women have *any* legal status under biblical law is "almost unique in the ancient world," as Bible scholar Gila Ramras-Rauch points out.[10]

What's more, an open-eyed reading of the Bible reveals that women play a crucial and dynamic role in the destiny of humankind, in both Jewish and Christian tradition. Inevitably, a woman figures decisively in the recurring theme of "the birth of the chosen one," starting with the matriarchs of the Hebrew Bible and culminating with the Virgin Mary in the Christian Bible. As we have already seen, Lot's daughters and Judah's daughter-in-law are examples of how the bearer of the "chosen one" is not passively impregnated with the seed of a patriarch; rather, these women take it upon themselves to defy the will of powerful men and sometimes God himself in order to bring about the crucial birth. Indeed, the Bible frequently singles out "the woman as initiator of events," as Ramras-Rauch puts it. "From Eve through Sarah and Esther, women have shaped sacred history through word and deed."[11]

GOD AND GYNO-SADISM

Still, a certain sexist sting can be felt in unexpected places in the Bible. Remarkably, even a woman so thoroughly victimized as the Levite's concubine still comes in for a bit of victim-blaming by the biblical author, at least in one version of the Bible. According to the Masoretic Text, an early and authoritative Hebrew version of the Bible, the Levite and the concubine are estranged because she "played the harlot against him" (Judg. 19:2 JPS), thus setting into motion the sequence of mishaps that reaches a sudden and unexpected crescendo of violence on that night in Gibeah.

But the phrase "play the harlot" does not appear in the Septuagint, an early Greek translation of the Bible that serves as the basis for many Christian Bibles, which says that the concubine "became angry with him" (RSV) and thus suggests only an ordinary squabble between husband and wife.[12] Indeed, we might conclude that she is the one sinned against, especially since the Levite displays such ardor in making his way to her father's house "to speak kindly unto her, to bring her back" (RSV).[13] In any event, the Levite's father-in-law seems very glad indeed to see him when he arrives in hot pursuit of his mate.*

The fact that the woman is described as a concubine, by the way, is probably *not* intended by the biblical author to demean her. A concubine is technically defined as a "a legal wife of secondary rank,"[14] a woman who "dedicate[s] herself to one particular man exclusively," and who "could partake of many aspects of regular marriage."[15] A concubine was *not* equivalent to a mistress or a harlot, at least according to biblical tradition and rabbinical law; the Bible regards concubinage as an

---

*In retelling the story of the Levite traveler and his concubine, I have imagined that the father-in-law insists on entertaining the Levite day after day, thus delaying his departure, only because his daughter has not yet consented to return with the Levite to his home in the hill-country of Ephraim.

unremarkable and perfectly honorable position in a household, and four of the twelve tribes of Israel descend from the sons of Jacob's concubines. But contemporary readers tend to feel otherwise, and at least one feminist Bible critic argues that the concubine ought to be regarded as a kind of sexual chattel: "Legally and socially, she is not the equivalent of a wife," insists Phyllis Trible, "but is virtually a slave, secured by a man for his own purposes."[16]

Trible goes even further in *Texts of Terror*, her collection of revisionist readings of the Bible, and suggests that the Levite himself may well be the murderer of the concubine and not merely an unwitting accomplice to her murder. The Septuagint plainly states that the concubine is dead when the Levite finds her outside the door of the old man's house in Gibeah. But the Masoretic Text is not so plainspoken: we are only told that the Levite calls to her, and she makes no answer. So Trible asks us to entertain the notion that the concubine was still alive on the morning after the gang rape, that she clung to life on the long journey back to the hill-country of Ephraim and died only when the Levite took out his butcher knife and went to work on her body.

"Is the cowardly betrayer," asks Trible, "also the murderer?"[17]

Such crimes and misdemeanors on the part of the Levite, real or imagined, are ultimately less troubling than the blood-shaking acts of violence against women that are so graphically depicted throughout the Book of Judges. The Gibeah Outrage is the single most grotesque example of what feminist Bible critic Anne Michele Tapp characterizes as "gyno-sadistic biblical texts,"[18] and the stories of Lot's daughters and Jephthah's daughter are only slightly less off-putting. "They are passive, resigned and helpless," she writes of all of these nameless women and their stories of abuse. "They suggest that women lived only as objects to be bartered, abused and sacrificed by men." What's worse, Tapp insists, the moral example of these Bible stories was (and perhaps still is) not merely sexist but actually life-threatening. "The ideologies expressed through these [stories]," writes Tapp, "are both degrading and deadly for women."[19]

Yet, remarkably enough, another feminist Bible scholar proposes that the author of the Book of Judges *is* a woman. What's more, she asks us to consider whether the physical violence and sexual abuse described in Judges is not so grotesque, so preposterous, that it amounts to an elaborate work of parody. Adrien Janis Bledstein wonders if whether the

Book of Judges was composed by "a deeply religious woman who is satirizing men who play God," a woman who is "[using] humor to deflate the arrogant."[20] And Bible scholar David Penchansky is willing to entertain the same intriguing notion: he detects "some radically feminist perspectives within the Hebrew Bible," and he goes on to imagine that Judges is the work of "a woman secretly harboring sympathies for the goddess, perhaps Asherah."[21]

By tradition, authorship of Judges was ascribed to the prophet Samuel, but the conventional wisdom among scholars is that the book was probably compiled from various stories and poems of the ancient Israelites by the same person (or, perhaps, persons) who authored the Book of Deuteronomy, a source known as "D" or the Deuteronomist. In fact, the Deuteronomist (or a source called the "Deuteronomistic historian") is thought to have authored—or assembled and edited—not only Deuteronomy itself but also the six books that follow in the Hebrew Bible, including Joshua, Judges, the First and Second Books of Samuel, and the First and Second Books of Kings.[22]

The Deuteronomist may have been a priest who lived and worked in the court of King Josiah, a descendant of King David during whose reign the scroll containing the Book of Deuteronomy mysteriously showed up in the Temple at Jerusalem.[23] Bible scholar Richard Elliott Friedman nominates the prophet Jeremiah as the man most likely to be the Deuteronomist. But Bledstein suggests that the Deuteronomist— and thus the author of Judges—may have been an otherwise obscure prophetess named Huldah who endorses the authenticity of "all the words of the book" that was found in the Temple (2 Kings 22:16).[24]

Regardless of the gender of its author, however, the fact remains that the Book of Judges depicts women as both heroines *and* martyrs, victims *and* victors. Indeed, if the nameless concubine who is gangraped to death is the single most victimized woman in the Bible, Judges also gives us a Bible-era guerrilla fighter who is arguably the single most valorous one. That woman is Jael, the only woman in the Hebrew Bible who slays an adversary with her own hands, and a woman whose story can be read as an ironic counterpoint to the Gibeah Outrage. Jael emerges from the woman's tent and, quite literally, strikes a blow against the worst excesses of "gyno-sadism."

"BETWEEN HER LEGS HE KNELT,
HE FELL, HE LAY"

The story of Jael is told twice in the Book of Judges, first in the biblical narrative and again in a lyrical interlude known as the Song of Deborah, a "priceless piece of archaic Hebrew poetry" that is thought to be among the oldest fragments in all of the Bible.[25] Indeed, the Song of Deborah is probably the remnant of a rich oral tradition that existed among the Israelites long before anyone thought to assemble the book we call the Bible.

Deborah is a prophetess who also serves as a judge of Israel, a position of authority and leadership in the days before a king reigned over Israel. Deborah calls on a man named Barak to lead the Israelites into battle against a Canaanite army under the command of a fierce and fearsome general named Sisera. Barak is a reluctant soldier, and he refuses to fight unless Deborah goes along with him. So the prophetess Deborah—whose name means "bee" in Hebrew and who is described by an obscure Hebrew word that suggests she is "a woman of flames"[26]—takes command of the army of Israel on the field of battle.

"I will surely go with thee, [but] the journey that thou takest shall not be for thy honour," Deborah taunts Barak, "for the Lord will give Sisera over into the hand of a woman" (Judg. 4:9).

That woman is Jael.

Jael is married to a man who belongs to the Kenites, a tribe that is not at war with the Canaanites; one Bible scholar describes her as "a bedawin housewife."[27] She is standing outside her tent when a lone figure approaches on foot. It is Sisera, who has fled from the victorious Israelites, abandoning his mighty war chariot and the vast army under his command; and now the defeated general seeks refuge from an unremarkable woman he takes to be a member of a neutral tribe.

"Turn in, my lord, turn in to me," says Jael to Sisera, and then—as if *he* had something to fear from *her*—she reassures him: "Fear not."

Sisera accepts her offer of refuge, and she hides him under a rug inside her tent. Thirsty from battle and flight, he asks for water, but she gives him milk, perhaps to lull him to sleep. He cautions her to turn away anyone who comes looking for him—and then he falls asleep. He is no longer afraid of his pursuers, and apparently feels that he has nothing to fear from the woman who is sheltering him.

Sisera is dead wrong. Jael picks up a hammer and a tent peg, slips silently into the tent, and drives the tent peg through the head of the sleeping general. When Barak shows up in pursuit of Sisera, Jael invites him into the tent and shows him the body of the warrior, now dead, his head pinned to the ground.*

The Song of Deborah reprises the incident in poetry that must have thrilled its original audience—and still has the power to thrill us.

> Above women in the tent shall she be blessed.
> Water he asked, milk she gave him;
> In a lordly bowl she brought him curd.
> Her hand she put to the tent-pin,
> And her right hand to the workmen's hammer;
> And with the hammer she smote Sisera, she smote through his
>   head,
> Yea, she pierced and struck through his temples,
> At her feet he sunk, he fell, he lay;
> At her feet he sunk, he fell;
> Where he sunk, there he fell down dead (Judg. 5:24–27).

Jael defies our worst fears of what is likely to happen when a soldier encounters a woman alone, whether in ancient Israel or contemporary Bosnia: we expect that the woman is at risk of rape, but here it is the soldier who is in danger. "Reversed rape" is how Bible scholars Danna Nolan Fewell and David M. Gunn describe the assault, and they read the Hebrew text to suggest that Jael thrusts her weapon into one of Sisera's bodily openings rather than his head. "Patriarchal expectation is turned upside down," they write, "as the warrior's mouth is penetrated by an unmistakably phallic tent peg."[28] The contrast between Jael and the Levite traveler's concubine is heartrending but somehow also highly satisfying: the concubine is a nameless victim of violence against women, a victim of her own husband and the men to whom he

---

*Jael's weaponry—a hammer and tent peg—complies with the dictates of Deuteronomy 22:5 ("A woman shall not wear that which pertaineth to a man"), which the rabbis interpreted to mean that a woman is forbidden to use a sword, a spear, or a dagger. Elsewhere in Judges, a wicked Israelite prince named Abimelech is grievously wounded by a millstone dropped on his head by a woman; Abimelech orders his armor-bearer to finish him off with a sword lest it be said: "A woman slew him" (Judg. 9:53–54).

abandoned her, but Jael is a courageous and resourceful warrior who singlehandedly prevails over a mighty warrior. Notably, Jael is *not* an Israelite, but she acts to vindicate the "standard of faith" of Israel when the menfolk, symbolized by the fearful Barak, are reluctant to carry the flag into battle.[29]

That the biblical author chose to include both stories in the same book is itself a telling irony. The nameless concubine is the victim of a gang rape in which her own husband is an accomplice, but Jael is the heroine of a tale that can be understood as "a polemic against rape," as contemporary Bible scholar Susan Niditch points out. The image of Sisera lying dead at her feet can be seen as "a hideous parody of soldierly assault on the women of a defeated foe"[30] and "an ironic glance at the time-honored martial custom of rape."[31] In both the original Hebrew and Niditch's lyrical English translation, the moment of Sisera's death at the hands of Jael is suffused with an ominous sensuality:

> Between her legs he knelt, he fell, he lay
> Between her legs he knelt, he fell,
> Where he knelt, there he fell, despoiled (Judg. 5:27).[32]

The ancient rabbis interpreted the verse to signify that Jael engaged in sexual intercourse with Sisera seven times before slaying him![33] Indeed, the very words used by the biblical author in describing the encounter between Jael and Sisera emphasize the interplay between eros and thanatos, sex and death. The Hebrew word for "legs" or "feet," as we have seen, is a common biblical euphemism for sexual genitalia, whether male or female. "Between her legs" echoes the most blood-curdling of the many curses that will befall Israel if the Lord is not strictly obeyed. "[H]er afterbirth that comes out from between her feet and her children whom she bears," says Moses in the Book of Deuteronomy, "she will eat them secretly" (Deut. 29:57 NEB). "Kneeling" recalls the despairing words of Job, who imagines his wife serving other men in every sense. "May my wife grind for another," says Job. "May others kneel over her!" (Job 31:10). The mighty Sisera ends up "despoiled" by a woman—a word that is used elsewhere in the Bible to describe the defeat of a hated enemy in battle (Jer. 47:4) and the harlotry of a faithless Israel: "And when thou art spoiled, what wilt thou do?" rails the prophet Jeremiah. "Though thou clothest thyself with crimson, . . . thy lovers will despise thee, they will seek thy life" (Jer. 4:30 Scofield KJV).[34]

As if to emphasize the startling reversal of traditional roles in the story of Jael—the fact that a woman is the victor and a man is the vanquished—the Song of Deborah ends with a poignant but sharply ironic scene in the house where Sisera's mother waits in vain for her son to return from battle. "Why is his chariot so long in coming?" says his fretful mother. One of the princesses in attendance on the old woman seeks to reassure her by suggesting that Sisera has been victorious in battle and is even now dividing the spoils of war, including "[a] damsel, two damsels to every man" (Judg. 5:30). The Hebrew word variously translated as "damsel" (JPS) or "wench" (NEB) or "maiden" (RSV) or "girl" (NRSV) has been rendered even more forcefully by contemporary Bible scholars: "womb," the literal meaning of the Hebrew word. But Adrien Janis Bledstein pointedly insists on giving a coarse and offensive but idiomatically correct translation—"cunt"—in order to confront us with the fact that Sisera, if victorious, would have regarded the women of Israel as nothing more than booty to be used and discarded in just the same way that the men of Gibeah abuse the concubine. The irony, of course, is that Sisera has fallen victim to Jael, and not the other way around. "Little do these arrogant women know," writes Bledstein, "that one of the 'cunts' has gored the neck of their hero."[35]

Jael is unique among the women in the Bible in her use of a weapon to slay a male adversary with her own hands, but she is also a trickster in the tradition of Rebekah, Tamar, Rahab, and Ruth. According to the Bible, she offers food and shelter in order to lure Sisera into her tent. The ancient author known as Pseudo-Philo paints a more lurid scene in which she spikes his milk with wine and strews her bed with rose petals as a further enticement.[36] The rabbis preserve a tradition that Jael gave him milk from her own breast and "surrendered herself to Sisera's passion" as "the only sure means to get hold of him and kill him."[37] So Jael shows herself to be "a warrior *and* seducer, alluring and dangerous, nurturing and bloodthirsty."[38] When Sisera falls dead at Jael's feet in the tent where he sought shelter, we are reminded of the wretched concubine as she falls, dead or dying, at the door of the house where she, too, sought shelter—and a certain rough justice is done.

BLACK PROPAGANDA

The earliest narratives in the Bible, or so goes the consensus of modern biblical scholarship, were first collected and written down sometime after 1000 B.C.E., during or shortly after the reign of David as king of the united monarchy of Judah and Israel. Much of the Bible was edited and revised during the reigns of the monarchs who descended from the House of David and succeeded him to the throne. So it is no surprise that many of the biblical authors regard David as *the* most important figure in the Bible—and he even figures in the Gibeah Outrage, although only in a secret subtext that is hidden between the lines of Holy Writ.

David is not actually named in the Book of Judges, which describes the troubled era when "there was no king in Israel." Indeed, the author of Judges is trying to convince the Israelites that they should submit themselves to royal authority by showing in such stomach-turning detail what can happen when they are kingless. By the time we reach the last and worst abomination in Judges, a gang rape that leads to civil war and near-genocide, the moral is unmistakable. "[D]o with them what seemeth good unto you," says the old man who offers the mob his own daughter and his guest's concubine, thus echoing the thematic phrase that we find more than once in the Book of Judges: "[E]very man did that which was right in his own eyes" (Judg. 21:25).

But there is another and even more subtle subtext to the Book of Judges and, specifically, the Gibeah Outrage—an attack on the man who will become the first king of Israel, the failed monarch who will be anointed and then abandoned by God, the man who will be replaced on the throne by the glorious David. That man, of course, is Saul, and so the tale of the Levite traveler and his concubine can be understood as "an anti-Saul polemic"[39]—an effort by the biblical author to predict the moral flaws and political failings of King Saul, to blacken his reputation and sully his name, and thus to prepare the reader for the anointing of his rival and successor, David, as the savior-king.

The rise and fall of Saul—and the remarkable saga that is the life of David—are chronicled in the books that follow Judges in the Hebrew Bible: First and Second Samuel, First and Second Kings, First and Second Chronicles. But the biblical author uses the Book of Judges to prepare us for these momentous events in the history of Israel. Above all, the author feels obliged to explain why Saul is unworthy to sit on the throne of Israel and deserves to be replaced by David. To the readers of the Bible in ancient Israel, the subtext of the Gibeah Outrage and its aftermath must have been plain and perhaps even faintly comical, even though neither David nor Saul is mentioned at all in the Book of Judges.

The "sons of hell" who threaten to sodomize the Levite and who gang-rape his concubine are men of the tribe of Benjamin—and so is Saul.

Gibeah, the place where the outrage against the Levite and his concubine takes place, is Saul's hometown and the capital of his kingdom. To make sure that the reader does not overlook the scene of the crime, the author manages to mention the name of the town twenty-two times in three brief chapters.[40]

The assembly of the tribes where the war of extermination against the Benjaminites is planned takes place at Mizpah, the same place where the prophet Samuel will later convene a gathering of the tribes and designate Saul as the first king of Israel. (Saul himself, by the way, turns up missing at the crucial moment, and the befuddled prophet is forced to inquire of God about Saul's whereabouts. "Will the man be coming back?" Samuel asks the Almighty in a comic aside, and God points out that Saul has concealed himself without explaining exactly why. "There he is," says God, "hiding among the baggage" [1 Sam. 10:22–23 NEB].)

Jabesh-gilead is the town whose population is slaughtered and whose virgin daughters are kidnapped and given as brides to the survivors of the tribe of Benjamin—and an attack on Jabesh-gilead by the Ammonites is the first crisis of Saul's reign as king of Israel. At the very end of his life, when Saul kills himself to avoid capture in battle, the townsfolk of Jabesh-gilead bring his body back from the battlefield and bury his remains under a tree (1 Sam. 31:12–13).

To convince the tribes of Israel to make war on the Benjaminites, the Levite traveler dismembers his slain concubine and sends a piece of her body to each tribe as a grisly call to arms. So, too, does Saul cut up a couple of oxen and dispatch the pieces to the tribes in order to compel them to join him in fighting the Ammonites: "Whosoever cometh not forth after Saul and after Samuel, so shall it be done unto his oxen" (1 Sam. 11:7).

Finally, when the Israelites ask God to designate the tribe that will lead them into battle against the Benjaminites, God says: "Judah first." Saul, the first king of Israel, is a member of the tribe of Benjamin—and David, the man who will succeed him on the throne, is a member of the tribe of Judah.

The Book of Judges, then, can be understood as one long argument in favor of monarchy among a people who have been governed so far only by patriarchs, prophets, and judges. The Israelites have acted abominably, we are given to understand. They have strayed from the strict faith of the patriarchs; they have been preyed upon by their pagan neighbors; and, at the end, they have fallen upon each other with a degree of barbarism that exceeds the worst excesses of their enemies. Only a king will be able to save them from their enemies and themselves—but, as the Book of Judges seems to predict, the first man to sit on the throne of Israel will fail. And so the scene is set for the greatest king in the history of Israel and the *real* hero of the Bible.

CHAPTER FOURTEEN

TAMAR AND AMNON

"Behold, I will raise up evil against thee out of thine own house. . . ."

—2 SAMUEL 12:11

Amnon sat glumly at the far end of the long banquet table, chewing on a crust of bread and glaring now and then at his father, the king, who held forth with broad gestures and grand words at the head of the table.

Even though he was the king's oldest son and heir apparent to the throne of Israel, Amnon was plainly a troubled young man. A scowl was fixed on his dark features, and his brown eyes glowed with a certain strange light, as if a fire burned inside him. Everyone in the court of King David saw Amnon's unhappiness—his wives, his generals, his priests, even his servants, all of them except the king himself.

David had many sons, and seldom did he bother to look at any of them. More often than not he was surrounded by a small crowd of courtiers, all of whom noisily competed for his attention. Even when the king found himself at table with Amnon, which happened rarely, he had much else on his mind. The long war against the Ammonites had finally ended in a victory, to be sure, and David now wore the gold crown that had once crowned the head of the king of Ammon himself. But David could not forget the dire words of that dour old prophet,

> *"Wherefore hast thou despised the word of the Lord, to do that which is evil in My sight? Uriah the Hittite thou has smitten with the sword, and his wife thou hast taken to be thy wife, and him thou has slain with the sword of the children of Ammon. Now therefore, the sword shall never depart from thy house. . . . Behold, I will raise up evil against thee out of thine own house. . . ."*
>
> —2 SAMUEL 12:9–11

Nathan, who afflicted him with unsettling messages from God even at his moments of greatest glory.

" 'The sword shall never depart from the House of David,' " Nathan had said, quoting the words of the Almighty as uttered to the prophet in yet another one of his dismal visions. " 'I will raise up evil against thee out of thine own house.' "

These words of warning were never far from David's thoughts, even as he held forth at the banquet table with yet another wry and slightly ribald tale about the days when he was but a humble shepherd and not yet a king. Distracted by his own tale, bloated with rich food and perhaps a bit drunk, the king surveyed the table without pausing to glance at Amnon.

Nor did Amnon watch his father with the keen interest displayed by the others around the table, who listened to the king's familiar story as if hearing it for the first time and laughed admiringly at his old jokes. What held Amnon's attention was the young woman sitting at the king's right hand, where Amnon felt *he* ought to be seated. Tamar was the king's daughter, Amnon's half sister, and she smiled with obvious pleasure whenever the king inclined his head to whisper something into her ear. Now and then, the two of them laughed at a secret joke—and something burned in Amnon's heart every time he saw their foreheads touch.

The king clearly took pleasure from the company of his daughter, whose sweet disposition and undemanding nature were such a contrast to the grasping and carping of his sons. David had so many sons, and all

> *And it came to pass at eventide, that David arose from off his bed, and walked upon the roof of the king's house; and from the roof he saw a woman bathing; and the woman was very beautiful to look upon. And David sent and inquired after the woman. And one said: "Is not this Bath-sheba, the daughter of Eliam, the wife of Uriah the Hittite?" And David sent messengers, and took her; and she came in unto him, and he lay with her . . . and she returned unto her house.*
>
> —2 SAMUEL 11:2–4

of them needy and troubled in one way or another, but he had fathered only one daughter. Her name was Tamar, and everyone—even the king himself—remarked on how very beautiful she was.

The king did not know it, but the gloomy words of the prophet Nathan were being whispered all over Jerusalem as the latest bit of gossip about the king's sordid affair with the woman named Bathsheba. Amnon had been among the first to hear of the incident, if only because more than one of the courtiers had already begun to cultivate Amnon in the confident belief that he would one day follow King David to the throne.

As the rumors had it, King David had first spied Bathsheba from afar as she bathed on the roof of her house. No one blamed *him* for *that*—indeed, one sniggering priest suggested that Bathsheba had fully intended to catch the king's eye by brazenly showing herself, naked and wet, within plain sight of the palace roof, where David was known to take the night air from time to time. Indeed, it was not unusual for some of the excitable young women of Jerusalem to lie in wait for David in the streets leading up to the palace and to shriek with excitement when the handsome king was spotted on the ramparts above their heads.

When it came to Bathsheba, however, it was the king himself who was smitten and lovesick. So he dispatched one of his more discreet attendants to invite Bathsheba into the royal bedchamber, and—like so many other women on so many other warm summer evenings—she did

> *And the woman conceived; and she sent and told David, and said: "I am with child." And David sent to Joab [saying]: "Send me Uriah the Hittite. . . ." And when Uriah was come unto him, David asked of him . . . how the people fared, and how the war prospered. And David said to Uriah: "Go down to thy house, and wash thy feet. . . ." But Uriah slept at the door of the king's house with all the servants of his lord, and went not down to his house. . . . And Uriah said unto David: ". . .[T]he servants of my lord are encamped in the open field; shall I then go into my house, to eat and to drink, and to lie with my wife? as thou livest, and as thy soul liveth, I will not do this thing."*
>
> —2 SAMUEL 11:5–11

> *And when David had called him, he did eat and drink before him; and he made him drunk; and at even he went out to lie on his bed with the servants of his lord, but went not down to his house.*
>
> —2 SAMUEL 11:13

not refuse. Still, apart from David's wives and a few of the fussier priests, no one in the royal palace regarded the fling as much of a sin, even if Bathsheba's husband, a soldier named Uriah, was serving in the king's army in the war against Ammon while she reclined on the king's bed.

But the whispers grew hotter when it was the time of the month for Bathsheba to purify herself at the ritual bath, and she declared herself to be with child. Now the king panicked, and he devised a devilish plan to blame the pregnancy on Uriah. The king summoned Uriah all the way back from the battlefield to the royal palace on the laughable pretense of asking him if the army was well and the war was going well. "Yes, well," replied the puzzled but dutiful soldier. His curiosity satisfied, David urged Uriah to avail himself of his own bed and his own wife as long as he was in Jerusalem. Uriah, still puzzled, refused the king's suggestion.

"My comrades are camped on the battlefield," said Uriah. "How, then, can I eat and drink in comfort and then sleep with my wife?"

So, night after night, the loyal soldier insisted on sleeping at the door of the royal bedchamber along with the servants, much to the consternation of the king himself. Not even an abundance of the king's wine weakened his resolve: the stalwart soldier drank himself drunk but did not stray from the king's door. Finally the king abandoned his goal of seduction and sent Uriah back to the battlefield in service of an even more sinister plan to solve the problem of the pregnant Bathsheba.

On the night before Uriah returned to the front, the king scribed a short letter to Joab, general of his army in Ammon. "Put Uriah into battle where the fighting is fiercest," the king wrote, "and then order your men to fall back so Uriah is alone." The message was unmistakable: Uriah was meant to die alone at the hands of the enemy. David sealed the letter himself, handed it to Uriah with complete confidence that he would not even try to pry it open and read it, and sent the obedient soldier back to the front with his own death sentence in his hand.

And it came to pass in the morning, that David wrote a letter to Joab, and sent it by the hand of Uriah. And he wrote in the letter, saying: "Set ye Uriah in the forefront of the hottest battle, and retire ye from him, that he may be smitten, and die."

—2 SAMUEL 11:14–15

And the messenger said unto David: ". . .[T]hy servant Uriah the Hittite is dead also." Then David said unto the messenger: "Thus shalt thou say unto Joab: Let not this thing displease thee, for the sword devoureth in one manner or another; make thy battle more strong against the city, and overthrow it. . . ."

—2 SAMUEL 12:23–25

Later, when Joab sent word to King David that Uriah had been killed in the fighting under the walls of the Ammonite fortress, David painted an expression of sorrow on his handsome features.

"Don't fret about Uriah—sometimes the sword devours one way, sometimes another," the king instructed his messenger to tell the general back at the front. "Just strengthen your assault on the city and raze it to the ground!"

The general did as he was told, the Ammonite fortress fell at last, and the rich plunder was soon on its way back to Jerusalem. David crowned himself with a victor's crown—and he took Bathsheba, now well along in her pregnancy, as his latest wife. Except for the gloomy predictions of the prophet Nathan, the future of David and his royal house seemed glorious indeed, just as glorious as God himself had promised.

Whenever Amnon pondered the vile way his father had secured Bathsheba as his latest wife, he experienced a palpable disgust that seemed to ball up in his stomach and rise into his throat. Here was yet another wife in the royal harem, yet another son in the noisy brood of royal mouths to feed. The man was an insatiable beast, Amnon told himself, a shameless philanderer who had no place sitting on the throne. When the king finally died—one way or another—and it was *his* turn to reign, Amnon told himself, the people of Israel would recognize and honor him as a righteous man and an upright king.

Such thoughts burned in Amnon's head as he spent long hours at the window of the house allotted to him in the royal compound. Since the king gave him little else to do, Amnon watched the minions who scurried back and forth across the courtyard around which the royal houses were clustered—captains, priests, and scribes in abundance, sometimes the lord of some great estate on his way to the throne room with a petition in hand, now and then a convoy of concubines headed toward the palace under an escort of armed soldiers, and always a teeming crowd of random servants and servitors. Amnon watched as if in a trance, and he imagined the day when they would be serving him instead of his father.

From time to time Amnon's eye fell on one man in particular who simply could not be overlooked even in a crowd—the commanding figure of Absalom, one of his many half brothers, the son of one of

David's wives, Maacah. Absalom was younger than Amnon, but he seemed to outshine his older brother in so many other ways: Absalom was taller, he was fairer, he was stronger and yet more graceful, he was more genial and thus better-liked among the courtiers. To Amnon's consternation, Absalom was regarded by more than one of the busybodies in the court of King David as a more promising candidate to be the next king of Israel than Amnon himself, the rightful heir.

To Amnon's relief, he did not encounter Absalom except on formal occasions, and he never found reason to seek out his half brother. Only when Amnon spotted him in the crowded courtyard was he forced to ponder why Absalom always seemed so good-natured and high-spirited when he himself, the future king of Israel, was always so angry and despairing.

One day, as Amnon stared down from his window, he spotted Absalom and the equally familiar figure of Tamar as they emerged from the palace and headed across the courtyard in the direction of Absalom's house. Like Absalom, Tamar was the daughter of Maacah, and she shared her brother's appealing features and graceful bearing. Amnon had grown up in the same household with the two of them, but Tamar had always clung to Absalom and allowed him to shield her from the playful attention of the other sons of the king. Now Absalom and Amnon had been allotted houses of their own by the king, but Tamar was not yet married and still lived in the palace. So Amnon did not encounter his half sister except on formal occasions when *everyone* gathered to listen to the king's tired old tales.

Today, however, Amnon found himself staring at Tamar with new interest. He watched from his high window as she walked with long strides across the courtyard, looking up at Absalom and laughing at something he said. Amnon noticed that she was taller than he remembered, her hair longer, her body more womanly. She wore the gown of a royal princess—rich, colorful, and concealing—but the long sleeves and the generous folds of the skirt did not entirely hide from Amnon's eyes a certain voluptuousness in her limbs and hips. Indeed, Amnon did not take his eyes off his half sister until she disappeared into Absalom's house on the far side of the courtyard.

And it came to pass after this, that Absalom the son of David had a fair sister, whose name was Tamar; and Amnon the son of David loved her.

—2 SAMUEL 13:1

And Amnon was so distressed that he fell sick because of his sister Tamar; for she was a virgin; and it seemed hard to Amnon to do any thing unto her. But Amnon had a friend, whose name was Jonadab, the son of Shimeah David's brother; and Jonadab was a very subtle man. And he said unto him: "Why, O son of the king, art thou thus becoming leaner from day to day? Wilt thou not tell me?" And Amnon said unto him: "I love Tamar, my brother Absalom's sister."

—2 SAMUEL 13:2–4

Amnon felt vaguely ill at ease as Tamar disappeared from sight. He swallowed involuntarily, as if something were caught in his throat—a sensation not unlike the one he felt when he recalled his father's exploits with Bathsheba and the baby that grew even now in her womb. But he was aware of something else, too: a certain breathlessness that came upon him when he envisioned the movement of Tamar's long legs as she walked across the courtyard and imagined what it might be like to stroke her long black hair or touch her smooth skin with his fingertips.

A servant interrupted his reverie, but Amnon waved away the food and drink that was offered. Later in the afternoon, the servant appeared with another meal. Amnon waved him away again, and the dish of food simply gathered flies on the floor of the corridor outside his door. At last, Amnon undressed and slumped into his bed. The next morning he was up early and spent the day at the window, hoping to catch a glimpse of Tamar in the courtyard below. By the third day of his vigil, the servants were concerned enough at Amnon's inexplicable fast to send for the only man they knew to be his friend, a cousin by the name of Jonadab.

"Son of the king!" Jonadab said with mock formality as he bulled his way into Amnon's quarters. "Why do you sit so glumly morning after morning? You are wasting away for want of food! What's wrong with you?"

"It's Tamar," said Amnon without turning away from the window.

"Tamar?" repeated his cousin. "Your sister? What about her?"

Amnon sat in silence for a moment, then stood up and faced his cousin.

"Tamar," he said in an insistent voice, "is *Absalom's* sister."

"So tell me what it is about Tamar," Jonadab persisted, "that makes you act like you are sick with a plague."

"I think," said Amnon slowly, "that I am in love with her."

Jonadab laughed out loud—and then, when he saw the grave expression on Amnon's face, his laughter turned into a sudden fit of coughing and he looked away in embarrassment. "Better the plague," he muttered to himself, "than to be lovesick over your own sister."

"Well, what am I supposed to do about it?" Amnon demanded. "I can't eat. I can't sleep. All I can do is think about how to get her into my bed. But I can't even get her to talk to me, much less to come into my bedchamber!"

Jonadab pondered these shocking words for a moment. He was Amnon's closest friend, perhaps his *only* friend, and Amnon would be king someday. And so Jonadab resolved to act as the friend of a future king ought to act.

"Get under the covers," he said, "and pretend that you are sick."

"I *am* sick," said Amnon miserably.

"We'll send word to your father that you are ailing," Jonadab continued. "He will be worried, of course. After all, the illness of the next

---

And Jonadab said unto him: "Lay thee down on thy bed, and feign thyself sick; and when thy father cometh to see thee, say unto him: Let my sister Tamar come, I pray thee, and give me bread to eat, and dress the food in my sight, that I may see it, and eat it at her hand."

—2 SAMUEL 13:5

king of Israel is a matter of the gravest concern. He will come to see you—"

"So what?" said Amnon. "It's Tamar I want to see, not my father."

"When the king comes to see you," Jonadab continued, "you will ask him to send Tamar to nurse you back to health. Tell him you don't trust the servants to prepare your meals properly. Tell him that's why you are ill and cannot eat. 'Let my beloved sister Tamar come and make a couple of hearty dumplings for me,' you will tell the king. 'Then I'll eat out of her hand.' "

Amnon stirred when he heard the sound of hushed voices outside the door of his quarters, and he peered out from beneath the covers to see what was astir. He heard one familiar voice—his servant's—and a couple that he did not recognize. One voice belonged to a woman, and his heart raced at the thought that Jonadab's wild plan might have actually succeeded in bringing Tamar to his bedchamber. Then he let his head fall back against the pillow—and waited.

Quite to Amnon's surprise, the first and crucial step in his cousin's plan had been successful. King David himself, attended by a small crowd of guards and retainers, had appeared briefly the previous day, spent not more than three minutes in Amnon's presence, and then bustled out again without saying more than three words. The king had seemed unconcerned over his son's ill health, just as Amnon had expected, and seemed to take more interest in the view from the window of Amnon's room than in Amnon himself. But at least the king had listened to Jonadab's somber appraisal of Amnon's ill health, and he had even stayed long enough to hear Amnon recite his lines. "Let my sister come and take care of me," Amnon had pleaded, "and I will nibble on those

---

So Amnon lay down, and feigned himself sick; and when the king was come to see him, Amnon said unto the king: "Let my sister Tamar come, I pray thee, and make me a couple of cakes in my sight, that I may eat at her hand."

—2 SAMUEL 13:6

Then David sent home to Tamar, saying: "Go now to thy brother Amnon's house, and dress him food." So Tamar went to her brother Amnon's house; and he was lying down.

—2 SAMUEL 13:7–8

luscious heart-cakes right out of her hands." After his father left, he had fretted over his choice of words and his unfeigned ardor in speaking them—perhaps the king would detect what he *really* wanted from Tamar.

"Do you think it will work?" Amnon had asked anxiously when the house was finally cleared of visitors.

"Of course it will work," Jonadab had responded cheerfully. "And when you have Tamar in your arms, dear cousin, please do not forget who put her there!"

Now Amnon waited, breathless again, his heart racing, as the servant made a noise at the door and peeked inside the dark room.

"Lord, your sister Tamar is calling on you," said the servant in a whisper. "Shall I send her away?"

Amnon sat upright in bed and fairly shouted "No!" Then, fearing that he sounded rather too healthy, he reclined again and spoke in a hoarse whisper. "No, no, do not send her away—I am always happy to see my cherished sister."

A moment later, the very thing that had occupied his long hours of reverie for so many days finally came to pass. Tamar stood before him, and his heart gladdened at the expression of concern and even affection that he imagined he saw in her face.

"Thank you, dearest Tamar," he croaked, "for coming to me."

Tamar, more curious than caring, cast a long appraising glance at Amnon.

"Father sent a messenger to summon me," she said. " 'Go to Amnon,' the messenger said, 'and fix him some dumplings.' "

Tamar paused for one long moment, as if to signal to Amnon how strange it seemed to her to be summoned to his house for such an odd favor. Then she continued: "The king commanded me to come, and so here I am."

> *And she took dough, and kneaded it, and made cakes in his sight, and did bake the cakes. And she took the pan, and poured them out before him; but he refused to eat.*
>
> —2 SAMUEL 13:8–9

"Thank you, dear sister," Amnon said, "for attending me in my illness."

"You don't *seem* very ill, dear brother," said Tamar. She paused again before adding: "Thank God."

"Yes, thank God, I am feeling much better now that you are finally here," said Amnon, watching her with a fixed gaze that unnerved her. "Suddenly, I find myself very hungry. Will you make some dumplings for me as I asked?"

"Yes, brother," Tamar allowed, "that's what I came here to do."

Now Tamar gestured to a young woman who stood in the corridor with a covered basket, and the servant began unpacking the ingredients for the meal: a jar of flour, a jug of water, a small cruse of oil, some seasonings folded into the corner of a cloth and tied with string, and an earthenware mold in the shape of a heart. The servant set to work at the big fireplace at the far end of the room, and soon the water was boiling. As Amnon watched in utter silence but with rapt attention, Tamar kneaded the water and flour into dumplings, pressed the thick dough into the mold, dropped them into the boiling water, then fished them out again with a long wooden spoon that the servant handed to her. An aromatic scent of spices and yeasty dough wafted through the darkened room. Finally, Tamar heaped the steaming dumplings onto a platter and handed it to her servant, who crossed the room and stood dutifully at the side of Amnon's bed.

"There's what you wanted," called Tamar. "Go ahead and eat."

Amnon looked at the platter of dumplings, then back at Tamar, and finally he glared at the others who stood expectantly around the room—a couple of Tamar's servants, and his own servant, too, and even one of the youngsters who tended the stove in the kitchen and now sat in the doorway with wide eyes. Everyone was watching him; everyone,

And Amnon said: "Have out all men from me." And they went out every man from him. And Amnon said unto Tamar: "Bring the food into the chamber, that I may eat of thy hand." And Tamar took the cakes which she had made, and brought them into the chamber to Amnon her brother.

—2 SAMUEL 13:9–10

And when she had brought them near unto him to eat, he took hold of her, and said unto her: "Come lie with me, my sister." And she answered him: "Nay, my brother, do not force me; for no such thing ought to be done in Israel; do not thou this wanton deed. . . ."

—2 SAMUEL 13:11–12

it seemed, wanted to witness the end of the remarkable encounter between Amnon and his sister.

"Get out!" he cried out, suddenly finding his old voice and shouting harshly at the servants. "Get everybody away from me!"

All of them stirred and scattered. Tamar's servant handed her the plate of dumplings, waited a moment for her nod, and then left the room. His own servant was the last one to leave the room, and he thought to pull the door closed behind him. Only Tamar remained, standing solemnly near the window and watching her brother in silence from across the room.

Amnon shivered uncontrollably as he lay alone in his bed, and he felt suddenly flushed with fever, as if he really *were* ill after all.

"Bring the food to me," Amnon called, his voice suddenly thick and hoarse, "so I can eat out of your hand."

Tamar approached the bed where Amnon lay, casting a brief glance toward the door, and held out the platter of dumplings.

Amnon reached out and seized the wrist of her right hand. The platter fell to the floor and the dumplings rolled in the dust. She cried out in fright and surprise, but Amnon held her fast and pulled her bodily toward him.

"Come on, sister," he growled. "Lie with me!"

Tamar stared at her brother and leaned away from him with the weight of her body, but he did not let go of her wrist. Her skin began to burn as he twisted her wrist to force her to come closer. She cast one more desperate glance at the door, and then cried out.

"Brother—don't!" she ordered. "I will not lie with you!"

Amnon grinned crazily at Tamar's words, as if he were encouraged in his attack by the sound of her voice speaking aloud his secret thoughts, and he pulled her toward him with new strength.

"A brother and sister together—such a thing isn't done in Israel!" Tamar said. "Don't commit such a sacrilege!"

Amnon relaxed his grip ever so slightly, then tugged sharply on her arm, and Tamar tumbled headfirst into his bed. He rolled on top of her, pinning her long legs with his own legs and pressing down on her hips with his own hips. Soon, only her head was free, and she whipped back and forth like a snake.

"What will become of me, brother!" she pleaded. "Where will I take myself after you have shamed me? And what about you, dear brother— you will make yourself an outcast in Israel, and you will have nowhere to hide from your deed."

Amnon considered these words for one grave moment, and Tamar sensed an opportunity to persuade her mad brother to break off his assault.

"Perhaps there *is* a way, Amnon!" she whispered urgently but intimately into his ear, her voice now assured and commanding. "Speak to

---

"And I, whither shall I carry my shame? and as for thee, thou wilt be as one of the base men in Israel. Now therefore, I pray thee, speak unto the king; for he will not withhold me from thee." Howbeit he would not hearken unto her voice; but being stronger than she, he forced her, and lay with her.

—2 SAMUEL 13:13–14

the king! Ask him for my hand in marriage! The king won't keep me from you, I promise!"

But Tamar's words seemed to provoke Amnon rather than reassure him, and he jerked his head away at the very sound of her words: *The king won't keep me from you. . . .* Abruptly, Amnon renewed his assault on Tamar. He tore away her maiden's garb and pawed at her body with both hands, using his own body as a weapon to overpower her. Amnon had his way with his sister in a series of brutal thrusts that betrayed more anger than passion. A few moments later, it was over. Amnon released his sister from his grip, then rolled away and seemed to sleep. Tamar, bruised and bleeding, lay next to him as she pondered what she ought to do now. She surprised herself by not weeping, and she pondered the faint sensation of some warm fluid turning cold on her bare thighs. Was it blood, she thought to herself, or something else?

Amnon awoke a few minutes later and looked at the ravaged young woman who lay beside him, mostly naked and marked here and there with ugly bruises that were even now turning black-and-blue. Suddenly a wave of revulsion not unlike nausea welled up out of his belly and choked him. Whatever it was he had felt toward Tamar a few moments before—love or lust or some other unspeakable passion—now turned instantly and massively into its opposite. The very sight of Tamar sickened him, and so he planted a bare foot on her naked hip and kicked her out of the bed with one powerful thrust. Tamar tumbled to the floor, where she lay among the dumplings she had offered him a few moments earlier.

"Get up!" he said, fighting back the inexplicable rage that tasted like bile in the back of his throat. "Go away!"

Tamar struggled to her feet and stood unsteadily in front of him. The bodice of her gown was torn on both sides, exposing her breasts and her battered hips, and blood oozed from her nose and the corner of her mouth and between her legs.

"Don't send me out like this, brother!" she said in a low voice that barely concealed her own dangerous rage. "To send me into the street like this is even worse than—"

Tamar fell suddenly silent, and Amnon started shouting for his servant.

"Get this *thing* away from me!" he bellowed. "Put her out! And bolt the door behind her!"

Then Amnon hated her with exceeding great hatred; for the hatred wherewith he hated her was greater than the love wherewith he had loved her. And Amnon said unto her: "Arise, be gone." And she said unto him: "Not so, because this great wrong in putting me forth is worse than the other that thou didst unto me." But he would not hearken unto her. Then he called his servant that ministered unto him, and said: "Put now this woman out from me, and bolt the door after her."—Now she had a garment of many colours upon her; for with such robes were the king's daughters that were virgins apparelled.—And his servant brought her out, and bolted the door after her.

—2 SAMUEL 13:15–18

And Tamar put ashes on her head, and rent her garment of many colours that was on her; and she laid her hand on her head, and went her way, crying aloud as she went.

And Absalom her brother said unto her: "Hath Amnon thy brother been with thee? but now hold thy peace, my sister; he is thy brother; take not this thing to heart." So Tamar remained desolate in her brother Absalom's house.

—2 SAMUEL 13:19–20

The servant of the future king of Israel obeyed his master, and Tamar found herself sprawled in the courtyard outside the door of Amnon's house. She struggled once again to her feet, and she stood with the bearing that befitted the daughter of the king. She covered herself as best she could in the torn and tattered gown. But she did not set off in the direction of the palace. Instead, she headed toward Absalom's house, weeping bitterly as she made her way through the curious crowd.

———

> *But when king David heard of all these things, he was very*
> *wroth. And Absalom spoke unto Amnon neither good nor bad;*
> *for Absalom hated Amnon, because he had forced his sister*
> *Tamar.*
>
> —2 SAMUEL 13:21–22

Absalom was summoned by the house servants to the entry where his sister had collapsed. He tried to sooth her in his own clumsy way as he led her to a bedchamber where she might find some privacy and some rest.

"Hush, sister, it could have been worse—at least it was your brother and not a stranger," he said by way of consolation. "Don't take it to heart."

But his words only seemed to provoke her, and he decided to leave her alone with her grief for awhile. When he returned, to his amazement, he saw that Tamar had heaped ashes on her head and rent her garment like one in mourning.

Tamar put on the black garb of bereavement and never took it off again, and she spent the rest of her days in desolation under the roof of her brother's house.

When David heard of the outrage that had been committed against his daughter by his eldest son, he thundered and cursed and generally made a proper show of kingly temper to all who were in attendance at that terrible moment—but he did nothing more than that. Absalom waited in vain for the day when the mighty King of Israel would chasten the man who had raped the king's daughter. But the day never came, and soon it appeared that David had forgotten the whole unpleasant incident.

Absalom said nothing more of the matter to the king or anyone else, including the desolate Tamar. Except for the fact that he refused to speak a single word to Amnon, good or ill, it appeared that Absalom, too, had forgotten what had happened to Tamar. Then, fully two years later, Absalom arranged for a banquet to celebrate the sheepshearing in Baal-hazor. He invited King David and all of his sons, including

Amnon, to attend the festivities. Every one of the princes accepted Absalom's invitation, even the unsuspecting Amnon, who regarded the banquet as a pitiable effort by Absalom to ingratiate himself with the future king after his long and insulting silence. Only King David declined to make the journey to Baal-hazor and join his sons at the banquet table.

A great disappointment it was to Absalom that his father was not there. Absalom would have preferred David to see with his own eyes how Absalom gave the command to his men-at-arms: "Strike down Amnon!" He would have preferred David to see how Amnon, silly with wine, struggled so comically to protect himself against the sword blows. He would have preferred David to see his firstborn son bleeding to death like a slaughtered calf. Then, Absalom thought to himself, David would have realized how a man should behave who is worthy to sit on the throne of Israel.

CHAPTER FIFTEEN

THE RAPE OF TAMAR

The Politics of Love and Hate
in the Court of King David

DAVIDISM ✛ THE CONSPIRACY OF THE "LIBIDO CAKES"
"A CHARIOT AND HORSES AND FIFTY MEN" ✛ HEAT
"WONDERFUL WAS THY LOVE TO ME"
THE BLESSING AND THE CURSE
"THEY SHALL NOT HURT NOR DESTROY"

Much of the Book of Samuel is the work of an anonymous biblical author who seems to possess an intimate knowledge of the official history *and* the dirty little secrets of King David and his royal family. The Court Historian, as he is sometimes called, is not merely an archivist and chronicler in service to an ancient potentate—he has been called "the first true historian,"[1] and the Book of Samuel is regarded as one of the earliest and most enduring works of literature and history in the Western tradition. The story of Tamar illustrates how the Court Historian uses an intimate scandal to illuminate the destiny of a nation: Amnon's private crime against his sister sets into motion a chain reaction of very public crimes that shake the throne of King David and, in a real sense, continue to resonate down through history.

The achievement and courage of the biblical author who composed the portions of Samuel known among scholars as the Court History of David (or the Succession Narrative) are all the more extraordinary when we compare the stories of David in Samuel and Kings to what passed for history elsewhere in the ancient Near East. Instead of the customary assortment of king lists and battle lists, the inventories of enemies ruined and spoils taken, and the glorification of reigning monarchs by their scribes, all the standard stuff of the servile propaganda that passed for official history in distant antiquity, the Court Historian writes boldly of the flaws and weaknesses of the monarch, the challenges to royal authority, the scandals of the royal court, and the least glorious moments in the lives of the monarch and his many wives and children.

"It is real history," wrote Sigmund Freud, "five hundred years before Herodotus, the 'Father of History.' "[2]

David comes across in the Bible as an extravagant monarch who does not hesitate to use his kingly power to indulge his appetites, sexual and otherwise—and the author of Samuel does not hesitate to tell us so. The Court Historian, for example, reveals exactly what happens when King David celebrates his conquest of Jerusalem by bringing the Ark of the Covenant, the holiest relic in the faith of ancient Israel, to the capital of the newly united monarchy of Judah and Israel.* King David leads the procession of thirty thousand soldiers, priests, musicians, and dancers who accompany the Ark on its slow and solemn journey to Jerusalem, and the king himself puts on an ecstatic display of "leaping and dancing before the Lord" (2 Sam. 6:16). In fact, the king is so ecstatic—and the priestly apron (or *ephod*) he wears is so brief—that David ends up flashing his genitals to the crowds that have gathered to watch the sacred spectacle. When the king finally reaches his palace, he is rebuked by his wife Michal, daughter of the former king, who has watched the festivities from the palace window and now scolds him for his bawdy and provocative display.

"Didn't the king of Israel do himself honor today," complains the sarcastic Michal, "exposing himself . . . in the sight of the slavegirls of his subjects, as one of the riffraff might expose himself!"

"It was before the Lord who chose me instead of your father . . . !" taunts an unrepentant David. "I will dance before the Lord and dis-

---

*The Bible tells us that the Ark of the Covenant was a chest containing the stone tablets on which God inscribed the Ten Commandments. The Ark was fashioned of acacia wood and decorated with two cherub figures (not the fat angels of Renaissance art but fierce beasts), and was imagined to be the throne on which God sat during earthly visitations. The Ark was carried by the ancient Israelites on their wanderings through the wilderness and into battle with their enemies, but it was David who first brought the Ark to Jerusalem and Solomon who installed it in the innermost sanctum of the Temple at Jerusalem, the Holy of Holies. The Ark disappeared from the Bible—and from history—with the destruction of Solomon's Temple during the Babylonian Conquest.

honor myself even more, and be low in my own esteem, but among the slavegirls you speak of I will be honored" (2 Sam. 6:20–22 New JPS).

These tabloidesque details tend to distract us from the real purpose of the biblical author in telling the story in the first place. To be sure, we are meant to understand that David is a lusty and rambunctious king who refuses to restrain his sexual impulses even when they lurch toward exhibitionism and casual sex with slavegirls. But we are also meant to understand the political repercussions of the spat between the king and his wife: David, angry and embittered, apparently declines to sleep with Michal, and she dies childless. No descendant of Saul, the man whom David replaced as king of Israel, will contend for the throne. But David sires plenty of sons by his various other wives, and several of these ambitious young men will soon reveal themselves to be contentious indeed. "I will raise up evil against thee out of thine own house," God later vows to David when his sexual excesses cost the life of an innocent man, and his sons fulfill the Almighty's vow (2 Sam. 12:11).

The use of the intimacies and passions of private life to illuminate the destiny of the nation is a technique of history-writing that strikes us as very modern indeed: "[R]eal historical facts," as one scholar describes the Court History, "in strongly stylized dress."[3] And so the ordeal of the royal princess named Tamar, so beautiful and yet so ill-used by her own father and brother, can be understood as an early augury of the decline and fall of the greatest king who ever sat on the throne of ancient Israel. Tamar is condemned to a life of suffering, humiliation, and despair by the brutal act of Amnon—and, as the Court Historian allows us to understand, so is David.

DAVIDISM

The name of David* is mentioned more than a thousand times in the Bible,[4] and David figures so prominently in the history and destiny of

---

*Actually, some scholars have suggested that "David" may be a title or a throne name rather than a personal name, which may help to explain why Samuel tells us first that someone named David slew Goliath (1 Sam. 17:50) and later credits a man named Elhanan with the same deed (2 Sam 21:19). Were David and Elhanan one and the same? If not, we have stumbled across yet another biblical mystery about who really did what to whom.

Israel that one scholar has proposed the term "Davidism"[5] to describe the worshipful attitude of certain biblical authors toward the celebrated king. Against the background of Samuel and Kings, where the stirring saga of David's life is first told, the rape of Tamar is only a brief and often-overlooked incident, even if her ordeal serves as the fateful first blow to David's kingship and the first act of defiance of kingly authority by one of his ambitious sons.

The formal biography of David is told in Samuel, Kings, and Chronicles, but the eminent Bible scholar Gerhard von Rad insisted that his story is also the "undersong" of the whole biblical narrative attributed to the source called the Yahwist. "[T]he figure of David, far more than Moses, is the hero of the Hebrew Bible," argues Harold Bloom.[6] And David has figured prominently in Western art and literature, both sacred and secular, for a couple of thousand years. From Donatello and Michelangelo to D. H. Lawrence and William Faulkner, the figure of David has been celebrated, sometimes reverentially and sometimes in burlesque. For example, the seventeenth-century British author John Dryden invoked the dubious moral example of King David when lampooning the libertinage of King Charles II.

> Then, *Israel's* Monarch, after Heaven's own heart,
> His vigorous warmth did, variously, impart
> To Wives and Slaves; And, wide as his Command,
> Scatter'd his Maker's Image through the Land.[7]

David is *still* impossible to ignore or overlook. "I've led a full, long life, haven't I? You can look it up," King David is imagined to say of himself in Joseph Heller's darkly comic novel, *God Knows*. "And God certainly knows that I was always a vigorous, courageous, and enterprising soul, overflowing with all the lusty emotions and desires of life. . . . I've got wars and ecstatic religious experiences, obscene dances, ghosts, murders, hair-raising escapes, and exciting chase scenes."[8]

Indeed, the saga of David's rise to power is among the most familiar texts in the Bible, even if the Sunday school version invariably accentuates the positive and leaves out the incidents of exhibitionism, voyeurism, adultery, mayhem, and murder. We all know David as the handsome young shepherd who plays the harp to soothe the troubled King Saul (1 Sam. 16:22–23) and the courageous boy warrior who slays

Goliath with a slingshot and a single stone (1 Sam. 17:48–49), but not quite so many of us are aware that David sallies forth to separate two hundred Philistines from their foreskins as a bride-price for Michal (1 Sam. 18:26–27), or that David and his men put themselves in service to an enemy king as a bandit army, pillaging the countryside at will and slaying everyone in sight "[l]est they should tell on us" (1 Sam. 27:11).

At the height of his power and glory, David conquers the city of Jerusalem and establishes his capital on the future site of the Temple, subdues the enemies of Israel on all sides, and extends the reach of his empire to the farthest boundaries once promised to Abraham by God himself: "from the river of Egypt unto the . . . Euphrates" (Gen. 15:18). The reign of David is the high-water mark of sovereignty in the long history of Israel—never before David did the Israelites enjoy such blessings, and never again will they enjoy them after his passing.

David has come to be regarded as an exalted figure in both Jewish and Christian tradition, the prototype of the monarch who reigns by the grace of God. He is described by the prophet Samuel as someone chosen by God above all others, "a man after His own heart" (1 Sam. 13:14), and David describes himself as "the man raised on high, the anointed of the God of Jacob" (2 Sam. 23:1). Despite his flawed character, his weakness for women, and his bloodthirsty conduct toward his fellow men, David emerges from the biblical narrative as the bearer of God's blessing, the model for all earthly kings, and the man from whose loins will spring the Messiah.

"I took thee from the sheepcote, from following the sheep, that thou shouldest be prince over My people," God tells David in what one scholar calls "the theological highlight" of the Book of Samuel.[9] "And I have been with thee whithersoever thou didst go, and have cut off all thine enemies from before thee, and I will make thee a great name, like unto the name of the great ones that are in the earth" (2 Sam. 7:9).

And yet the adoration of David in the Bible is counterbalanced by a frank and sometimes harsh account of his misdeeds. David's dalliance with Bathsheba and his conspiracy to murder her husband are described in an open-eyed account that confronts us with the king's appalling crime. Even David's role in the rape of Tamar is recounted without the "spin" we might expect from a court historian: the king is shown to be an accomplice, perhaps an unwitting one but perhaps not, and he does nothing to punish the rapist or vindicate his victim after the crime has been exposed. In fact, the biblical author artfully echoes David's affair with Bathsheba in his account of Amnon's rape of Tamar: both stories begin with a lustful glance, escalate into a forbidden sexual encounter, and reach a climax of bloody murder that can be ignored but not erased from the pages of Holy Writ.

THE CONSPIRACY OF THE
"LIBIDO CAKES"

To the contemporary reader, the rape of Tamar is all the more repugnant because she is the sister of her own rapist. But some Bible commentators, ancient and modern, have tried to cleanse Amnon's ugly crime of the still uglier notion that it was an act of incest, too. Because Tamar is only Amnon's *half* sister, we are asked to believe, the rape is not truly incestuous. And the fact that Tamar holds out the prospect of marriage supposedly reveals that the relationship between half siblings is not considered intimate enough to prohibit marriage. Thus, it is argued by some apologists, the sexual assault that follows could be regarded as rape but not incest.[10]

The notion of a sanctified sexual union between Amnon and Tamar comes from the lips of Tamar herself: "I pray thee, speak unto the king," she implores her brother in the terrible moments leading up to the rape, "for he will not withhold me from thee" (2 Sam. 13:13). But the most compelling meaning of her words—and the most heartrending, too—is that Tamar is simply trying to talk her brother out of raping her by holding out the faint hope of marriage. Whether she offers to marry Amnon with full knowledge that such a marriage would be contrary to divine law—or, as one scholar has suggested, she does so in "her naive belief that the king could dispense from the law"[11]— Tamar uses the only weapon available to her at that moment, the weapon of words.

Still, some scholars try to pretty up Amnon's crime of sexual violence against Tamar by entertaining the notion that marriage between brother and sister was somehow acceptable in ancient Israel. To do so, they have to explain away the fact that sexual intercourse with one's sister is unequivocally and repeatedly forbidden by biblical law: "The nakedness of thy sister, the daughter of thy father, or the daughter of thy mother, thou shalt not uncover" says Leviticus 18:9, using the familiar biblical euphemism for sexual intercourse. The fact that Tamar is Amnon's *half* sister makes no difference in Amnon's culpability under biblical law, since Leviticus specifically extends the taboo to half siblings, too: "[Thou shalt not uncover] the nakedness of thy father's wife's daughter, begotten of thy father, she is thy sister" (Lev. 18:11). Just in case anyone missed the point in Leviticus, the same rule is repeated even more fiercely in Deuteronomy: "Cursed be he that lieth with his sister, the daughter of his father, or the daughter of his mother" (Deut. 27:22).

Still, some apologists have argued that the plain language of these commandments and curses does not apply to Amnon and Tamar. According to strict biblical chronology, the law codes that are found in Leviticus and Deuteronomy were handed down long *before* the reign of King David and thus would have ruled out a marriage between brother and sister. Modern scholarship, however, suggests that the text of Leviticus and Deuteronomy was actually created by priestly authors and editors *after* the period described in the Book of Samuel, and so "a prohibition of marriage between brother and half sister was not recognized in the urban setting of Jerusalem in David's time."[12]

Other commentators argue that Tamar's proposition of marriage ought to be taken seriously on the strength of the bizarre episode in Genesis where Abraham passes off Sarah as his sister to the king of Gerar. As we have already seen, Sarah ends up in the king's bed, and only the last-minute intervention of God himself prevents the king from sleeping with her. Later, when the king complains to Abraham about his deception, the patriarch insists that he told only half a lie: Sarah is his wife *and* his sister, says Abraham, although only a *half* sister, "the daughter of my father, but not the daughter of my mother" (Gen. 20:12). On the strength of Abraham's feeble protestations to the king of Gerar, we are asked to believe that, both in his era and as late as the reign of King David, a man might marry his own half sister without censure.

The argument defies not only biblical law ("Cursed be he that lieth with his sister . . .") but common sense, too. Abraham has already lied to the king of Gerar by telling him that Sarah is his sister when, as far as we know from the biblical text, she is his wife—and only his wife. When Abraham comes up with the remarkable news that she is also his half sister, it comes as a surprise to the king of Gerar—*and* the rest of us, since the fact is nowhere else mentioned in the Bible! The sensible reading of Genesis 20:12 is that Abraham is *still* lying when he comes up with the cock-and-bull story about Sarah being his half sister. After all, the whole charade "is fully in line with Abraham's trickster character," as one scholar points out, and both Abraham and Sarah profit richly by the deception when the king bestows upon them flocks and herds, servants of both sexes, and a thousand pieces of silver (Gen. 20:2, 16). "Abraham and Sara[h] act as a team—perhaps a team of con artists."[13]

So, too, does Tamar "con" her brother by bringing up the prospect of marriage—but her proposition is only a desperate ruse to put off the rapist. Nothing in the Bible suggests that she holds the slightest affection for Amnon; nor can we take Amnon at his word when he declares his "love" for Tamar while he is plotting the sexual ambush with his cousin. Clearly, Amnon *lusts* after his sister, but he certainly does not *love* her, before *or* after the rape. Amnon betrays his real feelings toward Tamar when the rape is over and he brusquely orders his servant to throw her out of the house. "Put this woman out from me" is the standard English translation of what Amnon says (2 Sam. 13:17), but a more accurate rendering of the biblical Hebrew reveals that he regards Tamar as nothing more than an object of perverse and momentary pleasure. "Put this *thing* out from me" is what Amnon actually says.[14]

What is really happening at the moment before the assault is a cunning if desperate ploy by Tamar to talk her way out of being raped. The words she chooses are calculated to suggest that Amnon might get what he wants later on, and, at the same time, to caution him about the consequences of taking what he wants against her will. "Speak unto the king," says Tamar to her brother, thus holding out the possibility that she *would* sleep with him under different circumstances, and yet reminding him that he will be defying the king's authority and risking the king's wrath by forcing her into his bed. Of course, the words that Tamar speaks to Amnon do not deter him from carrying out his elaborate plan to rape her. As it turns out, King David has *not* withheld Tamar from Amnon—it was the king who commanded Tamar into Amnon's bedchamber in the first place!—and David does nothing to punish Amnon afterward.

Why is the king so passive in the face of an incestuous rape within the royal household? Perhaps it is because David is too guilt-ridden over his own sexual misadventures to chastise his son for doing much the same thing, as one scholar suggests.[15] Perhaps it is because the king insists on pampering and indulging his firstborn son and heir apparent—the Dead Sea Scrolls and an early Greek version of the Bible known as the Septuagint explain that David "did not rebuke Amnon his son because he loved him, since his firstborn was he," a line of text that simply does not appear at all in the Masoretic Text.[16] Or perhaps, as some Bible critics have boldly suggested, David does not think to single out Amnon for punishment because the king himself played such a dubious role in setting up the encounter in the first place. In fact, some Bible critics go so far as to accuse David of complicity and even conspiracy in the rape of Tamar, something that Tamar herself may suspect when she seeks refuge with her brother rather than her father after the deed is done.

According to one ingenious reading of the biblical text, David is tipped off to his son's real intentions toward Tamar when Amnon describes the kind of food he wants his sister to prepare for him. The specific word that Amnon uses in his plea to King David—*lebibot*—is usually translated into English as "bread" (JPS) or "cakes" (Scofield KJV) or "dumplings."[17] But the translation does not capture the sensual overtones of the Hebrew word: *lebibot* is an "erotic pun"[18] that plays on the Hebrew word for "heart" and evokes images of arousal and excitement. In fact, the delicacy that Amnon desires to eat from his sister's hand is rendered as "hearty dumplings" in the Anchor Bible and may have been literally heart-shaped.[19] To convey the erotic subtext of Amnon's demand on his sister, one Bible critic bluntly renders the Hebrew word as "libido cakes."[20]

"[B]y asking that Tamar prepare the dumplings," cracks another Bible commentator, "[Amnon] is privately anticipating more than the restoration of his health."[21]

Does David know what Amnon *really* wants from Tamar? The case against King David turns on the very words used by Amnon to describe the food he asks his sister to prepare. By describing the "hearty dumplings" for which he hungers in such erotic language, it is argued, Amnon is subtly asking permission of David to have his way with his sister—and, by agreeing to send Tamar to Amnon's house, the king is not only tacitly approving a sexual encounter of some kind between brother and sister but "delivering her into the hands of his son, her rapist."[22] Indeed, one scholar finds it "difficult to believe that David, himself the author of much subtler intrigues, would have been completely taken in by such transparent designs as this one."[23]

One of the sharper ironies in the Book of Samuel, a work of profound and persistent irony, is the fact that the outrage against Tamar takes place during the reign of a supposedly righteous king. At the end of the Book of Judges, as we have already seen, the biblical author holds out the promise that a king on the throne of Israel will preclude the kind of sexual violence that befell the Levite traveler's concubine in Gibeah. (see chapter thirteen.) Yet Tamar discovers that even the most glorious and powerful king in the history of Israel does nothing to prevent *or* punish the outrage to which she is subjected by her own brother. "Behold, the princes of Israel, every one according to his might, have been in thee to shed blood," God will later instruct the prophet Ezekiel to say, itemizing the "abominations" that have been committed within "the bloody city" of the Chosen People. "[A]nd each in thee hath defiled his sister, his father's daughter" (Ezek. 22:11).

"A CHARIOT AND HORSES AND FIFTY MEN"

Tamar disappears into her brother's house after the rape, never to be seen or heard again in the streets of Jerusalem *or* the pages of the Bible. But Tamar does not disappear from history—her rape sets into motion a chain reaction of assassination, insurrection, and civil war that threatens to topple King David from the throne and continues to afflict the royal house until the very end of his days. The rape of Tamar, we come to understand, may have been an intimate personal ordeal for the woman herself, but it was a crime with very public and distinctly political implications for the rest of her family and the nation of Israel.

Tellingly, Amnon himself, firstborn son of the king and heir apparent to the throne, is unconcerned about the authority or even the anger of his father when he sets out to sexually exploit Tamar. His insouciance is an early signal that David is no longer taken quite seriously by his own sons. Tamar obliquely invokes the threat of royal punishment in the moments before the rape—"speak unto the king"—but Amnon ignores his sister's subtle reminder that he will have to contend with their father if he does what he is threatening to do. Amnon simply does not care what his father will do, and he proceeds to commit a sexual outrage against the royal princess in a manner that seems calculated to bring the incident to the attention of the king, the royal court, and the public at large: not content with raping his sister, Amnon makes a spectacle of the ruined princess by ordering her to be thrown into the street.

If the rape of Tamar amounts to a test of the king's authority, then David fails the test miserably when he fails to punish or even admonish his audacious son. The lesson that Amnon and the rest of the court learn from the whole sordid affair is that the crown prince can do *anything* that strikes his fancy, no matter how outrageous, because the king is too passive, too indecisive, and too indulgent of his heir to do anything about it. From the moment of Tamar's rape, the once-mighty King David is marked as a monarch in sharp decline, and his apparent weakness excites the ambitions of his other sons.

King David's passivity is carefully noted by Absalom, the king's third-born son and Tamar's full brother, who is shown to be as thoroughly ambitious and calculating as his father. Absalom seems to draw at least a couple of ominous conclusions from the rape of Tamar. First, if anyone is going to exact revenge on Amnon for raping Tamar, it must be Absalom himself. Second, by striking down Amnon, Absalom will put himself within striking distance of his father's throne. Once Amnon is good and dead, all that stands between Absalom and absolute power is the impotent and indecisive David—and Absalom, embittered by the leniency of the king toward his sister's rapist and covetous of the crown, is perfectly willing to take on his own father in open insurrection.

After the assassination of Amnon at the sheepshearing festival at Baal-hazor, Absalom puts himself beyond the reach of David by seeking refuge in the court of his maternal grandfather, the king of a neighboring country called Geshur. Three years pass before David, bereaved over the death of one son and the self-exile of another son, is persuaded to invite Absalom back to Jerusalem, and another two years go by before the king consents to see his errant son. At last, a poignant reunion is arranged. "[Absalom] bowed himself on his face to the ground before the king," the biblical author tells us, "and the king kissed Absalom" (2 Sam. 14:33).

But, once again, we are observing an expert con artist at work.

Absalom is only faking the role of remorseful son. Just as Amnon had feigned illness while plotting to rape his sister, Absalom feigns obeisance toward his father while plotting to dethrone him. The plot goes public when Absalom acquires "a chariot and horses and fifty men to run before him" (2 Sam. 15:1)—a showy entourage worthy of a king and an unmistakable act of defiance toward King David. Sure enough, Absalom arranges to be crowned as king in Hebron, the very place where David was first anointed king over Judah, and thus goes into open rebellion against his father. "As soon as ye hear the sound of the horn," Absalom instructs the provocateurs that he scatters throughout Israel, "then ye shall say: 'Absalom is king in Hebron' " (2 Sam. 15:10).

David abandons his palace in panic and terror—he is literally barefoot and weeping as he escapes over the Mount of Olives—and flees from Jerusalem into the wilderness with a few loyal courtiers and a band of foreign mercenaries to protect him from his own son and his own people. Meanwhile, the newly crowned Absalom makes a very public display of his kingship by engaging in sexual intercourse with ten of David's concubines in a specially erected pavilion on the roof of the royal palace, "in the sight of all Israel" (2 Sam. 16:22). Thus comes to pass the very fate that the Almighty decreed for David to punish him for his infidelities with Bathsheba and his murder of Uriah.

"I will take thy wives before thine eyes," God has already vowed through the prophet Nathan. "For thou didst it secretly; but I will do this thing before all Israel, and before the sun" (2 Sam. 12:11–12).

David musters an army and goes to war against Absalom to reclaim his throne. At last, David seems to recapture the courage, charisma, and sheer good luck that once blessed his efforts in war and politics. His soldiers put the army of Absalom to rout and some twenty thousand men are slain in the forest of Ephraim, where David is able to put his youthful experience as a guerrilla fighter to good use in the rugged terrain.[24] "[T]he forest devoured more people that day than the sword devoured," the biblical author observes (2 Sam. 18:8). Even in victory, however, David is incapable of dealing harshly with a rebellious son. "Deal gently for my sake with the young man," David instructs his commanders, "even with Absalom" (2 Sam. 18:5).

But Absalom, as it turns out, is doomed to die by reason of a freak accident on the way to the battlefield. The biblical author has already told us that Absalom, like his sister Tamar, is beautiful to behold—

"Now in all Israel there was none to be so much praised as Absalom for his beauty" (2 Sam. 14:25)—and his crowning glory, so to speak, is a long and luxuriant head of hair, so abundant that it weighs out at two hundred shekels (two or three pounds) when he gets his annual haircut. But it is Absalom's hair that betrays him—his mule carries him under a large oak tree, and his head is caught in the low-hanging branches. "[H]e was taken up between the heaven and the earth," writes the biblical author, rendering the faintly comical scene in grandiloquent language, "and the mule that was under him went on" (2 Sam. 18:9).

Absalom is found by Joab, the same general who had arranged for the murder of Uriah at David's command. Absalom is still alive, but Joab defies the king's order to spare him—Joab strikes Absalom in the heart with three darts and then sets ten of his armor-bearers upon the helpless and wounded young man, thus bringing Absalom's life and brief reign to an ignoble end. Joab is apparently less sentimental than David on the subject of rebellious sons, and his "Machiavellian sense of public morality"[25] prompts the general to make an example of Absalom, if only to deter would-be pretenders to the throne. Upon learning of Absalom's death, King David does not rebuke Joab for disregarding his order to spare Absalom, but he famously proclaims his grief. "O my son Absalom, my son, my son Absalom!" the king wails. "Would I had died for thee, O Absalom, my son, my son!" (2 Sam. 19:1).

Absalom's death seems even more poignant when we recall that his sister remains in his household back in Jerusalem, a desolate woman now utterly lacking a protector or a provider. But the Bible allows us one intriguing hint of Tamar's destiny. Absalom, we are told, is the father of four children of his own, three sons and a daughter. His daughter, like his sister, is "a woman of fair countenance" (2 Sam. 14:27), and both women are named in honor of the *first* Tamar, a distant ancestress who so boldly and courageously wrote herself into history. (See chapter six.) The Bible does not tell us what becomes of these two Tamars, but we might imagine that they befriend one another and somehow manage to survive in spite of the sorry fate that has befallen them.

HEAT

King David's decline begins with Bathsheba and the adulterous affair that leads to the birth of Solomon, but we do not encounter her again until the very end of the king's reign, when he is old and feeble and no longer much interested in pleasures of the flesh. Bathsheba boldly enters the king's bedchamber even as a luscious young concubine named Abishag is "ministering" to the king's needs. We don't know exactly what Abishag is doing, but the biblical author allows us to understand that her ministrations will not excite the sexual jealousy of Bathsheba because the old king is impotent.

"Let her lie in thy bosom, that my lord the king may get heat," urge the solicitous courtiers who have recruited Abishag for service in the royal bedchamber. But David's once-mighty sexual appetites have flagged, and we are told that "the king knew her not" (1 Kings 1:2, 4).

Bathsheba reenters the biblical narrative at a crucial point in the saga of King David—indeed, it is really *the* decisive moment of the Court History, which is also sometimes called the Succession Narrative because of what happens next. She implores David to anoint their son, Solomon, as his chosen successor to the throne of Israel. And she informs David that another one of his many sons, Adonijah, has already declared himself to be king and is running around Jerusalem even now with the same kind of entourage that Absalom once used to announce *his* kingship—a chariot and horses and fifty men.

"And now, behold, Adonijah reigneth," says Bathsheba to the failing king, "and thou . . . knowest it not" (1 Kings 1:18).

While Bathsheba and the prophet Nathan are lobbying David in favor of Solomon, Adonijah is lining up his own allies, including the general who so often played the role of the royal hit man, the faithful Joab. But Bathsheba succeeds in extracting what she wants from David—"Assuredly Solomon thy son shall reign after me," says the weary old king, "and he shall sit upon my throne in my stead"—and Bathsheba bows to the floor in gratitude. "Let my lord king David live for ever," she says.

Bathsheba's words are to no avail. David lives only long enough to advise Solomon on whom he ought to trust and whom he ought to kill when David is gone. In a scene later artfully copied in *The Godfather*, David obliquely instructs Solomon to arrange for the murder of Joab, just as Joab once arranged for the murder of Uriah and Absalom. "[L]et not his hoar head go down to the grave in peace," says David. Then, after a bloody reign of forty years, the remarkable life of the old king is finally over: "And David slept with his fathers," the incomparable story-teller of Samuel and Kings concludes (1 Kings 2:6, 10).

But Solomon is not quite yet secure on the throne of David, and the Succession Narrative is not yet over. Adonijah renews his bid for the throne by audaciously asking Bathsheba to petition King Solomon for one little souvenir of their father—David's tempting but untouched concubine, Abishag. Readily if rather disingenuously, Bathsheba agrees to carry Adonijah's message to Solomon, knowing full well that her son will not mistake the real intent behind Adonijah's request. Just as Absalom had once staked his claim on David's throne by sleeping with the king's ten concubines on the roof of the palace, Adonijah is now asserting his own right to reign as king of Israel by seeking to wed the last of the king's wives. Solomon listens to the message that his mother brings to him, marks Adonijah as a deadly enemy, and resolves not to let *his* hoar head go down to the grave in peace. "God do so to me, and more also," vows Solomon, "if Adonijah have not spoken this word against his own life" (1 Kings 2:23).

The Succession Narrative ends on the same note of sexual irony that was struck at the very beginning. What appears to be one man's lust for a beautiful woman—first David's seduction of Bathsheba, then Amnon's rape of Tamar, and finally Adonijah's bid for Abishag—is shown to be an act with unmistakable political meanings and cata-strophic political consequences. Solomon himself goes on to indulge his own gargantuan passions—he accumulates some seven hundred wives and three hundred concubines—and he is seduced into worshipping their pagan gods and goddesses, with further disastrous consequences for the Royal House of David. Solomon builds the Temple at Jerusalem, thus crowning the achievements of his father, but the united monarchy of Judah and Israel is already beginning to crack—and the mighty empire of King David will begin to fall apart upon the death of Solomon.

"WONDERFUL WAS THY LOVE TO ME"

The frank descriptions of human passion *in extremis* that are preserved in the Book of Samuel are mostly overlooked by pious Bible readers, who seem to prefer David's psalms to his sexual adventures. Even some Bible scholars are uncomfortable with the candor of the biblical author about what one commentator delicately calls David's "failures in the area of moral restraint."[26] For example, Louis Ginzberg's *The Legends of the Jews*, a vast anthology of rabbinical legend and lore that bulks up to seven fat volumes, spares only two dismissive sentences* for Tamar and her suffering at the hands of her half brother: "Tamar cannot be called one of the children of David, because she was born before her mother's conversion to Judaism," the rabbis argued. "Consequently, her relation to Amnon is not quite of the grave nature it would have been in the strict sense of the terms."[27]

Then, too, the homoerotic overtones in David's life story have been stubbornly ignored by Bible critics until very recently. Pious commentators have long celebrated the intimate friendship between David and Jonathan as "the ideal of male friendship,"[28] for example, but they have refused to acknowledge the possibility that physical as well as spiritual intimacies passed between these two men. "The soul of Jonathan was knit with the soul of David," the Bible tells us plainly enough, "and Jonathan loved him as his own soul" (1 Sam. 18:1). On the eve of battle, Jonathan strips off his own cloak and tunic, his armor and weaponry, and tenderly dresses David in his apparel as a pledge of friendship (1 Sam. 18:4). And when Jonathan is later slain, David's oft-quoted and much-celebrated elegy speaks plainly enough of their bond. "Very pleasant hath thou been unto me," sings David, the "sweet psalmist" of Israel. "Wonderful was thy love to me, passing the love of women" (2 Sam. 1:26).

Remarkably, a certain squeamishness is *still* displayed by some contemporary scholars toward the sexual excesses in the Bible and, especially, the story of David. For example, the Bible shows Bathsheba as a

---

*One astonishing rabbinical pronouncement that Ginzberg left out is an explanation of why Amnon's "love" for Tamar turns so abruptly to hatred—Amnon, the Talmud proposes, sustained an embarrassing and painful injury when he found himself entangled in Tamar's pubic hair during the rape!

seductress who seeks to catch the king's eye, and at least one scholar speculates that "more than one Bathsheba in the neighborhood of the royal residence . . . hopefully took a bath where she could be seen from the roof of the King's house." But feminist critic J. Cheryl Exum complains that she is put off by the story of David and Bathsheba and similar "pornographic elements" in the biblical accounts of the Gibeah Outrage and the rape of Tamar. According to Exum, Bathsheba—not unlike Tamar—is "raped by the pen" because Bible readers are invited to put themselves "in the position of voyeurs" and watch what happens to Bathsheba when she catches the eye of the king while bathing on the rooftop. "This is no love story," Exum concludes. "[T]he scene is the biblical equivalent of 'wham bam, thank you, ma'am': he sent, he took, she came, he lay, she returned."[29]

In fact, some of the biblical authors themselves were clearly uncomfortable with the candor displayed in Samuel and Kings. So we are given a *second* version of the lives of David and Solomon in First and Second Chronicles, which appear as a kind of afterthought at the very end of the Hebrew Bible. David's love for Jonathan, his adulterous and murderous affair with Bathsheba, the rape of Tamar, and the insurrection of Absalom are never mentioned by the author of Chronicles, and other incidents in the reign of King David are boldly revised and rewritten to serve the author's theological agenda—the legitimacy and longevity of the Davidic line. For example, it is plainly reported in the Second Book of Samuel that David is ordered by God to conduct a census of the Israelites, something regarded as odious by ancient Israelites because a census was the first step toward taxation and conscription—and then, rather perversely, God turns around and punishes David and the Israelites when the king complies! (2 Sam. 24:1, 15). But the propagandist who composed Chronicles simply erases the name of God and writes in the name of Satan when retelling the very same story: "And *Satan* stood up against Israel, and moved David to number Israel" (1 Chron. 21:1).

Of course, it is precisely because the forbidden tales of the Bible have always made so many people so uncomfortable that they have come to be censored or suppressed or simply ignored. But if we read the Bible—and especially the story of David—with open eyes, we can readily see that the biblical authors regard even a human being who is as deeply flawed as David to be worthy of the loftiest blessings of the Almighty. And so it turns out that David, a man of war, will be the fore-bear of the Prince of Peace.

THE BLESSING AND THE CURSE

Four fateful covenants between God and humankind are described in the Hebrew Bible. The first deal is struck with Noah: "Never again shall the waters become a flood to destroy all living creatures," promises a remorseful God (Gen. 9:11 NEB). The second covenant is the one between God and Abraham, who is destined to become "the father of a multitude of nations" and whose descendants will be given the Promised Land "for an everlasting possession" (Gen. 17:4, 8). The third covenant is God's vow to Moses to make the Israelites "a kingdom of priests, and a holy nation" (Exod. 19:5–6) if they will agree to observe his commandments, which add up to 613 by the closing pages of the Five Books of Moses. And the fourth covenant is the one between God and David, a promise that has come to be understood by Jews and Christians alike as God's solemn commitment to redeem our own world from suffering once and for all.

"When thy days are fulfilled, and thou shalt sleep with thy fathers, I will set up thy seed after thee . . . and I will establish his kingdom," God tells David. "My mercy shall not depart from him . . . , [a]nd thy kingdom shall be made sure for ever before thee; thy throne shall be established for ever" (2 Sam. 7:12, 15–16).

In fact, the royal house of David ruled the ancient kingdom of Judah for some four hundred years[30]—a dynasty of unprecedented length and stability in the ancient world and, especially, the ancient Near East. The Almighty's promise to David was recalled each time one of his descendants ascended to the throne of Judah: "And thy house and thy kingdom shall be made sure for ever" (2 Sam. 7:16). And, according to ancient tradition, each new king in the Davidic line was anointed with holy oil during the ritual of coronation. For that reason, each new king in the line of David was regarded as an "anointed one"—the Hebrew word is *mashiach*, but we are more familiar with the Greek ren-dering of the same word: *Messiah*.

But the divine promise to David was not kept. The Davidic line of kings finally ran out in 587–586 B.C.E., when the Babylonians conquered the southern kingdom of Judah and destroyed the temple that Solomon had built at Jerusalem. According to the Book of Kings, the last heir of David to actually sit on the throne of Israel in Jerusalem is Zedekiah, a young man who serves at first as a quisling king appointed by Nebuchadnezzar, king of Babylon, but later rises up against his overlord. Zedekiah's rebellion fails, and the last sight he is allowed to see is the slaying of his children. Then his eyes are put out, and he is carried off in chains to Babylon, where he is put to work as a slave in a mill (2 Kings 25:7). No heir of David ever takes the throne in Jerusalem again.

To explain why God apparently reneges on his solemn promise to David, a later biblical author argues that God's promise of kingship to David and his "royal seed" is conditioned on the strict observance of divine law by the monarchs and their people. The fact that the Davidic kings, starting with Solomon and continuing through Zedekiah, engaged in pagan worship and other "abominations" explains why God does not regard himself as obliged to live up to his end of the bargain with David. Indeed, the Book of Kings gives us a scene in which David explains to Solomon that God's covenant comes with a big "if."

> If thy children take heed to their way, to walk before Me in truth with all their heart and with all their soul, there shall not fail thee, said He, a man on the throne of Israel (1 Kings 2:4).

So it is the faithlessness of Israel, and not a breach of contract by God, that leads to the destruction of Israel, according to the revisionist version of the covenant between God and David. Indeed, the prophets work themselves into a frenzy of blame in their efforts to convince the Israelites that their long ordeal of conquest, occupation, and dispersion is their own fault. "[T]he rulers transgressed against Me," God complains to the prophet Jeremiah, and "all the families of the house of Israel," too (Jer. 2:4, 8).

> Wherefore should I pardon thee?
> Thy children have forsaken Me,
> And sworn by no-gods;
> And when I had fed them to the full, they committed adultery,

And they assembled themselves in troops at the harlots'
    houses.
They are become as well-fed horses, lusty stallions,
Every one neigheth after his neighbour's wife.
Shall I not punish for these things? (Jer. 5:7–9).

The theological revisionism that we find within the pages of the
Bible is probably the work of priests and scribes who lived around the
time of King Josiah, a distant descendant of David and a fierce religious
reformer of ancient Israel. In 622 B.C.E., a book of sacred law mysteriously turned up in the Temple at Jerusalem; it was the Book of
Deuteronomy, according to recent Bible scholarship, or at least a significant chunk of it. Deuteronomy embodied a new and stern theology that
blames all of the woes of ancient Israel on the breach of God's covenant
with Moses. By worshipping strange gods and goddesses, thereby defying
the "statutes and ordinances" of divine law, the author of Deuteronomy
declares, the Israelites will forfeit the blessings that God promised to his
Chosen People and, instead, call down upon themselves the curses that
are set forth at length and in bloodcurdling detail in the Book of
Deuteronomy.

"I have set before thee life and death, the blessing and the curse,"
says Moses in Deuteronomy. "Therefore choose life, that thou mayest
live, thou and thy seed" (Deut. 30:19).

Significantly, the influence of the Deuteronomist can be detected in
several other books of the Bible: Joshua, Judges, First and Second
Samuel, and First and Second Kings, all of which are known among
scholars as the Dueteronomistic History. And the Deuteronomist displays a none-too-subtle agenda throughout these several books of the
Bible: he too seeks to validate the royal house of David as the legitimate
rulers of Israel, but he also seeks to explain the unhappy destiny of Israel
by blaming various of David's descendants for committing "abominations" in violation of God's law. One king after another "did that which
was evil in the eyes of the Lord," the Deuteronomist insists, and that is
why God withdrew his blessing from his Chosen People.

The sorry and squalid history of the descendants of King David
gives the Deuteronomist much to complain about. David is not fault-
less, as we have seen, and Solomon commits the ultimate sin of worshipping pagan gods and goddesses. All but one of David's descendants

are found wanting by the Deuteronomist in one way or another. Only a single Davidic monarch is singled out for unqualified praise[31]—King Josiah, a white-hot religious reformer who transformed the religious practices of ancient Israel in the early seventh century B.C.E. Until Josiah came along, and the Book of Deuteronomy was discovered, the religious practices of ancient Israel encompassed the worship of Baal and Asherah, the adoration of the sun and the moon and the stars, even the sacrifice of children to the god known as Moloch (2 Kings 23). To the joy of the Deuteronomist, Josiah vows to purge the nation of Israel of all but the strictest form of worship.

Josiah has been characterized by some contemporary critics as *Davidus redivivus*[32]—a resurrected David—and the otherwise obscure king is praised even more lavishly than David by the biblical authors because of his efforts to purify the faith of ancient Israel. King Josiah is credited with purging the Temple of paraphernalia for the worship of Baal and Asherah, pulling down "the houses of the sodomites" where women were put to work at making such paraphernalia, suppressing the worship of pagan gods and goddesses at the altars and "high places" in Jerusalem and elsewhere around ancient Israel, slaying the renegade priests who presided over such ceremonies, and burying the sites of pagan worship under "the bones of men" (2 Kings 23:4–20). For his efforts, King Josiah is described with a fervor that the Deuteronomist reserves for only one other man in all of the Bible—the prophet and lawgiver, Moses.

"And like unto him was there no king before him," the biblical author writes of Josiah, echoing the very words and phrases that are used to describe Moses, "that turned to the Lord with all his heart, and with all his soul, and with all his might, according to all the law of Moses; neither after him arose there any like him" (2 Kings 23:25).

Because Josiah alone enjoys such unreserved adulation, contemporary biblical scholarship suggests that the books of the Bible known as the Deuteronomistic History were first composed while Josiah sat upon the throne. Indeed, the Book of Deuteronomy itself has been called a "pious fraud" because the book is presented as one of the Five Books of Moses—"These are the words which Moses spoke unto all Israel beyond the Jordan" (Deut. 1:1)—when Deuteronomy was obviously composed by a different (and later) author than the ones who composed the other four books.[33] The authors of the Deuteronomistic History lionized King

Josiah, the otherwise obscure monarch under whom they lived and worked, because they endorsed his policy of centralizing and standardizing the worship of Yahweh to the exclusion of the other gods and goddesses that the Israelites seemed to find so alluring.

So the Bible, as we know it, preserves a snapshot of the court politics and the theological priorities at a single moment in the long history of ancient Israel. But the doing of "that which was evil in the sight of the Lord" by the Israelites and the monarchs who ruled them does not end with Josiah. The kings that come after Josiah are no better than the ones that came before him, according to the author of the Book of Kings, and the Davidic line comes to a final and sorrowful end with the Babylonian Conquest and the destruction of the Temple. As it turns out, no descendant of David will take the throne again. So the biblical authors find themselves with an awkward question to answer: If God has promised King David that his descendants will sit on the throne of Judah "for ever," when and how will God's promise be kept?

"THEY SHALL NOT HURT NOR DESTROY"

Solomon is an unlikely figure to succeed David to the kingship of the united monarchy of Judah and Israel. After all, he is the offspring of a marriage that was brokered through adultery and assassination, and he stands no closer than tenth in the line of succession. The Succession Narrative is intended to show how war and politics, intrigue and conspiracy, bloodshed and betrayal combined to bring him to the throne of Israel. Yahweh, reduced once again to the role of "a god of convenience,"[34] is rarely seen or heard, and the Court Historian allows us to see David and his contemporaries as "men who no longer walk by faith in the cultic religious symbols of the past," as one scholar puts it, "but contend for temporal power and freedom of self-expression in the mundane world."[35]

Still, as it turns out, the mundane world was not kind to the House of David or the united monarchy that he founded, and ancient Israel was soon reduced to civil war, conquest, occupation, and exile. Confronted with the harsh realities of their history, the Israelites began to reinterpret the divine promise to David in new and momentous ways. Since the throne of David was empty and no descendant was at hand, the next king in the Davidic line came to be understood as someone who would appear at some unknowable moment in the future and usher in an era of perfect peace and harmony—a rescuer, a redeemer, a savior. The "anointed one"—the Messiah—was slowly and subtly transformed from yet another flesh-and-blood monarch into a mysterious and miraculous figure who would fulfill God's original promise to King David.

"For a child is born unto us," the prophet Isaiah declares in a familiar biblical passage that fairly burns with the messianic yearnings of an oppressed people. "A son is given unto us; and the government is upon his shoulder."

> And of peace there be no end,
> Upon the throne of David, and upon his kingdom,
> To establish it, and to uphold it
> Through justice and through righteousness
> From henceforth even for ever (Isaiah 9:5–6).

Here we come to the fork in the road where Judaism and Christianity move off in different directions, so fatefully and with such bloody consequences. Jewish tradition regards the Messiah as a divinely anointed but thoroughly human figure who will "execute justice and righteousness in the land" (Jer. 23:5)—and, crucially, the Jewish faith holds that we are *still* awaiting the arrival of the Messiah. Christian tradition regards the Messiah as the Son of God and the source of heavenly salvation—and the Christian faith interprets the words of Isaiah and other prophets of the Hebrew Bible to identify Jesus of Nazareth as *the* Messiah, a word that is translated into Greek as *Christos* and is rendered in English as "Christ." From this fundamental difference of opinion about the identity of the final heir of David, more than two thousand years of hatred, oppression, suffering, and death have flowed, and no end is yet in sight.

More than one bitter irony is at work in these crucial biblical texts. David is regarded as "a man after God's heart," and yet God is not much in evidence in the Book of Samuel and, especially, in the rape of Tamar. Her ordeal, one of the most harrowingly realistic accounts in the Bible, is used by the biblical narrator to foreshadow the realpolitik of the court of King David, a place that fairly sizzled with Machiavellian intrigue and cynical power politics. The fact that David is an inadvertent accomplice to her rape—and, more troubling still, the fact that he does nothing to vindicate her or punish her rapist—is entirely overlooked by the Almighty.

But, then, the Book of Samuel allows us to understand that God does not much care about the high crimes and sexual misadventures of King David. When the Almighty first resolves to punish David for his adultery with Bathsheba and his role in the foul murder of her husband, it is an innocent baby who bears the brunt of divine wrath! As for David's brutality in politics and war—his path to the throne is littered with the dead bodies of his rivals and adversaries—the only punishment from on high is that Solomon, rather than David, will have the honor of building the Temple at Jerusalem. "Thou shalt not build a house for My name," God says, "because thou art a man of war, and thou hast shed blood" (1 Chron. 28:3). All is forgotten, all is forgiven, by the time God bestows his eternal blessing on David and decrees that his dynasty will ultimately bring forth the Prince of Peace, the Messiah.

"The Lord rewarded me according to my righteousness," boasts David. "According to the cleanness of my hands hath He recompensed me" (2 Sam. 22:21).

The greatest (and cruelest) irony of all is the fact that so much blood has been spilled over so many centuries precisely because we cannot agree on what the Bible says and means about the coming of the Messiah. Both Christians and Jews share a common belief, however, that the Messiah will be (or is) a descendant of David—"a shoot out of the stock of Jesse," as Isaiah puts it, referring to the father of David (Isa. 11:1). And so we must pray, Christian and Jew alike, that *all* of the words of prophecy will be realized in a time and place where deadly enemies make peace, where children are no longer at risk, a world where Tamar need not fear Amnon, and Amnon need not fear Absalom, and Absalom need not fear David.

> And the wolf shall dwell with the lamb,
> And the leopard shall lie down with the kid;
> And the calf and the young lion and the fatling together;
> And a little child shall lead them.
> And the cow and the bear shall feed;
> Their young ones shall lie down together;
> And the lion shall eat straw like the ox.

And the sucking child shall play on the hole of the asp,
And the weaned child shall put his hand on the basilisk's den.
They shall not hurt nor destroy
In all My holy mountain (Isa. 11:6–9).

To which *all* readers of the Bible, Christian or Jew or Muslim, agnostic or atheist, ought to be able to say: *Amen.*

CHAPTER SIXTEEN

GOD'S NOVEL HAS SUSPENSE

THE FACE OF GOD ✛ WHAT DOES GOD WANT?
MIDRASH ✛ GOD'S NOVEL

When you visualized a man or woman carefully, you could always begin to feel pity—that was a quality God's image carried with it. When you saw the lines at the corners of the eyes, the shape of the mouth, how the hair grew, it was impossible to hate. Hate was just a failure of imagination.

—GRAHAM GREENE
THE POWER AND THE GLORY

Jack Kerouac tells a story in *On the Road* about a young drifter who has just been released from a prison where he served time for grand theft. To avoid sitting on the cold stone floor of his cell during a long stretch in solitary, he used a prison-issue Bible as a kind of cushion. But the jailors objected to his impiety (or, more likely, his comfort) and replaced the fat tome with "a leetle pocket-size one so big," as the chatty ex-con puts it.

"Couldn't sit on it so I read the whole Bible and Testament," says the young man of his prison revelation. "[Y]ou know they's some real hot things in that Bi-ble."[1]

At first blush, of course, what's "hot" about the forbidden stories of the Bible are the shocks and surprises that await the reader who expects to find only Sunday school stuff—the frank and mostly nonjudgmental accounts of seduction, exhibitionism, voyeurism, adultery, incest, rape, and murder. Sometimes it is hard to make out the moral example that the biblical authors intend us to see in these tales of human passion. And that is why the stories we have explored here have been censored, banned, mistranslated, or simply ignored by preachers and teachers who found them too hot to handle.

But these stories are "hot" in quite another sense. As we have seen, the Bible is littered with the artifacts and relics of ancient beliefs and practices that come as a surprise to anyone who has been taught to regard the Bible as a single-minded manifesto of ethical monotheism. The depiction of God as a mischievous and sometimes even murderous deity is shocking to anyone who envisions the Almighty as a heavenly father and "King of the Universe," benign and compassionate, slow to anger and quick to forgive. By the time we finish reading and pondering these troubling stories, we are left with the unsettling realization that something very odd was going on in ancient Israel before the priests and scribes came along and cleaned up the biblical text—and we have only a faint if provocative notion of what it was.

So the theological hot spots in the Bible turn out to be even more unsettling than the incidents of human misconduct. While it may seem scandalous that in both Jewish and Christian tradition David is regarded as "a man after God's heart," the very model of a just and righteous king, and the progenitor of the Messiah, it is even harder to explain away the fact that his son and successor, the wise King Solomon, sacrifices to the Canaanite goddess called Ashtoreth, among other pagan deities, and yet is never punished for his "abominations." David's sins are purely human failings, but Solomon's act of apostasy defies what we are taught to regard as the essential teaching of the Bible and the three religions that regard the Bible as Holy Writ: "Thou shalt have no other gods before Me" is, quite literally, written in stone by the finger of the Almighty (Deut. 5:7)!

So we might conclude from an open-eyed reading of the forbidden texts of the Bible that the fundamental truth is that there is no fundamental truth. Instead, we are invited to join the rest of humanity in a restless, ceaseless search to discern some moral order in a chaotic universe. We are challenged by the Bible itself to figure out who God is and what God wants—and that is the most disturbing revelation of all. The plain fact is that the Bible offers many visions of God, many explanations of God's will, many prophecies of humankind's destiny, and the real challenge is to discern the ones that make sense and ring true, the ones that hold out the promise of peace in a troubled and dangerous world.

THE FACE OF GOD

"A god-shaped hole" is how the French existential philosopher Jean-Paul Sartre once described the fundamental yearning for the divine that aches in the hearts and minds of human beings in all ages and all places. Gods and goddesses have been depicted in the sacred art of *every* culture, ranging from the crude stick figures of cave paintings to the glorious images that adorn the Sistine Chapel. But the fantastic variety of these images explains why we cannot agree on the outline of that god-shaped hole in the human soul. Even the Bible does not pin itself down on who God is, what God looks like, why God acts the way he does, or what God wants of us.

Starting with the very first words of the Bible, the biblical authors simply cannot agree on how to describe and depict the One True God, and so we are given *two* versions of what happens "in the beginning."

The first account of Creation in Genesis depicts God only as a cosmic something-or-other, the kind of abstract deity that astrophysicists invoke when they gaze on some far-distant supernova and describe what they have seen as "the face of God." "Now the earth was unformed and void," goes Genesis 1:2, "and the spirit of God hovered over the face of the waters." When the formless God of Genesis 1 pauses to create man and woman "in His own image" (Gen. 1:27), he accomplishes the feat with hands-off verbal commands. Indeed, as we read the first account of creation in Genesis, we cannot really say that God *has* hands: "Let the earth bring forth the living creature after its kind," God decrees. "And it was so," the biblical author concludes (Gen. 1:24).

Quite a different deity shows up in the second account of Creation, where we are introduced to a strikingly earthy version of God who hunkers down in the muck and mire of the newly created planet and sculpts the first man out of clay with his own hands: "Then the Lord God formed man of the dust of the ground, and breathed into his nostrils the breath of life; and man became a living soul" (Gen. 2:7). Later, the touchy-feely God of Genesis 2 is seen strolling through the Garden of Eden "in the cool of the day" and chatting up the man and woman whom he has created with his own hands (Gen. 3:8–9). Significantly, the all-knowing and all-seeing Yahweh does not see or know where Adam and Eve are or what they have been up to or why they are suddenly wearing those famous fig leaves.

"Where art thou?" God calls out to the mortals he has just created, suddenly full of urgent questions. "Who told thee that thou wast naked? Hast thou eaten of the tree, whereof I commanded thee that thou shouldest not eat? . . . What is this thou hast done?" (Gen. 3:9, 11, 13).

The Bible goes on to conjure up countless visions of God. Sometimes the Almighty is a vagrant who shows up at the door with dusty feet and gratefully tucks into a meal of chops and curds (Gen. 18:8). Sometimes he is "the pillar of cloud by day, and the pillar of fire by night" (Exod. 13:22). Sometimes he is the "ancient of days," a white-haired celestial monarch on a fiery throne, attended by angelic courtiers numbering a "thousand thousands" (Dan. 7:9–10). Sometimes he is a changeling—an ordinary human being one moment, trudging through the desert on foot, and a thundering mountain god the next, casting down hellfire and brimstone from the heavens (Gen. 19:23–24).

Significantly, the biblical vision of God that is often invoked by clergy nowadays is an elusive and oblique one, a kind of postmodernist deity who disdains the flash-and-dazzle that he displayed in the Book of Exodus or the pomp-and-circumstance that surrounds him in the Book of Daniel. The existentialist version of God appears in the First Book of Kings, where the biblical author describes how the Almighty agrees to manifest himself for the prophet Elijah on a rocky mountaintop in ancient Israel.

> And, behold, the Lord passed by, and a great and strong wind rent the mountains, and broke in pieces the rocks before the Lord; but the Lord was not in the wind. And after the wind an earthquake; but the Lord was not in the earthquake. And after the earthquake a fire; but the Lord was not in the fire. And after the fire a still small voice (1 Kings 19:11–14).

Today, we are struggling to hear that still small voice amid the cacophony that attends the birth of a new millennium. A great many voices are shouting out *their* versions of what God wants us to believe, to know, to do. But the whole point of the Bible is that God cannot be understood as *one* manifestation to the exclusion of all others. God is capable of acting in ways that we find baffling, troubling, even outrageous. If the first principle of the Bible-based religions is Imago Dei—

the human aspiration to make ourselves over in the image of God—then we must be prepared to tolerate a range of human behavior that goes beyond the bland certainties that are taught in the typical sermon or Sunday school class. God and humanity are simply not that simple.

"God is no saint, strange to say," writes Jack Miles in *God: A Biography*. "Much that the Bible says about him is rarely preached from the pulpit because, examined too closely, it becomes a scandal."[2]

WHAT DOES GOD WANT?

The Bible encompasses so many contradictory laws, rituals, and commandments that we are forced to pick and choose the moral instruction that we find most compelling. Of course, there are plenty of people who are willing to make the choice for us, and that is one of the reasons why the Bible is such an unfamiliar book to so many people—many of us rely on teachers and preachers to tell us what matters in the Bible and what can be disregarded.

Over the centuries, and never more so than today, we have tended to be drawn to the kinder and gentler moral imperatives that can be found in the Bible. "And what doth the Lord require of thee?" writes the prophet Micah, whose message is especially compelling because it is so compassionate—and so simple. "Only to do justly, and to love mercy, and to walk humbly with thy God" (Mic. 6:8).

But a simple credo does not go far enough; wars have been fought (and are still being fought), men and women have been tortured (and are still being tortured), and lives have been lost (and are still being lost) over the question of what is just and what is merciful. The history of the Bible-based religions is also the history of book-banning and book-burning, inquisition and excommunication, holy war and holy crusade, martyrdom and mass murder, the rack and the auto-da-fé, martyrdom and murder. "[R]eligious intolerance," as Freud observed, "was inevitably born with the belief in one God."[3] The real challenge of the Bible, then, is to reach some common understanding of how an article of faith translates into a concrete act of human conduct—and that is why we hunger for words of moral instruction from the Almighty to fill

Sartre's god-shaped hole in our soul, words that can be understood and acted on, not in heaven but here and now.

Much attention has always been paid to the externals of religious practice, but the Bible depicts God as having little interest in such matters. Elaborate ceremonies of worship, no matter how solemn and reverent, are meaningless in the eyes of God if they are not accompanied by mercy and justice, as we are told by the prophet Isaiah. "Your new moons and your appointed seasons, My soul hateth; they are a burden unto Me; I am weary to bear them," God warns Isaiah. "Yea, when ye make many prayers, I will not hear" (Isa. 1:14–15). In a passage from Isaiah that is read aloud in contemporary Jewish congregations on the fast day of Yom Kippur, the Day of Atonement, the holiest day in the Jewish calendar, the prophet tells us what God really wants of us in simple, straightforward, and specific terms:

> It is to share your bread with the hungry,
> And to take the wretched poor into your home;
> When you see the naked, clothe him,
> And not to ignore your own kin (Isa. 58:7).[4]

Perhaps even more crucial in our afflicted and benighted world is a fundamental biblical teaching that suggests the Bible itself should not be used as a weapon to punish someone whose beliefs or skin color or nationality are different from our own. If the biblical authors were capable of tolerating such a wide range of human conduct, so many different conceptions of God, so should we. Spoken in the still small voice of a compassionate God, the teaching is often hard to hear in our noisy world. But the civilizing moral instruction that we find in the Book of Exodus ought to be taken to heart no less urgently in London or Los Angeles than in Belfast or Sarajevo or Jerusalem.

"And a stranger shalt thou not wrong, neither shalt thou oppress him; for ye were strangers in the land of Egypt," the Almighty reminds us in the Book of Exodus. "[F]or if they cry at all unto Me, I will surely hear their cry" (Exod. 22:20–22).

In fact, God requires us to do something more than respect and protect the stranger. As we have now seen, the Bible often regards the stranger (*ger*) as an object of fear and loathing. At certain ugly moments, a genocidal rage toward the stranger breaks forth. And yet, remarkably enough, the Bible also commands us to *love* the stranger, a fact that has been as thoroughly suppressed as any of the stories in this book over the last couple of millennia.

Only three times in the Torah we are *commanded* to love. "[T]hou shalt love the Lord thy God with all thy heart," goes Deuteronomy 6:5. "[T]hou shalt love thy neighbour as thyself," we are told in Leviticus 19:18. But Leviticus 19:34 elevates the love of the stranger to a sacred duty:

> "The stranger that sojourneth with you shall be as the home-born among you, and *thou shalt love him as thyself*. . . ."

The commandment to love the stranger is decidedly *not* reserved to some vague and distant messianic future—it is meant to be obeyed here and now. To be sure, the biblical authors sometimes indulged in flights of fancy and soaring mystical speculation, but most of what is told and taught in the Hebrew Bible is intended for the day-to-day lives of real people. Moses ascends to the peak of Sinai and experiences the "glory" of God in some unknowable way that defies mere words and images— but Moses comes back down the mountain bearing tablets of common stone, and the God-given laws are meant for ordinary men and women.

> "For this commandment which I command thee this day, it is not too hard for thee, neither is it far off. It is not in heaven, that thou shouldest say: 'Who shall go up for us to heaven, and bring it unto us, and make us to hear it, that we may do it?' " (Deut. 30:11–12).

Rather, Moses insists, all of us are capable of performing the commandment right here and right now: "But the word is very nigh unto thee, in thy mouth, and in thy heart, that thou mayest do it" (Deut. 30:14). To do justice to the stranger, even to love the stranger, is not too hard for us, even if five thousand years of human history and today's newspaper headlines suggest otherwise.

MIDRASH

Salman Rushdie, a modern author who has suffered a medieval ordeal as punishment for writing a book, once invoked Sartre's "god-shaped hole" in an effort to explain why he persists in his efforts. "I, too, possess the same God-shaped hole," Rushdie explains. "Unable to accept the unarguable absolutes of religion, I have tried to fill up the hole with literature."[5]

The enterprise that Rushdie describes—the effort to understand God through literature—has been undertaken not only by secular writers in the late twentieth century but also by true believers throughout the ages. The Bible was fixed in its current form at some unknowable point in distant antiquity, but the tradition of explaining and elaborating upon the Bible, which went on even while the Bible was still being written, has never stopped for a moment. *Midrash* is the Hebrew word that describes the ancient and honorable tradition of telling stories in order to reveal the inner meaning of sacred texts.

Midrash translates roughly as "exegesis" and is broadly defined as "a reflection or meditation on the Bible" in which "[t]he biblical message is adapted to suit contemporary needs."[6] Its earliest practitioners were the ancient sages whose commentaries are collected in the vast anthologies of rabbinical literature known as the Talmud and the Midrash. These learned and pious commentators often drew upon the rich accumulation of Jewish legend and lore generally known as Haggadah to illustrate the meanings that they detected in the biblical text. Storytelling, they realized, is what makes the Bible *and* biblical commentary come fully alive.

The same tradition can be found in "rewritten" Bibles like the *Biblical Antiquities* of Pseudo-Philo (see chapter eleven) or the scenes and dialogue that were boldly inserted into early Aramaic translations of the Bible known as Targums. Indeed, the First and Second Book of Chronicles, two books of the Hebrew Bible that tell a cleaned-up version of the saga of David and Solomon, are regarded by some scholars as a midrash on the First and Second Books of Samuel and the First and Second Books of Kings. So it turns out that teachers and preachers of Jewish tradition—ancient, medieval, and modern—brought their own lively imaginations to bear on Holy Writ and felt perfectly free to retell the stories of the Bible in colorful and sometimes provocative ways.

Thus the legend and lore called Haggadah became the raw material for pious musings that were intended not only to instruct and inspire but also to amuse. "The high aim of the Haggadah is religious and moral instruction and edification, but its authors are aware that to catch and hold the attention [of the reader] it must make itself interesting," explains one contemporary Bible scholar, "and it is not beneath its dignity to be entertaining." Precisely because a retold story is "only loosely connected with the Bible, and bears the teacher's or preacher's own individual stamp," the tradition is "characterized by a 'free diversity.' In other words, there is no such thing as 'orthodox' haggadah."[7]

Today, the term "midrash" has come to be applied to *any* earnest effort to understand and explain the Bible, and it is often used nowadays to describe the retelling of Bible stories in new and imaginative ways to shed light on the ancient texts. The need of human beings "to hear and tell stories," as Reynolds Price puts it, explains why we are drawn to storytellers, and the "god-shaped hole" in the human heart and soul, as Sartre puts it, explains why stories that help us understand who God is and what God wants are especially compelling.

For some readers, the Bible is a work of human authorship that may have been divinely inspired but does not amount to Holy Writ. "I myself do not believe that the Torah is any more or less the revealed Word of God," insists Harold Bloom in *The Book of J*, "than are Dante's *Commedia*, Shakespeare's *King Lear*, or Tolstoy's novels, all works of comparable literary sublimity."[8] Regardless of its authorship, however, the Bible itself has always inspired human beings to try their hands at explaining what they find in its hallowed pages. And so, if I may echo Bloom's words, I do not believe that the Talmud and the Midrash are any more or less illuminating as commentary on the Bible than are Thomas Mann's *Joseph and His Brothers*, Joseph Heller's *God Knows*, Jack Miles's *God: A Biography*, or Bloom's own *Book of J*, "all works of comparable literary sublimity."

GOD'S NOVEL

One author whose life's work can be understood as a contemporary midrash is Isaac Bashevis Singer, the master storyteller whose books and stories, all of them first written in Yiddish, were honored with a Nobel

Prize in 1978. When I was a young man who aspired to be what Singer liked to call a "scribbler," I came across an essay in which he summarized his own credo as a writer, a bit of confessional writing that discerns in God himself the humor, irony, and ingenuity of a novelist. "Yes," Singer wrote, "God is a writer, and we are both the heroes and the readers."[9]

> We know that the angels have nothing but praise. Three times
> a day they sing: Sublime! Perfect! Great! Excellent! But there
> must be some angry critics, too. They complain: Your novel,
> God, is too long, too cruel: Too little love. Too much sex. They
> advise cutting. . . . But about one quality we all agree: God's
> novel has suspense.[10]

So Singer, whose novels were often serialized in the Yiddish-language *Jewish Daily Forward* before publication in English, encourages us to regard all of life as the daily episodes in a serial that began with Genesis: "One keeps on reading it day and night," Singer concluded. "The fear of death is nothing but the fear of having to close God's book."[11]

What both Singer and the biblical authors understood is that ordinary men and women are not plaster saints. Real life includes moments of passion and pain, sin and scandal, just like the ones that we find in the forbidden and forgotten texts of the Bible. Indeed, the landscape that is described in the Bible is so alluring—and the Bible itself is so enriching and so enduring—precisely because it is peopled with men and women who are capable of both joy and sorrow, good works as well as great evil, acts of compassion and acts of cruelty.

The path across the biblical landscape is not straight and narrow, nor does it always lead to a city on a hill where all is goodness and light. Rather, as we have now seen, the Bible road wanders through some dangerous and yet tantalizing places where both skeletons and treasures are buried. Hidden away among all those psalms and proverbs, the "begats" and the "thou shalt nots," are groves of enchantment *and* killing fields—but these places are not easy to find, and few guides will point the way to them. And sometimes, as we travel toward some shimmering spiritual truth that beckons on the far horizon, we should be careful not to overlook the intriguing and instructive sights that can be seen at the side of the road.

WHO *REALLY* WROTE THE BIBLE?

THE SCROLL AND THE BOOK
THE TORAH AND THE NEW TESTAMENT
THE CLOSING OF THE CANON ✣ AUTHOR! AUTHOR!
DID A WOMAN WRITE THE BIBLE? ✣ "PLINK" ✣ WITNESSES
LET THERE BE LIGHT

For some true believers today, the Bible is the Revealed Word of God, and nothing else need be said about its authorship.

For other believers, the first five books of the Hebrew Bible were conveyed in their entirety "from the mouth of God to the hand of Moses," according to the prayerful words still recited in synagogues today. The remaining sacred books of the Bible, according to tradition, were authored by various prophets and kings: Samuel, Isaiah, Jeremiah, and Daniel, for example, are thought to be the authors of the books that bear their names; King Solomon wrote the Song of Songs; David wrote the Psalms; and so on.

A century of modern Bible scholarship suggests otherwise.

Today, the Bible is regarded by most scholars and critics as a patchwork of legend, lore, and law that was created over a thousand years or so in distant antiquity by countless unknown chroniclers and lawgivers and storytellers, collected and compiled and corrected by generation after generation of editors (or "redactors"), and canonized by the ancient rabbis only toward the end of the biblical era. Thus, even if we regard what we find in the Bible as divinely inspired, the words themselves were spoken aloud by human voices and set down in writing by human hands. What's more, the creation of the Bible as envisioned by contemporary scholarship is hardly less miraculous than the account embraced by orthodox believers of various faiths. We are invited to imagine the ancients at some distant and irretrievable moment in history: they have remembered and passed down their sacred stories from generation to generation, but only in the form of poems and songs committed to memory. Some of these stories are so old that no one remembers when or why they were first told; some are borrowed from the faith and folklore of travelers and sojourners, allies and enemies, invaders and conquerors; some are concocted by bards whose motives are not much different from those of Homer or Shakespeare, Mark Twain or Rudyard Kipling.

Over the centuries, the storytelling traditions were expanded and elaborated upon by priests and scribes whose goal was to formalize the stories and make them fit into the official faith of ancient Israel. The priests themselves promulgated law codes and prescribed elaborate rituals for high holy days and day-to-day life. At the same time, the archivists and chroniclers in service to the early monarchs began to write down official accounts of royal births and deaths, victories and defeats in wartime, international trade and treaties in peacetime. Then, in times of crisis, along came the seers and sermonizers whom we call the Prophets, and their visions and scoldings and exhortations were added to the sacred literature of ancient Israel.

Over the span of several centuries, starting around 1000 B.C.E. and ending sometime after 200 B.C.E., all of these many strands of storytelling, poetry and song, sacred law, priestly ritual, and court history were written down, gathered up, stitched together, and offered to the people of ancient Israel and their posterity in the form of the book that we know as the Bible. Today, the end product of a process that began in antiquity is *still* regarded by three religions as Holy Writ, and with no less fervor than at any earlier time in the Bible's long history.

THE SCROLL AND THE BOOK

"Bible" is derived from the Greek word *biblion* which means "book" or "papyrus," the plant from which paper was first made. In fact, the Greek word derives from the name of a Phoenician city in the ancient Near East, Byblos, where a papermaking industry first appeared. Strictly speaking, "bible" is more accurately defined as "little books" because the Bible actually consists of a great many separate writings, some quite short and none very long, that have come to be regarded as a single sacred text by all three Bible-based religions: Judaism, Christianity, and Islam.

In antiquity, however, the Hebrew Bible was not a book at all. Rather, the various writings were copied out on sheets of parchment by a scribe using a quill pen and handmade ink, and the sheets were sewn together and rolled up into scrolls. Only during the Christian era did the book (or "codex") replace the scroll as the common way to preserve and pass along writings of all kinds, including sacred writings. Because a book was easier than a scroll to carry, store, and use, the advent of books represented a technological revolution in the ancient world—and the early Christians were among the first to make use of the new technology in making their sacred texts widely available.

By the Middle Ages, both Christians and Jews favored the book for day-to-day use of their sacred writings, and the very first book to be printed with movable type in the the late fifteenth century was the Gutenberg Bible. Even today, however, Jewish congregations in synagogues around the world still read the first five books of the Bible—the Torah—from a scroll that has been copied out by hand on parchment in precisely the same way that it was done by the scribes of ancient Israel two or three thousand years ago.

THE TORAH AND THE NEW TESTAMENT

The Hebrew Bible is known in Jewish usage as the *Tanakh*, an acronym made up of the Hebrew names for its three major sections: *Torah* (also called the Five Books of Moses), *Nevi'im* (the Prophets), and *Kethuvim* (the Writings).

The first five books of the Hebrew Bible are known to most readers in the modern world by titles that are derived from the early Greek and Latin translations of the Bible: Genesis, Exodus, Leviticus, Numbers, and Deuteronomy. According to Jewish tradition, the same five books are titled with words that appear in the Hebrew text itself; thus, for example, Genesis is known in Jewish usage as *Bereshith*, the Hebrew word that means "In the beginning" and appears as the very first word in the Bible. These five books are collectively known as the Torah, a Hebrew word that means "teaching," or the *Chumash*, a Hebrew word derived from the number five. In Christian and scholarly usage, the same five books are also called the Pentateuch, a Greek word that means "five scrolls," or the Five Books of Moses, because of the tradition that attributes authorship to Moses by way of dictation from the Almighty on Mount Sinai.

According to Christian and secular usage, the Hebrew Bible is known as the Old Testament and the sacred writings of Christianity are called the New Testament, which is intended to distinguish between the original covenant between God and the Patriarchs of ancient Israel and the new covenant offered by Jesus of Nazareth. When Christian readers and scholars refer to "the Bible," they generally mean *both* the Old Testament and the New Testament. However, the phrase "Old Testament" is not used in Jewish circles because of its theological implications, which is why I have used the phrase "Hebrew Bible" rather than "Old Testament" in this book.

The next twenty-one books of the Hebrew Bible are collected under the general heading of the Prophets, or *Nevi'im*. These include the Former Prophets (Joshua, Judges, First and Second Samuel, and First and Second Kings), the Latter Prophets (Isaiah, Jeremiah, and Ezekiel), and the Twelve Minor Prophets (Hosea, Joel, Amos, Obadiah, Jonah, Micah, Nahum, Habakkuk, Zephaniah, Haggai, Zechariah, and Malachi).

The remaining thirteen books of the Hebrew Bible are collected under the heading of the Writings, or *Kethuvim*: Psalms, Proverbs, Job, the Song of Songs, Ruth, Lamentations, Ecclesiastes, Esther, Daniel, Ezra, Nehemiah, and First and Second Chronicles.

Christian Bibles generally present the books of the Hebrew Bible in a different order than the one used in Jewish Bibles. For example, the Book of Ruth comes immediately after Judges in most Christian Bibles, while Ruth appears in the Hebrew Bible in the section called the Writings along with the Book of Esther, the Song of Songs, and other works.

The ordering of the Bible in Christian practice follows an early Greek translation of the Bible called the Septuagint, which differs from the Hebrew Bible in the selection and order of sacred books. (See below.)

The Bibles used by the Roman Catholic, Orthodox, and many Protestant churches also include several ancient writings that are *not* recognized in Jewish tradition as part of Holy Writ, including such books of the late biblical era as Tobit, Judith, Sirach, Baruch, the Wisdom of Solomon, and several others. These books are generally known as the Apocrypha in Protestant usage and the Deuterocanon in Catholic usage, but none of them are included in the Hebrew Bible.

THE CLOSING OF THE CANON

"Canon" comes from the Greek word for a measuring stick, and the word is applied in Bible studies to describe the collection of biblical writings that have come to be regarded as sacred. At some point in ancient history, the Hebrew Bible was finalized (or "canonized") in its current form—some books had been regarded as sacred for centuries, some were added to the canon at a relatively late date, and some were excluded altogether by the rabbis who acted as guardians of the Bible. Indeed, the rabbinical literature preserves some of the heated debates over specific books and their worthiness for inclusion in the Bible, and the Song of Songs, a collection of erotic love poetry that somehow found its way into the Bible, inspired a notably hot controversy among the ancient sages.

According to one popular tradition, the Hebrew Bible was canonized at a rabbinical assembly held in the coastal town of Jabneh in Palestine in 90 C.E., but modern scholarship suggests that the process of canonization actually took many centuries. The Five Books of Moses were probably recognized as Holy Writ no later than 400 B.C.E., and the Prophets were generally accepted around 200 B.C.E. By the time of the Jabneh assembly, the problem faced by the rabbis was to pick and choose among a vast assortment of more recent writings on sacred themes, including a proliferation of commentaries on the earlier holy books, a number of so-called apocalyptic writings that predicted the end of the world, and the new Christian teachings. Thus, the final act of rabbinical authority at Jabneh was to close the *Jewish* biblical canon once and for all. The Christian canon, of course, remained open to receive the sacred writings that we know as the New Testament.

AUTHOR! AUTHOR!

Soon after the Hebrew Bible was canonized, some attentive readers began to notice certain oddities and curiosities in the biblical text. The very first can be found "in the beginning" of the Bible, where as we saw in chapter sixteen, we are given two quite different versions of the creation of the first man and woman in the Book of Genesis (Gen. 1:27, 2:7, 22). Only a few verses later in Genesis, we find two different versions of the familiar story of Noah and the Ark. In one version, Noah is commanded by the Almighty to bring *two* of every living thing aboard the ark, male and female of each species (Gen. 6:19). Then Noah abruptly receives a second set of divine instructions: God orders him to bring *seven* pairs of every "clean" animal but only one pair of the "unclean" animals (Gen. 7:2). We are told first that the flood lasts 40 days (Gen. 7:17) and later that it lasts 150 days (Gen. 7:24). On two different occasions, Noah sends out a bird to search for dry land, first a raven and then a dove (Gen. 8:7, 8).

Such repetitions of the same story in two different (and sometimes inconsistent) versions, which scholars call a "doublet," are found throughout the Bible. Indeed, we have already encountered one of the rare "triplets" in the Bible: the story of a patriarch who tries to pass off his wife as his sister is told three times, twice about Abraham and Sarah and once about Isaac and Rachel. (See chapter three.) But these unexplained repetitions were not the only puzzles in the Biblical text. We notice, for example, that God is sometimes called Yahweh and sometimes Elohim. We are told that Moses wrote the first five books of the Bible—but the last of these books, Deuteronomy, actually describes the death of its own author! Such flaws and contradictions turned out to be the crucial first clues in the search for an answer to the question of who really wrote the Bible.

Efforts were made to explain away these awkwardnesses by pious scholars of late antiquity and the Middle Ages, both Jewish and Christian. But as the centuries passed and Bible readers grew more demanding, the tortured explanations of the early apologists no longer sufficed. Thomas Hobbes and Spinoza, among many others, insisted on pointing out the obvious if slightly heretical conclusions to be drawn from such evidence. "It is . . . clearer than the sun at noon that the Pentateuch was not written by Moses," Spinoza declared, "but by someone who lived long after Moses."[1]

The pioneering Bible scholars of the nineteenth century, including such commanding figures as Karl Heinrich Graf and Julius Wellhausen, proposed a way to explain the apparent inconsistencies that have come to be accepted as a first principle of Bible scholarship. The Bible, they suggested, was drawn from many sources, written down by many hands, and revised over the centuries by many redactors, each with a different theological agenda, a specific historical frame of reference and political subtext, and a distinctive literary style. What we regard as the Holy Scripture is a patchwork quilt fashioned by human hands, and we can learn to recognize the styles and motifs used by the various contributors to the finished work.

Of course, we cannot know with certainty the identities of the biblical authors—their names, places of residence, dates of birth and death. We cannot really know whether the men and women who authored and edited the Bible were individuals working alone or members of a "school" or "tradition." Indeed, biblical scholarship has detected layer upon layer of additions and deletions, revisions and redactions, and so it is likely that the biblical text was worked and reworked by countless hands over the centuries. Still, the various threads of authorship are usually identified in scholarly writing as if they *were* the work of specific individuals.

"J," or "the Yahwist"

The oldest strand of biblical narrative is attributed to an author who calls God by his personal name, Yahweh, which appears in the Hebrew Bible as the four Hebrew letters corresponding to YHWH. Since the scholars who pioneered the study of biblical authorship in the nineteenth century were German, the German rendering of God's personal name (Jahveh) is used to identify the biblical author who calls God by that name—the author is called J, or the Yahwist. Scholars believe that he (or she) worked in the southern kingdom of Judah sometime after the reign of King David, perhaps in the tenth or ninth century B.C.E. Some of the richest and most intriguing material in the Bible is attributed to J, including many of the stories collected and retold in this book.

"E," or "the Elohist"

A parallel strand of biblical narrative is attributed to a different author who is known as E, or the Elohist, because he tends to refer to God by the Hebrew term *Elohim*. E, who displays a marked reverence for Moses and the line of priests descended from Moses, may have been a Levite priest from the northern kingdom of Israel who was working at a slightly later period in history than J, perhaps 900 or 800 B.C.E. It is the Elohist, for example, who shows us Aaron—the brother of Moses but also his rival—as he fashions a golden calf and disputes the primacy of Moses as God's chosen prophet, all with disastrous results for himself and the Israelites who follow his example.

"D," or "the Deuteronomist"

The Book of Deuteronomy, which stands apart from the rest of the Torah in its distinct literary style and theological concerns, is attributed to an author (or a group of authors) known as D, or the Deuteronomist. According to Richard Elliott Friedman's superb study of biblical authorship, *Who Wrote the Bible?*, the prophet Jeremiah may have been the Deuteronomist. The Book of Deuteronomy is thought to be "the book of the Law" that was rather mysteriously found in the Temple at Jerusalem during the reign of King Josiah in the seventh century B.C.E. (2 Kings 22:8). For that reason, some scholars have suggested that Deuteronomy is a "pious fraud" that was concocted to justify the reforms of Josiah, which marked a sea change in the nature of religious dogma and practice in ancient Israel. For example, the announcement of the death of Moses, which now appears at the very end of Deuteronomy, may have been borrowed from the Book of Numbers by D in order to enhance the credibility of a book that differs significantly from the other four books of the Torah.

The Book of Deuteronomy is also regarded by scholars as the keystone of a longer biblical narrative known as the Deuteronomistic

History, which includes not only Deuteronomy itself but also the books of Joshua, Judges, First and Second Samuel, and First and Second Kings. The authors and editors who created the Deuteronomistic History, collectively known as the Deuteronomistic Historian, are thought to have collected, combined, and edited the various stories, traditions, and histories sometime shortly before or during the Babylonian Exile.

"P," or "the Priestly Source"

The biblical authors whose work focuses largely on sacred law and ritual matters are collectively known as P, or the Priestly Source. All but a few passages of the Book of Leviticus are attributed to the Priestly Source, and it is likely that P was also responsible for combining the narratives of J and E into the biblical text so familiar to us today. The Priestly Source is notably lacking in playfulness—it is P's version of the story of Creation that features an aloof and indistinct God who summons man into existence (Gen. 1:27), while J imagines God as a kind of divine sculptor who hunkers down in the mud and makes the first man with his own hands (Gen. 2:7). P devotes much attention to the minutiae of ritual observances and paraphernalia, but we find no talking animals, no dreams, and not a single angel in the biblical text attributed to the Priestly Source—and, significantly, P never once uses the Hebrew word for "mercy."

"R," or "the Redactor"

At a relatively late stage of biblical authorship, various priests and scribes collected these many strands and fragments of biblical authorship, assembled them into a series of continuous narratives, and added their own glosses, interludes, and linkages. The gifted editors who stitched together the Bible are collectively known as R, or the Redactor, although it is likely that R, like P and D, represents the work of a school or a tradition rather than a single author or editor. The Redactor seems to put a "spin" on the older passages in service of a specific theological and political agenda. For example, the stern and sometimes brutal attitude toward intermarriage and idol worship that can be found at places in the biblical text may reflect the anxieties of the priestly redactors who were struggling against the threat of assimilation in the unsettled period after the end of the Babylonian Exile and the return of the Israelites to Canaan.

Other Biblical Authors

Bible scholarship has suggested the existence of other authors whose work can be detected in the Hebrew Bible. Portions of the Second Book of Samuel and the First Book of Kings, for example, are traced to a source variously known as the Succession Narrative or the Court History of David, and the author is sometimes called the Court Historian because he may have been an official chronicler of the royal House of David and demonstrates a lively interest in promoting the legitimacy of the Davidic dynasty.

Another example is the Book of Isaiah, where the bulk of the text is traditionally regarded as the work of the prophet Isaiah, who appears to have lived in Jerusalem in the eighth century B.C.E., but chapters 40–66 are attributed by scholars to a different (and much later) author who is identified as Deutero-Isaiah ("second Isaiah") and probably lived and wrote during the era of the Babylonian Exile.

Now and then, as we have seen, new and surprising candidates are nominated by enterprising scholars for authorship of important portions of the Bible. Sigmund Freud, drawing on the scholarship of his era, reported in *Moses and Monotheism* that "modern research workers think they can recognize the priest Ebjatar, a contemporary of King David," as the Yahwist.[2] And Bible scholar Adrien Janis Bledstein proposes that the Deuteronomist may have been an otherwise obscure prophetess named Huldah who lived during the reign of King Josiah. (See chapter thirteen.)

Lost Books of the Bible

The Bible itself refers to several intriguing works that are now lost to us, including the Book of Yashar, the Book of the Battles of Yahweh, and the Chronicles of the Kings of Judea. We can only speculate on what these books contained and why they were not preserved along with the books of the Bible and various noncanonical writings that survive as the

Apocrypha, but it is clear that the biblical authors knew and used these other sources.

DID A WOMAN WRITE THE BIBLE?

The sacred texts of the Bible were probably under the guardianship of the priesthood of ancient Israel, a caste that was exclusively male. For that reason, Bible scholars have generally assumed that the Bible is a work of male authors and male editors. The Bible itself, however, offers some clues that suggest at least some of the biblical text—including the most intriguing and influential passages—were written by women.

For example, what may be the single oldest fragment in the Bible, the Song of Deborah (Judg. 5), is conventionally attributed to the prophetess Deborah, and in fact the striking role attributed to a woman in the victory of the Israelites over their enemies suggests that it is the work of a woman writer. (See chapter thirteen.) On a vastly greater scale, however, the thread of biblical narrative attributed to J—which makes up a substantial portion of Genesis and can be found elsewhere in the Bible—may be the work of a woman, too.

The biblical author known as J writes a great deal *about* women, who are almost invariably depicted in a sympathetic, insightful way, and often in a playful light. Indeed, the matriarchs are often more dynamic than their husbands, who seem rather pallid by comparison. J displays an intimate and comfortable knowledge of "the manner of women," as the Bible refers to menstruation, and gives us the account of how Rachel's father searches her tent for his missing household idols—she has hidden them in the camel-saddle on which she is sitting during the search, and she dissuades her father from looking under the saddle by claiming that she is menstruating (Gen. 31:30–35). And in the story of Tamar and Judah, a courageous and resourceful woman defies the will of a patriarch in order to claim what is due to her under biblical law. (See chapter seven.) Both of these texts are cited as evidence that J may have been a woman.

The argument is persuasively made in *The Book of J* by Harold Bloom and David Rosenberg. Bloom discerns a woman's sensibilities at work in the biblical narrative attributed to J, whom he characterizes as the original Jewish mother. "J's attitude toward Yahweh," he writes, "resembles nothing so much as a mother's somewhat wary but still proudly amused stance toward a favorite son."[3] Ironically, Bloom's conclusions have been criticized by some feminist commentators as being sexist, and yet Bloom makes a provocative and intriguing case for the notion that "J is a *Gevurah* ('great lady') of post-Solomonic court circles, herself of Davidic blood, who began writing her great work in the later years of Solomon, in close rapport and exchanging influences with her good friend the Court Historian, who wrote most of what we now call 2 Samuel."[4]

"PLINK"

Although the oldest fragments of the Bible were first composed in the form of songs and poems as early as the second millenium B.C.E., the oldest *written* copies of the Bible are much more recent. Indeed, until the mid-twentieth century, the oldest complete copy of the Hebrew Bible dated back to the ninth and tenth centuries of the modern era, and the oldest copy of a complete Christian Bible was only a few hundred years older. Then, with the discovery of the so-called Dead Sea Scrolls at a place called Qumran near the Dead Sea in 1947, Bible scholars suddenly found themselves in possession of biblical manuscripts that date all the way back to the second century B.C.E. or so.

According to a beloved story that has attached itself to the Dead Sea Scrolls, a young Bedouin shepherd was idly casting pebbles into a desert cave when he heard a "plink" and the sound of breaking pottery. Inside the cave—and, as it turned out, several other caves nearby—was a cache of ancient ceramic jars containing the remains of the sacred library of a Jewish sect known as the Essenes. These writings are the Dead Sea Scrolls.

Only one complete book of the Bible, the Book of Isaiah, was found intact at Qumran. However, fragments of *every* book of the Hebrew Bible except the Book of Esther were also found among the Dead Sea Scrolls. Significantly, the Dead Sea Scrolls demonstrate how *little* the text of the Bible has changed over the last two thousand years or so. Although some words and phrases of the manuscript fragments found among the Dead Sea Scrolls vary from the text of the Bible as we know it today, the differences are small in number and modest in significance. In fact, the text of the Book of Isaiah as preserved in the Dead Sea Scrolls is substantially identical to what we find in modern Bibles.

WITNESSES

One of the most intriguing pieces of evidence suggesting multiple sources of the Bible is the simple fact that there are so many versions— or "witnesses," as Bible critics put it—of the ancient biblical text. Although some scholars imagine that all of the many versions of the Bible derive from a single original text—a so-called Ur-text—no such work has actually been found. Rather, it seems more likely that a great many versions of the sacred texts proliferated in the ancient world and found different expressions among the various peoples and cultures who preserved them and passed them along from generation to generation. Whatever the reason, the fact remains that more than one version of the Bible has survived over the centuries. The texts discussed below remain in common use around the world.

The Masoretic Text

Jewish tradition regards the so-called Masoretic Text as the most authoritative version of the Hebrew Bible. "Masorete" is derived from an Aramaic word that means "tradition," and the Masoretes were rabbinical scholars and scribes who dedicated themselves to preserving the integrity of the biblical text by adopting a single standard version to be used in making copies of the Bible. Starting sometime around 500 C.E., and continuing for a period of five centuries or so, the Masoretes corrected what they regarded as scribal errors, standardized the words and phrases of the text itself, indicated the correct pronunciation of the biblical Hebrew, and thus established the definitive version of the Bible for Jewish usage.

The Masoretes adopted a system of symbols to indicate the vowelization of the Hebrew words in the Bible, since the Hebrew language is written in consonants only, and they also introduced the practice of dividing the biblical text into verses; both of these innovations have become indispensable for Bible readers and scholars. (The division of the text into chapters, however, was introduced in the thirteenth century by an English bishop who finally made it possible to quote the Bible by "chapter and verse" for the first time in its long history.)

The Bible that I have used in this book, except where otherwise indicated, is an early twentieth-century English translation of the Masoretic Text. From time to time, I have cited other versions of the Bible, generally for the purpose of pointing out the differences—sometimes slight but often significant in meaning—between the Masoretic Text and the other "witnesses" of the biblical text described below.

The Septuagint

The Bible was originally written in classical Hebrew, although a few passages are rendered in an ancient sister-language called Aramaic. But the early and repeated dispersions of the Jewish people from the Holy Land resulted in the growth of large expatriate communities where Greek and other tongues were spoken in place of Hebrew as the language of daily life. For that reason, translations of the Hebrew text became crucial to the preservation of the Bible, both in Jewish and in Christian usage.

The most important and influential translation of the Hebrew Bible is a Greek version called the Septuagint. The name is derived from a Latin word that means "seventy," and it refers to the tradition that seventy rabbinical scholars participated in the making of the translation. For that reason, the Septuagint is often identified in scholarly writing as LXX. A story is told that all of the rabbis worked separately but miraculously arrived at precisely the same translation!

The earliest portions of the Septuagint date back to the third century B.C.E., when the translation was first undertaken for use by the growing Jewish expatriate community in Alexandria and elsewhere in the Greek-speaking world. However, the Septuagint was also favored by early Christians, who adopted Greek as the language of their sacred writings, and thus most of the quotations from the Hebrew Bible that appear in the New Testament are taken from the Septuagint rather than the underlying Hebrew text. For that reason, too, the Septuagint was used as the basis for several Christian translations of the Bible into Latin and other languages. Since the Septuagint adopted a different order of books than the one used in the Masoretic Text, and included several of the apocryphal books, these elements found their way into Christian Bibles.

The Septuagint also gives us some of the familiar divisions of the biblical text into two paired books. The Book of Samuel, for example, can be accommodated on a single scroll when rendered in Hebrew, which contains only consonants and takes up much less space on a sheet of paper or parchment than the same text in a language that includes both vowels and consonants. The Septuagint, by contrast, required *two* scrolls to accommodate the Greek translation of the Book of Samuel, and so the translators divided the text into what we know today as the First and Second Books of Samuel. The same technique is preserved in other biblical works that are conventionally divided into first and second volumes in modern Bibles.[5]

The Targums and Other Ancient Translations

Late in the biblical era, Aramaic replaced Hebrew as the day-to-day language of the Holy Land, and so the original Hebrew text was translated into Aramaic. Several Aramaic translations, each one known as a Targum, have survived from antiquity, and they reveal that the early translators felt at liberty to embroider upon and explain the biblical text, sometimes to avoid embarrassing or difficult-to-explain passages and sometimes to highlight a particular moral or theological point of view. Some scholars regard the Targums as a kind of "rewritten Bible" rather than a faithful rendering of the original Hebrew text. Still, the sense of freedom that the Aramaic translators brought to their work seems to suggest that the Bible was *not* regarded as so sacrosanct that it could not be imaginatively rewritten and reinterpreted.

The Bible was also translated into other languages of the ancient Near East, and some of these translations are still regarded as authoritative by various churches in our own times. The Samaritans, a people who split off from the Israelites in antiquity, have preserved their own version of the Pentateuch, including an original Hebrew text and various translations into Aramaic, Arabic, and Greek. An ancient translation of the Bible into the Syriac language, a form of Aramaic, is still used by the Syrian Orthodox and Maronite churches, and an early translation of the Bible into the Coptic language is still used by the Coptic Orthodox Church. These and other early translations of the

Bible illustrate that the biblical text has been preserved in a great many different forms—one scholar, for example, counted some six thousand textual differences between the Masoretic Text and the Pentateuch used by the Samaritans.

The Vulgate

The first translation of the Bible into Latin was the Vulgate, which was completed by St. Jerome at the direction of the Bishop of Rome at the beginning of the fifth century C.E. The Latin text of the Vulgate was relied upon by some of the earliest translators of the Bible into European languages, including English. Only after the revival of ancient languages and the retrieval of ancient writings during the Renaissance did Western European scholars go back to the original texts of the Bible in Hebrew and Greek to create their translations.

The King James Version

The familiar words and phrases that strike most readers as "biblical" are found in the so-called King James Version, a Shakespearean-era English translation of the Bible by fifty or so Anglican clerics who completed their work at the behest of King James I in 1611. The so-called KJV has been revised extensively over the centuries—and has been replaced in many churches by contemporary translations—but the ringing phrases of the original text can still be found in many English-language Bibles, including the 1917 Jewish Publication Society translation of the Masoretic Text that I have used as my "proof text" in this book.

Although the King James Version is a fundamental work of Western literature, it has come to be regarded as passé and politically incorrect in many circles nowadays. Some modern translators are much more forthcoming about the "forbidden" elements of the Bible than the KJV—the superb Anchor Bible, for example, offers fresh and lucid translations of both the Hebrew and the Christian books of the Bible and explains the real meanings of the biblical text in line-by-line annotations. Still, the newer Bible translations that have replaced the stately old KJV have not matched its grandeur and resonance of language. The new translations are more accurate in their scholarship, more forthcoming in their exploration of history, linguistics, and theology, but something has been sacrificed in the process.

Here is a comparison of Genesis 1:1–3 as it appears in a 1909 edition of the King James Version and two more recent renderings of the Hebrew text.

King James Version (1909)	*New English Bible (1970)*	*New JPS Translation (1985)*
In the beginning, God created the heaven and the earth. And the earth was without form, and void; and darkness was upon the face of the deep, and the Spirit of God moved upon the face of the waters. And God said, Let there be light; and there was light.[6]	In the beginning of creation, when God made heaven and earth, the earth was without form and void, with darkness over the face of the earth, and a mighty wind that swept over the surface of the waters. God said, "Let there be light," and there was light; and God saw that the light was good, and he separated light from darkness.[7]	When God began to create heaven and earth—the earth being unformed and void, with darkness over the surfaces of the deep and a wind from God sweeping over the water—God said, "Let there be light"; and there was light.[8]

Since the debate over the proper approach to biblical translation is an old, contentious, and highly technical one, I will not belabor it here except to invite the reader to ponder which of the readings of Genesis he or she finds more resonant and meaningful.

LET THERE BE LIGHT

A terrible price was paid by the courageous observers who first proposed that the Bible was written by human beings. Spinoza was excommunicated by the Jewish community; the daring work of an early Bible scholar named Andreas Van Maes was banned by the Catholic Church; and the writings of a French Calvinist named Isaac de la Peyrere were burned. Even today, some true believers refuse to entertain the notion that men and women—merely mortal if also divinely inspired—put down the words on parchment and paper that so many seekers of truth all over the world regard as sacred.

What I have tried to suggest in this book is that some of the richest and most meaningful passages of the Bible—and some of the most instructive moral examples—can be found in stories that have been censored or suppressed precisely because they tell stories that are so deeply human. In a sense, then, the established religious authorities of all ages and all faiths have been far more comfortable with the notion that the Bible consists *only* of pristine moral pronouncements from on high and *not* the revelations of real men and women struggling with the messier challenges of life on earth.

Thankfully, however, it is no longer considered heresy to contemplate and explore the human authorship of the Bible—and, I suggest, the experience of reading the Bible is all the richer and more accessible if we do. "The sacred writer," as the Catholic Church conceded more than a half century ago, may be properly (and even piously) regarded as "the living and reasonable instrument of the Holy Spirit."[9] More recently, as we have already seen, Harold Bloom has put the same thought in slightly more secular terms, when he characterizes the Torah as no more and no less "the revealed Word of God" than Dante, Shakespeare, or Tolstoy.

So, even if we disagree on the outer limits of divine inspiration when it comes to the writing of books by mortal men and women, we all seem to start at the same place: the Bible.

CHRONOLOGY

The dating of many events and works in early biblical history is the subject of much controversy among scholars, and thus all dating is approximate and, in many instances, speculative. I have adopted the designation Before the Common Era (B.C.E.) in place of the more familiar Before Christ (B.C.) to indicate events that occurred before the birth of Jesus, and the designation Common Era (C.E.) in place of Anno Domini ("In the Year of Our Lord," or A.D.).

BEFORE THE COMMON ERA (B.C.E.)

	Biblical Events	Stories in The Harlot by the Side of the Road
1800–1700	The wanderings of the Patriarchs (Abraham, Isaac, and Jacob) and the Matriarchs (Sarah,	Lot and His Daughters (Chapter Two); The Rape of Dinah (Chapter Four);Tamar and Judah (Chapter Six)

Biblical Events	*Stories in* The Harlot by the Side of the Road
	Rebekah, Rachel, and Leah) and the early sojourn of the Israelites in Canaan
1700–1600	Joseph in Egypt; the settlement and enslavement of the Israelites in Egypt
1280	Exodus of the Israelites from Egypt under Moses	*Zipporah and Moses* (Chapter Eight)
1240–1200	Conquest of the Land of Canaan by the Israelites	*Jephthah and His Daughter* (Chapter Ten); *The Traveler and His Concubine* (Chapter Twelve)
1020–1000	Reign of King Saul	
1000–960	Reign of King David	*Tamar and Amnon* (Chapter Fourteen)

Biblical Events	*Authorship of the Bible*
960–920	Reign of King Solomon	Court Historian at work
922	Division of the United Monarchy of David and Solomon into Northern Kingdom (Israel) and Southern Kingdom (Judah)	
900		Yahwist (J) at work
800		Elohist (E) at work
722	Conquest of the Northern Kingdom of Israel by the Assyrians and Destruction of the "Lost Ten Tribes"	

	Biblical Events	Authorship of the Bible
700–600		Deuteronomist (D) at work
622		Discovery of the Book of Deuteronomy
587–586	Destruction of the Temple at Jerusalem, Fall of the Southern Kingdom of Judah, and Commencement of the Babylonian Exile	
500		Priestly Source (P) at work
538	End of the Babylonian Exile and Return of the Israelites to Jerusalem	
520–515	Construction of the Second Temple at Jerusalem	
400		Redactor (R) at work
250–100		Translation of the Hebrew Bible into Greek (Septuagint)
100		Earliest surviving Hebrew texts of the Bible at Qumran (Dead Sea Scrolls) (Discovered in 1947)

COMMON ERA (C.E.)

70	Destruction of the Second Temple at Jerusalem	
90		Final canonization of the Hebrew Bible

Biblical Events	*Authorship of the Bible*
405	First translation of the Christian Bible from Greek into Latin (St. Jerome's Vulgate)
500–1000	Standardization of Hebrew text by the Masoretes (Masoretic Text)
1526	First translation of the Bible into English (William Tyndale's Pentateuch)
1611	King James (Authorized) Version of the Bible

ENDNOTES

CHAPTER ONE

1. Susan Niditch, "The Wronged Woman Righted," *Harvard Theological Review* 72, nos. 1–2 (January–April 1979): 149.

2. Marvin H. Pope, "Euphemism and Dysphemism in the Bible," in *The Anchor Bible Dictionary*, 6 vols., ed. David Noel Freedman (Garden City, N.Y.: Doubleday, 1992), vol. 1, 725.

3. Pope, *ABD*, vol. 1, 725.

4. G. Vermes, "Baptism and Jewish Exegesis," *New Testament Studies* 4 (1957–1958) (Cambridge, England: Cambridge University Press, 1958): 314.

5. Ralph Klein, "Chronicles, Book of, 1–2," in *ABD*, vol. 1, 997.

6. Robert Gordis, *The Biblical Text in the Making* (Philadelphia: Dropsie College for Hebrew and Cognate Learning, 1937), 30.

7. Pope, *ABD*, vol. 1, 721.

8. Pope, *ABD*, vol. 1, 722.

9. Leonard J. Greenspoon, "Rahab (Person)," in *ABD*, vol. 5, 611.

10. Murray L. Newman, "Rahab and the Conquest," in *Understanding the Word*, ed. James T. Butler, Edgar W. Conrad, and Ben C. Ollenburger (Sheffield, England: JSOT Press, 1985), 180, fn. 34, citing John L. McKenzie, *The World of the Judges* (Englewood Cliffs, N.J.: Prentice-Hall, 1966), 48.

11. Jack Miles, *God: A Biography* (New York: Alfred A. Knopf, 1995), 125. "The word *kabod* can have a spiritual meaning—its usual translation is 'glory'—but also a visceral one: It is the standard word for 'liver.' According to the eminent linguist and Bible

scholar Marvin H. Pope, *kabod* probably alludes to male genitalia at Job 29:20, where 'glory' is still the correct translation, even though genitalia are to be understood."

12. Roland E. Murphy, "Song of Songs, Book of," in *ABD*, vol. 6, 153–54.

13. Sid Z. Leiman, "The Canonization of Hebrew Scripture," *Transactions* 47 (February 1976): 72.

14. Murphy, *ABD*, vol. 6, 153–54.

15. Julian Pitt-Rivers, *The Fate of Shechem, or The Politics of Sex* (Cambridge: Cambridge University Press, 1977), 156.

16. Pitt-Rivers, 146.

17. Pitt-Rivers, 126.

18. "Potiphar," *Joseph and the Amazing Technicolor Dreamcoat*, copyright 1969 The Really Useful Group plc (PRS). Rights in the United States administered by Colgems-EMI Music, Inc. (ASCAP).

19. Mordechai Richler, *St. Urbain's Horseman* (New York, Alfred A. Knopf, 1972), 242–43.

20. Michael Ventura, "Letters at 3 A.M.," *LA Village View* (December 24–30, 1993): 5.

21. Reynolds Price, *A Palpable God* (San Francisco: North Point Press, 1985), 3.

CHAPTER THREE

1. Larry R. Helyer, "The Separation of Abraham and Lot," *Journal for the Study of the Old Testament* 26 (June 1983): 77.

2. Louis Ginzberg, *The Legends of the Jews*, 7 vols. (Philadelphia, Jewish Publication Society, 1909–1938), vol. 5, 240, n. 171. See also T. Desmond Alexander, "Lot's Hospitality," *Journal of Biblical Literature* 104, no. 2 (June 1985): 289–91.

3. Haim Z'ew Hirschberg, "Lot," in *Encyclopaedia Judaica*, 7 vols. (Jerusalem: Keter Publishing House), vol. 11, 507.

4. Ginzberg, vol. 5, 243, n. 188.

5. "Minyan" in *EJ*, vol. 12, 67.

6. Ginzberg, vol. 1, 252.

7. George W. Coats, "Lot," in *Understanding the Word*, ed. James T. Butler, Edgar W. Conrad, and Ben C. Ollenburger (Sheffield, England: JSOT Press, 1985), 120.

8. Sharon Pace Jeansonne, "The Characterization of Lot in Genesis," *Biblical Theology Bulletin* 18, no. 4 (October 1988): 123, citing Bruce Vawter, *On Genesis: A New Reading* (Garden City, N.Y.: Doubleday, 1977), 235–36.

9. Jeansonne, 126.

10. Jeansonne, 123, citing Claus Westermann, John Skinner, and Bruce Vawter.

11. Coats, 129.

12. J. H. Hertz, ed., *The Pentateuch and Haftorahs*, 2d ed. (London: Soncino Press, 1981), 67, n. 8.

13. Raphael Patai, *The Arab Mind* (New York: Charles Scribner's Sons, 1976), 85–86.

14. Patai, 84, 133–135.

15. R. E. Clements, "The Relation of Children to the People of God in the Old Testament," *Baptist Quarterly* 11, no. 5 (January 1966): 196. See also Neh. 5:1–5, 2 Kings 4:1–7, and Exod. 21:7–8.

16. Roland de Vaux, *Ancient Israel* (New York: McGraw-Hill, 1965), vol. 1, 41.

17. Jeansonne, 124, citing John Skinner, *A Critical and Exegetical Commentary on Genesis* (Edinburgh: T. & T. Clark, 1930), 307.

18. Gerhard von Rad, *Genesis*, rev. ed. (London: S. C. M. Press, Ltd., 1972), 218.

19. L. Hicks, "Lot," in *Interpreter's Dictionary of the Bible* (New York: Abingdon Press, 1962), vol. K–L, 163.

20. Jeansonne, 127, citing Gen. 34 (see chapter four), Gen. 38 (see chapter six), Judg. 19 (see chapter twelve), and 2 Sam. 13 (see chapter fourteen).

21. C. J. H. Wright, "Family," in *The Anchor Bible Dictionary*, 6 vols., ed. David Noel Freedman (Garden City, N.Y.: Doubleday, 1992), vol. 2, 767–68. "[T]here is much in the [Old Testament] to indicate that love, joy, care and honor were to be found in the Israelite home."

22. Jeansonne, 124.

23. Coats, 123–24.

24. Warren Kliewer, "The Daughters of Lot," *ILIFF Review* 25, no. 1 (winter 1968): 27.

25. Alexander, 291.

26. Gerald A. Larue, *Sex and the Bible* (Buffalo, N.Y.: Prometheus Books, 1983), 91.

27. Larue, 91–92.

28. Edmund Leach, "Why Did Moses Have a Sister?" in *Structuralist Interpretations of Biblical Myth*, ed. Edmund Leach and D. Alan Aycock (Cambridge [England] and New York: Cambridge University Press, 1983), 59–60, fn. 35.

29. Larue, 95.

30. Larue, 93.

31. E. A. Speiser, tr., intro., and notes, *Genesis*, Anchor Bible (Garden City, N.Y: Doubleday, 1986), 91–93.

32. Von Rad, 167.

33. Julian Pitt-Rivers, *The Fate of Shechem, or The Politics of Sex* (Cambridge, England: Cambridge University Press, 1977), 151–152, citing Speiser, de Vaux, and von Rad.

34. Speiser, 92–93.

35. Speiser, 93.

36. Anson Rainey, "Concubine," in *EJ*, vol. 5, 862.

37. Ginzberg, vol. 1, 264.

38. Speiser, 155, n. 9.

39. Coats, 123.

40. Larue, 99. "Expulsion because of jealousy seems too harsh. . . . [E]xpulsion because of molestation seems more natural."

41. von Rad, 217.

42. von Rad, 217.

43. Carol A. Newsom, "Angels," in *ABD*, vol. 1, 249.

44. Speiser, 139, n. 11.

45. Bernard J. Bamberger, "Angels and Angelology," in *EJ* vol. 2, 957.

46. Karen Armstrong, *Jerusalem* (New York: Alfred A. Knopf, 1996), 27–28.

47. Joseph Blenkinsopp, "Abraham and the Righteous of Sodom," *Journal of Jewish Studies* 33, nos. 1–2 (spring-autumn 1982): 119, n. 1.

48. T. S. Eliot, *The Waste Land*, in *The Harper Anthology of Poetry*, ed. John Frederick Nims (New York: Harper & Row, 1981), 574–575.

49. Speiser, 142.

50. Hermann Gunkel, *The Legends of Genesis* (New York: Schocken Books, 1964), 34.

51. D. Alan Aycock, "The Fate of Lot's Wife" in *Structuralist Interpretations of*

Biblical Myth, ed. Edmund Leach and D. Alan Aycock (Cambridge [England] and New York: Cambridge University Press, 1983), 116.

52. Ginzberg, vol. 1, 255.

53. Aycock, 118.

54. Aycock, 115.

55. The young woman whose dance so charmed Herod that he granted her wish and gave her John the Baptist's head on a platter is not named in the New Testament (Matt. 14:6–8; Mark 6:22–25), but the ancient historian Josephus gives her name as Salome. RSV, 1189–1190, n. 14.1–12.

56. Ginzberg, vol. 5, 243, n. 188.

57. Ginzberg, vol. 5, 243, n. 188.

58. von Rad, 223.

59. Clements, 201.

CHAPTER FIVE

1. Michael Maswari Caspi, "The Story of the Rape of Dinah," *Hebrew Studies* 26, no. 1 (1985): 29, citing *Midrash Rabbah Genesis*.

2. Louis Ginzberg, *Legends of the Jews*, 7 vols. (Philadelphia: Jewish Publication Society, 1909–1938), vol. 1, 395.

3. Ita Sheres, *Dinah's Rebellion* (New York: Crossroad, 1990), 6–7.

4. Meir Sternberg, *The Poetics of Biblical Narrative* (Bloomington: Indiana University Press, 1985), 446.

5. Martin Kessler, "Genesis 34—An Interpretation," *Reformed Review* 19, no. 1 (September 1965): 4, fn. 6, citing Gerhard von Rad.

6. E. A. Speiser, tr., intro., and notes, *Genesis*, Anchor Bible (Garden City, N.Y.: Doubleday, 1986), 262.

7. Sheres, 1.

8. Sternberg, 446.

9. Danna Nolan Fewell and David M. Gunn, "Tipping the Balance," *Journal of Biblical Literature* 110, no. 2 (summer 1991): 207.

10. Fewell and Gunn, 196, n. 4.

11. Julian Pitt-Rivers, *The Fate of Shechem, or The Politics of Sex* (Cambridge, England: Cambridge University Press, 1977), 146–47.

12. Gila Ramras-Rauch, "Fathers and Daughters," in "Mappings of the Biblical Terrain," ed. Vincent L. Tollers and John Maier, *Bucknell Review* 33, no. 2, 1990, p. 161, citing the work of Samuel Sandel.

13. James Kugel, "The Story of Dinah in the *Testament of Levi*," *Harvard Theological Review* 85, no. 1 (1992): 2.

14. Fewell and Gunn, 200; Sheres, 86.

15. Sheres, 83, 85–86.

16. Caspi, 41.

17. Sheres, 86–87, 89.

18. Kugel, 16.

19. Kugel, 14, citing David Weiss Halivni, *Midrash, Mishnah, and Gemara: The Jewish Predilection for Justified Law* (Cambridge, Mass.: Harvard University Press, 1986), 30–34.

20. Victor H. Matthews, *Manners and Customs in the Bible* (Peabody, Mass.: Hendrickson Publishers, 1988), p. 14.

21. Susan Niditch, "The Wronged Woman Righted," *Harvard Theological Review* 72, nos. 1–2 (January–April 1979): 145.

22. Ramras-Rauch, 162. "[A]s a defiled woman she is doomed to a life of disgrace if she is returned home unmarried, while as the wife of the converted Shechem she would have some status."

23. Pitt-Rivers, 147–48.

24. Roland de Vaux, *Ancient Israel* (New York: McGraw-Hill, 1965), vol. 1, 26.

25. Cynthia Ozick, *Metaphor and Memory* (New York: Alfred A. Knopf, 1989), 278–79.

26. Clinton Bailey, "How Desert Culture Helps Us Understand the Bible," *Bible Review* 7, no. 4 (August 1991): 20. "All males are obliged to defend and avenge each other, just as they are all liable to suffer revenge for the misdeeds of the one. This not only gives 'strategic depth' to any isolated Bedouin, it also deters one Bedouin from attacking another, lest he cause hardship to the members of his clan."

27. Sternberg, 470.

28. Fewell and Gunn, 207, fn. 24, citing Walter Brueggemann, *Genesis: A Bible Commentary for Teaching and Preaching* (Atlanta: John Knox Press, 1982), 278.

29. Kugel, 3–5.

30. Sternberg, 472–74.

31. Haim Hillel Ben-Sasson, "Self-Defense," in *Encyclopoedia Judaica*, 17 vols. (Jerusalem: Keter Publishing House), vol. 14, 126.

32. Menachem Begin, *The Revolt*, rev. ed. (Los Angeles: Nash Publishing, 1977), xxv.

CHAPTER SEVEN

1. Susan Niditch, "The Wronged Woman Righted," *Harvard Theological Review* 72, nos. 1–2 (January–April): 148.

2. Karen Armstrong, *Jerusalem* (New York: Alfred A. Knopf, 1996), 39–40.

3. Robert Alter, "A Literary Approach to the Bible," *Commentary* 60, no. 6 (December 1975): 76.

4. Elaine Adler Goodfriend, "Prostitution (OT)," in *The Anchor Bible Dictionary*, 6 vols., ed. David Noel Freedman (Garden City, N.Y.: Doubleday, 1992), vol. 5, 505 et seq.; and Karel Van Der Toorn, "Prostitution (Cultic)," in *ABD*, vol. 5, 511 et seq.

5. Eugene J. Fisher, "Cultic Prostitution in the Ancient Near East? A Reassessment," *Biblical Theology Bulletin* 6 (June–October 1976): nos., 2–3, 226.

6. Mayer I. Gruber, "Hebrew Qedeshah and Her Canaanite and Akkadian Cognates," *Ugarit-Forschungen*, band 198 (1996): 134.

7. Fisher, 230.

8. Gruber, 134.

9. Robert Alter, *The Art of Biblical Narrative* (New York: Basic Books, 1981), p. 9. See also Nachman Avigad, "Seal, Seals," in *Encyclopaedia Judaica*, 17 vols (Jerusalem: Keter Publishing House), vol. 14, 1072–73; and Bonnie S. Magness-Gardiner, "Seals, Mesopotamian," in *ABD*, vol. 5, 1062–63.

10. J. A. Emerton, "Judah and Tamar," *Vetus Testamentum* 29, no. 4 (October 1979): 412.

11. Francis I. Anderson and David Noel Freedman, tr., notes, and comm. *Hosea*, Anchor Bible (Garden City, N.Y.: Doubleday, 1986), 225.

12. Anderson and Freedman, 224.

13. "Cosmetics," in *EJ*, vol. 5, 980.

14. Niditch, 145.

15. Niditch, 144.

16. Niditch, 144–46, fn. 8.

17. Harold Bloom and David Rosenberg, *The Book of J* (New York: Grove Weidenfeld, 1990), 222. See also George W. Coats, "Widow's Rights," *Catholic Biblical Quarterly* 34, no. 4 (October 1972): 463.

18. Deut. 25:5–10. See also Coats, 463.

19. Anderson, 36.

20. Deut. 25:5–10. See also Coats, 463.

21. Gerhard von Rad, *Genesis*, rev. ed., (London: S.C.M. Press Ltd., 1972), 356.

22. Coats, 464.

23. Calum M. Carmichael, "A Ceremonial Crux," *Journal of Biblical Literature* 96, no. 3 (September 1977): 321–36.

24. Coats, 462.

25. Julian Pitt-Rivers, *The Fate of Shechem, or The Politics of Sex* (Cambridge, England: Cambridge University Press, 1977), 169.

26. Louis Ginzberg, *The Legends of the Jews*, 7 vols. (Philadelphia: Jewish Publication Society, 1909–1938), vol. 2, 35–36, and "Tamar," in *EJ*, vol. 15, 783.

27. Thomas Mann, *Joseph the Provider* (New York: Alfred A. Knopf, 1944), 214.

28. Mann, 200.

CHAPTER NINE

1. B. P. Robinson, "Zipporah to the Rescue," *Vetus Testamentum* 36, no. 4 (October 1986): 450, fn. 9.

2. Robinson, 449.

3. Julian Morgenstern, "The 'Bloody Husband' (?) (Exod. 4:24–26) Once Again," *Hebrew Union College Annual* 34 (Union of Hebrew Congregations, 1963): 38, 43. Morgenstern suggests that Exodus 4:24–26 reflects a primitive form of marriage in the ancient Middle East in which the husband's task is simply to impregnate his wife, who remains in the household of her own family. By taking it upon herself to circumcise her son, Morgenstern argues, Zipporah is performing a task traditionally assigned to a woman's eldest brother in such marriages.

4. Trent C. Butler, "An Anti-Moses Tradition," *Journal for the Study of the Old Testament* 12 (May 1979): 9, 11.

5. Morgenstern, 52.

6. G. Vermes, "Baptism and Jewish Exegesis: New Light from Ancient Sources," *New Testament Studies* 4 (1957–1958) (Cambridge, England: Cambridge University Press, 1958), 310, 312–13.

7. Robinson, 457.

8. Louis Ginzberg, *The Legends of the Jews*, 7 vols. (Philadelphia: Jewish Publication Society, 1909–1938), vol. 2, 295. Satan also appears in place of Yahweh as the attacker in the Book of Jubilees, a biblical-era work that was excluded from the Hebrew Bible but appears in the Apocrypha. Vermes, 314–15.

9. Moshe Greenberg, *Understanding Exodus* (New York: Burman House for the Melton Research Center of the Jewish Theological Seminary, 1969), 110.

10. Greenberg, 113.

11. New JPS, 90.

12. Marvin H. Pope, in *The Anchor Bible Dictionary*, 6 vols., ed. David Noel Freedman (Garden City, N.Y.: Doubleday, 1992), vol. 1, 721.

13. Morgenstern, 45–46.

14. G. Johannes Botterweck and Helmer Ringgren, ed. *The Theological Dictionary of the Old Testament* (Grand Rapids: William B. Eeirdmans Publishing Company, 1978), 270 et. seq.

15. Greenberg, 114, fn. 1.

16. Ginzberg, vol. 2, 329.

17. Lawrence Kaplan,." 'And the Lord Sought to Kill Him' (Exod. 4:24): Yet Once Again," *Hebrew Annual Reviews* (Department of Judaic and Near Eastern Languages and Literatures, Ohio State University), (1981): 66. See also Robinson, 456, fn. 17.

18. Nahum M. Sarna, *Understanding Genesis* (New York: Schocken Books, 1970), 131.

19. Roland de Vaux, *Ancient Israel*, vol. 1 (New York: McGraw-Hill, 1965), 46–47.

20. Morgenstern, 41.

21. Vermes, 309.

22. Robinson, 448.

23. Vermes, 314–315, fn. 1.

24. J. H. Hertz., *The Pentateuch and Haftorahs*, 2d ed. (London: Soncino Press, 1981), 219, fn. 10.

25. R. E. Clements, "The Relation of Children to the People of God in the Old Testament," *Baptist Quarterly* 11, no. 5 (January 1996): 198.

26. Robinson, 459.

27. Edmund Leach, "Why Did Moses Have a Sister?" in Edmund Leach and D. Allan Aycock, *Structuralist Interpretations of Biblical Myths* (Cambridge [England] and New York: Cambridge University Press, 1983), 34–35, 47.

28. Leach, 35.

29. Ilana Pardes, *Countertraditions in the Bible* (Cambridge: Harvard University Press, 1992), 89–92.

30. Cheryl Anne Brown, *No Longer Be Silent* (Louisville, Ky.: Westminster-John Knox Press, 1992), 26, 27.

31. Leach, 39. See also Pardes, 89.

32. Pardes, 90.

33. Pardes, 91–92.

34. Pardes, 87, citing Daniel Boyarin, *Intertextuality and the Reading of Midrash* (Bloomington: Indiana University Press, 1990), 98.

35. Harold Bloom and David Rosenberg, *The Book of J* (New York: Grove Weidenfeld, 1990), 273.

36. Julian Morgenstern, "The 'Bloody Husband' (?) (Exod. 4:24–26) Once Again," *Hebrew Union College Annual* 34 (Union of Hebrew Congregations, 1963): 43–44, fn. 27, citing the work of A. J. Reinach and Hugo Gressmann.

37. The notion that Exodus 4:24–26 depicts the symbolic deflowering of Zipporah by a lusty god or demon has also been embraced by other Bible scholars, including

Eduard Meyer, Georg Beer, and Elias Auerbach. See Hans Kosmala, "The Bloody Husband," *Vetus Testamentum* 12 (January 1962): 16.

38. Morgenstern, 1963, 43, fn. 27.

39. Hans Kosmala, 16–17. See also Morgenstern, 44, fn. 27 ("[S]o far-fetched and groundless . . . , so arbitrary and utterly without proof, that it would hardly merit presentation . . . were it not put forth by a scholar of high repute") and Martin Buber, *Moses* (New York: Harper & Row, 1958), 57, where Buber cites these readings of Exodus 4:24–26 as evidence of "the devastation which the excessive enticement and allure of ethnology has effected in the history of religion."

40. Sigmund Freud, *Moses and Monotheism* (New York: Vintage Books, 1967), 39, citing Eduard Meyer.

41. Sarna, 29.

42. Sarna, 158.

43. Northrop Frye, *The Great Code* (New York: Harcourt Brace Jovanovich, 1982), 184.

44. Morgenstern, 1963, 36.

45. Sarna, 158.

46. Morgenstern, 1963, 36.

47. Hertz, 201.

48. René Girard, *Violence and the Sacred* (Baltimore: Johns Hopkins University Press, 1977), 4.

49. Sarna, 157, 159.

50. Kaplan, 67, citing J. Blau, "Hatan Damim," *Tarbiz* 26 (1956): 1–3.

51. Kaplan, 68.

52. Greenberg, 117, n. 1.

53. Kosmala, 21.

54. Buber, 58.

55. Buber, 58. (Emphasis added.)

CHAPTER ELEVEN

1. Leila Leah Bronner, "Valorized or Vilified? The Women of Judges in Midrashic Sources," in *A Feminist Companion to Judges*, ed. Athalya Brenner (Sheffield, England: Sheffield Academic Press, 1993), 73

2. J. Cheryl Exum, "The Tragic Vision and Biblical Narrative," in *Signs and Wonders*, ed. J. Cheryl Exum (Society of Biblical Literature, 1989), 64, citing Y. Zakovitch.

3. Louis Ginzberg, *The Legends of the Jews*, 7 vols. (Philadelphia: Jewish Publication Society, 1909–1938), vol. 4, 43.

4. Gila Ramras-Rauch, in "Fathers and Daughters," in "Mappings of the Biblical Terrain," ed. Vincent L. Tollers and John Maier, *Bucknell Review* 33, no. 2 (1990): 165.

5. I. Mendelsohn. "The Disinheritance of Jephthah in the Light of Paragraph 27 of the Lit-Ishtar Code," in *Israel Exploration Journal* 4, (1954): 116.

6. Mendelsohn, 116, 118–19.

7. Exum, 1989, 73.

8. Robert G. Boling, tr. and intro., *Judges*, Anchor Bible (Garden City, N.Y.: Doubleday, 1975), 208.

9. Exum, 1989, 67, fn. 4.

10. Barry G. Webb, "The Theme of the Jephthah Story," *The Reformed Theological Review* 45, no. 2 (May–August 1986): 40.

11. Daniel Landes, "A Vow of Death," in *Confronting Omnicide*, ed. Daniel Landes (Northvale, N.J.: Jason Aronson, 1991), 11.

12. Exum, 1989, 66, citing the work of Phyllis Trible.

13. Exum, 1989, 66.

14. Exum, 1989, 79.

15. Amos Oz, "Upon This Evil Earth," in *Where the Jackals Howl and Other Stories* (New York: Harcourt Brace Jovanovich, 1981), 217.

16. Cynthia Baker, "Pseudo-Philo and the Transformation of Jephthah's Daughter," in *Anti-Covenant*, ed. Mieke Bal (Sheffield, England: Almond Press, 1989), 197.

17. Ben Zion Bokser, *The Jewish Mystical Tradition* (New York: Pilgrim Press, 1981), 9–10.

18. Bokser, 50, 107.

19. Landes, 7.

20. Boling, 211.

21. Ginzberg, vol. 4, 44.

22. Anne Michele Tapp, "An Ideology of Expendability," in *Anti-Covenant*, ed. Mieke Bal, 174, fn. 10.

23. Exum, 1989, 71, fn. 6.

24. Webb, 40.

25. Joseph M. Davis, "On the Idea of Covenant," *Conservative Judaism* 41, no. 4 (summer 1989): 26–27.

26. Landes, 8.

27. Landes, 8–9.

28. Northrop Frye, *The Great Code* (New York: Harcourt Brace Jovanovich, 1982), 185.

29. *Biblical Antiquities* 39.11, cited in Cheryl Anne Brown, *No Longer Be Silent* (Louisville, Ky.: Westminster-John Knox Press, 1992), 97.

30. Ginzberg, vol. 4, 43–44.

31. Ginzberg, vol. 4, 44.

32. Ginzberg, vol. 4, 44.

33. Boling, 197.

34. J. Cheryl Exum, "On Judges II," in *A Feminist Companion to Judges*, ed. Brenner, 140.

35. Peggy L. Day, "From the Child Is Born the Woman," in *Gender and Difference in Ancient Israel*, ed. Peggy L. Day (Minneapolis, Minn.: Fortress Press, 1989), 69, fn. 14, citing the work of Gustav Bostrom.

36. Boling, 209. Boling finds the suggestion "doubtful."

37. Frye, 185.

38. Ramras-Rauch, 167.

39. David Penchansky, "Staying the Night," in *Reading between Texts*, ed. Danna Nolan Fewell (Louisville, Ky.: Westminster-John Knox Press, 1992), 84. But Penchansky goes on to disassociate himself from his own speculations: "They all have serious flaws and lack any strong textual or artifactual support" (85).

40. Adrien Janis Bledstein, "Is Judges a Woman's Satire of Men Who Play God?" in *A Feminist Companion to Judges*, ed. Brenner, 46.

41. Exum, 1989, 70.

42. Richard Elliott Friedman, *Who Wrote the Bible?* (Englewood Cliffs, N.J.: Prentice-Hall, 1987), 34–35.

43. Stephen L. Harris, *Understanding the Bible*, 2nd ed. (Palo Alto, Calif.: Mayfield Publishing Company, 1985), 83.

44. Martin Noth, *The Old Testament World* (Philadelphia: Fortress Press, 1966), 177–78.

45. Speiser, 7, n. 26.

46. Harris, 3–4.

47. Gerald Cooke, "The Sons of (the) God(s)," *Zeitschrift für die Alttestamentische Wissenschaft*, band 76 (1964): 24.

48. Raphael Patai, *The Hebrew Goddess* (New York: Avon Books, 1978), 9.

49. Patai, 9.

50. Patai, 13.

51. Patai, 113–14.

52. Patai, 12.

53. Carole Fontaine, "The Deceptive Goddess in Ancient Near Eastern Myth," *Semeia* 42 (1988): 86.

54. Patai, 13.

55. Ben Zion Bokser, *The Jewish Mystical Tradition* (New York: Pilgrim Press, 1981), 21.

56. *Bib. Ant.* 40.5–6, in Brown, 110.

57. *Bib. Ant.* 40.4, in Brown, 106.

58. Baker, 202.

59. Murphy, *Pseudo-Philo* (New York: Oxford University Press, 1993), 267.

60. *Bib. Ant.* 40.4–7, in Baker, 206–7 (Translation by D. J. Harrington).

61. *Bib. Ant.* 40.6, in Brown, 110.

62. *Bib. Ant.* 40.4, 40.6, in Brown, 106, 110.

63. *Bib. Ant.* 40.5–6, in Brown, 110.

64. *Bib. Ant.* 40.6, in Brown, 110 (Format has been slightly adapted).

65. Brown, 94.

66. Tapp, 172.

CHAPTER THIRTEEN

1. Jean-Jacques Rousseau, *Oeuvres Complètes*, ed. Bernard Gagnelin and Marcel Raymond (Paris: Gallimard, 1964), vol. 2, 1214–15. Original translation by Adam Kirsch.

2. David M. Gunn, "Joshua and Judges," in *The Literary Guide to the Bible*, ed. Robert Alter and Frank Kermode (Cambridge: Belknap Press of Harvard University Press, 1987), 119.

3. Stuart Lasine, "Guest and Host in Judges 19," *Journal for the Study of the Old Testament* 29 (June 1984): 40.

4. Elizabeth Cady Stanton, *The Woman's Bible* (New York: European Publishing Company, 1898; reprint, New York: Arno Press, 1972), 12, 36.

5. Stanton, 7.

6. Carole Fontaine, "The Deceptive Goddess in Ancient Near Eastern Myth," *Semeia* 42 (1988): 84–85.

7. Johanna W. H. Bos, "Out of the Shadows," *Semeia* 42 (1988): 38, fn, 1, citing the work of Naomi Steinberg.

8. Esther Fuchs, "The Literary Characterization of Mothers and Sexual Politics in the Hebrew Bible," *Semeia* 46 (1989): 154.

9. Joseph Heller, *God Knows* (New York: Alfred A. Knopf, 1984), 5.

10. Gila Ramras-Rauch, "Fathers and Daughters," in "Mappings of the Biblical Terrain," ed. Vincent L. Tollers and John Maier, *Bucknell Review* 33, no. 2 (1990): 168.

11. Ramras-Rauch, 160.

12. Robert G. Boling, tr. and intro. *Judges*, Anchor Bible (Garden City, N.Y.: Doubleday, 1975), 273–74.

13. Phyllis Trible, *Texts of Terror* (Philadelphia: Fortress Press, 1984), 66–67.

14. J. Cheryl Exum, *Fragmented Women* (Sheffield, England: JSOT Press, 1993), 177.

15. Anson Rainey and Ben-Zion (Benno) Schereschewsky, "Concubine," in *Encyclopoedia Judaica*, 17 vols. (Jerusalem: Keter Publishing House), vol. 5, 862–65.

16. Trible, 66.

17. Trible, 79–80.

18. Anne Michele Tapp, "An Ideology of Expendability," in *Anti-Covenant*, ed. Mieke Bal (Sheffield, England: Almond Press, 1989), 173.

19. Tapp, 171. (I have used the word "stories" in place of the technical term "fabulae" that appears in the original passage. "Fabulae" is defined by Tapp as "a series of logically and chronologically related events that are caused or experienced by actors," a definition that she credits to leading feminist Bible scholar Mieke Bal.)

20. Adrien Janis Bledstein, "Is Judges a Woman's Satire of Men Who Play God?" in *A Feminist Companion to Judges*, ed. Athalya Brenner (Sheffield, England: Sheffield Academic Press, 1993), 34.

21. David Penchansky, "Staying the Night," in *Reading between Texts* (Louisville, Ky.: Westminster-John Knox Press, 1992), 84–85. (As previously noted, Penchansky raises but disassociates himself from these intriguing scenarios.)

22. Richard Elliott Friedman, *Who Wrote the Bible?* (Englewood Cliffs, N.J.: Prentice-Hall, 1987), 103.

23. Friedman, 117.

24. Bledstein, 53.

25. Boling, 1109.

26. Leila Leah Bronner, "Valorized or Vilified?", in Brenner, 78.

27. Barnabus Lindars, "Deborah's Song," *Bulletin of the John Rylands University Library of Manchester* 65, no. 2 (spring 1983): 173.

28. Danna Nolan Fewell and David M. Gunn, 1990, 394.

29. Bledstein, 52.

30. Susan Niditch, "Eroticism and Death in the Tale of Jael," in *Gender and Difference in Ancient Israel*, ed. Peggy L. Day (Minneapolis, Minn.: Fortress Press, 1989), 46, citing Robert Alter, "From Line to Story in Biblical Verse," *Poetics Today* 4 (1983): 633.

31. Niditch, 45–46, 52.

32. Niditch, 47.

33. Bronner, 89.

34. Niditch, 47–50.

35. Bledstein, 41–42, fn. 4.

36. Lindars, 174.

37. Louis Ginzberg, *The Legends of the Jews*, 7 vols. (Philadelphia: Jewish Publication Society, 1909–1938), vol. 4, 198, fn. 85.

38. Niditch, 45. (Emphasis added.)

39. Yairah Amit, "Literature in the Service of Politics," in *Politics and Theopolitics in*

the Bible and Postbiblical Literature, ed. Henning Graf Reventlow, Yair Hoffman, and Benjamin Uffenheimer (Sheffield, England: JSOT Press, 1994), 28.

40. Amit, 31.

CHAPTER FIFTEEN

1. Jared J. Jackson, "David's Throne," *Canadian Journal of Theology* 11, no. 3 (1965): 183.

2. Sigmund Freud, *Moses and Monotheism* (New York: Vintage Books, 1967), 51.

3. Leonhard Rost, *The Succession to the Throne of David* (Sheffield, England: Almond Press, 1982), 104.

4. David M. Howard, Jr., "David," in *The Anchor Bible Dictionary*, 6 vols., ed. David Noel Freedman (Garden City, N.Y.: Doubleday, 1992), vol. 2, 41.

5. Martin Noth, *The Old Testament World* (Philadelphia: Fortress Press, 1966), 376–81.

6. Harold Bloom and David Rosenberg, *The Book of J* (New York: Grove Weidenfeld, 1990), 40–41.

7. Raymond-Jean Frontain and Jan Wojcik, ed., *The David Myth in Western Literature* (West Lafayette, Ind.: Purdue University Press, 1980), 4.

8. Joseph Heller, *God Knows* (New York: Alfred A. Knopf, 1984), 5–6.

9. David M. Howard, Jr., "David (Person)," *ABD*, vol. II, 44.

10. J. P. Fokkelman, *Narrative Art and Poetry in the Books of Samuel*, vol. 1 (Assen, The Netherlands: Van Gorcum, 1981), 103.

11. Charles Conroy, *Absalom, Absalom!* Analecta Biblica (Rome: Biblical Institute Press, 1978), 17–18, fn. 3.

12. Conroy, 17–18, fn. 3.

13. Susan Niditch, "The 'Sodomite' Theme in Judges 19–20," *Catholic Bible Quarterly* 44, no. 3 (July 1982): 370.

14. George Ridout, "The Rape of Tamar," in *Rhetorical Criticism*, ed. Jared J. Jackson and Martin Kessler (Pittsburgh: Pickwick Press, 1974), 77.

15. John H. Otwell, *And Sarah Laughed* (Philadelphia: Westminster Press, 1977), 23.

16. Phyllis Trible, *Texts of Terror* (Philadelphia: Fortress Press, 1984), 53.

17. P. Kyle McCarter, tr., intro., notes, and comm., *II Samuel*, Anchor Bible (Garden City, N.Y.: Doubleday, 1984), 322.

18. Trible, 58, n. 16.

19. McCarter, 322.

20. Fokkelien van Dijk-Hemmes, "Tamar and the Limits of Patriarchy," in *Anti-Covenant*, ed. Mieke Bal (Sheffield, England: Almond Press, 1989), 140, citing a translation by Jonneke Bekkenkamp.

21. McCarter, 322.

22. Dijk-Hemmes, 140–41.

23. Jackson, 189.

24. McCarter, 405.

25. McCarter, 410.

26. John J. Davis, *The Birth of a Kingdom* (Grand Rapids, Mich.: Baker Book House, 1970), 149.

27. Louis Ginzberg, *Legends of the Jews*, 7 vols. (Philadelphia: Jewish Publication Society, 1909–1938), vol. 4, 118.

28. Frontain and Wojcik, 5.

29. J. Cheryl Exum, 1993, 174–75.

30. Stephen L. Harris, *Understanding the Bible*, 2d ed. (Palo Alto, Calif.: Mayfield Publishing Company, 1985), 94.

31. Richard Elliott Friedman, *Who Wrote the Bible?* (Englewood Cliffs, N.J.: Prentice-Hall, 1987), 110.

32. David M. Gunn, "In Security: The David of Biblical Narrative," in *Signs and Wonders*, ed J. Cheryl Exum (n.p.: Society of Biblical Literature, 1989), 143, fn. 6.

33. Friedman, 102.

34. David M. Gunn, "Joshua and Judges," in *The Literary Guide to the Bible*, ed. Robert Alter and Frank Kermode (Cambridge: Belknap Press of Harvard University Press, 1987), 1987, 119.

35. Jackson, 185.

CHAPTER SIXTEEN

1. Jack Kerouac, *On the Road*, Penguin Classics (New York: Viking Penguin, 1991), 256.

2. Jack Miles, *God: A Biography* (New York: Alfred A. Knopf, 1995), 6–7.

3. Sigmund Freud, *Moses and Monotheism*, (New York: Vintage Books, 1967), 21.

4. As rendered in English in Sidney Greenberg and Jonathan D. Levine, ed., *The New Mahzor for Rosh Hashanah and Yom Kippur (Mahzor Haddash)* (Bridgeport, Conn.: Prayer Book Press, 1978), 557.

5. Salman Rushdie, "The Book Burning," *The New York Review of Books*, vol. 36, no. 3, March 2, 1989, 26.

6. Geza, Vermes, *Scripture and Tradition in Judaism* (Leiden: E. J. Brill, 1961), 7.

7. Vermes, 2–3, citing G. F. Moore, *Judaism in the First Centuries of the Christian Era*.

8. Harold Bloom and David Rosenberg, *The Book of J* (New York: Grove Weidenfeld, 1990), 11.

9. Isaac Bashevis Singer, "If You Could Ask One Question about Life, What Would the Answer Be? 'Yes,' " *Esquire* 82, no. 6 (December 1974): 95 et seq. Copyright © 1974 Isaac Bashevis Singer.

10. Singer, 95 et seq.

11. Singer, 95 et seq.

APPENDIX

1. Richard Elliott Friedman, *Who Wrote the Bible?* (Englewood Cliffs, N.J.: Prentice-Hall, 1987), 21.

2. Freud, 50.

3. Harold Bloom and David Rosenberg, *The Book of J* (New York: Grove Weidenfeld, 1990), 26.

4. Bloom and Rosenberg, 19.

5. Stephen L. Harris, *Understanding the Bible*, 2d. ed. (Palo Alto, Calif.: Mayfield Publishing Company, 1985), 89.

6. Scofield KJV.

7. NEB.

8. New JPS.

9. Friedman, 27.

ACKNOWLEDGMENTS

My work on *The Harlot by the Side of the Road* was inspired and sustained by several mentors and muses, first among them my wife, Ann Benjamin Kirsch, who glimpsed the promise of a book on the Bible in a talk that I gave on the story of Judah and Tamar some years ago. As I discovered when I first met Ann at the age of fourteen, all good things begin with her.

Ann and our two children, Adam Benjamin Kirsch and Jennifer Rachel Kirsch, encouraged and supported the book in countless loving ways over the years of research and writing. Jenny, for example, devised a screen-saver in honor of the project, featuring a message that subtly reminded me of my deadline every time I booted up the computer!

Adam Kirsch, the young man to whom I once read Bible stories at bedtime (see chapter one), is now all grown up, a gifted writer in his own right, and I relied on his expert assistance in completing the research for *Harlot*. Drawing on the collections of the Andover-Harvard Theological Library, the New York Public Library, and the UCLA Research Library, he searched out, retrieved, and, in some cases, even translated the scholarly works that I consulted in writing this book.

Among my blessings I count my agent and guardian angel, Laurie Fox of the Linda Chester Literary Agency, a radiant being whom I cherished as a friend and admired as a fellow writer long before she offered to represent my work, and my publisher at Ballantine Books, Clare Ferraro, whose vision, energy, wisdom, and commitment I was privileged to witness as a book reviewer even before I was fortunate enough to become one of her authors.

I am deeply grateful, too, for the opportunity to work with Virginia Faber, my editor at Ballantine, whose discerning eye and deftly wielded pencil greatly enhanced the book, and the incomparable Linda Chester, who brings a unique blend of grace, savvy, and dazzle to her work as a literary agent.

Another friend of long standing who became a colleague on *Harlot* is Liz Williams, the West Coast publicity director for Ballantine, a woman of high spirits and profound spirituality, good humor and good ideas, and a tireless crusader for books and authors.

Indeed, the whole enterprise has been all the more rewarding because of the gifted and gracious people with whom I have been privileged to work, including Ellen Archer, Mark Bloomfield, Hillary Cohen, Betsy Elias, Janet Fletcher, Jim Geraghty, Kathleen Fridella, Rachel Tarlow-Gul, Alice Kesterson, Steven Oppenheim, Nate Penn, and Lewis Robinson at Ballantine; Joanna Pulcini and Gary Jaffe at the Linda Chester Literary Agency; Judith Kendra at Rider Books in London; and Linda Michaels and Teresa Cavanaugh at Linda Michaels Ltd. International Literary Agents.

Jack Miles, a colleague and good friend, encouraged my work as a book reviewer for the *Los Angeles Times* over the years and godfathered my writing on the subject of the Bible, both by his willingness to share his vast knowledge and by the shining example of his masterpiece of biblical exegesis, *God: A Biography*.

Tony Cohan, publisher of Acrobat Books, is the man of letters who put my legal writing into print by commissioning and publishing *Kirsch's Handbook of Publishing Law*—and graciously encouraged me to climb the mountain of biblical storytelling, too.

I am blessed, too, with the friendship and colleagueship of Dennis Mitchell, my law partner and dear friend, whose encouragement and support have been essential to my work as a lawyer *and* a writer. And I have been heartened by the daily pleasure of working with my other friends and colleagues in the practice of law—Judy Woo, Angie Yoon, Gold Lee, Stephanie Harker, Larry Zerner, Scott Baker, and Gregg Homer.

Raye Birk and Candace Barrett Birk are gifted performing artists, ardent readers, earnest seekers, and abiding friends who have listened to so many forbidden tales of the Bible over so many lively dinners with Ann and me that they will surely find *The Harlot by the Side of the Road* to be familiar terrain by now.

Jonathan Kirsch
Los Angeles
February 19, 1997

RECOMMENDED READING
AND BIBLIOGRAPHY

RECOMMENDED READING

The works listed in the Bibliography below are *all* of the sources that I consulted in researching and writing *The Harlot by the Side of the Road*. Special mention should be made, however, of a few works that I found to be especially useful and interesting. These are books that I recommend highly to any reader who wishes to learn more about the Bible.

The Anchor Bible Dictionary is an accessible, comprehensive, and intriguing reference tool for any Bible reader. Even in six volumes, it is remarkably compact for a work of such ambition and accomplishment, and it includes entries by the most distinguished scholars in the field of biblical studies.

The *Encyclopaedia Judaica* is a general encyclopedia on Jewish topics, but I found it particularly helpful in teasing out some of the intricacies of Bible history and exegesis, not only in the Jewish tradition but also in Christian and Islamic sources.

Who Wrote the Bible? by Richard Elliott Friedman is a superb introduction to recent scholarship in the field of biblical authorship. Friedman presents his research and analysis, much of it highly original, almost like a mystery story, and he even names his own most likely suspect for the authorship of the Book of Deuteronomy.

Three books that approach God as a literary or historical figure rather than a matter of theology were crucial in my work and, in a deeper sense, helped to inspire me to write this book in the first place.

The Book of J by Harold Bloom and David Rosenberg consists of Rosenberg's original and lyrical translation of the thread of biblical narrative attributed to the source called J, and Bloom's provocative literary study of J, whom he imagines to be a highborn woman living and working in the royal court of Judah in distant antiquity.

God: A Biography by Jack Miles, a Pulitzer Prize–winning study of God as a literary character in the Bible, is no less than a modern masterpiece of biblical exegesis. Miles's chapter on the Book of Job is the crowning achievement, but the entire work is essential for any reader who is willing to approach the Bible as a work of literature as well as theology and moral instruction.

If a single book beckoned me back to the Bible after years of sporadic and indifferent Bible reading, it was Joseph Heller's *God Knows*, a comic novel in which the story of King David is told in the first person by David himself with the patter and the point of view of a stand-up comic in a burlesque house. Heller, like Harold Bloom and Jack Miles, is a contemporary author who breathes new life back into a very old book.

BIBLIOGRAPHY

Bibles

When quoting from certain versions of the Bible, I have used abbreviations in the text to identify the source of the quote. These abbreviations are given in the list below, along with the full title and bibliographical information for the various bibles. Following the abbreviations list, there is a list of other versions of the Bible that I have consulted. Where no specific source is indicated in the text, the quotation is taken from the 1962 edition of the Jewish Publication Society's *The Holy Scriptures According to the Masoretic Text* (JPS).

JPS

The Holy Scriptures According to the Masoretic Text. Philadelphia: Jewish Publication Society, 1961.

KJV

The Holy Bible Containing the Old and New Testaments in the King James Version. Nashville: Thomas Nelson Publishers, 1985.

NAB

The New American Bible. Catholic Bible Association of America. Chicago: Catholic Press, 1971.

NEB

The New English Bible with the Apocrypha. 2d ed. New York: Oxford University Press, 1970.

New JPS

Tanakh, The Holy Scriptures: The New JPS Translation According to the Traditional Hebrew Text. Philadelphia: Jewish Publication Society, 1985.

NRSV

The New Oxford Annotated Bible with the Apocrypha. New Revised Standard Version. Edited by Bruce M. Metzger and Roland E. Murphy. New York: Oxford University Press, 1994.

RSV

The New Oxford Annotated Bible with the Apocrypha. Revised Standard Version, Containing the Second Edition of the New Testament. Edited by Herbert G. May and Bruce M. Metzger. New York: Oxford University Press, 1973.

Scofield KJV   *The Scofield Reference Bible*.
                               Authorized King James Version.
                               New York: Oxford University
                               Press, 1945.

Anderson, Francis I. and David Noel Freedman, tr., notes, and comm. *Hosea*. Anchor Bible. Garden City, N.Y.: Doubleday, 1986.

Boling, Robert G., tr. and intro. *Judges*. Anchor Bible. Garden City, N.Y.: Doubleday, 1975.

Hertz, J. H. ed. *The Pentateuch and Haftorahs*. 2d ed. London: Soncino Press, 1981.

McCarter, P. Kyle, Jr., tr., intro., notes, and comm. *II Samuel*. Anchor Bible. Garden City, N.Y.: Doubleday, 1984.

The Complete Parallel Bible Containing the Old and New Testaments with the Apocryphal/Deuterocanonical Books. New York: Oxford University Press, 1993.

Speiser, E. A., tr., intro., and notes. *Genesis*. Anchor Bible. Garden City, N.Y.: Doubleday, 1987.

General Reference Works

Interpreter's Dictionary of the Bible, New York: Abingdon Press, 1962.

Botterweck, G. Johannes, and Helmer Ringgren, eds. *The Theological Dictionary of the Old Testament*. Grand Rapids, Mich.: William B. Eerdmans Publishing Company, 1977.

Browning, W. R. F. *A Dictionary of the Bible*, Oxford and New York: Oxford University Press, 1996.

Freedman, David Noel. gen. ed., *The Anchor Bible Dictionary*. Vols. 1–6. New York: Doubleday, 1992.

Housman, M. Th. et al., eds. *E. J. Brill's First Encyclopaedia of Islam, 1913–1936*. Vols. 2, 5, and 7. Leiden and New York: E. J. Brill, 1987.

Encyclopaedia Judaica. Vols. 1–17. corrected ed. Jerusalem: Keter Publishing House, Ltd., n.d.

Books

Alter, Robert. *The Art of Biblical Narrative.* New York: Basic Books, 1981.

Alter, Robert, and Frank Kermode, eds. *The Literary Guide to the Bible.* Cambridge: Belknap Press of Harvard University Press, 1987.

Amit, Yairah. "Literature in the Service of Politics: Studies in Judges 19–21." In *Politics and Theopolitics in the Bible and Postbiblical Literature*, edited by Henning Graf Reventlow, Yair Hoffman, and Benjamin Uffenheimer, pp. 28–40. Journal for the Study of the Old Testament, supplement series 171, Sheffield, England: JSOT Press, 1994.

Armstrong, Karen. *Jerusalem: One City, Three Faiths.* New York: Alfred A. Knopf, 1996.

Atkinson, Clarissa W., Constance H. Buchanan, and Margaret Miles, eds. *Immaculate and Powerful: The Female in Sacred Images and Social Reality.* Boston: Beacon Press, 1985.

Aycock, D. Alan. "The Fate of Lot's Wife: Structural Mediation in Biblical Mythology." In *Structuralist Interpretations of Biblical Myth*, edited by Edmund Leach and D. Alan Aycock, 113–19.

Baker, Cynthia. "Pseudo-Philo and the Transformation of Jephthah's Daughter." In *Anti-Covenant*, edited by Mieke Bal, 195–209.

Bal, Mieke. ed. *Anti-Covenant: Counter-reading Women's Lives in the Hebrew Bible.* Sheffield, England: Almond Press, 1989.

Barnavi, Eli, gen. ed. *A Historical Atlas of the Jewish People: From the Time of the Patriarchs to the Present.* New York: Alfred A. Knopf, 1992.

Begin, Menachem. *The Revolt.* (orig. 1951) rev. ed. Los Angeles: Nash Publishing, 1977.

Biale, David. *Power and Powerlessness in Jewish History.* New York: Schocken Books, 1986.

Bimson, John J. *The Compact Handbook of Old Testament Life.* Minneapolis, Minn.: Bethany House Publishers, 1988.

Bledstein, Adrien Janis. "Is Judges a Woman's Satire of Men Who Play God?" In *A Feminist Companion to Judges*, edited by Athalya Brenner, 34–53.

Bloom, Harold, and David Rosenberg. *The Book of J.* New York: Grove Weidenfeld, 1990.

Bokser, Ben Zion. *The Jewish Mystical Tradition,* New York: Pilgrim Press, 1981.

Brenner, Athalya, ed. *A Feminist Companion to Judges.* Feminist

Companion to the Bible, vol. 4. Sheffield, England: Sheffield Academic Press, 1993.

Bronner, Leila Leah. "Valorized or Vilified? The Women of Judges in Midrashic Sources." In A Feminist Companion to Judges, edited by Athalya Brenner, 72–95.

Brown, Cheryl Anne. No Longer Be Silent: First Century Jewish Portraits of Biblical Women, Louisville, Ky.: Westminster-John Knox Press, 1992.

Buber, Martin. Moses: The Revelation and the Covenant, New York: Harper & Row, 1958.

Butler, James T., Edgar W. Conrad, and Ben C. Ollenburger, ed. Understanding the Word: Essays in Honor of Bernard W. Anderson. Journal for the study of the Old Testament, Supplement Series 3. Sheffield, England: JSOT Press, 1985.

Carlson, R. A. David, the Chosen King: A Traditio-Historical Approach to the Second Book of Samuel. Stockholm: Almqvist & Wiksell, 1964.

Coats, George W. "Lot: A Foil in the Abraham Saga." In Understanding the Word, edited by James T. Butler, Edgar W. Conrad, and Ben C. Ollenburger, 113–32.

Conroy, Charles. Absalom, Absalom!: Narrative and Language in 2 Sam. 13–20. Analecta Biblica. Rome: Biblical Institute Press, 1978.

Cross, Frank Moore. Canaanite Myth and Hebrew Epic: Essays in the History of the Religion of Israel. Cambridge: Harvard University Press, 1973.

Culley, Robert C. Studies in the Structure of Hebrew Narrative, Philadelphia: Fortress Press, 1976.

Davis, John J. The Birth of a Kingdom: Studies in I–II Samuel and I Kings 1–11. Grand Rapids, Mich.: Baker Book House, 1970.

Day, Peggy L. "From the Child Is Born the Woman: The Story of Jephthah's Daughter." In Gender and Difference in Ancient Israel, edited by Peggy L. Day, 58–74.

———, ed. Gender Differences In Ancient Israel. Minneapolis, Minn.: Fortress Press, 1989.

Dijk-Hemmes, Fokkelien van. "Tamar and the Limits of Patriarchy: Between Rape and Seduction (2 Samuel 13 and Genesis 38)." In Anti-Covenant, edited by Mieke Bal, 135–56.

Eliot, T. S. The Waste Land. In The Harper Anthology of Poetry, edited by John Frederick Nims, New York: Harper & Row, 1981.

Exum, J. Cheryl. *Fragmented Women: Feminist (Sub)versions of Biblical Narratives*, Journal for the Study of the Old Testament, Supplement Series 163. Sheffield, England: JSOT Press, 1993.

———. "On Judges 11." In *A Feminist Companion to Judges*, edited by Athalya Brenner, 131–44.

———. "The Tragic Vision and Biblical Narrative: The Case of Jephthah." In *Signs and Wonders*, edited by J. Cheryl Exum, 59–84.

———, ed. *Signs and Wonders: Biblical Texts in Literary Focus*. Semeia Studies. N.P.: Society of Biblical Literature, 1989.

Fewell, Danna Nolan. ed. *Reading between Texts: Intertextuality and the Hebrew Bible*. Louisville, Ky.: Westminster-John Knox Press, 1992.

Flanagan, James W. *David's Social Drama: A Hologram of Israel's Early Iron Age*. Sheffield, England: Almond Press, 1988.

Fokkelman, J. P. *Narrative Art and Poetry in the Books of Samuel*. Vol. 1 *King David, 2 Samm. 9–20 and 1 Kings 1–2*. Assen, The Netherlands: Van Gorcum, 1981.

Freud, Sigmund. *Moses and Monotheism*. Translated by Katherine Jones. New York: Vintage Books, 1967.

Friedman, Richard Elliott. *Who Wrote the Bible?* Englewood Cliffs, N.J.: Prentice-Hall, 1987.

Frontain, Raymond-Jean, and Jan Wojcik, eds., *The David Myth in Western Literature*. West Lafayette, Ind.: Purdue University Press, 1980.

Frye, Northrop. *The Great Code: The Bible and Literature*. New York: Harcourt Brace Jovanovich, 1982.

Gerstein, Beth. "A Ritual Processed: A Look at Judges 11:40." In *Anti-Covenant*, edited by Mieke Bal, 175–93.

Gilbert, Martin. *Atlas of Jewish History*. 3rd ed. New York: Dorset Press, 1984.

Ginzberg, Louis. *The Legends of the Jews*. Translated by Henrietta Szold. Vols. 1–7. Philadelphia: Jewish Publication Society, 1909–1938.

———. *On Jewish Law and Lore*. (orig. 1955). New York: Atheneum, 1981.

Girard, René. *Violence and the Sacred*. Translated by Patrick Gregory. Baltimore: Johns Hopkins University Press, 1977. *Semeia* 46, 1989, 151–66.

Gordis, Robert. *The Biblical Text in the Making: A Study of the Kethib-*

Qere, Philadelphia: Dropsie College for Hebrew and Cognate Learning, 1937.

Gottwald, Norman K. *The Tribes of Yahweh: A Sociology of the Religion of Liberated Israel, 1250–1050 B.C.E.*. Maryknoll, N.Y.: Orbis Books, 1979.

Greenberg, Moshe. *Understanding Exodus*. New York: Behrman House for Melton Research Center of the Jewish Theological Seminary, 1969.

Greenberg, Sidney, and Jonathan D. Levine, eds. *The New Mahzor for Rosh Hashanah and Yom Kippur (Mahzor Hadash)*. Bridgeport, Conn.: Prayer Book Press, 1978.

Gunkel, Hermann. *The Legends of Genesis: The Biblical Saga and History*. New York: Schocken Books, 1964.

Gunn, David M. "In Security: The David of Biblical Narrative." In *Signs and Wonders*, edited by J. Cheryl Exum, 133–52.

————. *The Story of King David: Genre and Interpretation*. Journal for the Study of the Old Testament, Supplement Series 6. Sheffield, England: JSOT Press, 1978.

————. "Joshua and Judges." In *The Literary Guide to the Bible*, edited by Robert Alter and Frank Kermode, 102–21.

Hackett, Jo Ann. "In the Days of Jael: Reclaiming the History of Women." In *Immaculate and Powerful*, edited by Clarissa W. Atkinson, Constance H. Buchanan, and Margaret R. Miles, 15–38.

Hanselman, Stephen W. "Narrative Theory, Ideology, and Transformation in Judges 4," *Anti-Covenant*, edited by Mieke Bal, 95–112.

Harris, Stephen L. *Understanding the Bible: A Reader's Introduction*. 2d. ed. Palo Alto, Calif.: Mayfield Publishing Company, 1985.

Hawk, L. Daniel. "Strange Houseguests: Rahab, Lot, and the Dynamics of Deliverance." In *Reading between Texts*, edited by Danna Nolan Fewell, 89–97.

Heller, Joseph. *God Knows*. New York: Alfred A. Knopf, 1984.

Heschel, Abraham J. *The Prophets: An Introduction*. New York: Harper Torchbooks, 1969.

Humphreys, W. Lee. "The Story of Jephthah and the Tragic Vision: A Response to J. Cheryl Exum." In *Signs and Wonders*, edited by J. Cheryl Exum, 85–96.

Jay, Nancy. "Sacrifice as Remedy for Having Been Born of Woman." In *Immaculate and Powerful*, edited by Clarissa W. Atkinson, Constance H. Buchanan, and Margaret R. Miles, 283–309.

Kamuf, Peggy. "Author of a Crime." In *A Feminist Companion to Judges*, edited by Athalya Brenner, 187–207.

Kerouac, Jack. *On the Road*. Penguin Classics. New York: Viking Penguin, 1991.

Kline, Meredith G. *By Oath Consigned: A Reinterpretation of the Covenant Signs of Circumcision and Baptism*. Grand Rapids: William B. Eerdmans Publishing Company, 1968.

Landes, Daniel. "A Vow of Death." In *Confronting Omnicide: Jewish Reflections on Weapons of Mass Destruction*, edited by Daniel Landes, 5–11. Northvale, N.J.: Jason Aronson, 1991.

Larue, Gerald A. *Sex and the Bible*. Buffalo, N.Y.: Prometheus Books, 1983.

Leach, Edmund. "Why Did Moses Have a Sister?" In *Structuralist Interpretations of Biblical Myth*, edited by Edmund Leach and D. Alan Aycock, 33–66.

Leach, Edmund, and D. Alan Aycock, eds. *Structuralist Interpretations of Biblical Myth*. Cambridge [England] and New York: Cambridge University Press, 1983.

Long, Burke O. "Wounded Beginnings: David and Two Sons." In *Images of Man and God: Old Testament Short Stories in Literary Focus*, edited by Burke O. Long. Sheffield, England: Almond Press, 1981, 26–34.

Magnusson, Magnus. *Archaeology of the Bible*, New York: Simon & Schuster, 1978.

Matthews, Victor H. *Manners and Customs in the Bible*. Peabody, Mass.: Hendrickson Publishers, 1988.

Miles, Jack. *God: A Biography*, New York: Alfred A. Knopf, 1995.

Miscall, Peter D. "For David's Sake: A Response to David M. Gunn." In *Signs and Wonders*, edited by J. Cheryl Exum, 153–64.

Murphy, Frederick J. *Pseudo-Philo: Rewriting the Bible*. New York: Oxford University Press, 1993.

Newman, Murray L. "Rahab and the Conquest." In *Understanding the Word*, edited by James T. Butler, Edgar W. Conrad, and Ben C. Ollenburger, 167–81.

Niditch, Susan. "Eroticism and Death in the Tale of Jael." In *Gender and Difference in Ancient Israel*, edited by Peggy L. Day, 43–57.

Noth, Martin. *The Old Testament World*. Translated by Victor I. Gruhn. Philadelphia: Fortress Press, 1966.

Otwell, John H. *And Sarah Laughed: The Status of Woman in the Old Testament*. Philadelphia: Westminster Press, 1977.

Oz, Amos. "Upon This Evil Earth." In *Where the Jackals Howl and Other Stories*. Translated by Nicholas de Lange and Philip Simpson. New York: Harcourt Brace Jovanovich, 1981.

Ozick, Cynthia. *Metaphor and Memory*. New York: Alfred A. Knopf, 1989.

Pardes, Ilana. *Countertraditions in the Bible: A Feminist Approach*. Cambridge: Harvard University Press, 1992.

Patai, Raphael. *The Arab Mind*. New York: Charles Scribner's Sons, 1976.

———. *The Hebrew Goddess*. New York: Avon Books, 1978.

Penchansky, David. "Staying the Night: Intertextuality in Genesis and Judges." In *Reading between Texts*, edited by Danna Nolan Fewell, 77–97.

Philo of Alexandria (Philo Judaeus). *The Essential Philo*. Edited by Nahum N. Glatzer. New York: Schocken Books, 1971.

Pitt-Rivers, Julian. *The Fate of Shechem, or The Politics of Sex: Essays in the Anthropology of the Mediterranean*. Cambridge: Cambridge University Press, 1977.

Price, Reynolds. *A Palpable God*. (orig. 1978). San Francisco: North Point Press, 1985.

Richler, Mordecai. *St. Urbain's Horseman*. New York: Alfred A. Knopf, 1972.

Ridout, George. "The Rape of Tamar: A Rhetorical Analysis of 2 Sam. 13:1–22." In *Rhetorical Criticism: Essays in Honor of James Muilenburg*, edited by Jared J. Jackson and Martin Kessler, 75–84. Pittsburgh: Pickwick Press, 1974.

Rost, Leonhard. *The Succession to the Throne of David*. Sheffield, England: Almond Press, 1982.

Rousseau, Jean-Jacques. *Oeuvres Complètes*. Vol. 2. Edited by Bernard Gagnelin and Marcel Raymond. Paris: Gallimard, 1964.

Sarna, Nahum M. *Understanding Genesis: The World of the Bible in the Light of History*. New York: Schocken Books, 1970.

Sheres, Ita. *Dinah's Rebellion: A Biblical Parable for Our Time*. New York: Crossroad, 1990.

Stanton, Elizabeth Cady. *The Woman's Bible*. New York: European Publishing Company, 1898. Reprint, New York: Arno Press, 1972.

Sternberg, Meir. *The Poetics of Biblical Narrative: Ideological Literature and the Drama of Reading*. Bloomington: Indiana University Press, 1985.

Tapp, Anne Michele. "An Ideology of Expendability: Virgin Daughter Sacrifice in Genesis 19.1–11, Judges 11.30–39, and 19.22–26." In *Anti-Covenant*, edited by Mieke Bal, 158–74.

Trible, Phyllis. *Texts of Terror: Literary-Feminist Readings of Biblical Narratives*. Philadelphia: Fortress Press, 1984.

Tucker, Gene M. "The Rahab Saga (Joshua 2): Some Form-Critical and Traditio-Historical Observations." *The Use of the Old Testament in the New and Other Essays*, edited by James M. Efird, 66–86. Durham, N.C.: Duke University Press, 1972.

Vaux, Roland de. *Ancient Israel: Its Life and Institutions*. Vol. 1. New York: McGraw-Hill, 1965.

Whitelam, Keith W. *The Just King: Monarchial Judicial Authority in Ancient Israel*. Journal for the Study of the Old Testament, supplement Series 12. Sheffield, England: JSOT Press, 1979.

Vermes, Geza. *Scripture and Tradition in Judaism: Haggadic Studies*. Leiden: E. J. Brill, 1961.

Von Rad, Gerhard. *Genesis: A Commentary*. revised ed. Translated by John H. Marks. London: S.C.M. Press, Ltd., 1972.

Scholarly Journals and Other Periodicals

Ackerman, James S. "Knowing Good and Evil: A Literary Analysis of the Court History in 2 Samuel 9–20 and 1 Kings 1–2." *Journal of Biblical Literature* 109, no. 1 (spring 1990): 41–60.

Alexander, T. Desmond. "Lot's Hospitality: A Clue to His Righteousness." *Journal of Biblical Literature* 104, no. 2 (June 1985): 289–91.

Alexiou, Margaret, and Peter Dronke. "The Lament of Jephthah's Daughter: Themes, Traditions, Originality." *Studi Medievali*, serie terza, anno XII, fasc. 2 (1971): 819–63.

Alter, Robert. "A Literary Approach to the Bible." *Commentary* 60, no. 6 (December 1975): 70–77.

Anderson, Francis I. "Israelite Kinship Terminology and Social Structure." *Bible Translator* 20 (1969): 29–38.

Auld, A. G. "Judges I and History: A Reconsideration." *Vetus Testamentum* 25, fasc. 3 (May 1975): 261–85.

Bailey, Clinton. "How Desert Culture Helps Us Understand the Bible." *Bible Review* 7, no. 4 (August 1991): 14–38.

Biblical Archaeology Review. "Have Sodom and Gomorrah Been Found?" (September/October 1980).

Blenkinsopp, Joseph. "Abraham and the Righteous of Sodom." *Journal of Jewish Studies* 33, nos. 1–2 (spring-autumn 1982): 119–32.

Bos, Johanna W. H. "Out of the Shadows: Genesis 38, Judges 4:17–22, Ruth 3." *Semeia* 42 (1988): 37–67.

Butler, Trent C. "An Anti-Moses Tradition," *Journal for the Study of the Old Testament* 12 (May 1979): 9–15.

Carmichael, Calum M. "A Ceremonial Crux: Removing a Man's Sandal as a Female Gesture of Contempt," *Journal of Biblical Literature* 96, no. 3 (September 1977): 321–36.

Caspi, Mishael Maswari. "The Story of the Rape of Dinah: The Narrator and the Reader." *Hebrew Studies* 26, no. 1 (1985): 25–45.

Clements, R. E. "The Relation of Children to the People of God in the Old Testament." *Baptist Quarterly* 11, no. 5 (January 1966): 195–205.

Coats, George W. "Widow's Rights: A Crux in the Structure of Genesis 38." *Catholic Biblical Quarterly* 34, no. 4 (October 1972): 461–66.

Cohen, Shaye J. D. "Solomon and the Daughter of Pharaoh: Intermarriage, Conversion, and the Impurity of Women." *Journal of the Ancient Near Eastern Society* 16–17 (1984–1985): 23–37.

Cooke, Gerald. "The Sons of (the) God(s)." *Zeitschrift für die Alttestamentlische Wissenschaft*, band 76 (1964): 24–47.

Davis, Joseph M. "On the Idea of Covenant." *Conservative Judaism* 41, no. 4 (summer 1989): 20–34.

Emerton, J.A. "An Examination of a Recent Structuralist Interpretation of Genesis XXXVIII." *Vetus Testamentum* 26, fasc. 1 (1976): 79–98.

———. "Judah and Tamar." *Vetus Testamentum* 29, fasc. 4 (October 1979): 403–15.

———. "The Riddle of Genesis XIV." *Vetus Testamentum* 21, fasc. 4 (1971): 403–39.

———. "Some False Clues in the Study of Genesis XIV." *Vetus Testamentum* 21, fasc. 1 (1971): 24–47.

———. "Some Problems in Genesis XXXVIII." *Vetus Testamentum* 25, fasc. 3 (1975): 338–61.

Fewell, Danna Nolan, and David M. Gunn. "Controlling Perspectives: Women, Men and the Authority of Violence in Judges 4 & 5." *Journal of the American Academy of Religion* 78, no. 3 (Fall 1990): 389–412.

———. "Tipping the Balance: Sternberg's Reader and the Rape of Dinah." *Journal of Biblical Literature* 110, no. 2 (summer 1991): 193–211.

Fisher, Eugene J. "Cultic Prostitution in the Ancient Near East? A Reassessment." *Biblical Theology Bulletin* 6, nos. 2–3 (June–October 1976): 225–36.

Fontaine, Carole. "The Deceptive Goddess in Ancient Near Eastern Myth: Inanna and Inaras." *Semeia* 42 (1988): 84–99.

Fuchs, Esther. "The Literary Characterization of Mothers and Sexual Politics in the Hebrew Bible." *Semeia* 46 (1989): 151–66.

———. "Structure and Patriarchal Functions in the Biblical Betrothal Type-Scene: Some Preliminary Notes." *Journal of Feminist Studies in Religion* 3, no. 1 (spring 1987): 7–14.

Gruber, Mayer I. "Hebrew Qedeshah and Her Canaanite and Akkadian Cognates." *Ugarit-Forschungen*, band 198 (1986): 133–48.

Harrelson, Walter, Bernhard W. Anderson, and G. Ernest Wright. "Shechem, Navel of the Land." *Biblical Archaeologist* 20, no. 1 (February 1957): 2–31.

Helyer, Larry R. "The Separation of Abraham and Lot: Its Significance in the Patriarchal Narratives." *Journal for the Study of the Old Testament* 26 (June 1983): 77–88.

Jackson, Jared J. "David's Throne: Patterns in the Succession Story." *Canadian Journal of Theology* 11, no. 3 (1965): 183–95.

Jeansonne, Sharon Pace. "The Characterization of Lot in Genesis." *Biblical Theology Bulletin* 18, no. 4 (October 1988): 123–29.

Kaplan, Lawrence. " 'And the Lord Sought to Kill Him' (Exod. 4:24): Yet Once Again." *Hebrew Annual Review* 5, Department of Judaic and Near Eastern Languages and Literatures, Ohio State University (1981): 65–74.

Kessler, Martin. "Genesis 34—An Interpretation." *Reformed Review* 19, no. 1 (September 1965): 3–8.

Kliewer, Warren. "The Daughters of Lot: Legend and Fabliau." *ILIFF Review* 25, no. 1 (winter 1968): 13–28.

Kosmala, Hans. "The 'Bloody Husband.'" *Vetus Testamentum* 12 (January 1962): 14–28.

Krappe, Alexander H. "The Birth of Adonis." *Review of Religion* 6, no. 1 (November 1941): 3–17.

Kugel, James. "The Story of Dinah in the *Testament of Levi*." *Harvard Theological Review* 85, no. 1 (1992): 1–34.

Lasine, Stuart. "Guest and Host in Judges 19: Lot's Hospitality in an Inverted World." *Journal for the Study of the Old Testament* 29 (June 1984): 37–59.

Leiman, Sid Z. "The Canonization of Hebrew Scripture: The Talmudic and Midrashic Evidence." *Transactions* 47 (February 1976), Archon Books.

Lindars, Barnabas. "Deborah's Song: Women in the Old Testament." *Bulletin of the John Rylands University Library of Manchester* 65, no. 2 (spring 1983): 158–75.

McCarthy, Carmel. "The Tiqqune Sopherim." *Orbis Biblicus et Orientalis* 36, Universitätsverlag Freiburg Schwitz and Vandenhoeck & Ruprecht, Gottingen (1981).

Marcus, David. "The Bargaining between Jephthah and the Elders (Judges 11:4–11). *Journal of the Ancient Near Eastern Society* 19, (1989): 95–100.

Matthews, Victor H. "Hospitality and Hostility in Judges 4." *Biblical Theology Bulletin* 21, no. 1 (spring 1991): 13–21.

Mendelsohn, I. "The Disinheritance of Jephthah in the Light of Paragraph 27 of the Lit-Ishtar Code." *Israel Exploration Journal* 4, (1954): 116–119.

Millard, A. R. "The Meaning of the Name Judah," *Zeitschrift für die Alttestamentische Wissenschaft*, 8, no. 2 (1974): 216–18.

Morgenstern, Julian. "The 'Bloody Husband' (?) (Exod. 4:24–26) Once Again," *Hebrew Union College Annual* 34, Union of American Hebrew Congregations (1963): 35–70.

———. "The Oldest Document in the Hexateuch." *Hebrew Union College Annual* 4, Union of American Hebrew Congregations (1927): 1–138.

Niditch, Susan. "The 'Sodomite' Theme in Judges 19–20: Family,

Community, and Social Disintegration." *Catholic Bible Quarterly* 44, no. 3 (July 1982): 365–78.

————. "The Wronged Woman Righted: An Analysis of Genesis 38." *Harvard Theological Review* 72, nos. 1–2 (January–April 1979): 143–49.

Ramras-Rauch, Gila. "Fathers and Daughters: Two Biblical Narratives," in Vincent L. Tollers and John Maier, eds., "Mappings of the Biblical Terrain: The Bible as Text." *Bucknell Review* 33, no. 2 (1990): 158–69.

Robinson, B. P. "Zipporah to the Rescue: A Contextual Study of Exodus iv 24–6." *Vetus Testamentum* 36, no. 4 (October 1986): 447–61.

Rodd, Cyril S. "The Family in the Old Testament." *Bible Translator* 18, no. 1 (January 1967): 19–26.

Rushdie, Salman. "The Book Burning." *New York Review of Books* 36, no. 3 (March 2, 1989): 26.

Singer, Isaac Bashevis. "If You Could Ask One Question about Life, What Would the Answer Be? 'Yes.' " *Esquire* 82, no. 6 (December 1974): 95 et seq.

Ventura, Michael. "Letters at 3 a.m.: The Book of Wildness." *LA Village View* (December 24–30, 1993): 5. (Reprinted from *Austin Chronicle*.)

Vermes, G. "Baptism and Jewish Exegesis: New Light from Ancient Sources." *New Testament Studies* 4 (1957–1958) Cambridge University Press, 1958, 309–19.

Webb, Barry G. "The Theme of the Jephthah Story." *Reformed Theological Review* 45, no. 2 (May-August 1986): 34–43.

Whitelam, Keith W. "The Defence of David." *Journal for the Study of the Old Testament* 29 (June 1984): 61–87.

INDEX

AUTHOR'S NOTE

I first discovered what is hidden away in the odd cracks and corners of the Holy Scriptures when, many years ago, I resolved to acquaint my young son with the Bible as a work of literature by reading aloud to him from Genesis. I chose the New English Bible, with its plainspoken translation of the hoary old text, so that my five-year-old would understand what was actually going on in the stories without the impedimenta of the antique words and phrases that give the King James Version such grandeur but sometimes make it hard to follow.

We began "In the beginning," of course, and continued through the highly suggestive tale of Eve and the serpent, then the bloody murder of Abel by his brother, Cain. I already knew that Genesis was not exactly G rated, but I reassured myself that we would soon reach the tale of Noah and the ark, an unobjectionable Sunday school story that would distract my son from the more disturbing passages that we had just read. Nothing had prepared me for what we found there, right after the familiar moment when the animals come aboard the ark, two by two.

At the end of the story of Noah, after the flood has subsided and God has signaled his good intentions toward humanity by painting a rainbow across the sky, we came across a scene that does not find its way into the storybooks or Sunday school lessons: Noah is lying alone in his tent, buck naked and drunk as a sailor on the wine from his own vineyards. One of his sons, Ham, blunders into the tent and finds himself staring at his nude and drunken father.

"When Ham, father of Canaan, saw his father naked, he told his two brothers outside," we read in Genesis. "So Shem and Japheth took a cloak, put it on their shoulders and walked backwards, and so covered their father's naked body; their faces were turned the other way, so that they did not see their father naked" (Gen. 9:20–24).

After that scene, so comical and yet so disquieting to any parent mindful of Freud, I read the Bible more slowly, rephrasing certain passages as I went along and omitting others altogether. My son, already media-wise at five, soon began to protest: If I paused too long over a troublesome passage, trying to figure out how to tone down or cut the earthier parts, he would sit up in bed and demand indignantly: "What are you leaving out?"

In a sense, his question prompted **THE HARLOT BY THE SIDE OF THE ROAD**. As I read the Bible aloud to my son, I found myself doing exactly what overweening and fearful clerics and translators have done for centuries—I censored the text to spare my audience from the juicy parts. And so my son's question is answered here: The stories collected in its pages are the ones that I—like so many other shocked Bible readers over the millennia—was tempted to leave out.

— Jonathan Kirsch
May 1997

THE FORBIDDEN TALES OF THE BIBLE

GENERAL QUESTIONS AND DISCUSSION TOPICS

- In **THE HARLOT BY THE SIDE OF THE ROAD**, Jonathan Kirsch examines seven of the Bible's most controversial and most frequently suppressed stories. As you read through these tales, think about other Bible stories that receive little attention from sermonizers and Sunday school teachers. What can these other stories tell us about the lives and beliefs of the real men and women who lived in ancient times? And what can they reveal to us about our own troubled world?

- Why is it important to understand the Bible?

- Why aren't Americans more familiar with the Bible?

- Once upon a time it could be assumed that everybody who went to college had been exposed to at least one Bible course. Despite the separation of church and state, should this practice be reinstated in our schools?

- Does the Bible celebrate or denigrate women? Is it possible, as one feminist Bible critic suggests, that certain books of the Bible were written by a woman?

- Have fundamentalists made the Bible less appealing to mainstream readers?

- How can we increase interest in the Bible among young people today? How can we do the same for adults?

- There has been a growing number of books, articles, and television programs about the Bible in recent years. What accounts for this increased attention to the Bible and the lessons it has to offer?

LOT AND HIS DAUGHTERS *(Gen. 19:30–38) Having narrowly escaped the carnage brought down on Sodom and Gomorrah, Lot and his two daughters face the possibility that they are the last survivors on earth. In order to insure the continuation of their race, the two girls ply their father with wine and couple with him while he's in a drunken stupor.*

READING GROUP QUESTIONS AND DISCUSSION TOPICS

1. Some Bible scholars believe Lot's wife looked back at Sodom because she was curious about what was happening there and could not resist the impulse to look and see. Others believe she was saddened at the prospect of leaving Sodom, a place that she loved despite (or, perhaps, because of) its sinfulness. Kirsch suggests she might have turned back because she despairs of the fate of her other daughters—the ones whose husbands laughed at Lot's warnings and refused to flee the city. Do you think it was curiosity, longing for her beloved hometown, or motherly concern that made Lot's wife look back?

2. Women in the Bible are often depicted (and mostly condemned) as the willful and wily seducers of men—other examples include Eve (Gen.), Potiphar's wife (Gen. 39:7), Delilah (Judg. 16:5), and Salome (Matt. 14:6–8). But neither Lot's daughters, nor Lot himself, is criticized in the Bible or the religious literature that tries to explain away their sexual misadventure. Why does the Bible seem to regard the incest of Lot and his daughters as sanctified?

3. How did the rest of the biblical world regard incest? The Book of Leviticus contains a long and detailed catalogue of forbidden sexual partners. Does this suggest that incest might have been commonplace among the Israelites? After all, if incest were not regarded as a fact of life in the biblical world, why would the biblical lawgiver feel a need to address it at length and in such tantalizing detail?

4. When it comes to the most grotesque conduct of Lot's—his willingness to cast his daughters to the mob—apologists offer two thin excuses: the ancient laws of hospitality imposed on Lot a sacred obligation to protect his guests, even at the risk of his own family and his own life; children were regarded as something less precious in biblical times than they are today, more nearly chattel than loved ones, and so a father was at liberty to do with his children exactly as he pleased. Are these reasons enough to exonerate Lot for offering his daughters to the mob? Why have scholars and sages over the centuries tended to overlook this episode of abhorrent conduct on the part of Lot?

5. Kirsch explores the shocking notion that Ishmael, the firstborn son of the patriarch Abraham, molested his five-year-old halfbrother Isaac. Reread Kirsch's arguments and the biblical texts to which he refers. Do you agree with his theory?

6. Kirsch writes, "To discourage ordinary men and women from entertaining the thought that God himself might show up at their door and sit down to supper, the scribes may have systematically inserted angels into the Bible text as intermediaries between God and humankind." What are the angels of the Hebrews really like? Is it possible that they are, as Kirsch suggests, tools of censorship used by priestly scribes who did not want to encourage their readers to believe that God appeared to mortals without their assistance and their elaborate rituals?

THE RAPE OF DINAH *(Gen. 34) Dinah, the daughter of Jacob, is raped by Shechem, a princely Canaanite suitor, who then begs for her hand in marriage. The bride-price, demanded by her brothers, is the circumcision of every man in Shechem's kingdom. After the ritual is carried out, the weakened Canaanites—recovering from their ordeal—are easy targets for Dinah's brothers who kill them all, much to the dismay of Jacob.*

READING GROUP QUESTIONS AND DISCUSSION TOPICS

1. One voice alone is not heard in the Bible's account of the rape of Dinah, the voice of Dinah herself. While the men make speeches and haggle and plot among themselves and against each other, no one bothers to ask her whether she wants to marry Shechem or see him slain. What do you think Dinah's silence tells us about the biblical author?

2. Who is the true hero of Dinah's story? Is it her sword-wielding brothers who slaughter a whole people in her name? Or is it Dinah herself—a young, unwed woman living among strangers who ventures out of her father's encampment to seek the companionship of local women and who defies the strict and narrow protocols that govern the lives of wives and daughters of the patriarchs?

3. Was Dinah really raped by the lovesick prince Shechem? Or were they a couple of star-crossed lovers who dared to love each other across tribal boundaries?

4. What do you think of the theory that the story of Dinah was inserted in the Bible to combat a threat to the very survival of Israel—a warning to men or women not to consider marrying a non-Israelite who might lure them to worship pagan gods?

5. The punishment for the crime of rape in the ancient Near East was

that the rapist pay his victim's father fifty shekels, and marry her as well. To avoid adding insult to injury, of course, the rapist was obliged to marry his victim only if the woman and her family were willing. And, unlike an ordinary marriage, the Bible decreed that the rapist was never permitted to divorce his victim turned wife. Does this transform Shechem's bizarre marriage proposal into a form of reparation?

6. At the time this event occurred, the legal codes of nearby Assyria suggested that a man might actually claim a wife by forcing himself upon her. Does this suggest that Shechem's motive (if not his method) may have been rather more honorable than the biblical text allows us to understand? Could he have been trying to win her hand in marriage?

7. According to Kirsch, a close reading of Genesis 34 allows us to see that the Bible offers two visions of the stranger and two approaches to dealing with him, one that exhorts us to make war, the other that encourages us to make peace and even, as the story of Dinah and Shechem may secretly suggest, make love. What lessons can be learned from the story of Dinah and Shechem about making peace in the modern Middle East?

TAMAR AND JUDAH (Gen. 38) Tamar, a Canaanite widow of an Israelite, is involved in a failed "Levirate marriage"—a custom that obliges a man to impregnate his dead brother's widow if the brother dies without a male heir. Since her brother-in-law has failed to sire the child who has been promised her, she positions herself at the side of a road, disguised as a harlot, to seduce—and be impregnated by—her father-in-law, Judah.

READING GROUP QUESTIONS AND DISCUSSION TOPICS

1. Is this story scandalous or sexist? What does it tell us about the deadly peril that confronted women of the biblical era who did not submit to the mastery of a male, whether father or husband? Is Tamar's desperation due to the fact that women in biblical times were defined by their ability to produce children and that childless women were sometimes seen as people cursed by God?

2. Old Testament themes consistently condemn marriage outside the Twelve Tribes of Israel. Kirsch suggests that Tamar's Canaanite nationality might have been even more embarrassing to rabbinical authorities than the fact that Judah slept with her and fathered a pair of sons by her. Do you agree?

3. Why is the Bible torn between hatred and loathing of the stranger and the commandment to love the stranger? In what way does the Bible accommodate two very different rabbinical traditions: one that tolerates and even celebrates marriage with non-Israelites, and one that bitterly condemns and forbids it?

4. The Levirate marriage was a custom that obliged a man to impregnate his dead brother's widow if the brother died without a male heir. What social or political reasons allowed biblical-era society to sanctify sexual union between a woman and her brother-in-law?

5. Kirsch writes, "The story of Tamar confirms that there were at least two kinds of prostitutes whom an Israelite man might have encountered in Canaan—a common whore (Zonah, according to the original Hebrew) and a temple or 'cultic' prostitute (Qedeshah) whose sexual practices were sanctified among the Canaanites because they functioned as a form of worship of the goddesses of fertility." Do you think there's a particular significance to the Bible's differentiation between these two classifications?

6. Is the reference to Tamar as a sacred prostitute, rather than a common whore, a suggestion that the biblical author was trying to dignify and elevate Judah's dealings with her?

7. Rather than being a cautionary tale, is it possible that the story of Tamar and Judah is really an erotic love story that was somehow slipped into the pages of the Holy Bible? Was Judah really fooled by Tamar's disguise or is the disguise merely a game that each of them plays by prior arrangement or by tacit consent—either to provide "plausible deniability" for a love affair or to titillate each other?

ZIPPORAH AND MOSES (Exod. 4:24–26) Moses, his wife, Zipporah, and their son Gershom are camped at an oasis while en route to Egypt. In the middle of the night, God (Yahweh) appears and attacks Moses. Zipporah uses the blood ritual of circumcision to defend her husband and son.

READING GROUP QUESTIONS AND DISCUSSION TOPICS

1. The original Hebrew text of Exodus 4:24–26 is especially difficult to decipher because only two of the players in the scene are identified by name. The Bible tells us that it is Zipporah and Yahweh who encounter each other by night at the lodging place, but Moses is not named at all. Nor are we allowed to see with clarity who is doing what to whom—or why. Who do you think God's attack is aimed at?

2. Why would God seek to kill Moses so soon after befriending him, anointing him as a prophet, and sending him on the crucial mission to liberate the Israelites from Egyptian slavery?

3. The traditional explanation of this story—known as the "Bridegroom of Blood"—is that Yahweh seeks to kill Moses because he has violated the single most important clause of the covenant between God and Abraham by failing to circumcise his firstborn son, Gershom. Do you agree? What do you think of Kirsch's suggestion that it might have been some priestly editor, rather than God, who cared so passionately about circumcision?

4. Some scholars believe that the night attack on Moses reveals the hidden traces of pagan gods and goddesses in the Hebrew Bible. Do you agree?

5. Throughout his life, Moses is forced to depend on women to preserve his life or rescue him from deadly peril—both human and divine. As an infant, he is spared from Pharaoh's death sentence on

the firstborn of the Israelites by two courageous midwives who refuse to carry out Pharaoh's decree. Moses's mother fashions an ark out of bulrushes and sets him adrift in the river, thus saving her son's life while appearing to comply with Pharaoh's order. His sister watches over the ark from afar to make sure that he is rescued, and it is Pharaoh's daughter who draws him out of the river and raises him as her adopted son. In this story, it is his wife who saves him. How does this revise our perceptions of Moses as a powerful and potent figure, a prophet who is privileged to encounter God face-to-face because he is so nearly godlike himself?

6. Kirsch theorizes that Zipporah might be patterned after goddesses of the ancient and classical world, such as Isis or Athena, who traditionally intervened on behalf of imperiled heroes. He also sees a specific link to one pagan goddess-rescuer in particular, the deity of ancient Egypt known as Isis. Do you agree with Kirsch's theories?

STORY FIVE

JEPHTHAH AND HIS DAUGHTER (Judg. 11) Jephthah, a mercenary, is asked to lead the armies of Israel against an invading force from a neighboring kingdom. He accepts the offer and impulsively promises God that, in exchange for victory, he will sacrifice whoever first comes out of his house to greet him on his return from battle. He emerges victorious from the conflict but, to his horror, has no choice other than to sacrifice his only daughter to fulfill his vow. She goes willingly to the slaughter, but only after taking two months to go to the mountains with her friends and "bewail her virginity."

READING GROUP QUESTIONS AND DISCUSSION TOPICS

1. What does the Bible tell us about the worship of pagan gods and goddesses in the ancient world? And why did the biblical prophets regard pagan worship and prostitution as one and the same thing?

2. Is there significance to the fact that the Bible—a book whose authors regard names and naming as something sacred—fails to mention the name of Jephthah's daughter?

3. The Bible asks us to regard Jephthah's daughter as an accidental but willing victim of human sacrifice. Is another interpretation possible? What do you think of Kirsch's suggestion that Jephthah's daughter and her friends might have done something so shocking that the biblical authors were forced to dress up her death in the trappings of sacrifice?

4. The Bible tells us plainly enough that the women of Israel traditionally celebrated victory on the battlefield "with timbrels and with dances." As a combat veteran who lived alone with his beloved daughter, Jephthah might have expected and even hoped for such a greeting from her. Although he bemoans the fact that she will need to die if he is to fulfill his promise to God, did he know—

390

when he made his promise—that his daughter would be the first one to greet him?

5. What does God really think about human sacrifice? The Bible is filled with countless pleas and demands from his people, stretching all the way back to when He first befriended Abraham. Only a few pages earlier in the Book of Judges, the Almighty answers a plea from Gideon by offering a sign that it is really God who has called Gideon to service. And yet when it comes to making and keeping Jephthah's vow, God falls wholly and ominously silent—and thus condemns his daughter to death. Why was Isaac spared and Jephthah's daughter allowed to die?

THE TRAVELER AND HIS CONCUBINE (Judg. 19–21) A *traveling Levite and his concubine are forced by a storm to seek shelter in the town of Gibeah. They are taken in by a countryman and his daughter. The men of Gibeah—members of the tribe of Benjamin—surround the house in the night and demand the Levite be sent outside so that they might sodomize him. Instead, the Levite and his host offer up the concubine and the host's daughter to satisfy the mob. The concubine is gang-raped to death. The Levite brings her body home, dismembers it, and sends the pieces to the four corners of Israel in the hope of inciting a war of revenge against the tribe whose men killed her.*

READING GROUP QUESTIONS AND DISCUSSION TOPICS

1. Does the Bible celebrate or denigrate women? Why do even the earliest feminist Bible critics tend to regard the Holy Scripture as hopelessly tainted by the sexism of the stern patriarchy that created the Bible in the first place?

2. Is it possible, as one feminist Bible critic suggests, that the Book of Judges was written by a woman? And is the physical violence and sexual abuse described in Judges so grotesque and so preposterous that it amounts to an elaborate work of parody?

3. Jael is the unsung heroine of the Bible, a woman who is unique among all the compelling women in the Bible because she strikes down an enemy with her own hands. What does her story tell us about the role of women in war and peace in the ancient world? How many strong female characters from the Bible can you name?

4. Do you agree with Kirsch's hypothesis—that there is a hidden political agenda in the story of the "Gibeah Outrage." If there is such an agenda, what do you think it is? Kirsch sees the Book of Judges as a propaganda-like argument in favor of monarchy among a people who have been governed so far only by patriarchs, prophets, and judges. Do you agree?

TAMAR AND AMNON (2 Sam. 13) After a sordid affair with Bathsheba, King David arranges for the death of her husband so that he might marry her. Shortly thereafter Amnon, David's oldest son and heir apparent to the throne of Israel, falls desperately in love with his half sister, Tamar. Amnon feigns illness and asks the king to send Tamar to nurse him back to health. When she arrives, he rapes her and throws her out in the street. King David hears about this outrage but does nothing.

READING GROUP QUESTIONS AND DISCUSSION TOPICS

1. Some Bible scholars have tried to cleanse Amnon's ugly crime by suggesting it is not a case of incest. Do you think their arguments have any merit?

2. Other scholars regard King David as a collaborator in Amnon's rape of his half sister, Tamar. Do you see King David as an unwitting or an intentional accomplice? Does David's guilt over his own sexual misadventures keep him from chastising his son for doing much the same thing? When Amnon asks David to order Tamar to nurse him back to health, does David know what Amnon really wants from her?

3. Kirsch sees the story of Tamar's ordeal as an early augury of the decline and fall of David, the greatest king who ever sat on the throne of ancient Israel. Do you agree with his assessment?

WHO REALLY WROTE THE BIBLE?

| READING GROUP QUESTIONS AND DISCUSSION TOPICS |

1. Is the Hebrew Bible the revealed word of God—or the work of many hands over many centuries?

2. Did a woman write the Bible—or at least the best parts of it?

3. Discuss the different biblical authors and the various versions of the Bible that have survived over the centuries and remain in common use around the world. What do they tell us about the different peoples and cultures who preserved them and passed them along from generation to generation?

ABOUT THE AUTHOR

Jonathan L. Kirsch is a book critic for the *Los Angeles Times* and has been reading and studying the Bible for more than twenty years. He writes and lectures extensively on literary and biblical topics. His book reviews appear in the Life & Style section of the *Los Angeles Times* on alternate Wednesdays and in the *Sunday Book Review*. Kirsch, an attorney in private practice with the law firm of Kirsch & Mitchell, also contributes publishing-law columns to the newsletters of the Publishers Marketing Association, the Western Publications Association, and the American Society of Journalists and Authors.

Before embarking on the practice of law, Kirsch was senior editor of *California Magazine* (formerly *New West Magazine*), where he specialized in coverage of law, government, and politics. Previously, he worked as West Coast correspondent for *Newsweek*, as editor for *West* and *Home* magazines at the *Los Angeles Times*, and as a reporter for the *Santa Cruz Sentinel*. As a freelance writer, Kirsch has also contributed to *California Lawyer*, *Los Angeles Lawyer*, *New West*, *Los Angeles Magazine*, *New Republic*, *Publishers Weekly*, *Performing Arts*, *Human Behavior*, *L.A. Architect,* and other publications.

Kirsch is a member of the National Book Critics Circle, PEN Center USA West, the Author's Guild, the Western Publication Association, California Lawyers for the Arts, the Los Angeles Copyright Society, and the Intellectual Property sections of the California State Bar and the Los Angeles County Bar Associations. A member of the Board of Trustees of the Los Angeles Copyright Society, Kirsch also serves as legal counsel to the Publishers Marketing Association, the Western Publications Association, and the Jewish Journal of Greater Los Angeles. He is the recipient of the Publishers Marketing Association 1994 Benjamin Franklin Award for Special Achievement in Publishing.

Kirsch, 47, was born in Los Angeles, attended high school in Culver City, and completed a bachelor of arts degree with honors in Russian and Jewish history and Adlai E. Stevenson College honors at the Santa Cruz campus of the University of California. A member of the California State Bar since 1976, he earned a juris doctor degree cum laude at Loyola University School of Law. Kirsch is married to Ann Benjamin Kirsch, Psy.D., a psychotherapist in private practice in Beverly Hills. They live with their two children in Los Angeles.